Ethical Hacking and Penetration Testing in Cybersecurity

Shafiullah Khan
Abdullah Al Salem University, Kuwait

Ali F. Almutairi
https://orcid.org/0000-0001-8254-1262
Abdullah Al Salem University, Kuwait

Jaime Lloret
https://orcid.org/0000-0002-0862-0533
Universitat Politecnica de Valencia, Spain

IGI Global
Scientific Publishing
Publishing Tomorrow's Research Today

Vice President of Editorial Melissa Wagner
Director of Acquisitions Mikaela Felty
Director of Book Development Jocelynn Hessler
Production Manager Mike Brehm
Cover Design Jose Rosado

Published in the United States of America by
IGI Global Scientific Publishing
701 East Chocolate Avenue
Hershey, PA, 17033, USA
Tel: 717-533-8845 | Fax: 717-533-7115
Website: https://www.igi-global.com E-mail: cust@igi-global.com

Library of Congress Cataloging-in-Publication Data

LCCN: 2025024578 (CIP Data Pending)
ISBN13: 9798337335360
Isbn13Softcover: 9798337335377
EISBN13: 9798337335384
British Cataloguing in Publication Data
A Cataloguing in Publication record for this book is available from the British Library.

Table of Contents

Detailed Table of Contents

focuses on autonomous AI-powered ethical hacking frameworks, federated learning for secure threat intelligence sharing, and AI-human collaboration for effective cybersecurity governance. As cyber threats become more sophisticated, leveraging AI responsibly will be essential for advancing cybersecurity defenses while ensuring transparency and ethical compliance.

P. Selvakumar, Department of Science and Humanities, Nehru Institute of Technology, Coimbatore, India
Swapna Siddamsetti, Neil Gogte Institute of Technology, India
Lumbini Bhaumik, Asansol Engineering College, India
K. Sowmya, Nitte Meenakshi Institute of Technology, Nitte University, India
Dharmendra Singh, Independent Researcher, India
S. Giriprasad, SRM Institute of Science and Technology, India

AI-driven tools to identify vulnerabilities, detect anomalies, and automate security testing. This integration enhances cybersecurity by enabling faster threat detection, improving penetration testing, and strengthening defense mechanisms against cybercriminals.technologies enhance cybersecurity by automating tasks, improving accuracy, and adapting to new threats. From intrusion detection and malware analysis to predictive analytics and behavioral anomaly detection, AI-driven ethical hacking is reshaping the digital security landscape.tools to test for vulnerabilities. However, AI and ML are now augmenting these efforts, making penetration testing more efficient and comprehensive. AI-driven ethical hacking tools can analyze large datasets, identifying weaknesses faster and reducing response times to cyber incidents. vulnerability scanning, and exploitation techniques. AI-driven tools can analyze security configurations, detect weaknesses, and even suggest patches or mitigation strategies.

Mayur Jariwala, University of the Cumberlands, USA

As cyber threats evolve in scale and complexity, ethical hacking must also advance beyond traditional approaches. This chapter explores how artificial intelligence (AI) and machine learning (ML) are revolutionizing penetration testing, from reconnaissance and vulnerability assessment to social engineering and blue teaming. It examines real-world applications, adversarial AI risks, and the ethical boundaries of automated attacks. The chapter also highlights regulatory implications and emerging trends such as explainable AI and autonomous red teaming. It provides a forward-looking perspective on how AI can responsibly augment cybersecurity practices in both offensive and defensive contexts.

Ethical hacking is key to improving the structure of cybersecurity. The Ethical hackers can look for flaws before they become evident but criminal hackers find them. This study considers the methods employed by ethical hacker and stresses their importance in penetration testing, vulnerability assessments, and incident response. By simulating actual attack scenarios, ethical hackers offer organizations a window into their security posture, helping them to take effective countermeasures. The research also addresses the ethical choices positioned around ethical hacking, including the importance of responsible disclosure and abiding by appropriate legal frameworks. This report illustrates in given cases that ethical hacking not only brings about real benefits for organizations, converting security awareness into action and proactive risk management are also its objectives. Underpinning this thesis is the point that ethical hacking should be integrated into broader cybersecurity strategies to effectively fight the many-faced digital threats in an age of 21st-century warfare.

In today's rapidly evolving digital landscape, cybersecurity has become a central concern for organizations globally. The increasing reliance on interconnected systems, cloud computing, and digital infrastructure exposes businesses to a wide variety of cyber threats, including malware, data breaches, and advanced persistent threats (APTs). These threats jeopardize data confidentiality, integrity, and availability, undermining trust in digital ecosystems. In this context, ethical hacking and penetration testing have emerged as crucial tools to identify and mitigate vulnerabilities within information systems, helping organizations safeguard their digital assets and maintain business continuity. Penetration testing, a key aspect of ethical hacking, is the systematic process of evaluating computer systems, networks, or applications for vulnerabilities that could be exploited by malicious actors. By mimicking the techniques, tactics, and procedures (TTPs) of real-world attackers, penetration tests provide actionable insights into an organization's security posture.

Legal, ethical, and compliance frameworks are crucial in guiding ethical hacking practices. Ethical hacking, also known as penetration testing, involves simulating cyberattacks to identify and rectify vulnerabilities within systems. Ethical hackers must navigate legal boundaries to avoid unauthorized access to systems and data breaches. Laws such as the Computer Fraud and Abuse Act set strict guidelines for what constitutes lawful hacking. Moreover, ethical hackers adhere to a code of conduct that emphasizes integrity and respect for privacy. Compliance with industry standards, such as GDPR and PCI DSS, ensures that ethical hacking practices protect sensitive information and maintain trust with stakeholders. Organizations often establish clear policies and training programs to ensure hackers operate within legal parameters. By incorporating these frameworks, businesses can improve their cybersecurity posture while minimizing legal risks. Ethical hacking must align with laws and ethical standards to create a safer digital environment.

As the deployment of Narrowband Internet of Things (NB-IoT) networks accelerates globally, their inherently constrained architecture and large-scale connectivity introduce critical security challenges. Hence, there is a need to present a penetration testing and risk assessment framework taxonomy specifically designed for NB-IoT ecosystems that would leverage ethical hacking methodologies. In this chapter, we conduct targeted vulnerability analysis using virtualized testbeds and industry-standard toolkits, simulating various attacks. We introduce a comprehensive risk taxonomy that categorizes threats across various NB-IoT network layers, including edge, core, device, and operational components. By mapping penetration testing results to this structured taxonomy, our study provides an effective means to evaluate risk severity, uncover security gaps, and recommend mitigation strategies. This work also addresses the ethical, and compliance aspects of penetration testing within

Preface

Cybersecurity has become one of the most critical challenges of the digital era. As information systems expand in scale and complexity, organizations across the world face an ever-growing landscape of cyber threats. Malicious actors continuously develop sophisticated techniques to exploit vulnerabilities in networks, applications, cloud platforms, and connected devices. In this evolving environment, reactive security strategies are no longer sufficient. Instead, proactive approaches that identify weaknesses before attackers can exploit them have become essential. Ethical hacking and penetration testing represent two of the most effective methods for achieving this goal.

Ethical hacking allows security professionals to adopt the mindset and techniques of attackers in a controlled and authorized manner. By simulating real-world cyberattacks, ethical hackers are able to uncover vulnerabilities that traditional security assessments might overlook. Penetration testing complements this approach by systematically evaluating the security posture of systems, networks, and applications through structured methodologies. Together, these practices play a fundamental role in strengthening organizational defenses, improving resilience, and ensuring the protection of sensitive digital assets.

The motivation for editing this book, *Ethical Hacking and Penetration Testing in Cybersecurity*, arises from the growing need for comprehensive resources that bridge the gap between theoretical knowledge and practical implementation. While many works address isolated aspects of cybersecurity, there remains a demand for a structured reference that integrates technical techniques, methodological frameworks, ethical considerations, and emerging research trends. This volume aims to provide such a resource by bringing together contributions from researchers, academics, and industry professionals who share expertise and practical insights in the field of ethical hacking and penetration testing.

This book is designed to provide readers with a thorough understanding of ethical hacking methodologies, tools, and strategies used to identify and mitigate security vulnerabilities. It covers a wide range of topics, including penetration testing methodologies such as black-box, white-box, and gray-box testing; vulnerability assessment techniques; web application and API security testing; mobile and wireless network penetration testing; and cloud security challenges. In addition, the book explores advanced areas such as exploit development, malware analysis, red teaming and blue teaming strategies, threat hunting, and incident response.

An important aspect emphasized throughout this volume is the ethical and legal framework that governs cybersecurity practices. Ethical hacking must always be conducted responsibly and in accordance with legal regulations and professional standards. Therefore, the book highlights compliance requirements, privacy considerations, and governance frameworks that ensure penetration testing activities are conducted ethically and lawfully.

The field of cybersecurity continues to evolve rapidly with technological advancements. Emerging technologies such as artificial intelligence, machine learning, Internet of Things (IoT), blockchain systems, and even quantum computing introduce both new opportunities and new vulnerabilities. Recognizing this dynamic landscape, the book also addresses emerging trends and research directions that are shaping the future of ethical hacking and cybersecurity defense mechanisms.

This volume is intended for a diverse audience. Cybersecurity professionals—including ethical hackers, penetration testers, security analysts, and SOC teams—will find practical guidance and best practices to enhance their technical capabilities. Researchers and academics can explore emerging research topics and case studies that contribute to advancing the discipline. Graduate and undergraduate students in cybersecurity, computer science, and information security will benefit from structured explanations that connect theory with real-world practice. Additionally, IT administrators, law enforcement professionals, and decision-makers responsible for organizational security will gain insights into how ethical hacking can strengthen security strategies and risk management frameworks.

The success of this book would not have been possible without the valuable contributions of the authors who shared their expertise and research in this rapidly evolving domain. We extend our sincere appreciation to all contributing authors for their dedication and commitment in producing high-quality chapters that collectively enrich this volume. We also thank the reviewers for their constructive feedback, which helped improve the clarity and rigor of the chapters.

CHAPTER OVERVIEW

In Chapter 1, the authors examine the growing influence of adversarial artificial intelligence in the domain of ethical hacking. The chapter discusses how techniques such as generative adversarial networks and automated red-teaming are enabling more realistic simulations of cyberattacks, allowing cybersecurity professionals to evaluate system resilience under highly dynamic threat conditions. By exploring both the opportunities and the challenges associated with adversarial AI, the chapter also addresses ethical considerations and the importance of interdisciplinary collaboration. It concludes by outlining a roadmap for researchers, practitioners, and policymakers to responsibly leverage adversarial AI technologies in strengthening digital security infrastructures.

Chapter 2 focuses on the transformative role of artificial intelligence and machine learning in advancing ethical hacking practices and cybersecurity defense mechanisms. The authors highlight how AI-driven systems are increasingly being used for automated vulnerability detection, malware analysis, phishing detection, and real-time intrusion monitoring. The chapter further explores advanced AI techniques, including deep learning and reinforcement learning, which enable more intelligent penetration testing and enhanced threat intelligence capabilities. At the same time, the chapter critically examines challenges such as adversarial attacks on AI systems, data privacy concerns, algorithmic bias, and the computational demands of large-scale models, while also discussing future directions such as federated learning and collaborative AI-human cybersecurity frameworks.

In Chapter 3, the discussion continues on the integration of AI and machine learning into ethical hacking workflows, emphasizing how these technologies enhance vulnerability detection, anomaly analysis, and automated security testing. The chapter highlights how AI-driven tools can process vast amounts of security data to identify weaknesses more efficiently than traditional approaches. By incorporating predictive analytics, behavioral anomaly detection, and intelligent vulnerability scanning, the authors demonstrate how AI-assisted ethical hacking can significantly improve threat detection speed and response capabilities while strengthening defensive cybersecurity strategies.

Chapter 4 further expands on AI-driven cybersecurity by exploring how artificial intelligence and machine learning are transforming both offensive and defensive security operations. The chapter provides insights into how AI technologies support multiple phases of penetration testing, including reconnaissance, vulnerability discovery, and social engineering simulations. It also examines the implications of adversarial AI, regulatory concerns, and the ethical boundaries of automated attack simulations. In addition, the chapter highlights emerging developments such as explainable AI and autonomous red-team systems, offering a forward-looking perspective on the responsible integration of AI into cybersecurity practices.

Chapter 5 presents a strategic perspective on ethical hacking as an integral component of modern cybersecurity frameworks. The authors explain how ethical hackers proactively identify system vulnerabilities before they can be exploited by malicious actors. Through penetration testing, vulnerability assessments, and simulated attack scenarios, ethical hackers help organizations better understand their security posture and develop effective mitigation strategies. The chapter also emphasizes ethical decision-making, responsible vulnerability disclosure, and compliance with legal frameworks, demonstrating how ethical hacking can support proactive risk management and strengthen organizational security culture.

In Chapter 6, the authors provide a broad overview of ethical hacking and penetration testing within the context of today's interconnected digital ecosystem. As organizations increasingly rely on cloud computing, distributed infrastructures, and digital platforms, the risks associated with cyber threats have expanded significantly. This chapter explains how penetration testing serves as a systematic method for evaluating system security by replicating real-world attacker tactics and techniques. By identifying vulnerabilities and assessing the resilience of digital systems, penetration testing provides organizations with actionable insights to enhance cybersecurity defenses and protect critical information assets.

Chapter 7 examines the legal, ethical, and compliance frameworks that govern ethical hacking practices. The chapter emphasizes that penetration testing must operate within clearly defined legal boundaries and ethical guidelines to avoid unauthorized system access or data misuse. It discusses relevant regulatory structures and industry standards, highlighting the importance of privacy protection, professional codes of conduct, and organizational policies that guide ethical hacking activities. By integrating legal and compliance considerations into cybersecurity operations, the chapter demonstrates how organizations can strengthen their security posture while maintaining trust and accountability.

Chapter 8 addresses the security challenges associated with Narrowband Internet of Things (NB-IoT) networks, which are rapidly expanding due to their role in supporting large-scale IoT deployments. The authors introduce a structured penetration testing and risk taxonomy framework designed specifically for NB-IoT environments. Using virtualized testing environments and standardized cybersecurity tools, the chapter analyzes vulnerabilities across multiple network layers, including devices, edge systems, and core infrastructure. By mapping penetration testing outcomes to a comprehensive risk taxonomy, the chapter provides valuable guidance for identifying security gaps, assessing threat severity, and implementing effective mitigation strategies.

In Chapter 9, the authors provide a structured overview of the penetration testing lifecycle, presenting a practical guide to the systematic stages involved in ethical hacking engagements. The chapter describes each phase of the process, including reconnaissance, threat modeling, vulnerability assessment, exploitation, and post-exploitation analysis. Particular attention is given to best practices, legal compliance, documentation, and communication with stakeholders. By emphasizing repeatable and responsible testing procedures, the chapter offers cybersecurity professionals a practical framework for conducting effective and methodical penetration testing activities.

Finally, Chapter 10 explores the critical role of red-team operations in strengthening organizational cybersecurity defenses. Through a practical case study conducted in a controlled and virtualized environment, the chapter demonstrates how red teams simulate real-world attacks to identify weaknesses in network infrastructures. The authors present the setup of penetration testing tools, the execution of red-team activities, and vulnerability scanning using widely adopted security tools. The chapter concludes with remediation strategies designed to address identified vulnerabilities, particularly those related to misconfigured or exposed network ports, highlighting the importance of proactive vulnerability management in modern cybersecurity strategies.

We hope that this book will serve as a valuable reference for understanding ethical hacking and penetration testing practices and will inspire further research, innovation, and collaboration in cybersecurity. By equipping readers with knowledge and practical insights, we aim to contribute to the development of stronger cybersecurity defenses and a safer digital ecosystem for organizations and individuals worldwide.

Shafiullah Khan

Abdullah Al Salem University, Kuwait

Ali F. Almutairi

Abdullah Al Salem University, Kuwait

Jaime Lloret

Universitat Politècnica de València, Spain

Chapter 1
Adversarial AI Challenges and Opportunities in Ethical Hacking

Zokir Mamadiyarov
Termez University of Economics and Service, Uzbekistan

Iroda Abdullaeva
Urgench State University, Uzbekistan

Gularam Masharipova
Alfraganus University, Uzbekistan

Munir Ahmad
http://orcid.org/0000-0003-4836-6151
Survey of Pakistan, Pakistan

ABSTRACT

Adversarial AI is redefining ethical hacking by enabling dynamic, high-fidelity simulations that better mirror real-world cyber threats. This chapter explores the integration of adversarial techniques, such as generative adversarial networks (GANs) and automated red-teaming, into cybersecurity practices, emphasizing their transformative impact on model testing and system defense. It discusses emerging best practices, ethical boundaries, and the need for interdisciplinary collaboration. The chapter concludes with a roadmap for industry, academia, and policymakers to responsibly harness adversarial AI, ensuring security and resilience in an increasingly AI-driven digital landscape.

DOI: 10.4018/979-8-3373-3536-0.ch001

INTRODUCTION

Adversarial artificial intelligence is a set of methods to decrease artificial intelligence and machine learning (ML) system performance by finding weaknesses in the algorithms used to control the systems. By creating adversarial examples (minute perversions in the data provided to an AI network, causing it to provide the wrong answers), bad actors can violate the integrity, confidentiality, and availability of the AI-based systems. Such attacks constitute a serious weakness in the network environment in regard to cybersecurity and anti-teaming, where AI finds a great application in threat identification, behavioral analytics, facial recognition, and network and system surveillance, among others. Adversarial AI may be used to make spam filters disappear, to outsmart malware classifiers, and to break biometric verification. With a growing degree to which AI is included in the cybersecurity infrastructure environment, the adversarial methodology is no longer merely a topic of relevance and interest, but also critical to ensuring reliable levels of digital absurdity and systemic strength (Baniecki & Biecek, 2024; Kong et al., 2021; Qiu et al., 2019).

The dual-use aspect of an adversarial AI is one of its distinct features. Adversaries can also use the same techniques to compromise machine learning systems, but defenders can use them to bolster them. As an example, using adversarial examples, the developers can determine the blind spots of an AI model and retrain it to be more resilient. This paradox, that is, the duo-competence of the adversarial AI in threatening as well as heightening security, questions multifaceted questions of access, intent, and control. Invasive actors use adversarial techniques to develop imperceptible attacks (Debicha et al., 2023), whereas cybersecurity researchers and ethical hackers use similar tools in their red-teaming, testing, and validation processes (Happe & Cito, 2023; Teichmann & Boticiu, 2023). Not only does the dual-use nature of this technology blur the boundaries between the use of offensive and defensive actions, but it also demands well-defined ethical and policy frameworks that would make sure that the technologies of such kind are safely deployed and utilized.

With the changing nature of the threat environment in the age of adversarial AI, ethical hacking, sometimes referred to as white-hat hacking, has assumed new substance. Conventionally, white hackers also pretend to perpetrate online attacks to check and enhance organizational strategies (Caldwell, 2011; Chauhan et al., 2024). The emergence of AI-powered threats, however, poses a different situation that requires an advanced strategy in which adversarial AI methodologies involve threats in the toolset of the ethical hacker. This involves the development of attacker-simulating inputs to test the hardness of the machine learning systems, attack modeling of AI-based detection, and red-team engagements to predict avenues of exploitation. Ethical hacking, thus, emerges as a defence mechanism as well as an offensive mode in anticipating AI-specific flaws. Adversarial AI techniques can help ethical hackers to keep abreast of rogue actors and make AI applications safer and more secure.

This chapter provides an in-depth analysis of AI as an adversarial technique in both offense and defense applications of cybersecurity. It examines the way in which adversarial AI is being used by rogue individuals and organizations to subvert the security protocols and how the cybersecurity experts and ethical hackers, in their turn, are turning to the same techniques to expose vulnerabilities and establish stronger security measures by using an AI weapon against weapon AI. The technical and operational barriers related to the use of adversarial AI in ethical hacking and aspects of model fragility, tool shortcomings, and explainability are discussed in the chapter as well. Also, it touches the ethical, legal, and political consequences of making use of such powerful technologies.

FOUNDATION OF ADVERSARIAL AI

The speed of the applied AI to cybersecurity systems, like intrusion detection systems, malware categorization, biometric authentication, and spam filtering etc, has immensely enhanced the effectiveness and efficacy of a digital defense. But with this joining, a new pose of cyber risk surfaced, as well as the attack of AI itself. Attackers have become active in exploiting the inherent weaknesses of ML by using subtle and sophisticated techniques called adversaries. Such malicious AI techniques pose a threat not only to the current cyber threat environment but also upend the efficacy of deployed traditional security systems.

Techniques Used by Malicious Actors

As the use of AI and ML systems has become a central element of the contemporary digital infrastructure revolution, as they are used in everything, such as facial recognition and fraud detection, to autonomous systems and cybersecurity, their weaknesses have also become hot spots on which attackers will pounce. Malicious parties are also using vulnerabilities inherent in the AI production chain to undermine the integrity of models, alter the outputs, and steal sensitive data. Such attacks are not only theoretical, but have also been experienced in real life by way of breaches that have necessitated quick measures to avoid such by way of specific risk mitigation control measures by the use of AI (Blauth et al., 2022; Houda, 2024; Villalón-Huerta et al., 2022). Figure 1 provides a structured overview of adversarial AI attack types, classified by their target phase in the AI lifecycle and functional intent. It highlights the primary mechanisms, evasion, poisoning, and privacy attacks, that adversaries exploit to compromise machine learning systems in cybersecurity.

Figure 1. Taxonomy of Adversarial AI Attacks

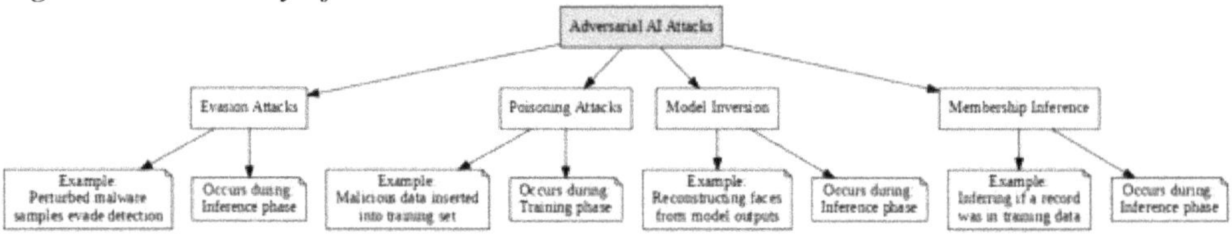

The present section is devoted to four broad categories of adversarial attacks, i.e., evasion attacks, poisoning attacks, model inversion, and membership inference, targeting each stage of the AI/ML pipeline. Performing such techniques singularly or in groups can severely sabotage confidence in the AI-balanced entities and increase the attack surface in high-priority areas of finance, defense, medical care, and critical infrastructure.

Evasion Attacks

Evasion attacks are a powerful type of adversarial strategy that weakens machine learning designs in the inference stage, once the system has been trained and is ready to use (Muthalagu et al., 2025; S. Wang et al., 2024). As opposed to poisoning attacks, which contaminate the training process, the evasion attacks are performed by manipulating a model's by subtly manipulating the stimulus data. Such attacks rely on the construction of adversarial samples. An adversarial sample is an input that is slightly perturbed in how it appears to a human, most commonly by adding noise, but discernibly changed in the way it is interpreted by a model.

In order to perform an evasion attack, the adversaries rely on special algorithms to calculate perturbations that will shift the input across the classification boundaries of the model. Among the most commonly used methods of generating such inputs are the Fast Gradient Sign Method (FGSM), Projected Gradient Descent (PGD), and Carlini-Wagner (C&W) attacks (Filipovich & Kovalev, 2023; Villegas-Ch et al., 2024). In FGSM, perturbations are computed by applying the sign of the gradient of the loss with respect to the input, and, in PGD, perturbations are computed via iterated gradient steps, having a norm-bounded constraint. The Carlini-Wagner method focuses on crafting inputs that are almost unnoticeable whilst still falling with high probability in the incorrect prediction category of the model on the basis of optimization of a particular loss. The most problematic issue with these techniques is that they do not need training data, but only the trained model or results, and can thus be performed even in a black-box-attack scenario.

The practical aspects of evasion attacks are long-term. In cybersecurity, adversaries can use binary obfuscation, padding, or code transformation to quietly modify malware so that it remains inoffensive to ML-based antivirus systems while still executing malicious actions. Such techniques can consistently bypass signature-based and behavior-based detection systems. Similarly, in face recognition systems, attackers might use adversarial patches, altered eyewear, or specially printed T-shirts to deceive the computer vision model. These visual artifacts exploit flaws in object detection and classification models, allowing attackers to impersonate other users or breach security in some cases.

When it comes to the field of self-driving cars, researchers have shown how the ability to misclassify the most important road signs can be found by placing small stickers on street signs or even by changing the texture of these signs (Hansson et al., 2021; Stilgoe, 2021). As an example, a handful of low-profile stickers can make an AI-based vision system confused about which sign to identify, i.e., Stop or Speed Limit 45. These errors of misclassification in real-time decision-making systems are very dangerous to safety, such as traffic violations, accidents, or the loss of control.

Evasion attacks also point to a systemic problem: the fragility of existing AI models to perturbations that are at scale, unnoticeable to humans. Where minor alterations in visual or textual content are typically insufficient to disrupt human cognition, neural nets tend to the opposite extreme, where variation in the input outside of the training distribution can disrupt deep learning systems. This vulnerability provides an opportunity to exploit the existing loopholes in the applications, including spam detection and voice command. With increasing dependability in mission-critical and safety-sensitive applications, the necessity of designing such resistant models that can be immune to adversarial perturbations becomes pressing. The AI countermeasures, which include adversarial training, input preprocessing, ensemble modeling, and anomaly detection, have to keep up with the latest attack methods in order to prevent disastrous outcomes relating to the integrity and reliability of the AI-based systems.

Poisoning Attacks

The second type of adversarial manipulation that could be the most dangerous in machine learning is poisoning attacks that aim at interfering with the initial phase of modelling creation, the training stage (Tian et al., 2023; Z. Wang et al., 2023; Xue et al., 2020). These attacks affect the integrity of the AI systems by corrupting the training dataset with malicious or misleading data so as to effectively taint the learning process of the model, accessing data down the line. The underlying weakness that this type of manipulation uses is that it is human nature and common to place a certain faith in the quality and authenticity of the training data provided by the developers. After being contaminated, a low fraction of spoiled gauge might possess significant and disproportionally harmful consequences affecting the behavior of the model, resulting in poor generalizations, false predictions, and security flaws.

Poisoning attacks are of two major types. The first is data poisoning, where the goal of the attacker is to undermine the performance of the model, in general. This is normally done through the input of noisy, mislabeled, or erroneous examples that obscure the decision boundaries of the model, such that such model would produce erroneous classification on new data (J. Chen et al., 2021; Y. Chen et al., 2023). The second, and usually more specific, is what is called a backdoor attack. In this, the model is trained on the particular pattern or trigger that is embedded in the training materials, and the result is to treat the model as it should in normal conditions, but yield an attacker-controlled response when activated (Gong et al., 2023; J. Zhang et al., 2022). The attacks are stealthy, and they are very difficult to detect since the normal measures of performance of the model might not be affected.

Poisoning is of particular concern to decentralized settings like federated learning or crowdsourced data systems. The model is trained on several devices or sources in such contexts, and the data is, in many cases, not centrally controlled. This opaqueness and non-auditability nature present an opportunity for adversaries to drop a corrupted sample that will not be able to raise a red flag on immediate detection. What it means to cybersecurity is huge. For instance, in AI-based intrusion detection systems, an attacker might seed the system with log entries that slowly normalize the interpretation of certain malicious activities in the AI model, such as port scanning or unauthorized access. This is a blind spot to actual threats, something that can easily counter the essence of the system's usage.

In biometric security systems, the corrupted training images forming the basis of a model with poisoned training data imbalances the capacity of the models in distinguishing individual persons. Worse still, backdoors could be installed in a way that the appearance of a specific facial expression, hairstyle, or accessory would provide access to an unauthorized user, such as glasses or an adversarial makeup. In like manner, in AI systems applied in the field of logistics and supply chain management, attackers may poison a dataset to bias demand predictions. This may result in involuntary excess stocking or intentionally reducing production, which will cost the company due to the heart of inventory control and loss in the other networks too.

Model Inversion Attacks

Model inversion attacks are an intensely invasive malicious AI attempt to recover or estimate sensitive input data on which a machine learning model was initially trained by querying it. The attacks especially work well on models that overfit their training data or output precise probabilities of the output, e.g., confidence scores, class distribution (Z. Zhang et al., 2023; Zhou et al., 2024). The idea of model inversion is essentially founded upon a systematic use of a relationship between model outputs with the respective inputs. By long-term poking the model by asking questions and observing the model's response, the adversaries can gradually learn the most likely feature inputs that would have created the observed outputs.

Mathematically, model inversion may be executed in numerous ways based on the level of access an attacker has. When the adversary can see both the model architecture and the model parameters (white-box), gradient-based approaches to optimization can recover the original inputs by optimizing to minimize a loss describing the difference between desired outputs and model outputs. Attackers in more advanced environments can use generative models like Generative Adversarial Networks (GANs) (Pan et al., 2019; Saxena & Cao, 2021) in order to generate the data distribution to create a credible reconstruction of training data. In even black-box models, in which the internal mechanics of the model are not exposed, some methods, such as probabilistic estimation and output probing, can produce a partial or approximate reconstruction, at least in cases where the model presents detailed confidence scores.

Domain context Specific consequences of model inversion are most serious in the domains that manage valuable personal data. A practical example can be used to explain this further in the field of health, where a machine learning model used to classify disease in scans of patients can be interrogated by the reveal of real medical images in the training set. Such recreated images might reveal identities, health status, or physical deviances of actual patients, which were not supposed to be reproduced, and go against the legal provisions of patient confidentiality, including the Health Insurance Portability and Accountability Act (HIPAA) (Lutkevich, 2019) or General Data Protection Regulation (GDPR) (Truong et al., 2020). Likewise, models deployed in criminal justice by carrying out risk assessment or facial recognition may be inverted to retrieve facial imagery or demographic features that disclose the identity and attributes of the people in the law enforcement databases. Such violations are not just technical and have serious ethical and legal consequences, particularly when the data is reused in profiling, surveillance, or even coercion.

In addition, the model inversion attacks reduce the trust that people place on AI systems, especially in high-stakes settings where implementations would require high standards of privacy. Disparagement of core values of responsible AI use is the risk of reverse-engineering of one of the biometric, medical, or behavioral data based on an output of the so-called anonymous model. Compliance systems are also vulnerable to such risks since data subjects can be unwillingly subjected to privacy risks despite lacking direct access to the information. Advancing model inversion methods requires powerful defenses, including differential privacy, output perturbation, model regularization, and limited output disclosures. Restricting the granularity of reaction and training models on resisting overfitting, the developers will be able to reduce the risk of inversion and preserve the confidentiality and ethical integrity of phone-based AI-driven systems.

Membership Inference Attacks

Membership inference attacks are a devious but effective type of attack where the purpose lies in determining whether a certain data point has been used to create a machine learning model. In this kind of attack, the difference in behavior based on the machine learning models between the training data and the new data is used as an attack. Such systems are particularly vulnerable to overfitting, such that instead of generalizing over the patterns, the model recalls specific training data. Overfitting usually causes a model to have greater confidence levels or lower prediction entropy of the points it has encountered during training. Given the model has been trained on a certain set of inputs and analyzed with precision on what the model is returning on one input, an adversary can deem, with high confidence, whether the input was present during the training data set (H. Hu et al., 2023; Niu et al., 2022, 2024; Rigaki & Garcia, 2024).

Adversaries usually apply shadow modeling techniques to conduct a membership inference attack. A shadow model is taught behavior to imitate the target model by supplying it with artificial datasets and watching the results. That adversary will then use the output patterns to train an inference model to help them identify the inputs that were present as part of the training set, as opposed to those that were not. When this discriminatory model is trained, it may be applied in order to check how the target model will respond to particular data points and draw conclusions on their membership status. The steps may be used even in black-box environments, where an attacker has no rights to the inner workings of the model, only to its API.

Membership inference attacks have especially disturbing implications at a privacy-sensitive level. A typical example in the field of healthcare is an attacker trying to query a disease prediction model that runs on a cloud system to find out whether data about a given patient was used in training the model. The simple validation that data have been included may indicate sensitive health data, including diagnoses, medical history, or affiliations with a demographic group. In a financial system, the analog attached to a credit-worthiness model would be an opportunity to use that on a respective finance-based system to determine whether a person had participated in the bankruptcy scheme, charged with tax fraud, or loan default. Membership inference in marketing analytics may reveal personal consumption habits, geographic whereabouts, or political alliances that the subject did not agree to share.

In addition to raising privacy issues, membership inference attacks raise significant legal and ethical issues, especially where such data protection laws are in effect, as in the internal market of the European Union with the GDPR or the United States with the HIPAA. Within these frameworks, a violation occurs in the form of unauthorized use or disclosure of personal information, even when indirectly inferred. In addition, the affected organizations can also undergo legal sanctions, reputation loss, and loss of credibility. It is expected that after anonymization or encryption, consumers and stakeholders would present their data, which would become unreconstructible and untraceable using AI.

Membership inference attacks should also be addressed proactively, rather than in a multilayered way. The overfitting behavior of the model could be substantially decreased using techniques such as differential privacy, dropout regularization, adversarial training, model calibration, and more. In addition, the system designers should reconcile model utility and privacy by either reducing inference of confidence scores or using output obfuscation techniques. After all, the avoidance of membership inference is a technical problem, but also a fundamental implementation need in the context of an ethical and lawful use of AI, especially in areas discussed publicly and with a high-risk profile. Table 1 presents the application of adversarial AI attacks across different sectors. These examples illustrate the versatility and severity of adversarial techniques, as well as the practical vulnerabilities in AI-dependent systems.

Table 1. Adversarial Attacks Across Domains

Domain	Attack Type	Description	Consequence
Autonomous Vehicles	Evasion	Modified stop signs misclassified as speed signs	Road safety compromised
Antivirus Systems	Evasion	Legitimate files flagged as malware (Cylance test)	False positives, operational disruption
Medical Imaging	Model Inversion / Evasion	Cancer scans are misdiagnosed via adversarial noise	Misdiagnosis risk
Facial Recognition	Evasion	Glasses used to spoof facial ID systems	Identity spoofing and system breach

ETHICAL HACKING AND ADVERSARIAL AI

Since AI systems are increasingly becoming a part of critical infrastructures, the importance of strong and robust AI security can hardly be overstated. Ethical hacking, which is the act of attacking systems to secure their defense, has adapted to use adversarial AI methods as well. In this new area, an ethical hacker with an operating space that might be more organized, such as in a red team or a penetration testing environment, can use adversarial AI to mimic the real-world threats, identify weaknesses of a system, and make sure that the AI-driven products do not become the worst protection tool of an organization.

Penetration Testing and Red-Teaming

Red-teaming in AI is a well-organized attack simulation that should help to find weaknesses in machine learning pipelines. In contrast to traditional red teams that hunt flaws at network or software levels, the AI-centered red teams replicate adversarial behavior particular to ML systems: the misclassification of the model, manipulation of the input, or leakage of the result. These simulations commonly exploit inference-time vulnerabilities, or data leakage, or biases under which the training has been conducted (Teichmann & Boticiu, 2023; Z. Wang et al., 2024; Zaydi & Maleh, 2025).

Formally, the red teams carry out evasion attacks to determine whether ML models can be misled by slight forms of data manipulation. In one example, an adversarial patch or camouflage clothes that confuses facial recognition software may be used with a vision-based surveillance system to test it. Likewise, chatbots also have language models that can be injected promptly or poisoned using toxic or biased inputs to determine whether the models generate toxic or biased outputs.

During penetration testing, hackers can act as adversaries to find the weak spots in an AI system prior to their exploitation by malicious hackers. A typical one is the beating of access gates in a biometric system. Ethical hackers can prepare attacks against the recognition algorithms: they can generate adversarial inputs, slightly deformed facial images or voice recordings, manipulated in order to trick an algorithm into allowing unauthorized access. Such adversarial tests assist in illuminating flaws in biometric authentication systems and can direct wavelength-based systems towards more robust systems.

Deception of fraud detection engines is another major area of adversarial penetration testing. Much like subtle adjustments in inputs, however, are made to datasets like transactional data, or in customer profiles, which will pass unnoticed to human decision makers, but will be purposefully in a position to elude machine learning-driven anomalous detectors. In the financial and e-commerce industries, this kind of red-teaming is especially useful as an adversarial practice that reflects tactics taken by criminals in cyberspace in order to prevent detection. Figure 2 illustrates a generalized workflow followed during adversarial AI red-teaming. This workflow spans from the identification of the AI system and threat model to the generation of adversarial examples and iterative evaluation of the system's response.

Figure 2. Adversarial AI Workflow in Red-Teaming Scenarios

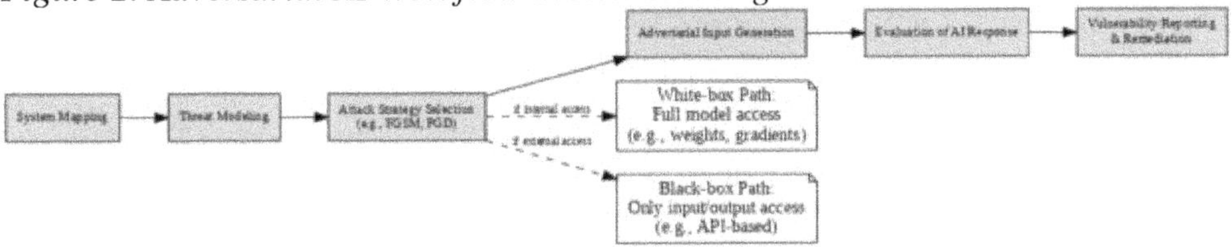

The next level of adversarial penetration testing is the ability to extract sensitive features or patterns regarding the deployed models. Ethical hackers can use either model inversion, gradient-based probing, or shadow modeling to reconstitute the characteristics of training data or reveal proprietary decision logic. These tests play a crucial role in assessing the possibilities that an AI system unintentionally leaks sensitive data in the form of its output, thus breaching privacy laws or exposing competitive secrets. With the help of such exercises, ethical hacking is not only a test of the soundness of the AI models, but it also helps form a secure-by-design AI infrastructure.

They are essential exercises where the resolution of these ML models is mandatory when used in sensitive and high-stakes environments such as border security, investment rating, and infrastructure safety.

Stress-Testing ML Models

Stress-testing is concerned with evaluating the behavior of AI systems in circumstances that are difficult to predict or when to may behave maliciously, e.g., when the distribution of the input differs from that seen during the training process or when deliberately malicious inputs are injected into the system (Flannery et al., 2025; W. Hu et al., 2025). Technically, testing of machine learning models entails subjecting them to a set of advanced attack-generating algorithms that target them extensively. The Fast Gradient Sign Method (FGSM) is one of the most popular methods, as the perturbations are made to the input data along the gradient of the loss function (Naqvi et al., 2023; J. Zhang et al., 2023). This small tweak may lead to the fact that a model misclassifies input samples, proving the vulnerability of decision boundaries in high-dimensional space.

FGSM can be extended to a more iterative signal, called Projected Gradient Descent (PGD). Instead of using a one-step perturbation, PGD itself makes a series of small changes in an established constraint (usually using the L-infinity norm) to improve the adversarial example in terms of its impact, but making it highly undetectable. It is a process that carries out a more realistic, continuous attack and is one of the strongest first-order adversaries (Ayas et al., 2022; He et al., 2024). Another family of adversarial techniques is the Carlini and Wagner (C&W) attacks, aimed at generating such weak perturbations that they will be almost unnoticeable (Fan et al., 2025). These attacks minimize a bespoke loss function, which concomitantly minimizes the distortion projecting to the input and maximizes the probability of misclassification. Their versatile nature comes with the fact that their changes are almost impossible to notice, yet the results in the output of the model are drastically different, which makes them exceptionally dangerous in systems that have to be safe.

In cases where the internals of models cannot be accessed, there is a black-box option through boundary attacks and decision-based attacks. These techniques only use the output of the model, i.e., class labels or confidence scores, and then iterate towards the formulation of adversarial inputs. These kinds of attacks are useful as approximations of the real world, where an attacker might not get system access to an AI service, but they might get API access to that service.

To assess the ability of the models to resist stress, these adversarial methods are used in a collection of testing settings. For example, in autonomous driving, the visual stressor will be presented by slightly altering the road signs with minor perturbations or stickers that will still be undetectable to human drivers but change the machine's perception. Within natural language processing (NLP) systems, prompt perturbations may generate biased or erroneous responses, manifesting the failures of the language model regarding comprehension or alignment. A related effective approach is synthetic data drift, in which samples used to train input data are slightly altered in their distributions, e.g., changing the lighting or dialect or representative demographic group, and checking whether a model trained on such data can still work well on shifted data. Collectively, these stress-testing techniques provide insights that would be valuable in knowing what a model can do, and they could tell the developers how to create robust and reliable AI systems.

Tools and Frameworks Supporting Adversarial Testing

Many open-source tools and frameworks to facilitate these adversarial testing activities have emerged, allowing ethical hackers to model a wide range of attacks. These frameworks make it difficult for adversarial methods to be reproduced into repeatable and modular processes that make experimentation and defending improvements quicker. To better understand the diversity and complexity of adversarial techniques used in stress-testing, Table 2 outlines key algorithms, their access requirements, and their strategic purposes. This comparison provides clarity on how these methods differ in terms of sophistication, visibility, and attack modality.

Table 2. Common Adversarial Attack Techniques and Their Characteristics

Attack Technique	Type	Access Level	Key Features	Use Cases
Fast Gradient Sign Method (FGSM)	White-box	Requires gradients	Single-step perturbation in the direction of the loss gradient	Baseline stress-testing
Projected Gradient Descent (PGD)	White-box	Requires gradients	Iterative, norm-constrained version of FGSM	Realistic adversarial simulation
Carlini & Wagner (C&W)	White-box	Requires gradients	Optimizes custom loss to minimize distortion and fool the model	Stealth attacks in critical systems
Boundary Attack	Black-box	No internal access	Uses model outputs to search the input boundary	External API red-teaming
Decision-Based Attack	Black-box	No internal access	Relies on label outputs to iteratively modify input	Model-as-a-service testing

One of the first adversarial ML open-source libraries is CleverHans, produced by Google Brain (Q. Hu, 2021; Vásquez-Venegas et al., 2024). It has a strong lineup of adversarial attack algorithms, such as FGSM, DeepFool, and Jacobian-based Saliency Map Attack (JSMA), with all being the expected tools to compare the model vulnerability with. CleverHans was designed to integrate smoothly with TensorFlow and PyTorch to allow researchers and practitioners to simply embed adversarial evaluations in their work as they might with other models of normal evaluation. The focus on reproduction and standardization has found it useful in comparing the robustness of the model across the architect and training methods.

The Adversarial Robustness Toolbox (ART), developed by IBM, presents a broader set of capabilities that is not limited to the common adversarial attacks (Agarwal & Nene, 2025). ART can be used both with white-box and black-box attack methodologies and can be used with several types of data, such as image, audio, and tabular data. Another advantage of ART is that it incorporates a broad range of defensive techniques besides the production of adversarial examples, including adversarial training, input preprocessing, estimation of model uncertainty, and the integration of the concept of differential privacy.

Another salient library is Foolbox, which has the best option in flexibility and convenience, particularly to practitioners of PyTorch and TensorFlow (Agarwal & Nene, 2025; Q. Hu, 2021). It accommodates various gradient-based and decision-based attack techniques and is auto-engineered to easily incorporate into testing pipelines. The thing that makes Foolbox stand out is the modular architecture. The user can set up attacks in a very customizable but still computationally efficient way. Such flexibility renders it an outstanding option in automated robustness testing in the development and deployment of models.

The Counterfit tool, developed by Microsoft, shows an alternative solution because it is a command-line framework that is more suitable for security teams red-teaming

AI systems. Counterfit enables the local and remote model testing and popular attack strategies such as FGSM, PGD, etc. It is also compatible with REST APIs and direct model interfaces, allowing it to be able to be heavily tested on different deployment environments. It is created with an eye toward reproducibility, and Counterfit allows automating adversarial attack pipelines, so it can be used in security audit reviews, continuous integration, continuous deployment, and compliance checks. A growing ecosystem of tools supports adversarial testing across different threat models, data types, and deployment environments. Table 3 summarizes the most widely adopted frameworks used by ethical hackers and red teams.

Table 3. Key Tools for Adversarial Testing

Tool	Developer	Supported Attacks	Model Compatibility	Use Highlights
CleverHans	Google Brain	FGSM, DeepFool, JSMA	TensorFlow, PyTorch	Academic benchmarking and standardized testing
ART (IBM)	IBM	White-box, Black-box, Poison	TensorFlow, Keras, PyTorch	Enterprise AI risk assessment
Foolbox	Robust Intelligence	FGSM, PGD, Score-based	PyTorch, TensorFlow	Flexible integration, automated pipelines
Counterfit	Microsoft	FGSM, PGD, API-level attacks	Local & remote models	Red-teaming automation in CI/CD

Taken together, such tools achieve much more than creating adversarial examples. They can be used to score robustness, a feature with which teams can measure and monitor the robustness of their models against adversarial examples. These also favour defensive training approaches, which retrain models on adversarial examples to achieve better generalization and robustness. Moreover, such frameworks facilitate the automation of the auditing procedure by utilizing a systematic application of a battery of attacks on numerous models and configurations. By so doing, they mutate abstract adversarial theory into red-teaming activities that transfer the education model into the practical application between ground-breaking research and applied security. Thus, these are unavoidable tools within any organization that tries to instill adversarial resilience in the AI lifecycle, from model development to the real world.

To integrate adversarial AI into ethical hacking is a progressive change in the landscape of cybersecurity and AI governance. Instead of hoping that attackers will be the first to discover AI systems' vulnerabilities, companies can undergo adversarial testing to find and patch the risks. As the primary defense against building trustworthy AI, some ethical hackers have adversarial skills and are accumulating a rising number of testing tools and methods. Hence, the incorporation of adversarial testing throughout the AI lifecycle, including development, production, and deployment, will make machine learning systems not only smart but also resilient and secure, and aligned with organizational risk reduction objectives.

TECHNICAL, ETHICAL, POLICY, AND OPERATIONAL CHALLENGES

With the further development of adversarial AI in the context of cybersecurity, a diversified field of problems of technical, ethical, operational, and policy nature emerges. Since the feasibility of applying adversarial techniques in performing stress tests and strengthening AI systems has a high potential, their actual implementation process is still associated with numerous limitations that require proper navigation.

Technical Challenges

Among the technical challenges is the inability to produce realistic simulated adversarial environments that reflect the dynamics of prediction scenarios that occur in the real world. Adversarial attacks that have been examined in literature most often assume that the environment is static, and do not consider either an adaptive adversary or noise in the environment. As another example, in autonomous driving or surveillance, the lighting conditions, occlusion, and other sensor imperfections play a major role in the way adversarial inputs can be realized. This means that ethical hackers can find it hard to duplicate these non-static and situational variables in controlled environments, and thus end up with an overestimation or underestimation of vulnerability in the system.

The second important technical concern is the extent of explainability and interpretability in the case of adversarial situations. Deep neural networks and other AI models are infamous for not being explainable in their decision-making process of making decisions. Under adversarial perturbations, it is even more difficult to interpret how a model wrongly classifies an input. This opacity hinders a desirable incident analysis, forensic investigation, and the feasible development of counterparts. Further, uninterpretable outputs place an ethical hacker and developer in the position of failing to persuade stakeholders that exposed vulnerabilities are significant or dangerous in a particular organization.

Technical issues are the model's robustness and generalizability. Generic attacks. A defense mechanism may provide robustness to some attacks (such as adversarial training or input preprocessing), albeit at the expense of model performance, runtime performance, or new threat generalization. Adversarial robustness is a moving target; although models can be trained to be robust to one type of perturbation, others may still be able to attack them, including those constructed with alternative norms or black-box assumptions. Also, defensive techniques are computationally expensive and not scalable to edge devices, so the practical applicability of defensive techniques is limited.

Operational Challenges

However, even the most powerful toolkits utilized today, such as CleverHans, ART, and Counterfit, have disadvantages: their scope is limited, they are not very easy to use, and none is standardized. Most of these tools have a high level of knowledge in the field of machine learning that is off-limits to the conventional security specialist. Natively, they have low levels of integration with wider cybersecurity tool sets, e.g., SIEM (Security Information and Event Management) or threat intelligence systems. The absence of user-friendly dashboards, reporting systems, and automation pipelines impedes the scaling operationalization of adversarial testing, particularly in the context of businesses with tens of AI models across divisions.

The operational barriers are further aggravated by the fact that the task requires highly qualified individuals with the ability to close the gap between cybersecurity and machine learning. The lack of cross-departmental aptitude limits the determination of institutional capacity to devise plans, carry out, and implement confrontational evaluations. Moreover, there are no streamlined workflows and best practices implemented that could make routine model audits easy and restrict the flow of integrating red-teaming into the pre-existing DevSecOps pipelines.

Ethical Challenges

Ethical issues are involved with the dual-use of adversarial AI research. Model-robustness techniques created to enhance model robustness can be turned against detection systems, used to create misinformation, or perform privacy attacks. The release of open-source code, pretrained models, and tutorials (based on their usefulness in terms of transparency and innovations) decreases this barrier of entry on the part of malicious actors. This brings to the fore critical concerns of assumed enlightened warning, accessibility, and publication standards, particularly in the academic and open science circles.

A trade-off between AI safety and AI security introduces new ethical challenges. The primary difference between safety research and security is that the former is aimed at a well-behaved environment and the latter at the existence of an adversary. Robustness-enhancing defense techniques such as input filtering or randomized smoothing may impair user experience, fairness, or accuracy. As an example, a trained algorithm, hardened to adversarial spam in email messages, might end up holding back legitimate messages, producing false positives. Such trade-offs should be taken into account contextually and their possible relevance to system criticality and impact on the user. To conceptualize the ethical tensions arising from adversarial AI, Figure 3 presents a dilemma map outlining key decision nodes and competing values faced by researchers, developers, and regulators.

Figure 3. Ethical Dilemma Map in Adversarial AI Research

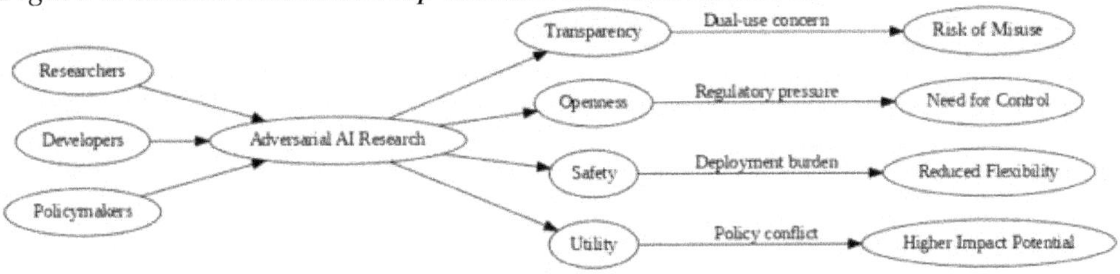

Ethical decision-making is also of great importance in establishing adversarial techniques that shall be released publicly and those that shall be maintained under controlled access. The absence of such generally accepted rules of ethics leads to researchers and developers being left to their own devices to sort out these areas of dilemma, and therefore leaves the door open to poor practice in consistency and safety.

Policy and Legal Challenges

There is an early form of legal and policy view on adversarial AI testing. Although there are approaches to traditional penetration testing, it is hard to make them applicable in relation to AI-based systems. Depending on the jurisdiction, crafting adversarial examples may or may not be legal, depending on the presence of consent, intent, and data usage agreements, particularly to the adversarial examples are being used against a third-party model or API. Moreover, there is also a regulatory gap when it comes to defining laws in national and international control of cybersecurity, as the peculiarities of adversarial machine learning have yet to be reflected in those. The lack of specialized laws means that organizations have to rely on general standards of cybersecurity, which, in most cases, lack the tools to inform adversarial practices related to AI.

The wider issue of AI governance also has to do with current policy gaps and includes data ownership, accountability in automated decision-making, and liability, as in the case of impairment caused by AI. Regulatory agencies have not been able to explain to whom such indemnities afforded by an adversarial vulnerability are directed: the developer of the model, the provider of the data, or the organization that uses it. This legal gray area makes it difficult to plan incident response, as well as discourages proactive adversarial testing. Due to the lack of unified global standards, legal interpretations of adversarial testing vary widely. Table 4 provides a comparative snapshot of legal stances in selected jurisdictions regarding adversarial testing of AI systems.

Table 4. Comparative Legal Ambiguities Across Jurisdictions

Country / Region	Legal Status of AI Pen Testing	Need for Consent	Relevance of Cybersecurity Laws	Notable Case Law or Guidance
USA	Ambiguous	Yes	Covered under CFAA	No specific ML guidance
EU	Emerging regulations	Yes	GDPR applies indirectly	Proposed AI Act may regulate adversarial use
Japan	Limited	Yes	Governed by local cybercrime law	No ML-specific rules
Canada	Unclear	Yes	PIPEDA and criminal law apply	No official AI-specific position
China	Strictly regulated	Required	National AI code under review	Emphasis on security testing by certified labs
Australia	Undefined	Yes	Covered under the Cybercrime Act	No ML-specific jurisprudence

Guidelines and Governance

In an attempt to alleviate these complex challenges, a number of organizations and multi-stakeholder alliances are starting to offer recommendations on responsible adversarial AI. These are the increased red-teaming transparency, ethical review boards to oversee dual-use research, reproducibility standards, and urging privacy-preserving methods. Nevertheless, more popular use of such constructs is not achieved, and there is an urgent need for cross-sector cooperation among governments, academia, industry, and civil society.

The guidelines should also aim at introducing limits to the responsible adversarial experimentation, introducing guidelines of consent to test the models of third party, and the structure of incentives to report bugs. Effective governance also requires the updating of governance measures to stay current, as well as their technical capabilities, to keep the advancement and application of adversarial AI consistent with more global societal goals of security, justice, and responsibility.

CONCLUSION

AI is fast taking the shape of a formidable resource and an exigent problem when it comes to cybersecurity. Its recent relevance in protecting AI systems against the current or emerging threats can be attributed to the growing trends in recent years, especially the emergence of automated red-teaming and the incorporation of episodes of generative adversarial networks (GANs), as well as the rising complexity of model stress-testing techniques. These technologies are changing the face of how hacking can be practiced by using dynamic simulations rather than translating vulnerability to moving to dynamic, learning-based scenarios that simulate real-world hackers with high fidelity.

As companies start to engage in adversarial AI as part of an ethical hacking process, a few best practices are taking shape. These comprise: integrating modular testing tool chains, being compliant with explainability and interpretability frameworks, frequent stress-testing of models in the development cycles, and consistent surveillance of distributional drift or threat patterns. By defining the boundaries to adversarial experimentation, like model ownership, consent, and intent, some of the most powerful tools will be used responsibly. Moreover, it is essential to develop an interdisciplinary team of experts specializing in cybersecurity, machine learning, and law to create an efficient environment of adversarial testing that will be not only resilient but also ethically informed.

In the future, there needs to be a roadmap that is being worked out in coordination across countries to find a path through adversarial AI that shows it is dual-use. In the context of industry, it means investing in secure-by-design AI systems, increasing training of developers, and encouraging transparency by using frequent red-teaming audits. The field of academia ought to be concerned with the responsible publication of research, the creation of uniform benchmarks, and the need to seek cooperation with policy institutions aimed at ensuring that the theoretical developments and their implementation and application in real life are connected. In the meantime, policymakers should revise some legal frameworks to respond to the reality of adversarial AI, facilitate open and safe AI development, and encourage multi-stakeholder governance approaches.

Adversarial AI has tremendous potential to enhance cybersecurity, yet this goal can be achieved only through maintaining a delicate dynamic between groundbreaking invention, accountability, and regulation. Integrating adversarial thinking in the design of the fundamentals of AI construction and security methods, ensuring cooperation across industries, we can, thus, create AI systems that will not be merely smarter, but safer, fairer, and better equipped to deal with the challenges of tomorrow.

REFERENCES

Agarwal, A., & Nene, M. J. (2025). Advancing Trustworthy AI: A Comparative Evaluation of AI Robustness Toolboxes. *SN Computer Science*, *6*(3), 1–16. DOI: 10.1007/s42979-025-03785-w

Ayas, M. S., Ayas, S., & Djouadi, S. M. (2022). Projected Gradient Descent Adversarial Attack and Its Defense on a Fault Diagnosis System. *2022 45th International Conference on Telecommunications and Signal Processing, TSP 2022*. DOI: 10.1109/TSP55681.2022.9851334

Baniecki, H., & Biecek, P. (2024). Adversarial attacks and defenses in explainable artificial intelligence: A survey. *Information Fusion*, *107*, 102303. Advance online publication. DOI: 10.1016/j.inffus.2024.102303

Blauth, T. F., Gstrein, O. J., & Zwitter, A. (2022). Artificial Intelligence Crime: An Overview of Malicious Use and Abuse of AI. *IEEE Access : Practical Innovations, Open Solutions*, *10*, 77110–77122. Advance online publication. DOI: 10.1109/ACCESS.2022.3191790

Caldwell, T. (2011). Ethical hackers: Putting on the white hat. *Network Security*, *2011*(7). DOI: 10.1016/S1353-4858(11)70075-7

Chauhan, R., Singh, R., Bartwal, R., Rawat, R., & Dhanalakshmi, R. (2024). An investigation of ethical hacking: White-hat hackers. *Challenges in Information, Communication and Computing Technology*, 769–774. DOI: 10.1201/9781003559085-132

Chen, J., Zhang, X., Zhang, R., Wang, C., & Liu, L. (2021). De-Pois: An Attack-Agnostic Defense against Data Poisoning Attacks. *IEEE Transactions on Information Forensics and Security*, *16*, 3412–3425. Advance online publication. DOI: 10.1109/TIFS.2021.3080522

Chen, Y., Zhu, X., Gong, X., Yi, X., & Li, S. (2023). Data Poisoning Attacks in Internet-of-Vehicle Networks: Taxonomy, State-of-The-Art, and Future Directions. *IEEE Transactions on Industrial Informatics*, *19*(1), 20–28. Advance online publication. DOI: 10.1109/TII.2022.3198481

Debicha, I., Cochez, B., Kenaza, T., Debatty, T., Dricot, J. M., & Mees, W. (2023). Adv-Bot: Realistic adversarial botnet attacks against network intrusion detection systems. *Computers & Security*, *129*, 103176. Advance online publication. DOI: 10.1016/j.cose.2023.103176

El Houda, Z. A. (2024). Cyber Threat Actors Review: Examining the Tactics and Motivations of Adversaries in the Cyber Landscape. In *Cyber Security for Next-Generation Computing Technologies*. DOI: 10.1201/9781003404361-5

Fan, L., Khairuddin, A. S. M., Liu, H., & Hasikin, K. B. (2025). Perceptual Carlini-Wagner Attack: A Robust and Imperceptible Adversarial Attack Using LPIPS. *IEEE Access : Practical Innovations, Open Solutions*, *13*, 1–1. DOI: 10.1109/ACCESS.2025.3588113

Filipovich, I., & Kovalev, V. (2023). Dependence of the results of adversarial attacks on medical image modality, attack type, and defense methods. *Diagnostic Biomedical Signal and Image Processing Applications with Deep Learning Methods*, 179–195. DOI: 10.1016/B978-0-323-96129-5.00004-4

Flannery, B. T., Sandler, H. M., Lal, P., Feldman, M. D., Santa-Rosario, J. C., Pathak, T., Mirtti, T., Farre, X., Correa, R., Chafe, S., Shah, A., Efstathiou, J. A., Hoffman, K., Hallman, M. A., Straza, M., Jordan, R., Pugh, S. L., Feng, F., & Madabhushi, A. (2025). Stress testing deep learning models for prostate cancer detection on biopsies and surgical specimens. *The Journal of Pathology*, *265*(2), 146–157. DOI: 10.1002/path.6373 PMID: 39660731

Gong, X., Chen, Y., Wang, Q., & Kong, W. (2023). Backdoor Attacks and Defenses in Federated Learning: State-of-the-Art, Taxonomy, and Future Directions. *IEEE Wireless Communications*, *30*(2), 114–121. Advance online publication. DOI: 10.1109/MWC.017.2100714

Hansson, S. O., Belin, M. Å., & Lundgren, B. (2021). Self-Driving Vehicles—An Ethical Overview. *Philosophy & Technology*, *34*(4), 1383–1408. DOI: 10.1007/s13347-021-00464-5

Happe, A., & Cito, J. (2023). Understanding Hackers' Work: An Empirical Study of Offensive Security Practitioners. *ESEC/FSE 2023 - Proceedings of the 31st ACM Joint Meeting European Software Engineering Conference and Symposium on the Foundations of Software Engineering*. DOI: 10.1145/3611643.3613900

He, L., Wang, Z., Yang, S., Liu, T., & Huang, Y. (2024). Generalizing Projected Gradient Descent for Deep-Learning-Aided Massive MIMO Detection. *IEEE Transactions on Wireless Communications*, *23*(3), 1827–1839. Advance online publication. DOI: 10.1109/TWC.2023.3292124

Hu, H., Salcic, Z., Sun, L., Dobbie, G., Yu, P. S., & Zhang, X. (2023). Membership Inference Attacks on Machine Learning: A Survey. *ACM Computing Surveys*, *54*(11s), 1–37. Advance online publication. DOI: 10.1145/3523273

Hu, Q. (2021). A survey of adversarial example toolboxes. *Proceedings - 2021 2nd International Conference on Computing and Data Science, CDS 2021*, 603–608. DOI: 10.1109/CDS52072.2021.00109

Hu, W., Shao, C., & Zhang, W. (2025). Predicting U.S. bank failures and stress testing with machine learning algorithms. *Finance Research Letters, 75*, 106802. DOI: 10.1016/j.frl.2025.106802

Kong, Z., Xue, J., Wang, Y., Huang, L., Niu, Z., & Li, F. (2021). A Survey on Adversarial Attack in the Age of Artificial Intelligence. *Wireless Communications and Mobile Computing, 2021*(1), 4907754. Advance online publication. DOI: 10.1155/2021/4907754

Lutkevich, B. (2019). What is HIPAA (Health Insurance Portability and Accountability Act)? In *WhatIs.com*.

Muthalagu, R., Malik, J., & Pawar, P. M. (2025). Detection and prevention of evasion attacks on machine learning models. *Expert Systems with Applications, 266*, 126044. DOI: 10.1016/j.eswa.2024.126044

Naqvi, S. M. A., Shabaz, M., Khan, M. A., & Hassan, S. I. (2023). Adversarial Attacks on Visual Objects Using the Fast Gradient Sign Method. *Journal of Grid Computing, 21*(4), 52. Advance online publication. DOI: 10.1007/s10723-023-09684-9

Niu, J., Liu, P., Zhu, X., Shen, K., Wang, Y., Chi, H., Shen, Y., Jiang, X., Ma, J., & Zhang, Y. (2024). A survey on membership inference attacks and defenses in machine learning. *Journal of Information and Intelligence, 2*(5), 404–454. Advance online publication. DOI: 10.1016/j.jiixd.2024.02.001

Niu, J., Ma, X., Chen, Y., Zhang, G., He, Z., Hou, Z., Zhu, X., Wu, G., Chen, K., & Zhang, Y. (2022). A survey on membership inference attacks and defenses in Machine Learning. *Journal of Cybersecurity, 7*(6). Advance online publication. DOI: 10.19363/J.cnki.cn10-1380/tn.2022.11.01

Pan, Z., Yu, W., Yi, X., Khan, A., Yuan, F., & Zheng, Y. (2019). Recent Progress on Generative Adversarial Networks (GANs): A Survey. *IEEE Access : Practical Innovations, Open Solutions, 7*, 36322–36333. Advance online publication. DOI: 10.1109/ACCESS.2019.2905015

Qiu, S., Liu, Q., Zhou, S., & Wu, C. (2019). Review of artificial intelligence adversarial attack and defense technologies. In *Applied Sciences (Switzerland)* (Vol. 9, Issue 5). DOI: 10.3390/app9050909

Rigaki, M., & Garcia, S. (2024). A Survey of Privacy Attacks in Machine Learning. *ACM Computing Surveys*, *56*(4), 1–34. Advance online publication. DOI: 10.1145/3624010

Saxena, D., & Cao, J. (2021). Generative Adversarial Networks (GANs). In *ACM Computing Surveys* (Vol. 54, Issue 3). DOI: 10.1145/3446374

Stilgoe, J. (2021). How can we know a self-driving car is safe? *Ethics and Information Technology*, *23*(4), 635–647. DOI: 10.1007/s10676-021-09602-1

Teichmann, F. M., & Boticiu, S. R. (2023). An overview of the benefits, challenges, and legal aspects of penetration testing and red teaming. *International Cybersecurity Law Review*, *4*(4), 387–397. Advance online publication. DOI: 10.1365/s43439-023-00100-2

Tian, Z., Cui, L., Liang, J., & Yu, S. (2023). A Comprehensive Survey on Poisoning Attacks and Countermeasures in Machine Learning. *ACM Computing Surveys*, *55*(8), 1–35. Advance online publication. DOI: 10.1145/3551636

Truong, N. B., Sun, K., Lee, G. M., & Guo, Y. (2020). GDPR-Compliant Personal Data Management: A Blockchain-Based Solution. *IEEE Transactions on Information Forensics and Security*, *15*, 1746–1761. Advance online publication. DOI: 10.1109/TIFS.2019.2948287

Vásquez-Venegas, C., Wu, C., Sundar, S., Prôa, R., Beloy, F. J., Medina, J. R., McNichol, M., Parvataneni, K., Kurtzman, N., Mirshawka, F., Aguirre-Jerez, M., Ebner, D. K., & Celi, L. A. (2024). Detecting and Mitigating the Clever Hans Effect in Medical Imaging: A Scoping Review. *Journal of Imaging Informatics in Medicine*, *2024*(4), 1–17. DOI: 10.1007/s10278-024-01335-z PMID: 39643820

Villalón-Huerta, A., Ripoll-Ripoll, I., & Marco-Gisbert, H. (2022). A Taxonomy for Threat Actors' Delivery Techniques. *Applied Sciences (Basel, Switzerland)*, *12*(8), 3929. Advance online publication. DOI: 10.3390/app12083929

Villegas-Ch, W., Jaramillo-Alcázar, A., & Luján-Mora, S. (2024). Evaluating the Robustness of Deep Learning Models against Adversarial Attacks: An Analysis with FGSM, PGD and CW. *Big Data and Cognitive Computing 2024, Vol. 8, Page 8*, *8*(1), 8. DOI: 10.3390/bdcc8010008

Wang, S., Ko, R. K. L., Bai, G., Dong, N., Choi, T., & Zhang, Y. (2024). Evasion Attack and Defense on Machine Learning Models in Cyber-Physical Systems: A Survey. *IEEE Communications Surveys and Tutorials*, *26*(2), 930–966. Advance online publication. DOI: 10.1109/COMST.2023.3344808

Wang, Z., Li, S., Zhang, L., Hu, C., & Yan, L. (2024). A Red Team automated testing modeling and online planning method for post-penetration. *Computers & Security*, *144*, 103945. DOI: 10.1016/j.cose.2024.103945

Wang, Z., Ma, J., Wang, X., Hu, J., Qin, Z., & Ren, K. (2023). Threats to Training: A Survey of Poisoning Attacks and Defenses on Machine Learning Systems. *ACM Computing Surveys*, *55*(7), 1–36. Advance online publication. DOI: 10.1145/3538707

Xue, M., Yuan, C., Wu, H., Zhang, Y., & Liu, W. (2020). Machine Learning Security: Threats, Countermeasures, and Evaluations. *IEEE Access : Practical Innovations, Open Solutions*, *8*, 74720–74742. Advance online publication. DOI: 10.1109/ACCESS.2020.2987435

Zaydi, M., & Maleh, Y. (2025). EMPOWERING RED TEAMS WITH GENERATIVE AI: TRANSFORMING PENETRATION TESTING THROUGH ADAPTIVE INTELLIGENCE. *EDPACS*, *70*(2), 41–66. DOI: 10.1080/07366981.2024.2439628

Zhang, J., Dongdong, C., Huang, Q., Liao, J., Zhang, W., Feng, H., Hua, G., & Yu, N. (2022). Poison Ink: Robust and Invisible Backdoor Attack. *IEEE Transactions on Image Processing*, *31*, 5691–5705. Advance online publication. DOI: 10.1109/TIP.2022.3201472 PMID: 36040942

Zhang, J., Qian, W., Nie, R., Cao, J., & Xu, D. (2023). Generate adversarial examples by adaptive moment iterative fast gradient sign method. *Applied Intelligence*, *53*(1), 1101–1114. Advance online publication. DOI: 10.1007/s10489-022-03437-z

Zhang, Z., Liu, Q., Huang, Z., Wang, H., Lee, C. K., & Chen, E. (2023). Model Inversion Attacks Against Graph Neural Networks. *IEEE Transactions on Knowledge and Data Engineering*, *35*(9), 8729–8741. Advance online publication. DOI: 10.1109/TKDE.2022.3207915

Zhou, S., Zhu, T., Ye, D., Yu, X., & Zhou, W. (2024). Boosting Model Inversion Attacks With Adversarial Examples. *IEEE Transactions on Dependable and Secure Computing*, *21*(3), 1451–1468. Advance online publication. DOI: 10.1109/TDSC.2023.3285015

Chapter 2
AI and Machine Learning Applications in Ethical Hacking: Advancing Cybersecurity Defense

R. Siva Subramanian
http://orcid.org/0000-0002-7509-9223
SRM Institute of Science and Technology, Tiruchirappalli, India

Venkata Ramana Kaneti
VNR Vignana Jyothi Institute of Engineering and Technology, India

G. Saranya
SA Engineering College, India

N. P. Ponnuviji
R.M.K. College of Engineering and Technology, India

ABSTRACT

The integration of Artificial Intelligence (AI) and Machine Learning (ML) in ethical hacking has significantly enhanced cybersecurity defense mechanisms. AI-driven techniques enable automated vulnerability detection, malware analysis, phishing prevention, and real-time intrusion detection, making security operations more efficient and proactive. Advanced AI models, including deep learning and reinforcement learning, strengthen penetration testing and threat intelligence. However, challenges such as adversarial AI attacks, data privacy concerns, biases in AI models, and high computational costs pose significant risks. Future research focuses on autonomous AI-powered ethical hacking frameworks, federated learning for secure threat intelligence sharing, and AI-human collaboration for effective cybersecurity

DOI: 10.4018/979-8-3373-3536-0.ch002

governance. As cyber threats become more sophisticated, leveraging AI responsibly will be essential for advancing cybersecurity defenses while ensuring transparency and ethical compliance.

1. INTRODUCTION

1.1 Overview of Cybersecurity Threats in the Digital Era

The advancement in technology and integration of various systems has resulted to a sharp rise in cybercrimes. Today, organizations in all sectors are dealing with new and changing threats like malware, ransomware, phishing, DoS and DDoS attacks, and APTs (Sharma, P., & Gupta, H. 2024). Today, cybercrime is becoming more and more complex and traditional security methods are not enough to contain such threats. They may result in business losses, negative publicity, stealing, and exposure of several sensitive details, which is why cybersecurity is an essential consideration today for governments, companies, and even individuals (Adejumo, A., & Ogburie, C. 2025). They noted that the rate of change is one of the most critical problems in cybersecurity today. Using automation, artificial intelligence and even augmented and sophisticated social engineering, cyber criminals exploit the systems. Furthermore, the growth of cloud, the Internet of Things (IoT), and mobile devices means a greater number and range of entry points to be hacked. Current security measures that have been employed in organizations like the signature-based detection and the rule-based threat management do not suffice the current the threats. This means that organization are seeking for proactive and intelligent measures to protect their networks hence making ethical hacking an essential component of the security system(Untawale, T. 2021).

1.2 Role of Ethical Hacking in Cybersecurity Defense

Ethical hacking is the process of testing the security of an organization's systems and networks by trying to breach them legally, or legally hacking into a system. Ethical hackers on the other hand use their talents in a positive way as they seek to find the vulnerabilities in the system with an aim of fixing them. Ethical hacking is useful in the field of cybersecurity since it involves testing a system for vulnerabilities before they are exploited by hackers(Kirubai, J. C. D., & Priscila, S. S. 2024).

Ethical hackers are hired by organizations so that they can test the organization's defenses, conduct vulnerability tests and enhance security. It is important to understand that ethical hacking is conducted using the methodologies that include black-box testing, white-box testing, and the gray-box testing. These approaches help the security professionals to view the security of an organization from different angles so as to give it adequate protection. Legal requirements such as the GDPR, HIPAA, and other industry standards that require routine assessment of networks are some of the regulatory bodies that encourage the use of ethical hacking. However, there are disadvantages of ethical hacking as well. Conventional penetration testing techniques require a lot of manual work and may take quite a lot of time in the process. In addition, the highly advanced cyber threats may not be easily identified by human expertise and therefore require the use of advanced software tools. This has paved way to increased incorporation of AI and ML in ethical hacking to improve efficiency and effectiveness of cyber security audits.

1.3 The Emergence of AI and Machine Learning in Ethical Hacking

The implementation of AI and ML in ethical hacking is quite significant and transformative as it has introduced an automate, smart, and self-learning security systems. AI-based hacking software is capable to process a large amount of security information, identify threats and estimate risks, compared to conventional techniques. Artificial intelligence can learn from previous attacks and recognize that certain patterns may pose a threat to the system, hence preventing them from executing their functions. Another important role of AI in ethical hacking is in the discovery of vulnerabilities which are automated(Prabhu et al., 2025). Most of the conventional vulnerability scanning tools are difficult to configure and even the results obtained have to be interpreted. On the other hand, AI-based scanners use machine learning and employ it to learn from the new threats and scan for vulnerabilities on its own without much human interaction. Further, AI integrated penetration testing tools can mimic real life attacks and this is very useful in assessing organizations' vulnerabilities. There is also another aspect that AI helps in ethical hacking, and that is adversarial testing. Red teaming with Artificial Intelligence leverages the use of algorithms to develop new and complex attack procedures, and procedures that allow an organization to analyze its defenses against cyber threats that employ Artificial Intelligence. This makes it easier for security teams to be prepared for any new threats since they are always on the lookout for them. Also, it is possible to note that using reinforcement learning techniques helps the AI systems to develop the penetration testing capabilities and learn from the previous security assessments. Nevertheless, there are some challenges that are associated with the use of AI in ethical hacking. AI models are vulnerable to adversarial attacks which are the techniques by which the AI system is tricked into relaxing security measures. In addition, the application of AI in hacking also has some issues in ethic and law, for example, the misuse of the AI hacking tools. It is crucial to ensure that the AI-based ethical hacking is well in line with the set ethical and legal policies to avoid adverse outcomes.

1.4 Objectives and Scope of the Survey

This chapter seeks to establish the application of AI and ML in ethical hacking and how the two technologies strengthen security systems. The following are the major objectives of this chapter:

1. To enable the reader to have a clear understanding of ethical hacking and the role it plays in the realm of cybersecurity.
2. To consider how ethical hacks and both AI and ML can improve the methods of information security.
3. To examine multiple practical uses of ethical hacking under the umbrella of artificial intelligence in encompassing vulnerability scanning and detection, malware analysis, intrusion and adversarial evaluation.
4. In order to identify the problems and difficulties that are connected with the usage of AI in ethical hacking.
5. In order to share ideas and views on what is yet to come in the field of AI use for cybersecurity defense.

This chapter focuses on the various AI and ML techniques that are applied in ethical hacking and these are the supervised learning, unsupervised learning, reinforcement learning and the adversarial AI. It also includes real-life examples, use cases, and applications of security solutions based on artificial intelligence. Furthermore, this chapter analyses ethical, legal, and regulatory issues of AI in ethical hacking, and the importance of a responsible approach to AI in cybersecurity. Thus, it can be stated that the importance of AI and ML in the cybersecurity defense will only grow in the future. It is critical for developing better and smarter security systems to understand how these technologies can be used for ethical hacking. This chapter will be useful for cybersecurity specialists, researchers, and anybody else engaged in the sphere of AI ethical hacking services and products.

2. FUNDAMENTALS OF ETHICAL HACKING AND AI-DRIVEN SECURITY

2.1 Ethical Hacking: Concepts, Methodologies, and Importance

Ethical hacking is the process of testing the computer systems, networks, and applications for vulnerabilities by an authorized person to find out how protected they are from unauthorized users. Ethical hackers employ the same methods as the hackers but for noble purposes of testing the systems with the aim of making them more secure. Companies from different sectors hire ethical hackers to identify their strengths and weaknesses so that they could fix vulnerabilities in their systems. The concept of ethical hacking can be centered on three major activities which include identification, assessment, and remediation of vulnerabilities. Ethical hackers are well-organized in their approach towards security testing and conduct it in stages including reconnaissance, scanning, exploitation, maintaining access and reporting of the vulnerabilities. These phases are also similar to those used by black-hat hackers; however, ethical hackers work legally and within the provided legal frameworks(Yamini et al., 2024).

Ethical hacking is a critical practice in cybersecurity since it involves identifying potential threats that are not easily apparent to a company's IT department. The threats are not new and are always adapting to new strategies; therefore, companies must be on the lookout for threats all the time. Ethical hacking allows the security personnel to 'attack' an organization and check its preparedness against threats. However, it is important to note that there are some disadvantages or limitations of ethical hacking. In general, traditional penetration testing presents a number of drawbacks, which are time-consuming, demands great expert knowledge, and may fail to detect sophisticated threats. As AI and ML are applied to cybersecurity, more and more enterprises are implementing intelligent and automated security into ethical hacking.

2.2 AI and ML in Cybersecurity: An Overview

AI and ML have become important in cybersecurity since it provides automated responses, intelligent, and adaptive security systems(Sinha, A. R et al 2023). The intelligent security systems can process hundreds of thousands of pieces of information, notice specific trends, and estimate risks in comparison with ordinary security technologies. The subfield of AI called machine learning enables systems, which are used to protect computer networks and personal data, to identify threats more effectively as the result of analyzing information about previous attacks. The following is the explanation of how AI and ML are used in ethical hacking Trade and Security: Enhancement of Penetration testing, vulnerability assessment, and Threat Intelligence. Automating security tools can help in identifying the potential threats and weaknesses by executing tests that would otherwise have to be done manually(Basak et al 2024). Also, ML algorithms can monitor the traffic patterns in a network, identify signs of an attack, and even forecast an attack before it happens. The first benefit of artificial intelligence use in the realm of cybersecurity is its malleability and capacity for learning. Conventional security measures are rule and signature-based, which means that they cannot identify attacks that exploit as yet unknown vulnerabilities or those that are newly developed. On the other hand AI based security measures employs behavioral analysis as well as the identification of incidents that deviate from normal use. This approach assists organizations to be a step ahead of the criminals and enhance on their security measures. But, there are certain drawbacks to the integration of AI in cybersecurity. AI models depend on large datasets of good quality for the process of learning to happen. This is the case since poor quality data or a biased training set will result in the wrong classification of threats as well as false alarms. Furthermore, the adversaries are now using adversarial AI approaches to breach the security measures making it mandatory for organizations to enhance AI security measures periodically.

2.3 Key Differences Between Traditional and AI-Powered Cybersecurity Approaches

In the traditional approach, cybersecurity measures include the use of detection systems, firewalls, anti-virus, and other methods such as penetration testing that is conducted by individuals. Though these methods have been useful in combating known threats, they are inadequate in handling the ever emerging threats. The artificial intelligence solution, in contrast, is based on automating the processes and applying trained algorithms and real-time analysis to fight cyber threats more efficiently. Some of the main distinctions between conventional and artificial intelligence security strategies are the capacity to process massive data. Traditional security systems simply have a list of rules and signatures which are used to detect threats and as a result cannot address emerging threats. On the other hand, AI techniques can handle big amount of network traffic data, logs, user activity and detect threats in real time. The other major difference is the speed at which threats are identified and neutralized or containments are made. The conventional security measures involve the use of human input and analysis in the detection and prevention of cyber threats, which may take a lot of time. On the other hand, the AI-driven systems can perform all these tasks without human intervention including, identification of security threats and defense against cyber threats. This real-time threat detection capability enhances an organization security posture, and cuts down on the probability of data breach. Also, conventional security measures are mostly post-incident, implying that they act after attacks have taken place. It is important to note that AI-based security solutions, though, offer a proactive approach as they are one step forward in identifying security threats and thereafter warding off attacks before the campaign commences. Thus, using machine learning models, one will be able to monitor the network activity and analyze it for the presence of any anomaly taking place in the network, and make necessary changes in the security measures. However, like any other technology, AI has its pros and cons in the cybersecurity context, and they include the following: AI has to be trained and fine-tuned before it can be used for any purpose and it is for this reason that cyber criminals are coming up with better ways of evading the AI-based detection systems. Moreover, AI-based security solutions consume more computational resources, and this is a disadvantage especially to SMEs. However, AI technology is slowly integrating itself into cybersecurity and ethical hacking, and therefore it will remain paramount as technology advances.

2.4 AI-Driven Penetration Testing and Vulnerability Assessment

AI in penetration testing and vulnerability assessment has now become the new trend in ethical hacking. The conventional styles of penetration testing are the manual probing, exploiting, and reporting of the security loopholes, which is a process that may take a lot of time and resource. These are several benefits that can be derived from automating such processes through AI-powered penetration testing. Automated tools of penetration testing are built with AI, which can learn different patterns and therefore scan network settings, application source code, and logs to find threats. These tools can mimic different attacks and determine the vulnerabilities that an organization's security system has. AI-based penetration testing is different from that of other penetration testing since it keeps on updating itself with the new threats and employs new strategies to counter the threats posed by the hackers. There are several uses of AI in penetration testing of which the most common is automated vulnerability scanning. Vulnerability scanners can automatically scan the code, find misconfiguration, and potential security issues in it with a high level of accuracy when it is created with AI. These scanners can also be programmed to filter the results by the level of risk, so that the most serious issues are addressed first. Another testing technique that is worth mentioning within the sphere of AI-based security testing is adversarial testing. There are also uses of AI for adversarial model generation, where AI is used to create situations that can be used to challenge the security systems and compare them to AI cyber threats. It assists in understanding an organization sector's preparedness against new-age security threats possible through deepfake phishing or AI-assisted malware attacks. In addition, it increases the efficiency of vulnerability assessment by offering threatening information in real-time. One can use AI-powered security platforms to collect data from sources such as the dark web, threat intelligence feed, and security logs in a given organization. This is because the preventive measures help organizations to prevent the vulnerabilities from being exploited by the cybercriminals. Nevertheless, there are some challenges that are associated with the use of AI in penetration testing. With AI models, it is possible to get false positives and that mean lot of alerts that in reality does not pose any security threat hence wasting resources. Another disadvantage of using AIs is that they require ongoing and regular updates for optimization against new threats. It is also important for organizations to consider ethical issues of AI-based penetration testing, specifically regarding the legal use of these tools.

When it comes to protection, AI and ML have made a significant change in ethical hacking as it is contributes to intelligent security. Ethical hacking, a process that was formerly done through manual means, discovered through penetration testing and vulnerability assessment, has been boosted by AI security tools that enable the constant identification of incursions. Comparing traditional and AI-based cybersecurity approaches, it is possible to conclude that AI has certain benefits that are helpful at analyzing vast amounts of data, increasing the speed of threat identification, and shifting from a reactive to a proactive security model. Penetration testing and vulnerability assessment using AI has a lot of advantages in determining the security weaknesses and the risks. However, there are some challenges that need to be solved to fully unlock AI in cybersecurity, these are adversarial AI, data quality and ethical issues. With the advancement of cyber threats, ethical hacking integrated with AI will have a significant role to ensure the protection of organizations from cyber threats.

3. AI AND ML APPLICATIONS IN ETHICAL HACKING

The use of AI and ML in ethical hacking has also increased as it has helped security professionals in automating vulnerability assessment, improving threat intelligence and developing better mechanisms to respond to threats. Previous methods of penetration testing and vulnerability assessment were carried out with much effort and time and were less accurate compared to the AI-based tools. Ethical hackers use artificial intelligence to discover vulnerabilities and also perform attacks and reconstruct them to gauge the extent to which the hacker can exploit them. In this section, the author discusses how AI and ML have been used in ethical hacking and their effectiveness in the current systems used for defending against cyber threats.

3.1 Automated Vulnerability Detection

In ethical hacking, the most important use of AI is to identify vulnerabilities by using automated tools. The traditional method of vulnerability scanning is highly dependent on rules of security and assessments where a large amount of work is done manually and the process is often lengthy and error-prone. This process is improved by the help of advanced scanning tools where AI uses big data to learn from the past attacks and identifies security weaknesses much effectively. Vulnerability scanners are AI-based and employ the use of ML algorithms to analyze patterns and come up with likely loopholes in software, networks, and applications. These tools are capable of updating their knowledge base from time to time by using the new attack vectors and security threats. AI-based vulnerability detection is not based on the signature-based detection approach, but focuses on behavioral analysis and anomaly detection methods, meaning that security teams can detect zero-day vulnerabilities, which are the new security flaws that hackers can use. The information about vulnerabilities can be learned by the machine learning algorithms, and they can estimate the probabilities of the system's exposure to particular threats. The changes in the system configurations, network logs, and codebases can be identified and predicted with the help of AI that will alert security personnel before such vulnerabilities are noticed by attackers. Also, AI-based exploitation tools can be used to conduct emulation for measuring the impact of threats in order to determine which ones should be addressed first(LA, A. G. 2026).

Figure 1. AI and ML Applications in Ethical Hacking

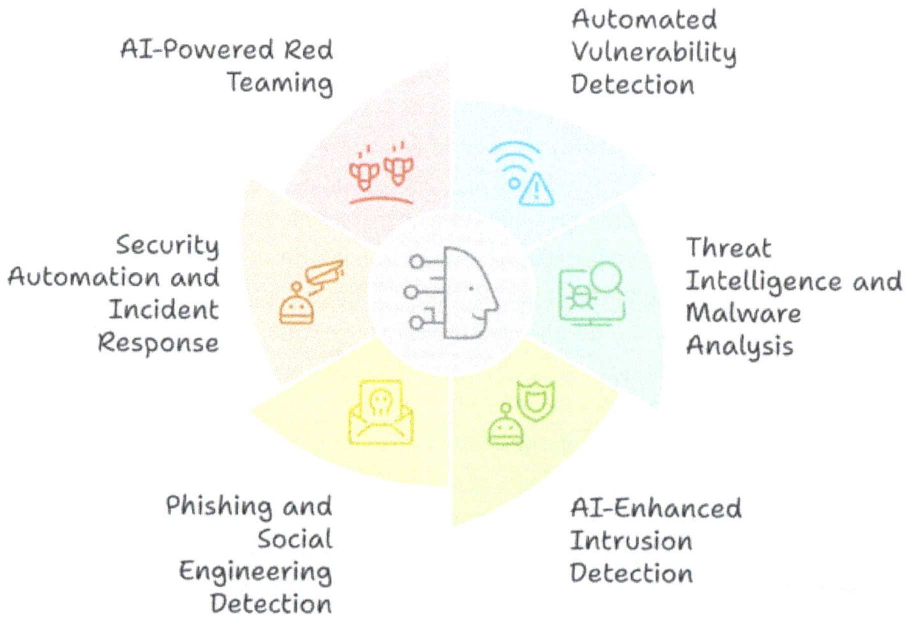

3.2 Threat Intelligence and Malware Analysis

Threat intelligence and malware analysis are some of the areas where AI and ML are very useful in the current world as they offer help to the security professionals to identify and categorize the new threats in a short span. The traditional approach to detect the malware and other cyber threats was based on signatures, which was not very effective in the dynamic environment. The above limitations are solved by the AI-based solutions that analyze the behavior of the malware and identify patterns that are linked to malicious activities. Using large datasets of known malware samples, ML can classify threats into such categories as trojans, ransomware, spyware, etc. Specifically, integrating AI in malware detection searches for characteristics in files, recognizes network activities, and reads logs to provide suspicious information. These tools can also detect metamorphic or polymorphic malware which are the type of viruses that change their form to avoid being detected. The second AI use in malware analysis is termed behavioral threat intelligence. It is done in contrast to simple statistical checks, which do not take into account how a file or an application behaves in a particular setting. Since AI-based security systems can detect unusual patterns and activities, new strains of malware may be easily spotted by such systems. This proactive approach greatly helps ethical hackers to identify new types of cyber threats(Ganesan et al 2023).

3.3 AI-Enhanced Intrusion Detection and Prevention Systems

Intrusion Detection and Prevention Systems (IDPS) can be considered as an important part of cybersecurity defense tools. The traditional approaches of IDPS are based on the use of rules and signature-based detection and therefore are not effective for the zero-day attack and other new forms of cyber threats(Ramalingam et al 2025). Conversely, AI integrated IDPS uses the ML and deep learning models to detect the security threats, and respond to them in real-time. IDPS that are based on artificial intelligence technologies utilize such approaches as anomaly detection to detect different types of threats such as unauthorized access to the network, or unusual network traffic or user activities. These systems involve the constant surveillance of the network, where any activities that are out of the ordinary are noted, and the potential cyber threats are identified early enough. Attack data make machine learning models more accurate in intrusion detection, and avoid false alarms and reaction to events, security teams must be engaged promptly(Jyothsna et al 2025). Also, it is to note that with the help of an AI-based IDPS, real-time counter measures can be applied. In the event of an intrusion attempt, these systems can prevent the IP addresses of the intruders from accessing the network, isolate infected devices, and send notifications to the security personnel to take further necessary actions. AI integration in intrusion prevention helps in improving on the capacity of an organization to prevent cyber threats hence minimizing on instances of data breaches and system compromises(Gracious, L. A. (2025).

3.4 Phishing and Social Engineering Attack Detection

Online scams and such tricks as phishing and social engineering are among those threats that are most dangerous to ordinary people and companies since they use e-mail, fake site, and other tricks to get personal information. Phishing is detected to a higher degree using AI because it can analyze the content of the email, the sender, and other characteristics of the domain. AI email filtering systems also employ NLP and ML in order to understand the text of the email messages, recognize phishing attempts, and suspicious links, or even dangerous attachments. While the current spam filters may fail to detect phishing emails due to their use of keywords, AI-based phishing detection counters this by changing with time to meet the new techniques used in phishing. Moreover, AI-based domain analysis tools investigate the new registered domains, and filter out those, which exhibit patterns, similar to phishing sites. Through such URL patterns, SSL certificates, and hosting patterns, AI-based security solutions are capable of identifying such websites before they are employed in phishing attacks.

The same way, ML models also assist in identifying social engineering attacks since it involves observing the user's behavior and communication. When used with artificial intelligence, security systems can detect irregularities in the users' behavior and thus, prevent impersonation scams and BEC attacks. This is proactive in enhancing the organizations' protection from being a target of phishing and social engineering.

3.5 AI for Security Automation and Incident Response

Security automation and incident response is one of the other domains where ethical hacking is improved by AI. Conventional approaches to handling incidents involve the use of human expertise; this takes time to contain threats. Security orchestration, automation and response (SOAR) platforms refer to applications based on Artificial Intelligence that make incident response less tedious given that they perform functions like threat detection, analysis, and mitigation. Security automation tools are implemented using ML algorithms to help the system correlate the alerts, rank threats and respond to cyber threats automatically. For instance, if an A transforms an attempt at unauthorized access detected by the AI-driven system, then the system can immediately cancel a user's privileges and isolation of affected devices. This feature ensures that the effects of the cyberattacks are limited and the damage is addressed to prevent further occurrence. Moreover, it is worth noting that AI is used in the automation of penetration testing as well. In traditional penetration testing, security administrators need to analyze the system vulnerabilities and attack the weaknesses by themselves. These processes are automated by penetration testing tools to help organizations to conduct these tests without involving people. These tools employ the use of the ML models to create different attack scenarios which can help an organization to understand its security position.

3.6 AI-Powered Red Teaming and Cyberattack Simulations

Red teaming is a security practice that involves the use of a team of specialists to conduct an attack on an organization to test its readiness in terms of defense. Red teaming elevates this process through a different approach whereby a team of information technology specialist's designs attack strategies that are dynamic due to incorporation of ML algorithms from the artificial intelligence. Red Teaming tools in the context of AI implementation are used to study an organization's security posture and find out how it can be breached. These tools can mimic the attack methods like exploiting vulnerabilities, going round the authentication measures, and gaining higher access. With dynamic and innovative approaches to their methods, AI red teams give security personnel a true representation of the state of their organization's security. Another area of AI application in the red teaming process is adversarial AI testing. This is mainly because hackers have started incorporating the use of AI in their activities in an effort to avoid getting detected and thus get past any security measures that have been put in place. Ethical hackers use AI to hack AI-powered security systems to assess the effectiveness of the security models against cyber threats opened by AI. Incorporating AI based cyber threat scenarios organizations can be able to prepare well in case of an attack, improve their analysis in the event of an attack and also generally have a better stand in as far as protection from cyber threats is concerned . This makes it possible for the security teams to be always ahead of the emerging threats and adapt their security strategies to counter the threats effectively.

The cases use of AI and ML in ethical hacking have improved chiefly in areas such as automated vulnerability scanning; threat intelligence; and incident handling. In particular, AI increases the effectiveness of security measures in hacking that help an organization assess and prevent situations with cyber threats. In penetration testing, cybersecurity with AI has provided a more strategic approach to the detection of security threats and vulnerabilities, phishing, and security automation. Nonetheless, adversarial AI, false positives, and ethical issues remain as the issues that are not easy to overcome. All organizations to develop AI security models and ensure adequate involvement with AI security solutions in accordance with further development of threats. Ethical hacking plays an intertwining crucial role in today's world since as AI develops, it will require more experts to maintain cybersecurity.

4. CHALLENGES AND LIMITATIONS OF AI IN ETHICAL HACKING

Despite the advancement made by AI in the realm of ethical hacking and cybersecurity, there are also having some issues and limitations. The integration of AI in security tools leads to having new threats such as adversarial attacks on AI systems, problems related to biased machine learning, ethical issues, and limitational problems. The following challenges should be considered to guarantee the efficiency and proper utilization of AI in cybersecurity. This section aims at identifying the major challenges that are likely to be faced in ethical hacking with the help of Artificial Intelligence.

4.1 Adversarial AI and Evasion Techniques

This has been a major concern when it comes to employing the use of AI in ethical hacking due to adversarial AI and evasion techniques. Hackers are now using Artificial Intelligence in developing new ways of attacking that can easily penetrate through the AI-based security systems. Adversarial AI is a process where input data is changed in a way that will mislead an AI into classifying threats or overlooking certain activities.

Some of the adversarial steps include:

Evasion Attacks: Making small changes to the malware samples to make it difficult for the AI-based malware detection tools to detect them.

Data Manipulation: The process of feeding AI systems with wrong data with the aim of making it to produce the wrong results.

Model Inversion Attacks: This is a type of attack where an attacker aims at extracting some specific information from a given AI model by making queries to the model, and analyzing its responses to arrive at the desired information.

For instance, current deep learning-based intrusion detection systems can be easily fooled to label the incoming traffic as normal by constructing network packets. Likewise, AI-based email security solutions aimed at detecting phishing can be easily avoided by modifying the phishing emails in a way that they would not be detected. To defend against adversarial AI, researchers are subsequently required to create better models of machine learning that can identify adversarial patterns that might be used to control the model & reflect on such patterns to identify & adapt to other new forms of attacks. Nevertheless, the development of AI models that are not vulnerable to adversarial inputs and can efficiently counter them remains a cumbersome problem in cybersecurity.

Figure 2 Challenges and Limitations of AI in Ethical Hacking

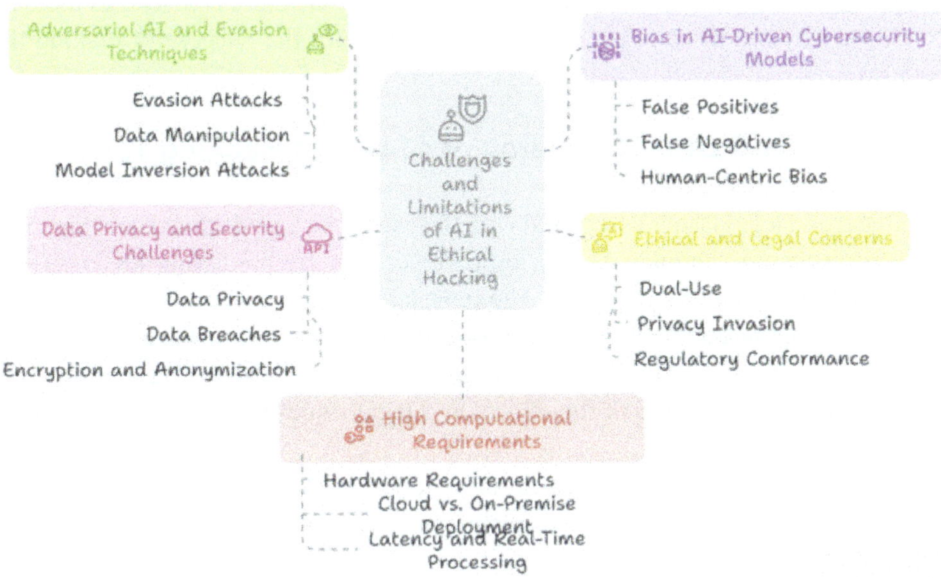

4.2 Bias in AI-Driven Cybersecurity Models

Another limitation that has been realised to affect the use of AI in ethical hacking is bias in AI models. This fact is extremely important: machine learning algorithms will never be better than the data that is taught to them. Any bias present in the training data will be replicated in the AI system, and this will affect the security assessment as well as decision making. When it comes to biases in AI cybersecurity models, there are potential risks that are fairly familiar with them namely: This is a major disadvantage of training AI system where they will learn from one kind of attack or in certain areas, they may not be effective on other types of attacks. The misrepresentation of facts makes the Artificial Intelligence flag genuinely innocuous activities as risky, this translates as false positives while on the other hand the models can fail to identify real threats hence false negatives leave security gaps. Human-Centric Bias: Security policies derived from human threat intelligence data are likely to have human bias, thus discriminating security. For instance, a fraud detection model that is developed using a dataset that consists of mainly financial transactions from one country is likely to fail to detect fraud patterns in other countries. Likewise, a skewed AI-based IDS can be programmed to identify some user activities as malicious as per the biased training data. Redundant attempts to reduce bias can be ensured through diverse, balanced sets of training data to be used by ethical hackers and cybersecurity experts. Moreover, there is a need to monitor the AI security models and adjust them as required for the purpose of making the models fairer.

4.3 Ethical and Legal Concerns of AI-Based Hacking Tools

Ethical and legal issues associated with the use of AI-based ethical hacking tools are also discussed. Though AI can improve security by predicting the risks and threats that may occur in cyberspace, the same technology can be used for malicious intents. The distinction between ethical hacking and cybercrime becomes difficult to make when these hacking tools are in the possession of the wrong parties.

The following are some of the ethical and legal issues that are related to AI in ethical hacking:

Dual-Use: The AI-based penetration testing tools that are used to check the vulnerabilities of a network or an organization's system can be used for malicious purposes by hackers.

Privacy Invasion: AI security monitoring systems may be a privacy invasion whereby the information being monitored is personal to the users.

Regulatory conformance: The implemented AI-based cybersecurity solutions must respect the general data protection standards or other regional norms.

For instance, the application of AI in hacking tools such as vulnerability scanning tools can be exploited by attackers to penetrate the corporate networks. Likewise, AI-based social engineering detection tools may violate the user's privacy rights by monitoring their personal messages.

In order to mitigate these concerns, it becomes imperative that organizations set down some ethical and legal standards for ethical hacking for AI. There is also the need for regulatory authorities to set standards to guide its usage in cybersecurity while at the same time denying any wrongdoers the opportunity to use AI for wrong means.

4.4 Data Privacy and Security Challenges in AI-Powered Security Systems

Artificial intelligence security systems require a high amount of data to feed and enhance the learning models and the detection of risks. But the problem that arises is how to manage and protect such data to ensure the privacy and security of the users. AI-based security solutions have to perform large scale data analysis while at the same time ensuring security of data.

Some of the major issues that come under data privacy and security are as follows:

Data Privacy: Some of the models used in AI security need the logs, usage data, and system settings, which may be sensitive to an organization. If not well managed, this data can easily be accessed by unauthorized persons.

Data Breaches: Sometimes the model itself becomes a target of the cybercriminals and they try to get the training data or change the behavior of the model.

Encryption and Anonymization: there is a need to protect sensitive data while making sure that the AI model can analyze them in the best way possible.

For instance, artificial intelligence-based intrusion detection systems that scan through the network traffic for suspicious activity may involve the use of PII, thus triggering compliance concerns with the data protection laws. The authors also establish that if an AI model is in any way penetrated, attackers will be in a position to obtain key security information, which they will use to breach security.

Thus, to address these risks, the firms need proper measures of protecting the data, including encryption, access control, and differential methods. Also, the periodic security assessment and compliance scan is important to ensure the AI security tool meets the regulatory requirements of privacy.

4.5 High Computational Requirements and Scalability Issues

Machine learning-based threat detection and penetration testing techniques in combination with other advanced AI based tools utilize a large amount of computational resources for data processing and analysis. The high computational costs required in ethical hacking by use of AI is a big issue when it comes to large organizations as it is expensive.

Key scalability issues include:

Hardware Requirements: The AI models must be installed on high-end GPUs, high-performance computing clusters, and large storage volumes to perform security tasks.

Cloud vs. On-Premise Deployment: It is noteworthy that while starting the service in the cloud may facilitate a horizontal scaling of the AI-based security system, there are data security and vendor lock-in concerns associated with the cloud deployment model.

Latency and Real-Time Processing: Since threat intelligence feeds are constantly running on AL-based security systems, high latency slows down its performance and ineffective response to cyber threats.

For instance, an AI-based Security Information and Event Management (SIEM) system that is used for processing real-time security log data from a number of sources. If the system is not capable of handling large amount of data, there will be significant delay in processing and identifying threats.

Due to the limitations of the available computational resources and the need for improving the security of organizations, there is a need to integrate AI solutions for security automation. Specifically, the employment of the hybrid-AI architectures, edge computing solutions, and efficient AI models are considered to address the computational limitation issue without compromising on the effectiveness of the AI-based security solutions.

However, a number of issues and drawbacks are present that impede the widespread use of AI and ML in ethical hacking and cybersecurity. AI is a threat to AI security models and there is the need for continued research in an effort to counter these adversarial threats. This chapter discusses how biases are present in AI-based cybersecurity tools and the measures that should be taken to eliminate them. Thus, ethical and legal issues related to AI hacking tools raise the matter of proper AI application in cybersecurity. The issue of data privacy and security poses another challenge to the implementation of AI based security solutions since they require a high level of data protection and to meet the set standards of the law. Finally, high computational requirements and problems related to scalability are the challenges that can be critical for organizations with limited resources. Nevertheless, it can be said that AI will remain relevant to the practice of ethical hacking in the future. Acknowledging these limitations, cybersecurity workers can fully leverage the potential AI in terms of improving threat detection, automation of different processes and increasing its efficacy as a tool to counter emergent cyber threats.

5. FUTURE TRENDS AND RESEARCH DIRECTIONS

AI and Machine Learning have now become integrated into ethical hacking to enhance the cybersecurity measures. Nevertheless, as the field of AI-based cybersecurity solutions is advancing, there is a set of new research avenues and technological developments that would help to overcome the mentioned limitations and improve the efficacy of AI in ethical hacking.

5.1 AI-Powered Autonomous Ethical Hacking Frameworks

Automated ethical hacking is the process of performing penetration testing, vulnerability assessment, and security analysis with little or no inputs from human beings. Traditional ethical hacking includes the manual processes of scanning, exploitation and reporting of vulnerabilities and it is a slow process that is likely to involve human errors. The future of ethical hacking involves having fully automated

AI systems that are capable of running assessments on an organization's systems in real time.

The future frameworks of ethical hacking with the help of artificial intelligence will rely on:

Reinforcement Learning (RL): The AI models trained under RL can ascertain the potential threats, penetrate the loopholes, and modify the strategy depending on the response received from the security systems. Self Learning Penetration Testing: It becomes quite beneficial when AI agents that can automatically perform penetration testing, modify attack vectors and design counter strategies without requiring human input. Validation through AI: When security is constantly monitored through the help of AI, it is easier to detect security issues as they occur and either recommend or implement the necessary security measures. For instance, an AI-driven automated ethical hacking solution can constantly probe for vulnerabilities in an organization's network, try to breach them and offer solutions on how the threats can be addressed immediately. It will also help to reduce the time taken to conduct security audits and also improve the response time to threats. However, there are still some issues that are yet to be addressed in a bid to ensure that autonomous ethical hacking tools are ethical, controlled and not to be used by the wrong parties. It is therefore important that there are policies that govern as well as regulate the use of such advanced ethical hacking frameworks powered by artificial intelligence.

5.2 Federated Learning for Decentralized Cybersecurity Defense

Federated learning is one of the AI techniques that allow training the machine learning models locally on multiple devices without sharing data. This is especially useful in cybersecurity since privacy and security of data are paramount in such a field. It is often the case that large-scale datasets are not possible due to data security and other compliance issues.

The following are some of the possibilities of federated learning in ethical hacking in the future:

Decentralized Threat Intelligence Sharing: This will allow security organizations and enterprises to train AI models on the decentralised cybersecurity data set without sharing of sensitive information.

Federated learning: This enables ethical hackers to build artificial intelligence models that help detect security breaches but without violating the privacy of the users, especially regarding the GDPR and CCPA guidelines.

Adaptive Security Models: AI models can be trained on localized attack patterns depending on the organization, type of organizations and geographical regions to increase accuracy.

For instance, using federated learning, it is possible to train an IDS using the AI model across different organizations without actually sharing logs or attack data. This enhances the collaboration of security intelligence for everyone without compromising the information of individual organizations.

However, FL also comes with some challenges for example, communication overhead, model synchronization and adversarial attacks on federated models. The challenges of poisoning attack and model update becomes significant in the federated learning framework hence future research should work towards mitigating them when dealing with data in federated learning setup.

Figure 3 Future Trends and Research Directions

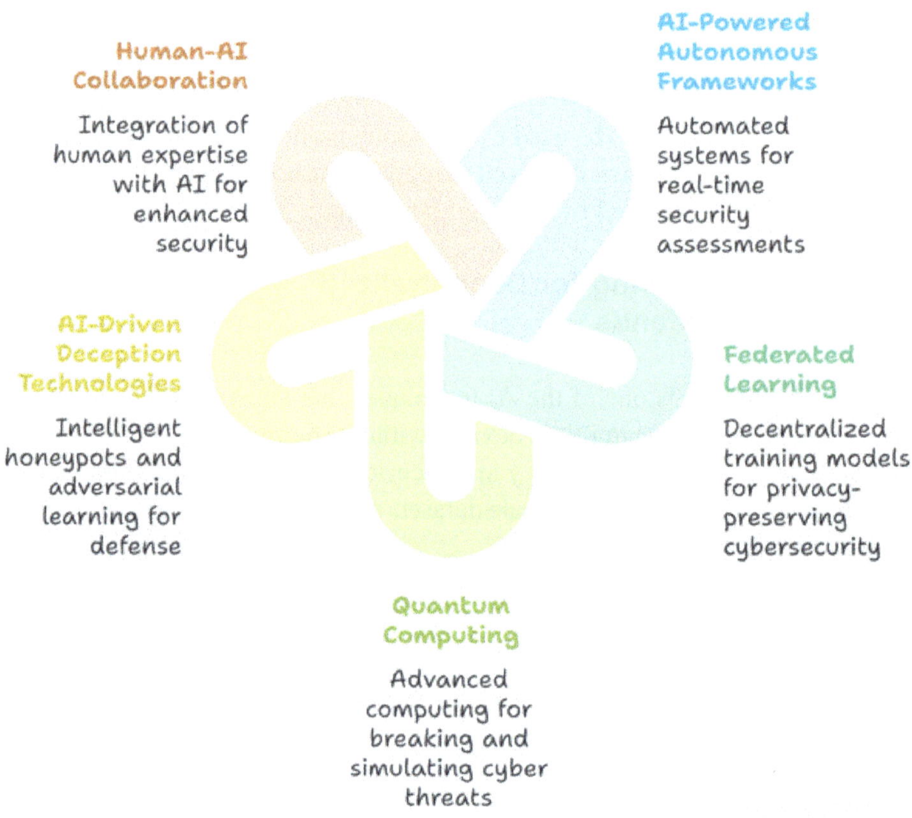

5.3 Role of Quantum Computing in Ethical Hacking

Quantum computing is on the verge of revolutionizing cybersecurity, the offense as well as the defense. Quantum computers differ from classical computers in that the former employs quantum bits (qubits) as opposed to the binary form of processing (0 and 1). This has a major significance in equally cyber threats and security measures.

As for the possible uses of quantum computing in ethical hacking, the following can be mentioned:

Quantum Cryptanalysis: Due to the existence of quantum algorithms like Shor's algorithm, it is possible to break classical cryptography, and therefore, there is a need for post quantum cryptography. Ethical hackers will have to determine the vulnerability of cryptographic systems against quantum threats.

Quantum AI for Threat Detection: Implementation of quantum machine learning can significantly improve the process of threat detection on the basis of complex patterns.

Simulation of cyberattacks with Quantum Computing: Quantum simulations can mimic cyber threats and thus, help the ethical hackers to defend the system against them.

For example, it would be possible to employ an AI system powered by a quantum computer to run virtually numerous cyberattack variants simultaneously and assess constantly the likeliness of the most typical attacks, while strengthening the cybersecurity measures and protections against them.

Nevertheless, quantum computing's application in cybersecurity is not yet fully developed and implemented. Further research should be devoted to the creation of the post-quantum cryptography and to the usage of the AI security models in the conditions of quantum computing.

5.4 Advancements in AI-Driven Deception Technologies

Adversarial machine learning could be considered as the tools that are becoming crucial in cybersecurity nowadays. AI is improving the deception-based security techniques by making the cyber threats more intelligent and thereby developing countermeasures for them.

The significant developments in AI technologies and especially the non-vendor deception technologies are as follows:

AI-Powered Honeypots: Honeypots are the systems designed to look like the actual systems in an organization or company and are used in trapping attackers. Advance honeypots can be used with artificial intelligence to allow them to change their behavior in response to the actions of the attacker, thus offering extended insights into threats.

Adversarial Machine Learning for Attack Simulation: The AI models can be trained in such a way that they can produce adversarial examples that mimic real cyberattacks for evaluating the security system.

Automated Threat Attribution: The use of AI in deception technology provides an automatic way of determining the behavior of the attackers, who they are, and what they are likely to do next in the process of enhancing active defense.

For instance, a honeypot system that is AI-driven can change its security settings on its own to ensnare the hackers into a trap and direct them to harmless decoys and not the actual systems that are valuable to the organization.

Although AI-driven deception technologies present a viable defense mechanism, the use of such technologies has some ethical and legal implications. It is imperative that the strategies used in deception conform to cybersecurity laws and do not cause harm to other legal users.

5.5 Human-AI Collaboration for Ethical Hacking and Security Governance

Thus, the human factor is still relevant in the analysis of threats, decision-making, and regulation of ethical hacking in the context of AI's continuous development in the sphere of cybersecurity. The advancement of AI in the field of ethical hacking will require the integration of man and machine to come up with better solutions in cybersecurity.

Some of the areas of interaction between humans and AI in ethical hacking are as follows:

AI-augmented security analysts: since mundane security tasks can be well automated, the analysts can devote their time to the actual analysis of threats.

AI in Ethical Hacking: As the AI models become more complicated, it is crucial to incorporate explainability in the ethical hacking tools to be developed.

Supervisory: There will be a need to set up legal and ethical standards for the use of AI in cybersecurity since it will be manned by people.

For example, the use of security automated systems such as security AI guard the ethical hackers by giving the necessary information on the security threats and the recommended measures to be taken by the security specialists in testing and enhancing the AI algorithms. However, AI is not a substitute for human ethical hackers. Rather, it is an augmentation technology that can improve human abilities in many ways and provide them with the necessary tools. The research should be directed towards the integration of artificial intelligence as supportive to the human experts in the governance of cybersecurity to remain effective and ethical.

AI in ethical hacking has garnered advanced progressions for the future that holds fascinating truths that will eventually lead to the change of strategies of defense mechanisms against cybercrimes. Smart self-defending and self-healing techniques will be developed using artificial intelligence machine powerful ethical hacking frameworks to continuously monitor and assess any vulnerabilities and risks, federated learning technique will allow for decentralized and privacy-preserving way to share intelligence information. New application of quantum computing will bring in new possibilities of threats and risks that will call for new and unique cryptographic solutions along with new attack models. Cognitive deception technologies will improve the security, the use of intelligent honeypots, and adversarial machine learning. Last but not the least, the involvement of human beings to work with AI in ethical hacking will be necessarily crucial to make AI ethical, transparent, and legal. In this chapter, the author takes the view that as cyber threats are continually changing, so must AI ethical hacking. Further research and development should be aimed at improving the stability, fairness, and security of the AI models to withstand the next level of attacks from cybercriminals. The ethical and regulatory issues will also play an important role in determining the right application of AI in cybersecurity. Thus, with the consideration of those future challenges and trends, AI remains a strong tool that will help in fortifying cybersecurity and defense.

6. CONCLUSION

Thus, the combination of AI and ML has succeeded in becoming a game-changer when it comes to ethical hacking and cybersecurity defense measures. Realising advanced vulnerability and threat detection, intrusion prevention, and security automation, AI-based tools help cyber defence in a considerable way. The use of automated vulnerability scanner and simulated penetration are more accurate and timely, while ethical hackers are able to detect vulnerabilities ahead of time. Malware analysis, phishing, and detection, as well as red teaming techniques have enhancing the cybersecurity protection through AI-intelligent data acquisition and forecasting. However, it is essential to understand that like any other tool, AI in ethical hacking also has its disadvantages. Adversarial AI techniques can be used to avoid being detected while there are implicit bias in AI models that may result in threats being missed or even flagged as harmless. The drawback includes ethical issues such as the possibility of hackers using this AI to hack and privacy issues in data. However, two important issues still persist, namely, high computational costs and high requirement of infrastructure. In this chapter, I will establish how the integration of artificial intelligence to ethical hacking has major impacts in the academic and corporate fields. The cyber security research areas basically significant for the AI-driven solutions are adversarial machine learning, explainable AI, in addition to quantum-resistant cryptography. The effectiveness of using federated learning models for developing cybersecurity intelligence can improve the exchange of threat data without sharing the information with others since it is sensitive. In the industries, AI is transforming security by automating most of them and enhancing the proactivity in responding to the threats. AI-based SOAR can help particular security teams to automate processes and reduce the involvement of people in the process. Deception-related technologies that incorporate AI will include new products like adaptive honeypots and adversarial machine learning — both will facilitate countering sophisticated cyber threats. However, there is the need to ensure that AI is well implemented in ethical hacking through the following robust governance frameworks. There is the need for organizations to put measures in place that will prevent the AI-based cybersecurity tools from being used for malicious purposes. Also, legal frameworks must be put in place by the regulatory bodies to ensure safe use of AI in cybersecurity. AI is all set to become an important tool in the fight against cybercrime, thus turning ethical hacking into a more strategic and intelligent proposition. The future trends include the use of artificial intelligence for ethical hacking, quantum computing in cybersecurity, and improved synergy of man and artificial intelligence. The future of ethical hacking based on artificial intelligence raises the issue of the proportion of artificial intelligence in ethical hacking, as well as the issue of transparency and fairness of decisions made by artificial intelligence. With the contemporary increase in the levels of threats targeting digital systems, AI will play a critical role in protecting such systems. However, to unlock the full potential of AI in ethical hacking some factors that include continuous innovation, ethical issues, and legal requirements will be significant.

REFERENCES

Adejumo, A., & Ogburie, C. (2025). The role of cybersecurity in safeguarding finance in a digital era. *World Journal of Advanced Research and Reviews, 25.*

Basak, S., Chatterjee, P., Biswas, D., Bhadra, P., & Das, R. (2024). Introduction to AI and ML Technologies and Their Potential Applications in Cybersecurity. In *Strategies for E-Commerce Data Security: Cloud, Blockchain, AI, and Machine Learning* (pp. 277-309). IGI Global. DOI: 10.4018/979-8-3693-6557-1.ch012

Ganesan, S., Shanmugaraj, G., & Indumathi, A. (2023). A Survey of Data Mining and Machine Learning-Based Intrusion Detection System for Cyber Security. *Risk Detection and Cyber Security for the Success of Contemporary Computing*, 52-74.

Gracious, L. A. (2025). The Convergence of Artificial Intelligence and Cybersecurity: Technologies, Challenges, and Future Directions. In *Deep Learning Innovations for Securing Critical Infrastructures* (pp. 463–476). IGI Global Scientific Publishing. DOI: 10.4018/979-8-3373-0563-9.ch028

Jyothsna, V., Sandhya, E., Kamalapuram, K. B., & Bhasha, P. (2025). AI-Driven Threat Detection in Cloud Environments. In Convergence of Cybersecurity and Cloud Computing (pp. 261-284). IGI Global Scientific Publishing.

Kirubai, J. C. D., & Priscila, S. S. (2024). Artificial Neural Network-Based Efficient Cyber Hacking Detection System Using Deep Learning Approaches. In Explainable AI Applications for Human Behavior Analysis (pp. 205-223). IGI Global.

LA, A. G. (2026). Machine Learning for Threat Detection: A Comprehensive Survey on Anomaly Detection Techniques. *Improving Threat Detection, Network Security, and Incident Response With AI*, 235-268.

Prabhu, D., & Sudha, L. MR, P. K., Adaikkammai, A., Aparna, P., & Sathya, V. (2025). Machine Learning in Cybersecurity: Challenges, Applications, and Future Directions. *Exploiting Machine Learning for Robust Security*, 25-48.

Ramalingam, R., Arthi, K., Bhavani, M. M., & Sunitha, T. (2025). AI-Enhanced Security Information and Event Management (SIEM) System. In *Deep Learning Innovations for Securing Critical Infrastructures* (pp. 75-94). IGI Global Scientific Publishing.

Sharma, P., & Gupta, H. (2024). Emerging Cyber Security Threats and Security Applications in Digital Era. In *2024 11th International Conference on Reliability, Infocom Technologies and Optimization (Trends and Future Directions)(ICRITO)* (pp. 1-6). IEEE. DOI: 10.1109/ICRITO61523.2024.10522181

Sinha, A. R., Singla, K., & Victor, T. M. M. (2023). Artificial intelligence and machine learning for cybersecurity applications and challenges. *Risk Detection and Cyber Security for the Success of Contemporary Computing*, 109-146.

Untawale, T. (2021). Importance of cyber security in digital era. *International Journal for Research in Applied Science and Engineering Technology*, *9*(8), 963–966. DOI: 10.22214/ijraset.2021.37519

Yamini, B. MAY, P. M. A., Shobana, R., TP, A., & Nalini, M. (2024, December). Cybersecurity: Strategies, Sector-Specific Challenges, and Future Prospects. In *2024 4th International Conference on Ubiquitous Computing and Intelligent Information Systems (ICUIS)* (pp. 1338-1345). IEEE.

Chapter 3
AI and Machine Learning Applications in Ethical Hacking

P. Selvakumar
http://orcid.org/0000-0002-3650-4548
Department of Science and Humanities, Nehru Institute of Technology, Coimbatore, India

Swapna Siddamsetti
http://orcid.org/0000-0003-2006-2367
Neil Gogte Institute of Technology, India

Lumbini Bhaumik
http://orcid.org/0009-0006-6702-5335
Asansol Engineering College, India

K. Sowmya
http://orcid.org/0000-0002-6223-4908
Nitte Meenakshi Institute of Technology, Nitte University, India

Dharmendra Singh
http://orcid.org/0009-0007-4274-6379
Independent Researcher, India

S. Giriprasad
http://orcid.org/0000-0002-7258-8056
SRM Institute of Science and Technology, India

ABSTRACT

AI-driven tools to identify vulnerabilities, detect anomalies, and automate security testing. This integration enhances cybersecurity by enabling faster threat detection, improving penetration testing, and strengthening defense mechanisms against cybercriminals.technologies enhance cybersecurity by automating tasks, improving accuracy, and adapting to new threats. From intrusion detection and malware analysis to predictive analytics and behavioral anomaly detection, AI-driven ethical hacking is reshaping the digital security landscape.tools to test for vulnerabilities. However, AI and ML are now augmenting these efforts, making penetration testing more efficient and comprehensive. AI-driven ethical hacking tools can analyze large datasets, identifying weaknesses faster and reducing response times to cyber

DOI: 10.4018/979-8-3373-3536-0.ch003

incidents. vulnerability scanning, and exploitation techniques. AI-driven tools can analyze security configurations, detect weaknesses, and even suggest patches or mitigation strategies.

INTRODUCTION TO AI AND MACHINE LEARNING IN ETHICAL HACKING

AI-driven tools to identify vulnerabilities, detect anomalies, and automate security testing. This integration enhances cybersecurity by enabling faster threat detection, improving penetration testing, and strengthening defense mechanisms against cybercriminals.technologies enhance cybersecurity by automating tasks, improving accuracy, and adapting to new threats. From intrusion detection and malware analysis to predictive analytics and behavioral anomaly detection, AI-driven ethical hacking is reshaping the digital security landscape.tools to test for vulnerabilities. However, AI and ML are now augmenting these efforts, making penetration testing more efficient and comprehensive. AI-driven ethical hacking tools can analyze large datasets, identifying weaknesses faster and reducing response times to cyber incidents. vulnerability scanning, and exploitation techniques. AI-driven tools can analyze security configurations, detect weaknesses, and even suggest patches or mitigation strategies. Uses reinforcement learning to perform intelligent penetration testing.PentestGPT: Leverages AI to generate security test cases.AI-powered Metasploit modules: Enhance traditional exploitation frameworks. Unsupervised learning models: Identify anomalies and unknown threats by detecting deviations from baseline behaviors.Deep learning models: Recognize complex attack patterns, even those disguised as legitimate activities. Examples of AI-based threat detection tools: IBM Watson for Cyber Security – Uses AI to analyze threat intelligence. Darktrace – Leverages machine learning for real-time anomaly detection. AI-driven malware analysis helps ethical hackers identify and neutralize malicious software. Traditional malware detection relies on signature-based methods, which struggle against polymorphic malware. Examining code structures without executing the program. Monitoring behavior during execution to detect malicious intent. Running suspicious files in a controlled environment to analyze their behavior. Uses AI for large-scale malware analysis (Ali et al., 2023).

AI enhances both offensive and defensive social engineering tactics: AI identifies phishing emails, malicious URLs, and deceptive messages by analyzing linguistic patterns and metadata. AI algorithms detect manipulated media, preventing identity spoofing and fraud. Behavioral Biometrics: AI-based authentication systems analyze keystrokes, (Aloqaily et al., 2022)voice patterns, and mouse movements to prevent impersonation attacks.AI-driven tools like Microsoft Defender for Office 365 and

Google's AI-based phishing detection help mitigate social engineering threats.Cortex XSOAR – Automates incident response. Splunk AI Security Analytics – Uses ML for security monitoring. IBM QRadar Advisor with Watson – AI-powered threat intelligence. Advantages of AI and Machine Learning in Ethical Hacking The integration of AI and ML into ethical hacking provides several advantages:. Speed and Efficiency: AI automates repetitive tasks, reducing the time required for security assessments Scalability: AI systems can analyze vast amounts of data in real-time, detecting threats across global networks.. Adaptability: Machine learning continuously evolves, identifying new attack patterns.. Accuracy: AI minimizes human error and enhances detection capabilities.. Cost-Effectiveness: Automated AI tools reduce the need for large cybersecurity teams.AI and machine learning are revolutionizing ethical hacking and cybersecurity. By automating penetration testing, enhancing must embrace AI-driven security solutions while ensuring ethical and responsible use of these powerful technologies.

THE CURRENT STATE OF ETHICAL HACKING: CHALLENGES AND OPPORTUNITIES FOR AI AND MACHINE LEARNING

Yet, they also introduce new challenges, including adversarial AI attacks, data privacy concerns, and the risk of AI-powered hacking tools being misused. This article explores the current state of ethical hacking, examines the major challenges faced by security professionals, and highlights how AI and ML can both support and complicate the field.Ethical hacking has evolved significantly from traditional manual penetration testing to AI-driven cybersecurity assessments. Organizations increasingly rely on ethical hackers to conduct security audits, simulate cyberattacks, and assess network vulnerabilities. The key areas of ethical hacking today include:. Penetration(Anthony, 2023) Testing: Simulating attacks on networks, applications, and hardware to uncover weaknesses.. Vulnerability Assessments: Systematically identifying and prioritizing security gaps.. Red Team vs. Blue Team Exercises: Ethical hackers (Red Team) test the effectiveness of security defenses maintained by defenders (Blue Team).. Social Engineering Testing: Evaluating how well employees and organizations resist phishing, impersonation, and manipulation tactics. While ethical hacking provides invaluable insights into security weaknesses, the increasing complexity of digital systems—cloud environments, IoT devices, AI-driven applications—poses new challenges that require innovative solutions.Modern IT environments encompass cloud services, IoT devices, AI-driven applications, and hybrid networks. Ethical hackers must navigate these complex ecosystems to uncover vulnerabilities, which often requires specialized knowledge in multiple domains.Cybercriminals now use advanced tactics such as AI-powered malware, zero-day exploits, and nation-state-sponsored attacks. Traditional ethical hacking techniques may struggle to detect highly evasive threats.Challenge: Manual testing methods may not be sufficient to detect stealthy attacks.AI and ML Opportunity: (Bergsten & Rivas, 2019)AI-driven threat intelligence can predict attack patterns, detect anomalies, and automate malware analysis.Traditional penetration testing is time-consuming and dependent on human expertise. Ethical hackers must manually identify vulnerabilities, test exploits, and document findings, which can delay security improvements.Challenge: Human limitations can slow down security assessments, leaving systems vulnerable for longer periods.AI and ML Opportunity: Automated penetration testing tools powered by AI can simulate attacks, identify weaknesses, and provide mitigation recommendations faster.Ethical hacking operates within strict legal and ethical frameworks. White-hat hackers must obtain explicit permission before testing systems, and any unauthorized access—even with good intentions—can lead to legal consequences.Challenge: Navigating complex cybersecurity laws and ethical dilemmas in different jurisdictions.

AI and ML Opportunity: AI-powered legal compliance tools can help ethical hackers ensure they follow the latest regulations and industry standards.Challenge: Cybercriminals are using AI to develop more advanced attacks that ethical hackers must counter.AI and ML Opportunity: Ethical hackers can use AI to test security models for vulnerabilities and strengthen defenses against adversarial attacks.Opportunities for AI and Machine Learning in Ethical HackingDespite the challenges, AI and ML provide immense opportunities to enhance ethical hacking capabilities. These technologies can automate tedious tasks, improve threat detection, and offer new methods for securing digital systems.. AI-Powered Automated Penetration TestingAI-driven penetration testing tools simulate cyberattacks, analyze security configurations, and identify vulnerabilities faster than traditional methods.Machine learning algorithms analyze network traffic, system logs, and user behavior to detect anomalies that may indicate cyber threats.Example Technologies:Darktrace: AI-powered network threat detection.IBM Watson for Cyber Security: AI-driven threat intelligence and pattern recognition.mpact: AI can identify attacks that traditional rule-based security systems might miss, enhancing overall security monitoring.. Predictive Threat IntelligenceAI models analyze historical attack data and predict future cyber threats, allowing organizations to take preventive measures before attacks occur.Example Applications:Machine learning-driven SIEM systems: Detect patterns in security events.Graph-based AI models: Map relationships between attack vectors.Impact: Ethical hackers can use AI-driven threat intelligence to anticipate and mitigate attacks before they happen.Ethical hacking is at a crossroads, facing growing cybersecurity challenges while benefiting from AI and machine learning advancements. While AI enhances penetration testing, threat detection, and malware analysis, it also introduces risks such as adversarial attacks and ethical concerns.To maximize AI's potential, ethical hackers must integrate AI-driven tools into their workflows, continuously update their skills, and collaborate with cybersecurity researchers to develop resilient defenses. As cyber threats become more sophisticated, the fusion of AI and ethical hacking will be crucial in protecting digital assets and ensuring cybersecurity resilience.

THE ROLE OF AI AND MACHINE LEARNING IN ETHICAL HACKING: AUTOMATING VULNERABILITY DETECTION AND EXPLOITATION

The Evolution of Vulnerability Detection in Ethical Hackingraditional Approaches to Vulnerability DetectionBefore AI and ML, ethical hackers relied on manual testing methods, including:. Network Scanning: Tools like Nmap and Wireshark were used to analyze network traffic and detect open ports. Static and Dynamic Analysis: Security professionals manually examined source code and executed programs in controlled environments to identify vulnerabilities.. Signature-Based Detection: Systems compared known attack patterns with current activity to detect threats.. Fuzz Testing: Ethical hackers fed random or unexpected inputs to applications to discover weaknesses.While these methods were effective, they had limitations, including the need for significant human expertise, time-consuming processes, and difficulty detecting sophisticated threats.Example Tools:AI-enhanced Nessus: Uses AI to prioritize vulnerabilities based on risk.Qualys AI-based Scanning: Leverages ML to refine threat intelligence.mpact: AI improves the accuracy of vulnerability scans, reduces false positives, and identifies weaknesses faster than manual methods. Machine Learning for Anomaly DetectionI-powered systems analyze network behavior to detect anomalies that may indicate security vulnerabilities. Traditional rule-based detection systems struggle with unknown threats, while ML models continuously learn from new data.Types of ML Models Used:Supervised Learning: Uses labeled attack data to classify threats.Unsupervised Learning: Identifies anomalies without prior knowledge of attack types.Reinforcement Learning: AI learns from interactions to optimize detection strategies.Example AI-Based Detection Systems:Darktrace: Uses ML to detect abnormal network activity.IBM Watson for Cybersecurity: AI-powered threat intelligence system.Impact:(Blythe et al., 2016) AI-driven anomaly detection allows ethical hackers to identify potential vulnerabilities even before an exploit occurs.. Predictive Vulnerability AnalysisAI can predict future vulnerabilities by analyzing historical attack data. By identifying patterns in past exploits, AI models can forecast potential security weaknesses and suggest preventive measures.

Map relationships between known vulnerabilities and emerging threats.Threat Intelligence Feeds: AI scans global databases to detect new attack trends.Example

Platforms:Splunk AI Security Analytics: Uses ML for predictive cybersecurity. Cortex XDR: AI-based threat prevention system.Impact: AI allows ethical hackers to proactively secure systems before vulnerabilities are exploited.AI in Exploitation: Automating Ethical Hacking AttacksWhile AI enhances vulnerability detection, it also plays a role in automating the exploitation phase of ethical hacking. AI-driven penetration testing tools simulate cyberattacks to evaluate the effectiveness of security measures.. AI-Augmented Penetration Testin Traditional penetration testing requires ethical hackers to manually identify attack vectors and exploit vulnerabilities. AI automates this process, increasing efficiency and accuracy(Bran et al., 2023).AI Tools for Penetration Testing:Deep Exploit: Uses reinforcement learning to improve penetration testing.PentestGPT: AI-powered vulnerability scanning and exploitation.mpact: AI-driven penetration testing reduces the time needed to identify and exploit security gaps, allowing organizations to patch vulnerabilities faster.. AI-Powered Exploit DevelopmentAI can assist in creating and optimizing exploit code. By analyzing existing exploits, AI models generate new attack techniques tailored to specific vulnerabilities.Example AI-Powered Exploitation Methods:Automated Reverse Engineering: AI deconstructs software to find security flaws.Exploit Generation Algorithms: AI writes custom exploit code for detected vulnerabilities. Example Tools:Metasploit AI Modules: AI-driven exploit development framework. AI-Powered Shellcode Generators: Automate payload creation for ethical hacking. Impact: AI streamlines exploit development, helping ethical hackers test security defenses more effectively.Challenges of AI and Machine Learning in Ethical HackingDespite its benefits, AI in ethical hacking presents challenges: Adversarial AI AttacksCybercriminals can manipulate AI models to evade detection, generating adversarial inputs that deceive machine learning systems.Solution: Ethical hackers must continuously update AI models and test them against adversarial attacks.. Data Privacy and Compliance IssuesAI-driven security tools require vast amounts of data, raising concerns about privacy and regulatory compliance.Solution: Organizations must implement strict data governance policies and ensure AI models adhere to privacy laws. models may generate false positives or biased results if trained on incomplete or skewed datasets.Solution: Ethical hackers should use diverse datasets and regularly retrain AI models to improve accuracy.Solution: Governments and cybersecurity organizations must establish strict regulations to prevent AI-based hacking tools from falling into the wrong hands.

AI and ML will continue to shape the future of ethical hacking in several ways Quantum AI in Cybersecurity: Strengthening encryption and security defenses using AI-driven quantum computing.As AI and ML evolve, ethical hackers must stay ahead by integrating these technologies into their security strategies while ensuring ethical and responsible use.onclusionAI and machine learning are revolutionizing ethical hacking by automating vulnerability detection and exploitation. AI-driven tools enhance penetration testing, anomaly detection, To maximize the benefits of AI in ethical hacking, organizations must implement robust AI governance, continuously update ML models, and combine AI-driven automation with human expertise. As cyber threats become more sophisticated, the fusion of AI and ethical hacking will be essential in protecting digital assets and ensuring a resilient cybersecurity landscape.

AI-DRIVEN VULNERABILITY SCANNING: USING MACHINE LEARNING TO IDENTIFY POTENTIAL THREATS

The Evolution of Vulnerability Scanning Vulnerability scanning has been an integral part of cybersecurity for decades, but traditional methods have limitations in dealing with the scale and sophistication of modern threats.. Traditional Vulnerability Scanning MethodsTraditional scanning relies on predefined signatures, manual assessments, and rule-based engines to detect vulnerabilities. Some of the common techniques include:Signature-Based Scanning: Comparing known vulnerability patterns to scanned data.Rule-Based Detection: Using predefined security rules to flag potential weaknesses.Manual Penetration Testing: Ethical hackers manually test for exploitable flaws.Patch Management Systems: Identifying outdated software that needs updates.While effective, these methods often generate false positives, miss novel attack vectors, and require significant human effort.. Introduction of AI in Vulnerability ScanningArtificial intelligence enhances traditional scanning methods by leveraging machine learning to analyze data dynamically, detect unknown threats, and reduce false positives. AI-driven scanners can process real-time security logs, network traffic, and application data to identify vulnerabilities with greater accuracy and efficiency.Key areas where AI improves vulnerability scanning include:Automated Threat Detection: Identifying security flaws without predefined signatures.Behavioral Analysis: Learning normal system behavior to detect deviations.Predictive Security Intelligence: Forecasting future vulnerabilities based on past data.How Machine Learning Enhances Vulnerability Detectio. Supervised Learning for Known VulnerabilitiesSupervised learning models are trained on labeled datasets containing past vulnerabilities and exploits. (Calderon, 2019)The model learns to recognize patterns associated with security flaws and applies this knowledge to detect similar vulnerabilities in real-world environments.Example Application:AI scans software codebases to identify coding patterns associated with security vulnerabilities.AI-based malware scanners detect known attack signatures based on previous datasets.Impact: Supervised learning improves the accuracy of vulnerability detection by learning from historical attack data.. Unsupervised Learning for Anomaly DetectionUnsupervised learning models do not rely on predefined labels. Instead, they analyze system behavior and detect deviations that may indicate potential vulnerabilities.Example Application:I monitors network activity and flags suspicious behavior.

ML algorithms detect unauthorized access attempts in real time.Impact: Unsupervised learning allows AI-driven scanners to detect zero-day vulnerabilities that do not match existing signatures.. Reinforcement (Eshita et al., 2016)Learning for Adaptive SecurityReinforcement learning enables AI systems to improve their vulnerability detection capabilities through continuous feedback and interaction with security environments.xample Application:AI-powered penetration testing tools learn how to exploit vulnerabilities more effectively.ML models adjust their scanning techniques based on real-world attack simulations.mpact: Reinforcement learning enables AI to refine its detection strategies, making vulnerabilit scanning more adaptive and efficient.AI-Powered Vulnerability Scanning ToolsSeveral AI-driven vulnerability scanning tools are revolutionizing cybersecurity by automating threat detection and analysis.. AI-Based Network Vulnerability ScannersDarktrace: Uses ML to detect network anomalies.CylancePROTECT: AI-driven endpoint security solution.Functionality: These tools analyze network traffic, detect suspicious patterns, and identify security vulnerabilities in real-time. AI-Enhanced Code Analysis ToolsCodex AI Security Scanner: Analyzes software code to identify vulnerabilities. Synopsys Coverity: Uses AI to detect security flaws in codebases.Functionality: These tools help developers detect vulnerabilities in applications before deployment.. AI-Powered Web Application ScannersAcunetix AI Scanner: Identifies vulnerabilities in web applications.Detectify: Uses ML to simulate real-world attacks on websites.Functionality: These scanners automatically test web applications for SQL injection, cross-site scripting (XSS), and other security flaws.enefits of AI-Driven Vulnerability Scanning. Faster and More Efficient DetectionAI-powered scanners analyze vast amounts of data in seconds, reducing the time needed for security assessmentsms to detect both known and unknown vulnerabilities.Despite challenges such as adversarial AI attacks and data privacy concerns, AI-powered scanners provide a proactive approach to cybersecurity, reducing risks and strengthening digital defenses. As AI technology evolves, organizations must integrate AI-driven scanning solutions into their security frameworks to ensure continuous protection against emerging cyber threats.By leveraging AI and machine learning, businesses and security professionals can enhance their vulnerability detection capabilities, minimize attack risks, and build a more secure digital future.

PREDICTIVE ANALYTICS FOR VULNERABILITY DETECTION: USING AI TO FORECAST POTENTIAL ATTACKS

AI-driven predictive models, organizations can identify weaknesses in their infrastructure, prioritize security patches, and preemptively defend against emerging threats. Machine learning algorithms analyze past attack trends, detect anomalies, and assess risk levels to provide actionable insights that strengthen cybersecurity defenses.This article explores the role of predictive analytics in vulnerability detection, the machine learning techniques used, the benefits and challenges of AI-powered forecasting, and the future of predictive security in combating cyber threats. In cybersecurity, predictive analytics helps identify potential vulnerabilities and anticipate cyberattacks before they occur. Data Collection: AI gathers data from past cyberattacks, threat intelligence feeds, and system logs.. Data Processing: Machine learning models analyze patterns and trends in historical vulnerabilities.. Threat Prediction: AI identifies potential attack vectors based on emerging threats.. Risk Assessment: Predictive models assign risk scores to vulnerabilities to prioritize mitigation efforts.. Proactive Defense: Organizations use insights to patch vulnerabilities before exploitation.Machine Learning Techniques for Predictive Vulnerability Detection. Supervised Learning for Predicting Known Vulnerabilities-Supervised learning trains AI models on labeled datasets of past cyberattacks and security incidents(Fast & Horvitz, 2017). These models learn to recognize patterns associated with vulnerabilities and predict similar threats in new environments.Example Applications:AI-based scanners detect software vulnerabilities based on past exploit data.ML-powered security tools classify potential risks based on historical attack patterns.Impact: Helps security teams prioritize vulnerabilities and address weaknesses before attackers exploit them.. Unsupervised Learning for Identifying Unknown ThreatsUnsupervised learning analyzes network traffic and system behavior to detect anomalies without predefined attack signatures.Example Applications:AI detects unusual login patterns indicating a potential cyberattack.ML(Fortes et al., 2022) models identify zero-day vulnerabilities by spotting deviations from normal behavior.mpact: Enhances security by detecting emerging threats that do not match known attack signatures.

Reinforcement Learning for Adaptive Security MeasuresReinforcement learning allows AI models to improve their predictions through continuous interaction with security environments.Example Applications:AI-driven firewalls learn to block new attack techniques over time.Predictive threat models adapt based on real-time security eventsImpact: Improves AI's ability to predict and prevent cyberattacks dynamically.AI-Powered Predictive Security Tools. Threat Intelligence Platforms with AI Prediction CapabilitiesIBM Watson for Cybersecurity: Uses AI to analyze security threats and predict vulnerabilities.Recorded Future: AI-driven threat intelligence platform for forecasting cyber risks.Functionality: These tools process global cyber threat intelligence data to anticipate attack trends.. AI-Enhanced SIEM SystemsSplunk AI Security Analytics: Uses predictive analytics to detect vulnerabilities.ortex XDR: AI-powered security monitoring and threat prediction. Functionality: Security Information and Event Management (SIEM) systems use AI to analyze logs and detect potential attack indicators.Kenna Security: Predicts which vulnerabilities are most likely to be exploited.Tenable Predictive Prioritization: AI-driven vulnerability risk assessment tool.Functionality: AI assigns risk scores to vulnerabilities, helping organizations prioritize patches.Benefits of Predictive Analytics in Vulnerability Detection1. Proactive Threat MitigationPredictive analytics helps organizations identify vulnerabilities before cybercriminals exploit them. Impact: Reduces the risk of successful attacks and minimizes security breaches.. Improved Incident ResponseI-powered predictive models provide early warnings about potential security threats.Impact: Security teams can respond to threats faster and prevent damage.. Reduced False Positives Machine learning improves the accuracy of vulnerability detection by filtering out irrelevant alerts.Impact: Reduces alert fatigue and ensures security teams focus on real threats.. Optimized Patch ManagementAI-driven risk assessments help organizations prioritize security patches based on the likelihood of exploitation.Impact: Ensures critical vulnerabilities are patched first, improving overall security posturemounts of threat intelligence data, detect anomalies, and assign risk scores to vulnerabilities.Despite challenges such as adversarial AI manipulation and data privacy concerns, AI-powered predictive analytics provides a significant advantage in mitigating cyber threats before they materialize. As AI technology continues to evolve, integrating predictive analytics into cybersecurity strategies will be essential for building a proactive and resilient defense against emerging threats.

DEEP LEARNING FOR VULNERABILITY CLASSIFICATION: USING NEURAL NETWORKS TO IDENTIFY VULNERABILITY TYPES

Before deep learning, vulnerability classification relied on manual analysis, rule-based systems, and signature-based detection. These approaches had several limitations:High False Positives: Traditional methods often misclassify benign activities as threats.Scalability Issues: Manual classification struggles with large datasets. Inability to Detect Zero-Day Vulnerabilities: Signature-based detection fails against novel attack patterns.Lack of Adaptability: Rule-based systems require frequent updates to remain effective.Deep learning overcomes these limitations by continuously learning from new cybersecurity data, detecting complex patterns, and improving classification accuracy. Role of Deep Learning in Vulnerability ClassificationDeep learning models analyze structured and unstructured cybersecurity data—such as logs, code repositories, and network traffic—to classify vulnerabilities. Key advantages include:Automated Feature Extraction: Neural networks identify patterns in vulnerability data without requiring manual input.High Precision and Recall: Deep learning minimizes false positives and false negatives.Adaptive Learning: Models refine their classification abilities over time, improving accuracy.By integrating deep learning, cybersecurity systems can classify vulnerabilities more effectively, helping organizations prioritize security patches and mitigate threats.Neural Networks for Vulnerability ClassificationSeveral deep learning architectures are used for vulnerability classification, each offering unique advantages.. Convolutional Neural Networks (CNNs) for Code and Log AnalysisCNNs, typically used for image recognition, have been adapted for cybersecurity by analyzing textual data such as software code, log files, and network traffic patterns.Example Applications:Detecting insecure coding practices in software repositories.Analyzing system logs for signs of vulnerabilities.Impact: CNNs enhance vulnerability classification by extracting hierarchical features from cybersecurity data.. Recurrent Neural Networks (RNNs) for Sequential Data AnalysisRNNs, particularly Long Short-Term Memory (LSTM) networks, excel at analyzing sequential data such as time-series logs and network traffic patterns.Example Applications:Identifying vulnerabilities in system logs by detecting abnormal sequences.Analyzing API call sequences for potential exploits. Impact: RNNs improve vulnerability classification by detecting temporal patterns in cybersecurity data. Transformer-Based Models for Context-Aware Classification

Transformer models like BERT (Bidirectional Encoder Representations from Transformers) and GPT (Generative Pre-trained Transformer) are used for natural language processing (NLP) tasks, including cybersecurity analysis.xample Applications: Extracting insights from vulnerability databases (e.g., Common Vulnerabilities and Exposures - CVE).Impact: Transformers provide context-aware vulnerability classification, improving accuracy in detecting new threats.AI-Powered Tools for Vulnerability Classification. AI-Enhanced Static Code Analysis ToolsDeepCode: Uses AI to detect security vulnerabilities in source code.Codex AI Security Scanner: Analyzes software repositories for insecure coding patterns.unctionality: These tools help developers classify vulnerabilities during the software development lifecycle.. (Hutter & Hutter, 2021) AI-Driven Network Security SolutionsDarktrace AI: Uses deep learning to classify network vulnerabilities.Recorded Future: Uses NLP and deep learning to classify cyber threats.IBM Watson for Cybersecurity: AI-driven vulnerability classification tool.unctionality: These platforms analyze security reports and threat intelligence data to classify emerging vulnerabilities.Benefits of Deep Learning in Vulnerability Classification. Improved Accuracy in Threat DetectionDeep learning models reduce misclassification rates, ensuring vulnerabilities are accurately categorized.Impact: Helps organizations prioritize critical security patchesDeep learning is transforming vulnerability classification by automating the detection and categorization of security threats. Neural networks—such as CNNs, RNNs, and transformers—enhance classification accuracy, scalability, and adaptability. AI-powered tools analyze code, network traffic, and threat intelligence data to improve cybersecurity defenses.Despite challenges such as computational demands and adversarial AI risks, deep learning provides a powerful solution for identifying and mitigating vulnerabilities.(Li, 2018) As AI continues to evolve, integrating deep learning into cybersecurity strategies will be essential for building proactive and resilient security infrastructures.By leveraging deep learning, organizations can improve vulnerability classification, enhance threat detection, and strengthen their overall cybersecurity posture, ensuring a safer digital environment.

MACHINE LEARNING FOR EXPLOITATION: USING AI TO AUTOMATE EXPLOIT DEVELOPMENT

Before AI, exploit development was a manual process requiring expertise in:Reverse Engineering: Analyzing compiled code to discover vulnerabilities.Fuzzing: Testing software with unexpected inputs to find weaknesses.Shellcoding: Writing malicious payloads to execute unauthorized commands.Exploit Crafting: Combining discovered vulnerabilities with exploit techniques.hile effective, traditional methods were time-consuming and required skilled human operators.. AI and ML in Exploit DevelopmentMachine learning models accelerate the exploitation process by:Identifying vulnerabilities faster than manual analysis.Generating exploit code based on past successful attacks.Optimizing payloads for greater effectiveness. Predicting potential attack vectors before they are publicly known.This shift has dramatically changed the cybersecurity landscape, enabling both ethical hackers and cybercriminals to develop exploits more efficiently.Machine Learning Techniques for Exploit Development. Supervised Learning for Exploit PredictionSupervised learning models are trained on labeled datasets of vulnerabilities and past exploits. These models can:Predict which vulnerabilities are most likely to be exploited. Suggest optimal exploit strategies for specific security flaws.Classify vulnerabilities based on exploitability risk.Example: AI-powered tools analyze the CVE (Common Vulnerabilities and Exposures) database to determine which vulnerabilities are easiest to exploit.. Unsupervised Learning for Discovering New Attack VectorsUnsupervised learning detects hidden patterns in data without predefined labels. It is used for:Automated fuzzing: Generating unpredictable test cases to find vulnerabilities. Zero-day detection: Identifying security flaws before they are publicly disclosed. Network anomaly detection: Recognizing deviations that indicate potential attack vectors.Example: AI-powered fuzzers like AFL++ use ML to generate new test cases that expose software vulnerabilities.. Reinforcement Learning for Exploit OptimizationReinforcement learning (RL) allows AI to improve exploit techniques over time by interacting with test environments and learning from successes and failures.

Self-improving exploits: AI agents refine attack methods through trial and error. Adaptive malware: AI modifies exploit payloads dynamically to evade detection. Automated privilege escalation: AI tests various strategies to maximize access control bypasseExample: DeepExploit is an AI-powered penetration testing tool that automatically finds ad executes exploits using RL techniques..(Looi et al., 2021) Generative AI for Crafting Exploit CodeGenerative AI, such as GPT-based models, can generate exploit scripts based on vulnerability descriptions.Automated exploit generation: AI writes attack scripts for known vulnerabilities.Exploit template creation: AI generates base code for exploit frameworks.olymorphic malware development: AI creates variations of known exploits to bypass detection.Example: OpenAI's Codex has demonstrated the ability to generate exploit code when provided with vulnerability details, raising both ethical concerns and security implications. AI-Powered Tools for Automated Exploit Development. AI-Driven Vulnerability ScannersZerodium AI Scanner: Uses ML to detect and classify exploitable vulnerabilities.Tenable.io Predictive Prioritization: AI ranks vulnerabilities based on exploit likelihood.Functionality: These tools analyze software for security weaknesses and predict how they could be exploited.. AI-Augmented Penetration Testing ToolsDeep-Exploit: Uses reinforcement learning to automate penetration testing.Metasploit AI Module: Enhances Metasploit's exploit framework with ML-powered recommendations.Functionality: These tools generate and execute exploits with minimal human input.. AI-Based Malware Development Platforms (Ethical Use Only)EvilModel (Research Purposes): Demonstrates how AI can create evasive malware.MalGAN: Uses generative adversarial networks (GANs) to bypass antivirus detection.Functionality: (Moriniello et al., 2024)These tools showcase how AI can be used to craft highly evasive exploits and malware.Benefits of AI in Exploit Development for Ethical Hacking. Faster Vulnerability ExploitationAI significantly reduces the time required to identify and exploit security flaws.mpact: Ethical hackers can improve penetration testing efficiency.. Enhanced Precision in Attack SimulationsAI improves exploit accuracy, minimizing errors in penetration testing.Impact: Helps organizations assess real-world attack risks more effectively.. Adaptive Security TestingMachine learning enables real-time adaptation to evolving security defenses. Impact: AI-powered ethical hacking can identify security gaps before attackers do.. Reduced Human Effort in Exploit ResearchI automates tedious exploit research tasks, allowing cybersecurity professionals to focus on strategy.Impact: Frees up human expertise for more complex security challenges.thical Concerns and Challenges of AI in Exploit Development. Dual-Use Dilemmament by automating vulnerability identification, exploit generation, and attack optimization. AI-powered tools enhance penetration testing, vulnerability research, and ethical hacking, enabling faster and more precise security assessments.However, AI's potential for misuse raises serious ethical concerns, making it essential to establish safeguards and regulations. By responsibly integrating AI into cybersecurity practices, organizations can strengthen their defenses against AI-driven threats while ensuring that ethical hacking remains a force for good.As AI continues to evolve, the cybersecurity industry must balance its benefits and risks, ensuring that advanced exploitation techniques are used to enhance security rather than compromise it.

AI-POWERED PENETRATION TESTING: USING MACHINE LEARNING TO SIMULATE REAL-WORLD ATTACKS

AI-powered penetration testing simulates real-world attacks with greater efficiency, accuracy, and scalability than traditional methods. By leveraging ML algorithms, ethical hackers can identify security gaps, predict attack strategies, and enhance cybersecurity defenses. This article explores how AI-driven penetration testing works, the benefits and challenges of AI in ethical hacking, and the future of intelligent security testing.Penetration testing, also known as ethical hacking, involves simulating cyberattacks to identify vulnerabilities in an organization's security infrastructure. This process typically includes:Reconnaissance: Gathering information about the target system.Scanning & Enumeration: Identifying potential entry points.Exploitation: Attempting to exploit vulnerabilities.Post-Exploitation & Reporting: Assessing the impact and suggesting mitigation strategies.Traditional penetration testing is largely manual and requires skilled professionals to analyze security flaws and craft exploits. While effective, it has limitations:Time-Consuming: Manual testing can take days or weeks.Limited Scope: May not cover all potential attack scenarios.High Costs: Requires significant investment in expert personnel.Human Error: Penetration testers may overlook certain vulnerabilities. AI-Driven Penetration TestingAI-powered penetration testing enhances traditional methods by automating key processes, including:Automated reconnaissance: AI gathers target information from public and private sources.Intelligent vulnerability detection: Machine learning algorithms analyze code, logs, and traffic patterns to detect security flaws.AI-generated exploit development: AI tools generate attack payloads for identified vulnerabilities.Adaptive attack simulations: AI continuously refies its approach based on real-world attack data.AI-driven penetration testing is faster, more accurate, and scalable, allowing organizations to proactively address security weaknesses.

Machine Learning Techniques for AI-Powered Penetration TestingSupervised Learning for Vulnerability DetectionSupervised learning models are trained on labeled datasets of past vulnerabilities and exploits to recognize common attack patterns.Example: AI models analyze historical penetration test reports to predict high-risk vulnerabilities.Unsupervised ML identifies unknown attack patterns by analyzing system behavior and detecting anomalies.Example: AI detects unusual network traffic that could indicate a zero-day attack.Impact: Hlps penetration testers discover new attack vectors.. Reinforcement Learning for Attack SimulationReinforcement learning (RL) enables AI to refine attack strategies through trial and errorExample: AI systematically tests different exploit techniques to find the most effective attack path.Impact: Simulates real-world attack scenarios with increasing sophistication.Generative (Mahadev Madgule et al., 2023)AI for Exploit DevelopmentGenerative AI can automatically create exploit code based on vulnerability descriptions.Example: AI-generated shellcode for buffer overflow vulnerabilities. mpact: Accelerates exploit development for penetration testers.AI-Powered Tools for Penetration Testing. AI-Driven Vulnerability ScannersTenable.io: Uses AI to prioritize vulnerabilities based on exploit likelihood.Qualys AI-Powered Scanner: Automates security assessments using machine learning.Nessus AI: Identifies security gaps with predictive analytics.. AI-Augmented Exploit FrameworksDeep-Exploit: AI-powered penetration testing tool that autonomously finds and executes exploitsMetasploit AI: Enhances the Metasploit framework with ML-based attack predictions.. AI-Based Threat Simulation PlatformsDarktrace AI: Simulates advanced persistent threats (APTs) using ML.CylanceOPTICS: AI-driven security analysis platform for real-time attack simulations.Benefits of AI-Powered Penetration Testing. Increased Speed and EfficiencyAI automates the penetration testing process, reducing the time required for vulnerability assessment.mpact: Organizations can identify and mitigate risks fasteAI-powered penetration testing is revolutionizing ethical hacking by automating attack simulations, (Nguyen, 2023)vulnerability detection, and exploit development. Machine learning enhances penetration testing by making it faster, more accurate, and scalable, allowing organizations to identify and address security threats before cybercriminals can exploit them.Despite challenges such as ethical concerns and the risk of AI misuse, AI-driven penetration testing is shaping the future of cybersecurity. As AI continues to evolve, organizations must adopt responsible AI practices to strengthen their security posture while ensuring that AI-driven penetration testing remains a force for good.

REINFORCEMENT LEARNING FOR PENETRATION TESTING: USING AI TO OPTIMIZE PENETRATION TESTING STRATEGIES

This article explores how reinforcement learning enhances penetration testing, the core techniques used, AI-powered tools for RL-based ethical hacking, challenges, and the future of RL-driven penetration testing.Reinforcement learning is a machine learning paradigm where an AI agent interacts with an environment, takes actions, and learns from feedback in the form of rewards or penalties. The goal is to maximize cumulative rewards by discovering the most effective strategy through repeated trials.Agent: The AI model performing penetration testing.Environment: The target system, network, or application being tested.Actions: The penetration testing techniques the AI agent can use (e.g., scanning, exploiting, privilege escalation).Rewards: The success or failure of an action (e.g., gaining access to a system provides a positive reward).Policy: The strategy the agent develops to maximize penetration testing success.. Why Use Reinforcement Learning for Penetration Testing?Traditional penetration testing follows predefined scripts and attack methodologies, making it predictable and limited in scope. RL overcomes these limitations by:Learning from experience: AI refines attack strategies based on trial-and-error interactions.Adapting to different environments: RL adjusts to different network architectures, security policies, and defenses.Optimizing attack paths: AI identifies the most efficient ways to exploit vulnerabilities.Automating complex penetration tests: RL reduces reliance on human expertise for repetitive tasks.By using RL, penetration testing becomes more intelligent, efficient, and capable of mimicking advanced cyber threats.How Reinforcement Learning Optimizes Penetration Testing Strategies. State-Space Exploration for Attack Path DiscoveryRL models explore possible attack paths within a target environment by:Mapping all possible states (e.g., open ports, running services, credentials).

Evaluating the best route to achieve a security breach.Learning how to bypass security controls dynamically.Example: An RL agent analyzing a corporate network may test different attack paths until it finds the optimal sequence of actions to escalate privileges. Reward-Based Learning for Exploit SelectionAI assigns rewards to successful exploit attempts and penalties to failed ones, allowing the RL agent to:Prioritize the most effective exploits.Avoid unnecessary or risky actions.Learn which vulnerability chains yield the highest success rates.Example: If a SQL injection attempt grants database access, the RL agent increasests preference for similar attacks in future scenarios.. Dynamic Adaptation to Changing DefensesReinforcement learning enables AI to adapt to evolving security defenses by:Continuously testing and adjusting attack strategies.dentifying new vulnerabilities that emerge over time. earning how to evade intrusion detection and prevention systems (IDS/IPS).Example:(Nguyen & Hekman, 2024) An RL-based penetration testing tool can detect and bypass web application firewalls by refining its attack patterns.Unlike traditional penetration testing, which follows a fixed methodology, RL-based systemsMake real-time decisions based on system responses.Adjust attack sequences dynamically. Discover unexpected vulnerabilities through exploration.Example: Instead of running a standard port scan, an RL agent might prioritize testing authtication mechanisms if it detects weak credentials.Key AI Models for Reinforcement Learning in Penetration Testing. Q-Learning for Exploit PrioritizationQ-learning is a popular RL algorithm where AI learns the best action to take in a given state based on a reward system. Use(Ouchchy et al., 2020) Case: AI prioritizes which vulnerabilities to exploit based on past success rates.Benefit: Reduces time spent on ineffective attack paths.. Deep Q-Networks (DQN) for Large-Scale TestingDeep Q-networks use deep learning to handle complex penetration testing scenarios with vast state spaces.Use Case: AI analyzes enterprise networks with thousands of potential attack vectors.Benefit: Finds optimal attack strategies faster than traditional methods. Monte Carlo Tree Search (MCTS) for Attack Path DiscoveryMCTS is an RL approach that explores different attack paths and selects the most promising ones.Use Case: AI tests multiple attack sequences to find the shortest route to system compromise.enefit: Enhances penetration testing efficiency in large-scale environments.AI-Powered Tools Using Reinforcement Learning for Penetration Testin. DeepExploitFunctionality: AI-driven penetration testing tool that autonomously finds and executes exploits.echnology: Uses reinforcement learning to optimize attack strategies.. CybER AIFunctionality: Simulates cyberattacks using RL-based decision-making.Technology: Adapts to different security defenses dynamically.. OpenAI Gym for CybersecurityFunctionality: Provides a simulated environment for training RL penetration testing agents. echnology: Enables AI models to refine attack techniques in a controlled setting. enefits of Reinforcement Learning in Penetration Testing.

Faster and More Efficient TestingRL-based penetration testing significantly reduces the time required for vulnerability assessments. Realistic Attack SimulationsAI mimics real-world cyber threats more accurately than rule-based penetration tests.. Reduced Human EffortAI automates repetitive tasks, allowing cybersecurity professionals to focus on strategic decisions. Continuous Learning and ImprovementRL models improve over time, making penetration testing more effective with each iteration.Challenges of Reinforcement Learning in Penetration Testing. Ethical and Legal ConcernsAI-powered penetration testing tools must be used responsibly to avoid unintended damage.Solution: Ensure legal authorization before deploying AI-driven penetration tests.. Complexity of Training AI ModelsReinforcement learning requires extensive training and computational reources.Solution: Use simulated environments before deploying RL agents in real-world systems. Risk of AI Misuse by CybercriminalsHackers could use RL-based penetration testing tools to automate attacks.Solution: Implement strict security controls on AI-driven offensive security tools.etration testing will continue evolving, with future advancements including:. Autonomous AI Red Teams: AI-driven systems continuously testing and strengthening enterprise defenses.. Self-Improving Security Models: RL agents that learn from every cyberattack to enhance future penetration tests.. AI-Driven Blue Teaming: Defensive AI using RL to predict and counter penetration test strategies.. Quantum AI for Cybersecurity: Quantum computing-powered RL models capable of handling ultra-complex attack simulations.As AI advances, reinforcement learning will become an essential tool in cybersecurity, providing organizations with proactive defense strategies against evolving cyber threatsWhile challenges such as ethical concerns and AI misuse remain, the future of RL-driven penetration testing promises greater efficiency, scalability, and resilience in the fight against cybercrime.

AI-DRIVEN INCIDENT RESPONSE: USING MACHINE LEARNING TO DETECT AND RESPOND TO CYBER THREATS

Traditional incident response follows a manual, human-driven process where security analysts detect threats, investigate incidents, and respond based on predefined protocols. Key steps includeDetection: Identifying suspicious activity through security logs, firewalls, and intrusion detection systems (IDS).Investigation: Analyzing logs, correlating data, and identifying the root cause of the attack.Containment: Isolating affected systems to prevent the spread of malware or unauthorized access. Eradication & Recovery: Removing threats, restoring systems, and implementing patches.Lessons Learned: Reviewing the incident and improving security policies. While effective, traditional incident response has limitations:Slow response times: Manual investigations take hours or days.High false positives: Security teams waste time on non-critical alerts.Limited scalability:(Zhai et al., 2020) Human analysts struggle to handle large-scale attacks.Reactive approach: Responds to threats after they occur, rather than preventing them.. Supervised Learning for Threat ClassificationSupervised ML models are trained on labeled datasets of past cyberattacks to recognize specific threats.Example: AI classifies malware types (e.g., ransomware, trojans) based on previous attack signatures.Impact: Improves detection accuracy and reduces false positives.. Unsupervised Learning for Anomaly DetectionUnsupervised ML models identify unknown or zero-day threats by detecting deviations from normal behavior.Example: (Wang et al., 2022)AI detects unusual login activity suggesting credential compromise.mpact: Ientifies novel attack patterns missed by traditional security tools..

Reinforcement Learning for Automated ResponseReinforcement learning (RL) allows AI to adapt its response strategies based on trial-and-error learning. Example: AI automatically blocks malicious IPs and refines firewall rules over time.Impact: Optimizes security policies dynamically to counter evolving threats.. Natural Language Processing (NLP) for Threat IntelligenceNLP enables AI to analyze unstructured security data from threat reports, logs, and social media.Example: AI extracts indicators of compromise (IoCs) from cybersecurity blogs and applies them to network defenses.Impact: Enhances real-time threat intelligence and situational awareness.ow AI Detects and Responds to Cyber Threats. AI-Powered Threat DetectionAI continuously monitors network traffic, endpoints, and cloud environments to detect malicious activities such as:Unusual data exfiltration (e.g., large file transfers to unknown servers).ateral movement within a network (e.g., attacker escalating privileges).Behavioral anomalies (e.g., a user accessing sensitive files at unusual hours).AI-driven incident response is transforming cybersecurity by automating threat detection, triaging alerts, and executing rapid responses. Machine learning enhances the ability to detect sophisticated attacks, reduce false positives, and adapt to evolving threats. Despite challenges, AI-powered security operations will continue to revolutionize how organizations defend against cyber threats in an increasingly digital world.

DEEP LEARNING FOR ANOMALY DETECTION: USING NEURAL NETWORKS TO IDENTIFY UNUSUAL NETWORK ACTIVITY

By leveraging neural networks, deep learning models can analyze vast amounts of network data, detect subtle deviations from normal behavior, and identify cyber threats that traditional systems might miss. This article explores how deep learning enhances anomaly detection, the key types of neural networks used, real-world applications, challenges, and the future of AI-driven cybersecurity.Anomaly detection refers to identifying deviations from normal behavior within a dataset. In cybersecurity, anomalies can indicate various types of threats, including:Network intrusions (e.g., unauthorized access attempts).Insider threats (e.g., employees exfiltrating sensitive data).Malware infections (e.g., ransomware encrypting files). DDoS attacks (e.g., excessive traffic from botnets).Traditional anomaly detection techniques rely on predefined rules or statistical methods, but these approaches have limitations:High false positive rates due to rigid detection rules.Inability to detect unknown threats (e.g., zero-day attacks).Lack of adaptability to evolving attack patterns.. Why Use Deep Learning for Anomaly Detection?Deep learning models excel at identifying complex patterns in large datasets. Unlike traditional methods, deep learning can:Automatically learn patterns without needing explicit rules.Detect unknown and zero-day threats by analyzing deviations from learned behaviors.Improve accuracy over time by continuously learning from new network activity.Deep Learning Techniques for Anomaly Detection. Autoencoders for Network Anomaly DetectionAutoencoders are unsupervised neural networks designed to learn efficient representations of data by compressing and reconstructing inputs. ow it Works.

Recurrent Neural Networks (RNNs) for Time-Series Anomaly DetectionRNNs are designed for sequential data analysis, making them effective (Vijayakumar et al., 2024)for monitoring network traffic over time.How it Works:RNNs analyze historical sequences of network activity.Deviations from learned sequences are flagged as anomalies.Use Case: Detecting slow, stealthy cyberattacks that evolve over time. Example: An RNN identifies an attacker escalating privileges over multiple login attempts.Impact:Detects subtle attack patterns missed by traditional systems.Improves over time by learning evolving attack behaviors.. Convolutional Neural Networks (CNNs) for Intrusion DetectionAlthough CNNs are typically used for image recognition, they can also detect network anomalies by analyzing traffic patterns.How it Works:Converts network traffic data into visual representations.Uses CNNs to classify traffic as normal or malicious.se Case: Identifying unusual packet flows in a network.(van Dijck, 2014)Example: A CNN detects a DDoS attack by recognizing abnormal traffic distribution.Impact:Enhances accuracy in detecting structured attack patterns.Enables fast, automated threat classification.. Generative Adversarial Networks (GANs) for Anomaly DetectioGANs consist of two neural networks: a generator and a discriminator, which work together to learn data distributions.ow it Works:The generator creates synthetic network traffic similar to normal activity. he discriminator learns to distinguish between normal and anomalous traffic.Use Case: Detecting adversarial cyberattacks designed to evade traditional security tools. Example: A GAN identifies an attacker attempting to bypass an intrusion detection system (IDS).Impact:Adapts to evolving cyber threats dynamically.Reduces false positives by refining detection thresholds.ow Deep Learning Identifies Unusual Network Activity1. Real-Time Threat DetectionDeep learning models process vast amounts of network data in real time, identifying threats as they emerge.Example: AI detects an unauthorized device connecting to a secure network.Benefit: Prevents attacks before they cause damage.. Behavioral Profiling of Users and DevicesDeep learning builds profiles of normal user and device behavior, flagging deviations. Example:(Page et al., 2018).

CASE STUDY: USING AI AND MACHINE LEARNING FOR VULNERABILITY DETECTION AND EXPLOITATION IN A REAL-WORLD SCENARIO

However, these approaches are often time-consuming, error-prone, and limited in their ability to detect zero-day vulnerabilities. AI and ML are revolutionizing this field by automating vulnerability detection, predicting exploits, and enhancing ethical hacking strategies.This case study provides an in-depth analysis of how AI and ML were used to identify and exploit vulnerabilities in a real-world scenario. We will explore the methodologies employed, the AI-driven tools used, the challenges faced, and the overall impact of AI in ethical hacking.Background: The Organization and Security LandscapeThe Target OrganizationThe case study focuses on a multinational financial services company that processes millions of transactions daily. Due to its extensive digital infrastructure, the company is a prime target for cybercriminals, including nation-state actors, ransomware groups, and insider threats. ecurity Concerns:The organization handles sensitive financial and personal data. The company's security team faced challenges detecting unknown vulnerabilities. AI-Driven Vulnerability Detection. Automated Scanning with Machine LearningThe company deployed an AI-driven vulnerability scanner capable of:Detecting misconfigurations in cloud environments.Identifying outdated software versions with known exploits.Analyzing network traffic for signs of weak encryption(Sugumaran et al., 2024).The AI system was trained using historical attack data, allowing it to recognize new vulnerability patterns.Results:he AI scanner detected 37 previously unknown vulnerabilities, including SQL injection flaws, misconfigured access controls, and API security gaps.AI reduced the time required for vulnerability scanning from 3 weeks to 4 hours compared to traditional methods. Behavioral Anomaly DetectionAn AI-powered behavioral analytics system monitored network activity to identify suspicious behavior.Key Findings:AI detected an unusual data transfer pattern from an internal database, suggesting possible data exfiltration.The system identified multiple failed login attempts followed by successful access, indicating potential brute-force attacks.Impact:The AI model reduced false positives by 43%, allowing security teams to focus on real threatsPhase 2: AI-Enhanced Exploitation Simulation. AI-Powered Penetration TestingAfter vulnerability detection, the company simulated (Ruckenstein & Pantzar, 2018)real-world exploitation attempts using an AI-driven penetration testing framework.How AI Enhanced Exploitation:AI automated reconnaissance by scanning for exposed assets and weak entry points.

A deepfake voice model was trained using public speeches and internal voice recordings of a CFO.The AI system generated a realistic phone call requesting urgent wire transfers.Outcome: out of 10 employees were deceived and nearly initiated unauthorized transactions.The company implemented stricter authentication protocols, including voice biometrics anmulti-factor authentication (MFA).. AI-Generated Exploit CodeA natural language processing (NLP) model was used to analyze security advisories, GitHub repositories, and darknet forums to generate potential exploit code for newly discovered vulnerabilities.Findings: developed a working exploit for an unpatched vulnerability in an internal web application.The security team was able to fix the flaw before a real attacker could exploit it.mpact:AI reduced exploit development time from several weeks to a few hours.The company patched 90% of vulnerabilities within 48 hours, improving remediation speed.Challenges and Ethical Considerations. Adversarial Attacks Against AI ModelsCybercriminals attempted to evade AI-based security measures by using adversarial techniques, such as:Data poisoning (injecting misleading data to deceive AI).Evasion attacks (modifying malware signatures to bypass AI detection).Mitigation:he company used adversarial training to harden AI models against manipulation.. AI Bias and False PositivesML models initially exhibited bias, flagging legitimate employee actions as suspicious.

FUTURE DIRECTIONS IN AI AND MACHINE LEARNING FOR ETHICAL HACKING: EMERGING TRENDS AND OPPORTUNITIES

One of the most significant trends in AI and ethical hacking is the development of fully autonomous (Strauß, 2018)AI-driven security systems. Currently, penetration testing and threat hunting require human intervention to analyze AI-generated results and refine attack strategies. However, future AI systems will operate independently, mimicking human ethical hackers while continuously learning from new attack patternsContinuous Security Assessments: AI will monitor and test enterprise networks 24/7, proactively identifying weaknesses before attackers do.AI-Orchestrated (Sreenivasulu et al., 2022)Cyber Ranges: AI-powered environments will simulate advanced cyberattacks in real time, allowing organizations to test their defenses dynamically.Opportunities:Ethical hacking will become more accessible, allowing smaller organizations to conduct automated security assessments without large teams of experts.AI-driven red teams will significantly reduce the time required to detect and patch vulnerabilities, strengthening cybersecurity resilience.Challenges:Ensuring AI remains ethical and does not become a security risk itself.Preventing AI from being weaponized by malicious actors for autonomous cyberattacks.. The Integration of Reinforcement Learning in Penetration TestingReinforcement learning (RL) is a branch of AI where agents learn through trial and error to optimize strategies.

Automated Privilege Escalation Strategies: RL-based AI will analyze misconfigurations and automatically attempt privilege escalationOpportunities:RL-based penetration testing will identify complex attack chains that human testers may overlook.AI will optimize attack sequences, reducing the time required to exploit vulnerabilities.Challenges:AI-generated exploits may be difficult to control, raising concerns about ethical use and potential misuse.RL-based penetration testing may become too aggressive, potentially disrupting critical systems.. AI-Powered Zero-Day Vulnerability DiscoveryTraditional vulnerability detection relies on signature-based methods and manual penetration testing. However, AI-driven models will increasingly predict and discover zero-day vulnerabilities before they are exploited.Key Developments: Generative AI for Code Analysis: Large language models (LLMs) trained on secure and insecure codebases will automatically identify potential zero-day flaws.AI-Powered Binary Analysis: Deep learning models will reverse-engineer compiled software, detecting vulnerabilities in closed-source applications.AI-Augmented Threat Intelligence: NLP-based AI will scan dark web forums, hacker marketplaces, and exploit databases to identify emerging threats in real time.Opportunities:AI-driven zero-day detection will significantly reduce the time between vulnerability discovery and remediation.Ethical hackers will enhance bug bounty programs by leveraging AI to find vulnerabilities faster.Challenges:Adversarial AI attacks: Hackers may use AI to create undetectable exploits, making defensive AI models necessary.AI-based zero-day discovery may lead to legal and ethical concerns if vulnerabilities are disclosed irresponsibly.. AI in Adversarial Cybersecurity and Deception TechnologiesAs AI is used to improve cybersecurity defenses, attackers are also using AI to bypass security measures. Future cybersecurity strategies will include AI-driven deception technologies to mislead attackers and disrupt their efforts.Opportunities:AI-based deception will turn cyberattacks against attackers, allowing defenders to gather inteligence on hacking groups.Advanced AI phishing detection will prevent social engineering attacks before they reach usersChallenges:(Rughini & Flaherty, 2022)Ensuring AI deception systems do not accidentally interfere with legitimate usersPreventing attackers from identifying and bypassing deception mechanisms.

RECOMMENDATIONS FOR ETHICAL HACKERS: USING AI AND MACHINE LEARNING TO ENHANCE CYBERSECURITY

Traditional vulnerability scanning methods can be time-consuming and prone to human error. AI-powered tools significantly enhance vulnerability detection by automating scans, analyzing large datasets, and identifying weaknesses faster.Key Recommendations:Use AI-based vulnerability scanners: Tools like AI-powered Nmap, Nessus, and OpenVAS use machine learning to improve accuracy in vulnerability detection.Leverage natural language processing (NLP) for threat intelligence: AI can analyze threat reports, security advisories, and dark web discussions to identify potential vulnerabilities before thy are exploited.Implement predictive analytics: Use ML models to analyze historical attack data and predict which vulnerabilities are most likely to be exploited.Best Practices:Combine AI-driven scans with manual validation to avoid false positives.Ensure AI models are trained on diverse and up-to-date datasets to improve accuracy.. Utilize Machine Learning for Intelligent Penetration TestingPenetration testing is essential for ethical hackers, but manual testing can be slow and inefficient. Machine learning enhances penetration testing by automating reconnaissance, vulnerability exploitation, and attack simulations. Key Recommendations:Use AI-powered penetration testing tools: Platforms like DeepExploit, Metasploit AI, and IBM Watson for Cybersecurity automate attack simulations.Implement reinforcement learning (RL) for attack strategy optimization: RL-based AI can autonomously learn which attack paths are most effective against specific security configuratins.Leverage AI for automated exploit generation: ML models can analyze security advisories and develop exploit code to test vulnerabilities safely.Best Practices:Always conduct AI-driven penetration tests in controlled environments to prevent accidental damage.Follow responsible disclosure policies when identifying vulnerabilities.

Enhance Threat Hunting with AI and Deep LearningThreat hunting involves proactively searching for cyber threats before they cause harm. AI and deep learning improve threat hunting by analyzing massive datasets and detecting hidden attack patterns.Key Recommendations:Deploy AI-powered Security Information and Event Management (SIEM) systems: Use tools like Splunk AI, Elastic Security, and Darktrace to identify threats in real time.Use deep learning for anomaly detection: Neural networks can identify suspicious activity that traditional rule-based systems might miss.pply AI to detect insider (Shanthi et al., 2023)threats: ML models can analyze user behavior and detect anomalies that indicate insider attacks.Security Operations Centers (SOCs) are responsible for detecting, analyzing, and responding to cyber threats. AI-driven SOCs use machine learning to accelerate incident response and reduce human workload.Key Recommendations:Use AI-based threat detection and response platforms: Tools like Cortex XSOAR, Microsoft Sentinel, and IBM Resilient automate incident response workflows.Implement AI-driven malware analysis: Machine learning models can detect and classify malware variants faster than traditional signature-based methods.Deploy AI-powered deception technologies: Honeypots and deception networks can be enhanced with AI to lure attackers and study their techniques.Best Practices:Ensure AI-based response actions are monitored by human analysts to prevent false alarms.Continuously update AI models with new attack patterns to maintain effectiveness. Develop Skills in Adversarial Machine LearningAs AI becomes more prevalent in cybersecurity, attackers are also using adversarial machine learning to evade detection. Ethical hackers must understand how adversarial AI works to develop effective defenses. ey Recommendations:Study adversarial attack techniques: Learn about evasion attacks, model poisoning, and adversarial perturbations that attackers use against AI-based security systems.Test AI security models for vulnerabilities: Conduct red team exercises to identify weaknesses in AI-driven threat detection tools.Implement adversarial training: Train AI models with adversarial examples to improve their resilience against attacks.Best Practices:Use open-source adversrial AI frameworks like CleverHans and Foolbox for security testingCollaborate with AI researchers to stay ahead of emerging adversarial(Ramakrishnan et al., 2022).

CONCLUSION

As cyber threats evolve, AI-powered solutions have become both a necessity and a double-edged sword—capable of fortifying defenses but also vulnerable to adversarial manipulation by malicious actors.This conclusion summarizes the key findings of AI and ML applications in ethical hacking, explores their impact on the future of cybersecurity, and highlights both the opportunities and challenges that lie ahead in this new era of AI-driven cybersecurity.Machine learning models are capable of predicting zero-day vulnerabilities by analyzing patterns in known exploits.AI-powered penetration testing tools can simulate real-world attack scenarios, providing more comprehensive security assessments. Machine Learning for Threat Intelligence and Cyber DefenseAI-powered threat hunting tools can identify hidden attack patterns, reducing response times for security teams.Deep learning models improve anomaly detection, allowing organizations to identify unusual network activity before a breach occurs.AI-based predictive analytics enables organizations to proactively address security gaps before they can be exploited. Reinforcement Learning for Optimized Cybersecurity StrategiesReinforcement learning (RL) allows AI models to continuously adapt and refine attack and defense strategies based on real-time data.I-driven penetration testing agents can learn from past attacks, making them more efficient over time.Organizations can leverage RL-based cybersecurity systems for automated and self-learning defense mechanisms. AI-Powered Incident Response and AutomationAI-driven Security Operations Centers (SOCs) improve incident response by automating threat detection and mitigation.Automated cybersecurity solutions reduce the burden on human analysts, allowing them to focus on complex security issues.AI-enhanced deception technologies, such as intelligent honeypots, can lure attackers into controlled environments, gathering intelligence on their tactics. The Double-Edged Sword: Ethical and Adversarial AIWhile AI strengthens cybersecurity, attackers are also leveraging AI for automated attacks, deepfake phishing, and adversarial ML attacks.Ethical hackers must stay ahead of adversarial AI techniques by continuously testing AI security models for vulnerabilities.The ethical implications of AI in cybersecurity must be carefully managed to prevent misuse and ensure compliance with legal frameworks.. The Future of AI in Ethical Hacking: Opportunities and ChallengesOpportunities for AI-Driven Ethical HackingAI-Powered Cybersecurity Platforms: Fully autonomous security systems capable of detecting, analyzing, and mitigating threats in real time.Quantum AI for Cyber Defense: AI will play a crucial role in developing post-quantum cryptography and securing data against quantum-based attacks.AI-Augmented Red Teaming: Future penetration testing will involve self-learning AI agents that continuously evolve to uncover vulnerabilities.Advanced Threat Prediction: AI-driven predictive models will allow security teams to anticipate and neutralize threats before they materialize. Challenges and Ethical ConsiderationsI Bias and False Positives: AI-driven security models must be carefully trained to reduce bias and minimize false alerts.Adversarial Machine Learning Risks: Attackers are already using adversarial ML techniques to evade detection by AI-based cybersecurity solutions.AI in Cyber Warfare: The use of AI by nation-state actors in cyber warfare raises concerns about AI-powered offensive cyberattacks.Legal and Compliance Issues: The adoption of AI in ethical hacking must adhere to strict legal and ethical guidelines to prevent misuse. Final Thoughts: Embracing AI Responsibly in Ethical HackingThe incorporation of AI and ML in ethical hacking has undoubtedly ushered in a new era of cybersecurity—one where automation, intelligence, and real-time threat detection redefine how organizations defend against cyber threats. Ethical hackers now have unprecedented tools at their disposal, enabling them to detect vulnerabilities faster, automate penetration testing, and predict cyberattacks with greater accuracy.However, with great power comes great responsibility. As AI continues to advance, ethical hackers must ensure that its use remains transparent, ethical, and aligned with cybersecurity best practices.

REFERENCES

Ali, A., Khan, M. A., Farid, K., Akbar, S. S., Taher, A. I., & Ghazal, M.. (2023). The effect of artificial intelligence on cybersecurity. *2023 International Conference on Business Analytics for Technology and Security (ICBATS)*, Dubai, United Arab Emirates, pp. 1–7. DOI: 10.1109/ICBATS57792.2023.10111151

Aloqaily, M., Kanhere, S., Bellavista, P., & Nogueira, M. (2022). Special issue on cybersecurity Management in the era of AI. *Journal of Network and Systems Management, 30*(3), 39–37. DOI: 10.1007/s10922-022-09659-3

Anthony, A. (2023). Cyber resilience must focus on marginalized individuals, not just institutions, carnegie endowment for international peace. Available at: https://carnegieendowment.org/research/2023/03/cyber-resilience-must-focus-on-marginalized-individuals-not-just-institutions?lang=en (Accessed July 2, 2024).

Bergsten, S., & Rivas, P. (2019). Societal benefits and risks of artificial intelligence: a succinct survey. Available at: https://www.semanticscholar.org/paper/Societal-Benefits-and-Risks-of-Artificial-%3A-A-Bergsten-Rivas/fc38e40fd709429633b31436814334cc7edb0092 (Accessed July 4, 2024).

Blythe, M., Andersen, K., Clarke, P., Clarke, R., & Wright, P. C. (2016). 'Anti-solutionist strategies: seriously silly design fiction', In *Proceedings of the 2016 CHI conference on human factors in computing systems*. New York, NY, USA: Association for Computing Machinery (CHI '16), pp. 4968–4978. DOI: 10.1145/2858036.2858482

Bran, E., Rughini , C., Nadoleanu, G., & Flaherty, M. G. (2023). 'The emerging social status of generative AI: vocabularies of AI competence in public discourse', In 2023 24th International Conference on Control Systems and Computer Science (CSCS), Bucharest, Romania. DOI: 10.1109/CSCS59211.2023.00068

Calderon, R. (2019). The benefits of artificial intelligence in cybersecurity, economic crime forensics capstones. Available at: https://digitalcommons.lasalle.edu/ecf_capstones/36

Eshita, M., Ashutosh, G., & Nidhi, G. (2016). Artificial Intelligence Impact on Cyber Security. *Journal of Management and IT, 7*, 100–107.

Fast, E., & Horvitz, E. (2017). Long-term trends in the public perception of artificial intelligence. Proc. AAAI Conf. Artif. Intell. 31, 963–969. DOI: 10.1609/aaai.v31i1.10635

Fortes, P. R. B., Baquero, P. M., & Amariles, D. R. (2022). Artificial intelligence risks and algorithmic regulation. *European Journal of Risk Regulation, 13*(3), 357–372. DOI: 10.1017/err.2022.14

Hutter, R., & Hutter, M. (2021). Chances and risks of artificial intelligence—A concept of developing and exploiting machine intelligence for future societies. *Applied System Innovation, 4*(2), 1–19. DOI: 10.3390/asi4020037

Li, J. (2018). Cyber security meets artificial intelligence: A survey. *Frontiers of Information Technology & Electronic Engineering, 19*(12), 1462–1474. DOI: 10.1631/FITEE.1800573

Looi, J. C. L., Bonner, D., & Maguire, P. (2021). Maslow's hammer: Considering the perils of solutionism in mental healthcare and psychiatric practice. *Australasian Psychiatry, 29*(6), 687–689. DOI: 10.1177/10398562211005438 PMID: 34014790

Mahadev Madgule, N. (2023). Mechanical properties and microstructure of activated TIG welded similar joints of Inconel alloys by desirability approaches. *Materials Today: Proceedings, 77*, 528–533. DOI: 10.1016/j.matpr.2022.12.250

Moriniello, F., Martí-Testón, A., Muñoz, A., Silva Jasaui, D., Gracia, L., & Solanes, J. E. (2024). Exploring the relationship between the coverage of AI in WIRED magazine and public opinion using sentiment analysis. *Applied Sciences (Basel, Switzerland), 14*(5), 1994. DOI: 10.3390/app14051994

Nguyen, D. (2023). How news media frame data risks in their coverage of big data and AI. Internet Policy Review. Available at: https://policyreview.info/articles/analysis/how-news-media-frame-data-risks-big-data-and-ai (Accessed July 4, 2024).

Nguyen, D., & Hekman, E. (2024). The news framing of artificial intelligence: A critical exploration of how media discourses make sense of automation. *AI & Society, 39*(2), 437–451. DOI: 10.1007/s00146-022-01511-1

Ouchchy, L., Coin, A., & Dubljević, V. (2020). AI in the headlines: The portrayal of the ethical issues of artificial intelligence in the media. *AI & Society, 35*(4), 927–936. DOI: 10.1007/s00146-020-00965-5

Page, J., Bain, M., & Mukhlish, F. (2018). *'The risks of low level narrow artificial intelligence', in 2018 IEEE international conference on intelligence and safety for robotics (ISR). 2018 IEEE international conference on intelligence and safety for robotics*. ISR.

Ramakrishnan, T., Mohan Gift, M. D., Chitradevi, S., Jegan, R., & Subha Hency Jose, P. Nagaraja, Rajneesh Sharma H.N., Selvakumar P., Sintayehu Mekuria Hailegiorgis, (2022). "Study of Numerous Resins Used in Polymer Matrix Composite Materials", Advances in Materials Science and Engineering, vol. 2022, Article ID 1088926, 8 pages, 2022. DOI: 10.1155/2022/1088926

Ruckenstein, M., & Pantzar, M. (2018). Beyond the quantified self: Thematic exploration of a dataistic paradigm. *New Media & Society*, *19*(3), 401–418. DOI: 10.1177/1461444815609081

Rughini , C., & Flaherty, M. G. (2022). The social bifurcation of reality: Symmetrical construction of knowledge in lay science-distrusting and science-trusting discourses. *Frontiers in Sociology*, *7*, 782851. DOI: 10.3389/fsoc.2022.782851 PMID: 35224088

Shanthi, R. R., Sasi, N. K., & Gouthaman, P. (2023). *A new era of cybersecurity: the influence of artificial intelligence. 2023 international conference on networking and communications*. ICNWC.

Sreenivasulu, A., & Manimozhi, T. Satheesh kumar P. and Singh P.,(2022). "The Model of Smart Sensing Device For Sensitive Nanoclusters Modification in Sensing Properties," 2022 2nd International Conference on Advance Computing and Innovative Technologies in Engineering (ICACITE), Greater Noida, India, 2022, pp. 1043-1047, DOI: 10.1109/ICACITE53722.2022.9823846

Strauß, S. (2018). From big data to deep learning: A leap towards strong AI or "Intelligentia Obscura"? *Big Data and Cognitive Computing*, *2*(3), 16. DOI: 10.3390/bdcc2030016

Sugumaran, K. M. D., Pandiyarajan V., Y. B S, and M. S, (2024). "Analysis of Electromyography Signals for Control of Mechanical Prosthesis using Machine Learning Techniques," 2024 2nd International Conference on Intelligent Data Communication Technologies and Internet of Things (IDCIoT), Bengaluru, India, 2024, pp. 1059-1067, DOI: 10.1109/IDCIoT59759.2024.10467707

van Dijck, J. (2014). Datafication, dataism and dataveillance: Big data between scientific paradigm and ideology. *Surveillance & Society*, *12*(2), 197–208. DOI: 10.24908/ss.v12i2.4776

Vijayakumar, G., Rajkumar, M., Rajiv Chandar, N., Selvakumar, P., & Duraisamy, R. (2024). Muniyandi Rajkumar, Rajiv Chandar N, Selvakumar P and Ramesh Duraisamy, (2024). Environmentally friendly TDS removal from waste water by electrochemical ion exchange batch-type recirculation (EIR) technique. *Environmental Science. Water Research & Technology*, *10*(4), 826–835. DOI: 10.1039/D3EW00793F

Wang, H., Yu, B., Chen, X., & Yan, H. (2022). Global pattern and determinants of COVID-19 vaccine coverage and progression: a global ecological study. Soc. Sci. Electr. Publish. Pres. Soc. Sci. Res. Netw. DOI: 10.2139/ssrn.4046662

Zhai, Y., Yan, J., Zhang, H., & Lu, W. (2020). Tracing the evolution of AI: Conceptualization of artificial intelligence in mass media discourse. *Information Discovery and Delivery*, *48*(3), 137–149. DOI: 10.1108/IDD-01-2020-0007

Chapter 4
AI-Driven Ethical Hacking and Machine Learning Applications in Offensive and Defensive Cybersecurity

Mayur Jariwala
http://orcid.org/0009-0008-1686-8791
University of the Cumberlands, USA

ABSTRACT

As cyber threats evolve in scale and complexity, ethical hacking must also advance beyond traditional approaches. This chapter explores how artificial intelligence (AI) and machine learning (ML) are revolutionizing penetration testing, from reconnaissance and vulnerability assessment to social engineering and blue teaming. It examines real-world applications, adversarial AI risks, and the ethical boundaries of automated attacks. The chapter also highlights regulatory implications and emerging trends such as explainable AI and autonomous red teaming. It provides a forward-looking perspective on how AI can responsibly augment cybersecurity practices in both offensive and defensive contexts.

DOI: 10.4018/979-8-3373-3536-0.ch004

1. INTRODUCTION

1.1 Overview of Evolving Cyber Threats and Penetration Testing

The threat landscape in cybersecurity has evolved dramatically over the past two decades. In the early 2000s, cyberattacks were often limited to website defacements, script kiddie exploits, and relatively unsophisticated worms. However, today's threat actors deploy advanced, persistent, and often state-sponsored campaigns that exploit zero-day vulnerabilities, weaponize artificial intelligence, and operate within intricate attack chains (Durgaraju et al., 2025). These developments are no longer confined to critical infrastructure or high-profile targets. From small businesses to multinational corporations, the digital ecosystem has become an equal-opportunity hunting ground for cybercriminals, hacktivists, and nation-state operatives.

One of the most compelling responses to these challenges has been the formalization and maturation of penetration testing, a practice that simulates cyberattacks in a controlled and ethical manner. Often colloquially referred to as "ethical hacking," penetration testing helps organizations proactively identify weaknesses before real adversaries do. It has transitioned from being a niche exercise performed annually to an integral component of continuous security assessment. Modern pen testing now spans across cloud environments, APIs, mobile apps, IoT networks, and even AI models themselves.

The speed at which vulnerabilities emerge, coupled with the growing sophistication of attack vectors, has made traditional pen testing models increasingly inadequate. Manual assessments, while still valuable, struggle to scale in dynamic environments characterized by rapid deployment cycles, microservices, and globally distributed infrastructure. Additionally, the skill gap in cybersecurity continues to widen, making it difficult for organizations to staff competent red teamers or ethical hackers consistently.

Consequently, the demand for automation, intelligence, and adaptability in penetration testing has grown. AI and machine learning have emerged as promising enablers, offering the potential to simulate attacks faster, adapt to changing network conditions, and even anticipate an adversary's next move (Çaylı, 2024). As this chapter will explore, the integration of AI into ethical hacking is not just a technical upgrade, it represents a paradigm shift in how we understand and execute offensive and defensive cybersecurity strategies.

1.2 Role of AI/ML in Transforming Ethical Hacking

Artificial Intelligence (AI) and Machine Learning (ML) have quietly but decisively started reshaping the cybersecurity landscape, particularly in the realm of ethical hacking. Traditional penetration testing has long relied on the intuition and manual expertise of human testers, navigating systems, probing for vulnerabilities, and crafting exploits. While these human-driven methods remain valuable, they are increasingly outpaced by the speed, scale, and adaptability required in today's digital environment. AI and ML step in not to replace the ethical hacker but to supercharge their capabilities, bringing a level of precision and automation previously unimaginable.

AI's role begins at the reconnaissance phase, where massive amounts of publicly available data can be scraped, analyzed, and contextualized in seconds (Al-Sinani & Mitchell, 2024). ML models trained on threat intelligence feeds, dark web chatter, and network telemetry can identify targets, predict vulnerabilities, and even prioritize them based on potential business impact. This front-loading of intelligence accelerates the pre-engagement phase and provides a more targeted attack surface for ethical hackers to engage with.

Further down the pipeline, machine learning is now being employed to automate exploit development, simulate lateral movement, and mimic human-like attack behaviors. Reinforcement learning models have shown promise in learning optimal attack paths through simulated environments, adapting dynamically to the defenses they encounter. This kind of agility is something even the most seasoned human testers struggle to maintain under time constraints.

The integration of AI in penetration testing introduces repeatability and consistency, two qualities often hard to achieve with purely manual testing (Al-Sinani et al., 2025). An AI model doesn't forget, doesn't get tired, and can be rerun against updated environments to spot new vulnerabilities introduced during software changes or infrastructure shifts.

However, this transformation is not without its caveats. Ethical concerns around autonomous decision-making, the risk of adversarial manipulation of AI models, and regulatory ambiguities remain open questions. As organizations begin to deploy AI-augmented ethical hacking tools, striking a balance between automation and accountability becomes essential.

Ultimately, AI and ML are not just enhancing ethical hacking, they are redefining what it means to test the security of systems. The future points toward intelligent red teaming agents, capable of running simulated attacks with human-like ingenuity, but at machine speed and scale. This chapter will delve into these innovations, laying the foundation for a new era of cybersecurity testing.

1.3 Motivation and Chapter Overview

The motivation behind this chapter stems from a pressing reality: as cyber threats become more intelligent, adaptable, and evasive, our testing methodologies must evolve at a similar pace. Conventional ethical hacking frameworks, while methodical and time-tested, are increasingly ill-equipped to assess the resilience of complex, dynamic systems operating across cloud-native, distributed, and AI-augmented environments. Organizations are no longer dealing with static networks, they're defending fluid digital ecosystems composed of ephemeral containers, APIs, serverless functions, and interconnected IoT devices. In such a volatile landscape, the question arises, how do we test for security gaps that are constantly shifting?

This chapter responds to that challenge by examining how artificial intelligence and machine learning are transforming the ethical hacking process from a largely manual, reactive craft into a partially autonomous, predictive discipline. Rather than being confined to scheduled assessments or compliance checklists, AI-enabled penetration testing can now operate in real time, continuously scanning for anomalies, modeling potential attack paths, and simulating intelligent adversaries. In doing so, it offers a new level of visibility into systems that were previously too vast or too complex to test comprehensively.

Beyond the technical imperative, there's also a broader strategic rationale. As security teams grapple with mounting workloads and a persistent talent shortage, AI presents an opportunity to scale ethical hacking capabilities without proportionally increasing human resource requirements. It helps organizations stay ahead of attackers, not merely by mimicking them, but by learning from every attempted breach, refining models, and anticipating future threats.

This chapter is structured to guide readers through this emerging domain with both breadth and depth. It begins with a foundational overview of machine learning concepts relevant to cybersecurity, before progressing into specific use cases such as AI-assisted reconnaissance, intelligent vulnerability scanning, automated exploitation, and adversarial machine learning. Further sections explore the application of AI in blue teaming, ethical and legal considerations, and real-world case studies from critical sectors like finance and healthcare. The chapter concludes with forward-looking insights into autonomous red teaming, quantum threats, and the future of explainable AI in penetration testing.

By the end, readers will gain not just technical knowledge but also a critical understanding of how AI-driven ethical hacking fits into the larger cybersecurity ecosystem, both as a tactical instrument and a strategic enabler for modern organizations.

2. FOUNDATIONS OF MACHINE LEARNING IN ETHICAL HACKING

2.1 Supervised Learning (Classification for Anomaly Detection)

Supervised learning, one of the most widely adopted branches of machine learning, plays a pivotal role in ethical hacking by enabling the classification and detection of anomalies within digital environments. At its core, supervised learning involves training a model on labeled data, that is, data where the input features are associated with known outcomes. In the context of cybersecurity, this often translates to training algorithms to distinguish between benign and malicious behaviors, effectively building classifiers that can detect suspicious activity in real-time.

Bierbrauer et al. (2021) explained in penetration testing scenarios, supervised learning algorithms are particularly adept at identifying patterns that deviate from the norm, such as unauthorized access attempts, abnormal user behavior, or irregular network traffic. For instance, decision trees, support vector machines (SVMs), and logistic regression models have been trained on historical attack data to recognize specific exploit signatures or identify malware embedded within seemingly benign payloads. Once trained, these models can act as automated sentinels, scanning logs, packets, or API calls to detect known attack vectors.

A compelling application of supervised learning in ethical hacking lies in the simulation of intrusion detection systems (IDS). Pen testers often leverage these models not just to bypass existing IDS but to build their own classifiers that emulate how an organization's detection systems might respond to various attack strategies. This allows ethical hackers to preemptively understand which of their tactics are likely to be flagged and adapt their techniques accordingly.

However, the power of supervised learning is also its limitation. Since the model's performance hinges on the quality and completeness of labeled training data, it may fail to recognize novel or previously unseen attack techniques, an issue known as the "zero-day blind spot."(Bello et al., 2025). Imbalanced datasets, where benign samples vastly outnumber malicious ones, can skew classification accuracy, leading to either false positives or dangerous false negatives.

To address these challenges, modern pen testing environments often incorporate techniques like oversampling, synthetic minority oversampling technique (SMOTE), or ensemble learning to improve classifier robustness. Ultimately, supervised learning provides a crucial starting point for AI-enabled ethical hacking by offering a structured, data-driven approach to threat classification, but it must be continually refined and supplemented to remain effective in the face of evolving threats.

2.2 Unsupervised Learning (Clustering for Behavioral Analysis)

While supervised learning thrives on labeled datasets, unsupervised learning excels in uncovering hidden patterns in data where no prior classifications exist. This makes it exceptionally valuable in ethical hacking, especially when conducting behavioral analysis or probing for unknown vulnerabilities and attack signatures. In contrast to signature-based detection, which is limited by known threat profiles, unsupervised algorithms operate with the freedom to discover anomalies and groupings that human analysts may overlook entirely.

One of the most prevalent applications of unsupervised learning in penetration testing is clustering, a method that organizes data points into groups based on shared characteristics. Algorithms such as k-means clustering, DBSCAN (Density-Based Spatial Clustering of Applications with Noise), and hierarchical clustering are frequently used to analyze large volumes of log data, user behavior, or network flows. By observing how data naturally clusters, ethical hackers can identify outliers, activities that deviate significantly from the norm and may represent suspicious or malicious behavior.

For instance, in behavioral anomaly detection, clustering models can highlight patterns such as unusual login times, unexpected access to sensitive files, or erratic API call frequencies. These deviations, once isolated, serve as starting points for deeper probing during a pen test. Ethical hackers can simulate attacks that mimic such anomalies to evaluate how effectively security controls respond to behavior-based threats rather than signature-based ones (Paradhi et al., 2024).

Unsupervised learning plays a crucial role in network traffic analysis. Clustering models can help segment traffic into legitimate usage patterns (e.g., typical DNS queries, HTTP requests) and less common, potentially malicious behaviors (e.g., lateral movement, port scanning). These insights are invaluable in crafting simulated attacks that remain undetected by traditional tools but could disrupt business operations if exploited by a real adversary.

What makes unsupervised learning particularly suited to ethical hacking is its adaptability. Unlike static rule sets, clustering models evolve with the data, making them capable of highlighting new or emerging threats without requiring explicit labels or definitions. This is especially important in zero-trust environments and cloud-native ecosystems, where user behavior and system configurations change frequently.

That said, the flexibility of unsupervised learning comes with interpretability challenges. Clusters don't inherently explain themselves; they require contextual analysis to infer their meaning (Pu et al., 2021). Without careful feature selection and domain knowledge, ethical hackers risk misinterpreting benign anomalies as threats, or worse, overlooking meaningful indicators. Still, when used judiciously, clustering enables a proactive approach to vulnerability discovery and attack surface mapping, making it an indispensable tool in the modern ethical hacker's arsenal.

2.3 Reinforcement Learning (Adaptive Attack Simulations)

Among the diverse branches of machine learning, reinforcement learning (RL) stands out for its ability to simulate decision-making in dynamic, uncertain environments, a capability that is remarkably well-suited for ethical hacking. Unlike supervised or unsupervised learning, reinforcement learning does not rely on labeled data or static groupings (Hu et al., 2020). Instead, it revolves around an intelligent agent that learns by interacting with an environment, taking actions, receiving feedback (rewards or penalties), and gradually optimizing its strategy to achieve a defined objective. In ethical hacking, this paradigm enables the modeling of adaptive cyberattacks, allowing simulated adversaries to evolve and exploit vulnerabilities in complex systems.

The application of RL in penetration testing often centers on the concept of attack path optimization. For example, an RL agent can be tasked with compromising a target system by navigating through a network, identifying exploitable services, avoiding detection, and escalating privileges, much like a real attacker would. Over time, the agent refines its tactics, learning which sequences of actions yield the highest reward, such as successful lateral movement, data exfiltration, or evasion of intrusion detection systems (IDS). The beauty of this approach lies in its adaptability: it doesn't require hardcoded attack scripts or rule sets; the agent learns organically, even in environments it hasn't encountered before.

One compelling framework in this space is the OpenAI Gym-based CyberBattleSim developed by Microsoft, which uses reinforcement learning agents to model adversarial behavior within enterprise networks (Ilić et al., 2023). These agents simulate cyberattacks by making a series of decisions in a test environment, gradually learning the most efficient way to achieve their objectives under varying levels of system defenses. For ethical hackers, this offers a novel way to train red team strategies, uncover unknown vulnerabilities, and evaluate how security postures hold up under persistent, learning-based attacks.

However, integrating RL into ethical hacking is not without challenges. The design of a meaningful reward function is critical, rewarding the wrong behavior can lead the agent to develop tactics that are either ineffective or unrealistic. Additionally, training RL models can be resource-intensive and time-consuming, requiring extensive simulations to reach optimal performance. In high-stakes environments, such as critical infrastructure or financial systems, deploying RL-driven pen testing agents must be approached cautiously to avoid unintended disruptions.

Despite these hurdles, the potential of reinforcement learning in ethical hacking is profound. It allows for the automation of sophisticated, multi-stage attacks that mimic real-world adversaries with a level of nuance and persistence that is difficult to replicate manually. As this field matures, RL is poised to become a cornerstone of autonomous red teaming and cyber range testing, where continuous adaptation and learning are not just advantages, they are necessities.

2.4 Popular ML Tools: Scikit-Learn, TensorFlow, PyTorch, AutoML

As machine learning continues to influence the evolution of ethical hacking, a diverse ecosystem of tools has emerged to support the development, training, and deployment of AI models. These platforms empower cybersecurity professionals, not just data scientists, to experiment with algorithms, automate workflows, and embed intelligence into penetration testing strategies.

Scikit-learn, a Python-based library, is widely regarded for its simplicity and accessibility (Haryono et al., 2021). It offers an extensive collection of supervised and unsupervised algorithms, including decision trees, SVMs, k-means clustering, and anomaly detection models. Its clean API and integration with tools like pandas and NumPy make it an ideal starting point for rapid prototyping of machine learning-based security solutions.

TensorFlow, developed by Google, provides a more robust, scalable environment for deep learning applications. With its support for neural networks, reinforcement learning, and large-scale training, TensorFlow is suitable for building complex models used in behavioral analysis, pattern recognition, or even adversarial input generation. Ethical hackers leveraging deep packet inspection or biometric spoofing simulations often turn to TensorFlow for its flexibility and GPU acceleration.

PyTorch, another leading deep learning framework, is particularly favored in research-oriented penetration testing. Known for its dynamic computation graph and intuitive debugging capabilities, PyTorch excels in scenarios where iterative experimentation is essential, such as modeling adaptive attacks or designing generative adversarial networks (GANs) for evasion testing (Lomonaco et al., 2023).

Lastly, AutoML tools like Google AutoML, H2O.ai, or Auto-Sklearn simplify the process of model selection and tuning. These platforms are valuable when time is constrained or expertise in algorithmic fine-tuning is limited, enabling ethical hackers to rapidly deploy models with minimal manual intervention.

Each of these tools plays a unique role, and ethical hackers often combine them, depending on whether the task at hand is exploratory, scalable, or focused on real-time exploitation or defense.

3. AI-POWERED RECONNAISSANCE AND INTELLIGENCE GATHERING

3.1 OSINT Automation Using ML and NLP

Open Source Intelligence (OSINT) is a cornerstone of the reconnaissance phase in ethical hacking, often serving as the initial, and arguably most critical, step in mapping a target's digital footprint. Traditionally, gathering OSINT involves manually scanning publicly accessible sources such as websites, social media, forums, DNS records, breach databases, and code repositories (Hamed et al., 2024). While effective, this manual process is time-consuming and prone to oversight. Machine learning (ML), particularly in combination with Natural Language Processing (NLP), revolutionizes OSINT by introducing automation, precision, and real-time adaptability.

Machine learning models can be trained to filter and prioritize vast volumes of data scraped from disparate sources. NLP algorithms can then be used to extract meaningful insights from unstructured text, emails, leaked credentials, personal information, or even indirect mentions of an organization's assets (Koushal et al., 2025). For instance, a custom NLP pipeline might scan job postings to infer the technologies used by a company, or crawl developer forums for misconfigurations linked to a target domain. Named Entity Recognition (NER) models can highlight sensitive information such as user IDs, email addresses, server names, and API keys with minimal human intervention.

ML-driven OSINT tools can be continuously updated to adapt to evolving data structures and platform-specific nuances. They can identify patterns over time, flagging emerging risks like domain squatting, impersonation attempts, or data leaks across underground forums. Tools like SpiderFoot, Maltego with NLP plugins, and customized Python scripts leveraging spaCy or BERT-based models are increasingly used in reconnaissance automation.

For ethical hackers, these capabilities offer a dual benefit: reducing effort while expanding scope. They can not only build a more accurate picture of the target's digital presence but also simulate the kind of adversarial intelligence gathering conducted by advanced persistent threat (APT) groups. This lays a powerful foundation for subsequent stages of the penetration test.

Koushal et al. (2025) proposed a predictive system leveraging the Common Vulnerability Scoring System (CVSS) and supervised ML to forecast the exploitability of software vulnerabilities. Their model emphasized preprocessing, feature selection, and yielded actionable insights for cybersecurity defense

3.2 AI for Profiling Targets From Dark Web Data and Social Networks

Target profiling has evolved beyond surface-level domain and IP enumeration. In modern ethical hacking engagements, especially those simulating nation-state or corporate espionage threats, understanding a target's human and infrastructural footprint is essential. Artificial Intelligence (AI) facilitates this by enabling automated, scalable analysis of data drawn from the dark web and social networks, uncovering both technical and social vulnerabilities that traditional reconnaissance might overlook.

On the dark web, large volumes of stolen credentials, confidential documents, and internal communications circulate across marketplaces, forums, and encrypted messaging platforms. AI models, particularly those designed for text classification, clustering, and named entity recognition, can parse and index this content far more efficiently than manual methods. Deep learning tools like BERT or RoBERTa can be fine-tuned to identify mentions of company names, employee identifiers, or exposed configuration files. These discoveries help ethical hackers understand whether a target has already been compromised, what data is at risk, and which entry points may be exploited further.

Similarly, social media platforms, LinkedIn, Twitter, GitHub, Reddit, serve as rich OSINT sources. AI systems can be used to mine and correlate user-generated content with organizational metadata. For example, employee LinkedIn profiles may unintentionally reveal internal technologies or projects. Public GitHub repositories can expose API tokens or internal documentation. AI-driven graph analysis can even uncover social engineering attack paths by mapping relationships between employees, vendors, and exposed credentials.

Importantly, AI allows this data to be contextualized. It's not just about extracting names or URLs, it's about building behavioral profiles, identifying weak links in the human chain, and forecasting potential exploitation paths. In a red team exercise, such profiling enables ethical hackers to craft spear-phishing campaigns or lateral movement strategies that are informed, personalized, and realistic.

Ultimately, AI transforms fragmented public data into a coherent attacker's map, making ethical hacking engagements both sharper and significantly more predictive.

3.3 Tools and Real-World Examples

AI-powered reconnaissance has gained momentum due to a growing suite of tools that automate and enhance traditional intelligence-gathering techniques. These tools are no longer just passive data collectors, they are dynamic systems capable of extracting, interpreting, and correlating information across multiple sources, often in real time. Ethical hackers are increasingly leveraging such platforms to streamline OSINT workflows and deepen the analytical value of reconnaissance efforts.

One widely used tool is Maltego, a link analysis software that visualizes relationships between people, groups, websites, domains, IPs, and social networks. With AI and NLP extensions, Maltego can automatically tag entities, highlight contextual keywords, and perform sentiment analysis on harvested social media content. It's often employed in social engineering simulations, helping red teams identify high-value individuals or uncover inadvertent data leakage through public channels.

SpiderFoot is another AI-enhanced tool that offers deep reconnaissance capabilities. With more than 200 modules, it integrates threat intelligence feeds, DNS data, WHOIS records, breach databases, and darknet crawlers. SpiderFoot uses machine learning to prioritize risk indicators and eliminate noise from large datasets, offering ethical hackers a curated list of actionable intelligence points (Rajamäki et al., 2024).

On the more experimental edge, frameworks like Recon-ng and custom Python pipelines built with spaCy, Transformers, or LangChain allow for automated scraping and contextual understanding of unstructured data. These tools are especially effective when scanning forums or chat logs, extracting sentiment or detecting anomalous behavior that may indicate pre-breach discussions.

In real-world assessments, AI-powered reconnaissance has enabled ethical hackers to identify exposed S3 buckets, vulnerable DevOps tools, or abandoned subdomains used for phishing (Kolade et al., 2025). In one noted engagement, a pen test team used automated GitHub scrapers trained on NLP models to uncover hard-coded credentials in an engineer's public repository, leading directly to system access.

These tools are not only increasing efficiency but elevating the precision and realism of penetration testing engagements, ultimately contributing to more resilient cybersecurity postures.

4. MACHINE LEARNING IN VULNERABILITY ASSESSMENT

4.1 Static vs Dynamic Analysis With ML Models

Vulnerability assessment has traditionally relied on two primary techniques: static analysis and dynamic analysis. Each offers distinct advantages in uncovering security flaws, and with the integration of machine learning (ML), both have evolved into powerful tools for ethical hackers aiming to identify exploitable weaknesses in software, systems, and networks.

Static analysis, often performed through Static Application Security Testing (SAST), involves examining source code, bytecode, or binaries without executing the program. ML enhances this by detecting subtle patterns that may indicate insecure code practices, such as improper input validation or misuse of cryptographic functions (Wang et al., 2021). Supervised learning algorithms, when trained on labeled datasets of vulnerable and non-vulnerable code, can automate the identification of risky constructs. Natural Language Processing (NLP) is also used to analyze code comments or documentation, which may contain hints about insecure implementations.

On the other hand, dynamic analysis, or Dynamic Application Security Testing (DAST), evaluates applications during runtime. It focuses on how the application behaves under various inputs and environments. ML models used here excel at spotting anomalies in system responses, memory usage, API behavior, and network traffic. Reinforcement learning and anomaly detection techniques help simulate sophisticated attack paths and monitor for deviations that suggest vulnerability exploitation, such as unauthorized data access or privilege escalation.

One key benefit of ML-driven dynamic analysis is adaptability. For instance, if a web application is configured differently in production versus staging, an ML model can learn these differences and adjust its testing behavior accordingly. This reduces false positives and increases the relevance of identified vulnerabilities.

Together, ML-enhanced static and dynamic analysis provide a more holistic approach to vulnerability assessment. By correlating findings from both techniques, ethical hackers gain richer context, allowing them to pinpoint not just where vulnerabilities exist, but how they might realistically be exploited under real-world conditions.

4.2 Predictive Vulnerability Modeling Using Supervised ML

Predictive vulnerability modeling using supervised machine learning represents a strategic advancement in ethical hacking, shifting vulnerability assessment from reactive detection to proactive risk anticipation. Instead of waiting for a vulnerability to surface through scans or attacks, supervised ML models aim to forecast potential weaknesses based on patterns derived from historical vulnerability data, code attributes, and system configurations.

Supervised ML relies on labeled datasets, examples where software components are marked as vulnerable or not vulnerable. These datasets may include information from sources such as the National Vulnerability Database (NVD), CVE repositories, and proprietary bug tracking systems. Features extracted from these datasets may include code complexity metrics (e.g., cyclomatic complexity), developer activity logs, API usage, dependency age, and previous bug-fix histories. Using algorithms like Random Forest, Gradient Boosting, or Support Vector Machines, ethical hackers can train models to predict the likelihood of vulnerabilities in unseen code.

For example, a model might identify that third-party libraries with infrequent updates and high dependency chains have a higher probability of containing exploitable bugs. When integrated into the CI/CD pipeline, these predictions can trigger deeper inspection of specific components before deployment, an approach that significantly enhances security posture without slowing development velocity.

Ethical hackers can also apply these models to prioritize findings during large-scale assessments. Rather than treating all discovered issues equally, AI can assign risk scores to vulnerabilities based on predicted exploitability and contextual relevance (Koushal et al., 2025). This risk-based triaging ensures limited resources are directed toward the most dangerous weaknesses.

However, predictive modeling is only as good as the data it's trained on. Biases in training data, evolving software architectures, and the emergence of new exploit techniques can reduce accuracy over time. Despite these limitations, supervised ML remains a valuable augmentation to the ethical hacker's toolkit, particularly when integrated into continuous, DevSecOps-aligned security workflows.

4.3 Use of CVSS Scores and MITRE Datasets

Machine learning models designed for ethical hacking benefit significantly from structured and authoritative vulnerability data sources, among the most influential are the Common Vulnerability Scoring System (CVSS) and the MITRE datasets, including the Common Vulnerabilities and Exposures (CVE) list and ATT&CK framework. These datasets offer standardized formats, metadata, and contextual threat models that can be harnessed to train intelligent systems for vulnerability assessment, exploitation prediction, and defensive simulation.

CVSS scores provide a quantifiable assessment of a vulnerability's severity based on factors such as attack complexity, privileges required, user interaction, and the potential impact on confidentiality, integrity, and availability. According to Ahn et al. (2022) Supervised machine learning models can ingest CVSS vectors as features, numerical representations of each component, and correlate them with exploitability data, threat intelligence feeds, and patch histories. This enables models to make more nuanced predictions, such as forecasting which newly disclosed vulnerabilities are most likely to be weaponized in the wild.

Similarly, MITRE's ATT&CK framework offers a comprehensive taxonomy of adversarial behaviors, mapping real-world tactics, techniques, and procedures (TTPs). By cross-referencing CVE entries with ATT&CK mappings, ethical hackers can build AI models that not only detect vulnerabilities but simulate how an attacker might exploit them in a stepwise, multi-stage operation. This strategic insight elevates ethical hacking from surface-level scanning to scenario-based simulation (Grigorescu et al., 2022).

MITRE's Common Weakness Enumeration (CWE) list is also instrumental in training AI systems to recognize code patterns associated with recurring vulnerabilities, such as buffer overflows or insecure deserialization. These classifications add an interpretive layer, helping ML models understand not just that a system is vulnerable, but why and how.

The structured richness of CVSS and MITRE datasets offers a dependable foundation for machine learning models in ethical hacking, bridging theoretical vulnerability scoring with real-world exploit context and adversarial modeling.

4.4 Tools: DeepExploit, VulnHunter, Microsoft Security Risk Detection

The integration of machine learning into vulnerability assessment has not only enhanced accuracy and speed but has also driven the development of specialized tools designed to automate and scale these capabilities. Among the most prominent in this space are DeepExploit, VulnHunter, and Microsoft Security Risk Detection, each offering a unique blend of intelligence, automation, and practical usability for ethical hackers.

DeepExploit, built on top of Metasploit, exemplifies the fusion of reinforcement learning and penetration testing. It operates by autonomously identifying vulnerabilities, selecting appropriate exploits, and adapting its behavior based on the environment's feedback (Guo et al., 2019). DeepExploit continuously learns from each execution cycle, optimizing its decisions to improve success rates over time. Its reinforcement learning engine reduces reliance on predefined scripts and enables it to function more like a human attacker, probing defenses, adjusting strategies, and even chaining exploits. Ethical hackers benefit from its ability to simulate persistent and adaptive threats in a controlled, measurable manner.

VulnHunter focuses more on machine learning-based vulnerability classification and prioritization. It leverages supervised learning to analyze both static and dynamic characteristics of software applications, ranging from source code complexity to runtime behavior. One of VulnHunter's strengths lies in its ability to reduce false positives, a persistent challenge in large-scale assessments. By learning from historical vulnerability data and developer behavior, the tool fine-tunes its predictions and offers prioritized alerts that align better with real-world exploitability.

Microsoft Security Risk Detection, formerly known as Project Springfield, represents a more enterprise-oriented implementation of ML for fuzz testing (Bajantri & Shariff, 2024). It uses cloud-based AI to model application behavior under stress, automatically identifying security-critical bugs through a combination of symbolic execution and constraint solving. Designed for use in production-grade applications, this tool integrates seamlessly into CI/CD pipelines, allowing developers and ethical hackers to assess software security early in the lifecycle. Its predictive capabilities enable proactive remediation before vulnerabilities are deployed into live environments.

Together, these tools highlight a shift from reactive vulnerability scanning to intelligent, context-aware assessment. As these platforms evolve, they will likely form the backbone of next-generation red teaming efforts, enabling ethical hackers to discover and validate security weaknesses with unprecedented precision and efficiency.

5. AI FOR EXPLOITATION AND ATTACK SIMULATION

5.1 Automated Fuzzing, Reinforcement Learning for Attack Paths

Exploitation is the most critical and technically demanding phase of penetration testing. Once vulnerabilities have been identified, ethical hackers must determine whether they can be practically exploited and what impact such exploitation may have. Traditional exploitation relies heavily on manual testing, custom scripting, and a deep understanding of system internals. However, with the emergence of AI, especially automated fuzzing and reinforcement learning, this process is becoming increasingly dynamic, scalable, and efficient.

Automated fuzzing involves sending large volumes of malformed or unexpected input to an application to observe how it responds, crashing, exposing memory, or revealing entry points. Historically, fuzzing has been a brute-force technique (Böttinger et al., 2018). But today's AI-enhanced fuzzers use machine learning to prioritize inputs that are more likely to trigger anomalous behavior. For example, coverage-guided fuzzers like AFL (American Fuzzy Lop) have evolved with ML-based extensions to focus on under-tested execution paths. More advanced models use recurrent neural networks (RNNs) or generative adversarial networks (GANs) to generate semantically valid but strategically malformed inputs that mimic real user data, increasing the chance of uncovering subtle logic bugs.

Reinforcement learning (RL) takes exploitation a step further by modeling the entire exploitation process as a sequential decision-making problem. Here, an intelligent agent interacts with the environment, such as a sandboxed system or emulated network, by performing actions like probing services, injecting payloads, and analyzing responses. The agent is rewarded for successful exploits, such as gaining shell access or achieving privilege escalation, and penalized for detection or failure. Over time, the RL model learns optimal attack paths, effectively mimicking an attacker's evolving tactics.

One key advantage of combining automated fuzzing with RL is adaptability. Unlike rule-based exploitation tools, AI-driven systems can dynamically adjust strategies based on system configuration, patch level, or runtime defenses. For ethical hackers, this reduces the trial-and-error burden while improving the realism of simulated attacks.

As AI-enhanced exploitation matures, it will not only automate low-level exploit generation but also facilitate multi-stage, context-aware attack simulations that mirror advanced persistent threat-giving defenders a clearer picture of their actual exposure.

5.2 Intelligent Fuzzing for Zero-Day Detection

Detecting zero-day vulnerabilities, those previously unknown to vendors or the public, remains one of the most elusive goals in ethical hacking. Traditional fuzzing techniques, although effective for exposing generic memory corruption or input-handling flaws, often fall short in identifying sophisticated, context-specific bugs. This is where intelligent fuzzing, powered by AI and machine learning, presents a compelling advancement.

Intelligent fuzzing enhances the brute-force nature of conventional fuzzers by learning from execution feedback. Instead of generating inputs randomly, AI-enhanced fuzzers analyze code paths, input patterns, and runtime behavior to create more precise and targeted payloads (Shinde & Shivalkar, 2025). By leveraging machine learning algorithms, such as decision trees, reinforcement learning, and deep neural networks, fuzzers can prioritize inputs that are statistically more likely to trigger anomalies.

For example, Neural Fuzzing, an emerging approach, uses recurrent neural networks (RNNs) to model input sequences that conform to the grammar of file formats, network protocols, or application logic. This approach increases test coverage and reduces redundant attempts. Similarly, semantic-aware fuzzers integrate static analysis with ML to understand the structure of the code under test, allowing for more effective mutation strategies.

AI also supports dynamic test-case prioritization, where feedback loops rank input efficacy based on crash likelihood, code coverage, or system response time. Over successive iterations, the system evolves to favor test cases that probe deeper or more vulnerable code regions, crucial in uncovering latent zero-day flaws.

Tools like Learn&Fuzz, Angora, and Microsoft's SAGE demonstrate how AI can convert fuzzing from an art of chance into a strategic, data-driven process. For ethical hackers, this shift improves not just detection rates but also the overall efficiency and realism of security assessments, aligning more closely with how skilled adversaries might discover and exploit unknown weaknesses.

5.3 Simulating Buffer Overflows and Shellcode Injection using AI

Buffer overflows and shellcode injections are among the oldest, yet still relevant, exploitation techniques in cybersecurity. While modern systems have introduced memory protection mechanisms such as ASLR (Address Space Layout Randomization), DEP (Data Execution Prevention), and stack canaries, improperly secured legacy code and low-level system components remain susceptible. AI brings a renewed edge to ethical hacking by simulating these attacks with greater precision, automation, and adaptability.

Lu et al. (2018) explained that traditionally, discovering buffer overflows required meticulous manual code review or rudimentary fuzzing to trigger segmentation faults. With AI, especially deep learning models trained on binary analysis or memory access patterns, penetration testers can now identify potentially vulnerable buffer zones more quickly and with higher accuracy. These models can recognize patterns in disassembly, source code, or binary files that correspond to dangerous constructs such as unchecked user input or unsafe memory operations.

In the case of shellcode injection, AI-driven tools can generate polymorphic or obfuscated payloads capable of bypassing basic intrusion detection systems. By leveraging reinforcement learning, an AI agent can experiment with different shellcode variations in a sandboxed environment to determine which payloads are most effective and stealthy. Additionally, generative models, such as those based on GANs, can simulate novel payloads that mimic benign behavior at first glance, making them harder to detect.

AI also plays a role in simulating post-exploitation stages. Once a buffer overflow leads to shell access, AI can be used to navigate the compromised system, extract data, or escalate privileges in a manner consistent with real-world attacker behavior. This holistic simulation provides organizations with deeper insights into what could happen after initial exploitation, helping them strengthen internal detection and response mechanisms.

By integrating AI into buffer overflow testing and shellcode delivery, ethical hackers gain a powerful toolkit for replicating sophisticated exploitation scenarios, ones that reflect both past threats and those still evolving in the wild.

6. ADVERSARIAL MACHINE LEARNING IN PENETRATION TESTING

6.1 Evasion and Poisoning Attacks

Adversarial Machine Learning (AML) has introduced a new frontier in ethical hacking, one where the target is not a system or a network, but the very AI models tasked with defending them. Among the most researched and simulated threat vectors in this field are evasion and poisoning attacks, both of which reveal critical vulnerabilities in security systems that rely heavily on machine learning.

Evasion attacks occur at inference time (Ghimire & Thapaliya, 2024). The attacker subtly manipulates input data so that it misleads a trained model without triggering human suspicion. In penetration testing, this is often demonstrated by crafting adversarial inputs, network packets, executable files, or API requests, that evade detection by intrusion detection systems (IDS), antivirus software, or spam filters. For instance, a penetration tester might use techniques like Fast Gradient Sign Method (FGSM) or Projected Gradient Descent (PGD) to modify malware signatures just enough to avoid classification as malicious while preserving the payload's functionality. These attacks are particularly effective against image classifiers, NLP-based spam filters, or behavioral detection models.

Poisoning attacks, on the other hand, occur during the training phase. Here, the adversary injects tainted data into the model's learning process, degrading its accuracy or manipulating its predictions. In a red teaming scenario, ethical hackers may simulate poisoning by altering logs, injecting misleading traffic into training datasets, or contributing manipulated code to open-source repositories used in model training. Poisoning can render models unreliable, causing benign activity to be flagged or allowing malicious behavior to go unnoticed (Mohammadian et al., 2024).

The importance of testing against these threats is growing rapidly, especially as AI becomes embedded in security tools. Ethical hackers equipped with AML capabilities can simulate how an intelligent adversary might bypass or corrupt machine learning defenses, helping organizations develop robust, adversarially resilient models. These simulations often reveal blind spots in AI-centric security deployments, highlighting the need for continual validation, model hardening, and input sanitization.

6.2 Defense Bypass and AI Model Vulnerabilities

As artificial intelligence becomes increasingly embedded in security infrastructure, ranging from next-gen firewalls to autonomous threat detection systems, it brings not only enhanced capabilities but also a new class of attack surfaces. One of the emerging challenges in ethical hacking is simulating how adversaries might bypass AI-driven defenses by exploiting intrinsic vulnerabilities in the machine learning models themselves.

Unlike traditional software vulnerabilities, which may stem from poor coding or configuration, AI model vulnerabilities are often more subtle and behavioral. For instance, a deep learning-based intrusion detection system may become overly reliant on certain features in training data, packet size, timing, or specific headers. A knowledgeable attacker can manipulate these features without altering the core payload, effectively bypassing detection while carrying out malicious operations. This vulnerability is known as model overfitting, where the system learns to focus too narrowly on specific patterns rather than generalizable threat behavior (Mmaduekwe et al., 2023).

Another critical flaw is model interpretability. Many AI-powered defenses operate as black boxes, making it difficult for security analysts to understand how decisions are made. This opacity can be weaponized; adversaries can experiment with inputs to probe and reverse-engineer model behavior, identifying thresholds or conditions that trigger alerts. Once these "tripwires" are known, attackers can deliberately stay just below the detection limit.

Penetration testers can simulate such bypass attempts using model extraction attacks, wherein APIs or output confidence scores are used to clone or approximate the target AI model (Çaylı, 2024). Once replicated, the model becomes a playground for adversarial testing, revealing weak points and helping defenders build more resilient systems.

Ethical hacking that targets AI model vulnerabilities is still an emerging discipline, but it is increasingly essential. As attackers begin to view AI not just as an obstacle but as a target, penetration testers must adapt, developing new tactics that account for the fragility, bias, and attackability of intelligent defense systems.

6.3 Use in Red Teaming vs Potential for Misuse

The growing adoption of adversarial machine learning (AML) techniques in red teaming exercises reflects a critical shift in ethical hacking, from traditional rule-based testing to dynamic, learning-based adversary simulation. Red teams are now integrating AML tools and strategies to test the resilience of machine learning-powered defenses, assess how easily detection systems can be fooled, and evaluate how organizations respond to subtle, AI-generated attack vectors. However, with this advancement comes a parallel concern: the dual-use dilemma, where the same tools developed for security testing can be repurposed for malicious intent.

In legitimate red teaming, AML is used to generate realistic adversarial samples, automate evasion testing, and simulate persistent threats that adapt to the environment in real time. For example, a red team might deploy an AI model that mimics advanced threat actors by continuously probing an AI-based intrusion detection system (IDS) and learning from its response. This iterative process reveals the IDS's blind spots, helping blue teams enhance detection thresholds and generalization.

AML in red teaming can simulate scenarios that traditional penetration testing often overlooks, like poisoning a threat detection model with tainted log files or reverse-engineering an AI-based spam filter to inject undetectable phishing emails. These exercises bring out vulnerabilities that would otherwise go unnoticed in static assessments.

Yet, these same techniques, if released without control, pose serious risks. Automated adversarial payload generators, when accessible to threat actors, could accelerate the creation of polymorphic malware or manipulate commercial AI systems in finance, healthcare, or content moderation. The line between research and exploitation becomes thin.

Therefore, while AML presents powerful opportunities for red teams, its use must be governed by strict ethical guidelines, responsible disclosure practices, and clear organizational oversight. Balancing innovation with accountability will be key to ensuring AML remains a force for cyber defense rather than a weapon for adversaries.

7. AI IN SOCIAL ENGINEERING AND PHISHING SIMULATIONS

7.1 NLP-Driven Phishing Email Generation

Phishing remains one of the most prevalent and effective cyberattack vectors, primarily because it exploits human behavior rather than system vulnerabilities. In ethical hacking, simulating phishing attacks has become a standard practice to test employee awareness and organizational resilience. However, with the advent of Natural Language Processing (NLP) and generative AI models, the realism, adaptability, and success rates of phishing simulations have increased dramatically, presenting both enhanced testing capabilities and new ethical dilemmas.

Traditionally, phishing emails were manually crafted, often containing generic content and predictable structures. Now, large language models (LLMs) like GPT-4 and open-source alternatives such as LLaMA or Bloom can be fine-tuned to generate context-aware, grammatically correct, and highly persuasive emails. These models analyze public data, such as job roles, social media posts, and organizational structure, to craft messages that appear tailored and authentic. A message targeting an HR executive, for example, might reference a recent LinkedIn post or an internal policy, making the deception harder to detect (Yigit et al., 2024).

From a red teaming perspective, NLP allows for rapid generation of multiple phishing variants, each with different tones, content styles, or psychological triggers. Emotional manipulation, urgency, or social proof can be embedded programmatically into the message body. This significantly enhances the realism of simulated phishing campaigns used in security awareness training.

Some ethical hackers now integrate NLP-generated emails into phishing-as-a-service (PhaaS) testing platforms, enabling large-scale, adaptive simulations across departments or regions. These tools measure click rates, credential submissions, and report rates, generating data to inform future security strategies.

Yet, the power of NLP also raises concerns about misuse. If deployed irresponsibly, even in simulated environments, such messages can blur the lines between awareness testing and psychological manipulation. Thus, while NLP dramatically improves the sophistication of phishing simulations, its use must be accompanied by clear ethical boundaries, transparency with stakeholders, and predefined fail-safes to ensure constructive, not coercive, training outcomes.

7.2 Deepfakes and Voice Spoofing for Vishing/Baiting Attacks

The convergence of deep learning and multimedia synthesis technologies has led to a new breed of social engineering threats, deepfakes and AI-generated voice spoofing. These tools are no longer confined to the realm of misinformation or political propaganda; they are now increasingly being explored, simulated, and tested within ethical hacking frameworks, particularly in vishing (voice phishing) and baiting scenarios.

Deepfakes, synthetic videos generated using Generative Adversarial Networks (GANs), can convincingly replicate the facial expressions and speech of real individuals. In a red teaming context, ethical hackers may simulate a deepfake impersonation of a senior executive requesting a wire transfer or sharing login credentials. When embedded in a phishing email or played during a video call, such simulations can test not only technical controls but also the human trust boundary within the organization.

Similarly, according to Kumar et al. (2024) voice cloning technologies, trained on short voice samples using deep neural networks, enable attackers to synthesize convincing audio messages. Tools like Descript's Overdub or open-source models like Coqui TTS can reproduce tone, cadence, and vocal tics of a known individual, making phone-based scams significantly harder to detect. In ethical hacking exercises, red teams use these tools to conduct vishing campaigns that simulate real-world attacks, such as fake IT support calls or HR inquiries.

The danger lies in how seamlessly these technologies exploit cognitive biases. People tend to trust familiar voices or visual cues. By leveraging this trust, adversaries can bypass digital defenses entirely and compromise systems through simple conversation.

Ethical deployment of such simulations must include clear rules of engagement, stakeholder consent, and psychological safeguards. While deepfake and voice spoofing simulations are powerful for raising awareness and measuring risk, they should never cross into manipulation or distress. Used responsibly, they provide a glimpse into the future of social engineering, where what you see or hear can no longer be taken at face value.

7.3 GPT-Based Chatbot for Phishing Simulation

The rise of large language models (LLMs) like GPT-3.5, GPT-4, and their open-source counterparts has unlocked powerful capabilities in conversational AI, some of which are now being integrated into phishing simulation frameworks within ethical hacking. These GPT-based chatbots offer a novel way to simulate real-time, interactive phishing attacks that go far beyond traditional static emails or pre-scripted lures (Mishra et al., 2025).

Unlike conventional bots, GPT-based agents are capable of generating human-like dialogue that adapts dynamically to user responses. In a phishing simulation, an ethical hacker can deploy a chatbot that initiates a conversation, posing as an IT administrator, HR representative, or third-party contractor. As the dialogue progresses, the chatbot intelligently adjusts its phrasing, urgency, and tone based on the user's reactions. This makes the simulation not only more realistic but also more effective in testing user susceptibility under varied social conditions.

For instance, a simulated chatbot may begin by confirming a user's email, proceed to "verify" system activity, and subtly guide them to click a malicious link or share login credentials. Because GPT can understand and mimic the nuances of workplace communication, the phishing attempt feels legitimate, triggering the same cognitive and emotional cues exploited in real attacks.

This capability, while valuable for training and awareness, raises critical concerns. If not properly constrained, GPT-based phishing simulations can veer into manipulative territory, especially when targeting non-technical employees. There's also the risk of overfitting responses that become too aggressive or intrusive. Ethical hackers must therefore implement defensive strategies such as content filters, intent throttling, and strict guardrails around topics and tone.

Red teams must work in tandem with compliance and HR teams to design GPT-based simulations that are informative without being exploitative. When handled responsibly, these simulations serve as a wake-up call, demonstrating that trustworthy communication can now be convincingly faked, and training must evolve accordingly.

8. BLUE TEAMING AND AI-ENHANCED DEFENSE MECHANISMS

8.1 Behavior-Based Threat Detection Using ML

In contrast to signature-based detection methods, which rely on known attack patterns or threat signatures, behavior-based threat detection aims to identify anomalies in system or user behavior that may indicate malicious activity. With the infusion of machine learning (ML), this paradigm becomes significantly more effective, enabling blue teams to monitor vast and complex environments for subtle indicators of compromise that would otherwise escape traditional tools.

Machine learning algorithms are particularly well-suited to behavior-based detection because they can learn baseline activity patterns from raw telemetry data, such as logins, file access, network connections, and process executions, and subsequently flag deviations that warrant investigation. These deviations may include actions like accessing sensitive files at unusual hours, using abnormal remote connections, or launching rarely used executable paths. Models such as isolation forests, autoencoders, and clustering techniques are frequently employed for unsupervised anomaly detection in this context.

Behavioral models can also be tailored to user-specific profiles, allowing for the detection of insider threats or account compromise. If an employee suddenly begins interacting with systems or data types unrelated to their role, the ML model can highlight this deviation as potentially suspicious, regardless of whether the action itself violates a predefined rule (Zhang et al., 2024).

One of the critical advantages of ML-driven behavior detection is its adaptability. As the organization's workflows, devices, and user habits evolve, the model continues to update and refine its understanding of "normal." This ensures that alerts are more relevant and reduces the noise associated with false positives, an ongoing challenge in security operations centers (SOCs).

Ultimately, integrating ML into behavior-based detection shifts blue team operations from reactive event triaging to proactive risk anticipation. Ethical hackers, too, benefit by testing the limits of such systems, probing where adaptive defenses succeed or fail in recognizing adversarial behavior patterns across endpoints, users, and networks.

8.2 SIEM + UEBA Systems Enhanced With AI

Security Information and Event Management (SIEM) systems have long served as the backbone of centralized threat monitoring, aggregating logs from endpoints, servers, firewalls, and applications. However, their effectiveness depends on accurate rule definitions and correlation logic, often struggling with false positives and missed anomalies. By integrating Artificial Intelligence (AI) and User and Entity Behavior Analytics (UEBA), modern SIEM platforms now offer smarter, more contextual threat detection.

AI-enhanced SIEM systems, such as Splunk, IBM QRadar, and Microsoft Sentinel, leverage machine learning to analyze massive datasets, identifying patterns across time, systems, and user activities. Unlike static rules, these systems dynamically adapt to changing behavior and evolving attack techniques. They learn what "normal" looks like for individual users or machines and flag behaviors that deviate from established baselines (Marri et al., 2024).

UEBA further deepens this capability by focusing on human and system behaviors rather than just technical events. For example, if a low-privilege user suddenly attempts to access administrative shares or a service account starts transmitting large amounts of data externally, the AI-powered UEBA engine will assign a risk score and escalate the incident.

For blue teams, this fusion of SIEM and AI/UEBA results in fewer false alarms and faster detection of stealthy attacks like insider threats, account takeovers, and lateral movement. Ethical hackers, when simulating adversarial actions, often test the responsiveness and adaptability of these systems, pushing the limits of their intelligence and helping refine detection models based on real-world tactics.

8.3 Closed Feedback Loop From Red Team Output

A critical advancement in AI-driven cybersecurity defense is the implementation of a closed feedback loop, a continuous learning system where blue teams refine their detection strategies based on insights generated from red team simulations. This loop transforms penetration testing results into actionable intelligence, creating a self-improving cycle of adversarial learning, response tuning, and defensive evolution.

In practice, this means that every red team engagement, whether conducted manually or with AI-enhanced tools, produces data on what tactics were successful, what attack paths went unnoticed, and how detection systems responded. This data is fed back into machine learning models powering behavioral analytics, SIEM correlation engines, and threat prioritization algorithms. Over time, the system becomes increasingly resilient, not just to known threats but to adaptive, evolving adversarial behavior.

For instance, if a red team successfully bypasses a UEBA system by mimicking normal user behavior, the blue team can retrain detection models using the session logs. Reinforcement learning algorithms can incorporate this experience to improve their decision-making, making it harder for similar tactics to succeed in the future.

This iterative process tightens the defensive perimeter while reducing reliance on static rule sets (Desetty, 2024).

Ethical hackers play a pivotal role in this feedback loop, not just by simulating threats but by providing structured insights into why specific attacks succeeded. These insights are especially valuable when integrated with AI, as they feed high-quality training data into models responsible for future anomaly detection, threat classification, and automated response orchestration.

A closed feedback loop ensures that defense strategies do not remain static. Instead, they evolve in lockstep with real-world threats, transforming penetration testing from a periodic activity into a strategic, AI-assisted, continuous improvement process.

9. ETHICAL, LEGAL, AND REGULATORY CONSIDERATIONS

9.1 AI Explainability and Fairness in Red Teaming

As AI-driven ethical hacking becomes more prevalent, the need for explainability and fairness in its implementation has gained urgency. When machine learning models are used to simulate adversarial behavior, whether for identifying vulnerabilities or testing human responses, there must be transparency regarding how these models arrive at decisions and whether those decisions align with ethical boundaries.

In red teaming scenarios, AI models are often used to generate attack paths, predict exploitable weaknesses, or craft social engineering content. Without proper interpretability, the rationale behind these actions may remain opaque, raising concerns about accountability. This lack of clarity can be particularly problematic when AI-generated decisions impact real users or systems, such as simulated phishing messages sent to employees or AI-directed attempts to exploit sensitive application logic (Zhang et al., 2024).

Explainable AI (XAI) techniques, such as SHAP (SHapley Additive exPlanations) and LIME (Local Interpretable Model-Agnostic Explanations), offer pathways to clarify why a model made a certain prediction or took a particular action. Integrating XAI into red team operations helps ensure that AI behavior is not only effective but also auditable and defensible under scrutiny.

Fairness is another critical dimension. AI models may unintentionally reflect biases from the training data, such as disproportionately targeting specific user behaviors, roles, or demographics in phishing simulations. Ethical hackers must evaluate whether these models reinforce harmful patterns or introduce inequities in their testing strategies.

Embedding fairness and explainability in AI-powered red teaming promotes trust, ensures compliance with emerging AI governance standards, and supports responsible innovation in cybersecurity assessment.

9.2 GDPR, HIPAA, ISO/IEC 27001 in Pen Testing With AI

As AI continues to transform penetration testing, organizations must navigate a complex web of data protection laws and security standards, ensuring that AI-driven assessments remain compliant. Regulations such as the General Data Protection Regulation (GDPR) in the European Union and the Health Insurance Portability and Accountability Act (HIPAA) in the United States impose strict limitations on how personal and sensitive data can be collected, processed, and used, even in controlled, simulated attacks.

For example, under GDPR, any use of personal data in AI models, such as behavioral logs used for anomaly detection or training phishing simulations, must have a legitimate legal basis. Red teaming that involves AI-generated content targeting employees must balance the need for realism with the right to privacy and informed consent. Similarly, in healthcare environments, HIPAA mandates that ethical hacking exercises avoid exposing protected health information (PHI), even when evaluating system vulnerabilities using AI-based tools (Leslie et al., 2024).

Standards like ISO/IEC 27001 provide a structured framework for managing information security risks during AI-assisted penetration testing. They emphasize principles such as data minimization, risk assessments, auditability, and third-party controls, all of which are essential when AI systems autonomously access or analyze sensitive environments.

To maintain compliance, ethical hackers must document how AI tools are trained, what data is used, and how outputs are controlled. Incorporating privacy-by-design principles into AI penetration testing workflows not only supports legal compliance but also helps build organizational trust and resilience against potential regulatory audits or litigation.

9.3 Ethics of Simulating Real Attacks Using Autonomous AI

Simulating real-world attacks using autonomous AI systems pushes the boundaries of ethical hacking into a new and uncharted territory. While such simulations offer unmatched realism and complexity, they also introduce significant ethical concerns. Chief among them is the potential for unintended harm, to individuals, systems, or data, especially when the AI operates with a level of autonomy that even its creators may not fully understand or control.

Autonomous AI red team agents may discover novel attack vectors, chain multiple exploits, or behave unpredictably depending on how they were trained (Helkala et al., 2023). If insufficient safeguards are in place, the simulated attack could unintentionally disrupt production environments, expose sensitive data, or generate outputs that closely mimic malicious activity, raising alarms within an organization or even across third-party monitoring systems.

These simulations blur the line between ethical assessment and real offense. Ethical hackers must ensure that autonomous AI is not replicating attacker behavior so effectively that it violates internal policies, industry norms, or legal boundaries(Valencia, 2024). Transparency, control, and human oversight become non-negotiable requirements in these exercises.

To preserve trust and accountability, red teams should define clear rules of engagement, maintain comprehensive logging of AI actions, and obtain stakeholder consent before initiating autonomous simulations. Only through responsible design and governance can AI be ethically deployed in simulations that resemble real-world attacks without crossing the line into uncontrolled experimentation.

10. FUTURE TRENDS AND RESEARCH DIRECTIONS

10.1 Autonomous Red Teaming Agents

The future of ethical hacking is increasingly pointing toward autonomous red teaming agents, AI-driven systems capable of independently conducting complex penetration testing operations with minimal human oversight. These agents are designed to mimic the adaptive, persistent behavior of real-world adversaries, dynamically learning from system responses and modifying their attack strategies in real time.

Built on reinforcement learning and decision-tree-based logic, autonomous agents can explore, exploit, and escalate privileges across multi-layered infrastructures without predefined playbooks. They ingest live telemetry, environmental variables, and historical red team data to refine their tactics, ultimately creating realistic and scalable attack simulations that evolve with organizational defenses.

Although still in developmental stages, such agents are being tested in military cyber ranges and enterprise environments, where they serve as adversarial AI counterparts to blue team defense systems. In the long term, autonomous red teaming is expected to complement human testers by continuously scanning for exploitable conditions and informing security updates with real-time adversarial feedback.

10.2 Explainable AI in Ethical Hacking Tools

As AI becomes more embedded in penetration testing, the demand for explainable AI (XAI) within ethical hacking tools is rapidly growing. Many current models operate as black boxes, delivering results, such as risk scores or vulnerability predictions, without transparency into the reasoning behind those outputs. This opacity undermines trust, limits auditability, and creates barriers to adoption in regulated industries.

Explainable AI introduces methods that help ethical hackers and security teams understand how and why an AI system made a specific decision. Techniques like SHAP (SHapley Additive Explanations), LIME (Local Interpretable Model-Agnostic Explanations), and decision tree visualizations are now being integrated into next-generation AI-driven tools to enhance interpretability.

In penetration testing, XAI can illuminate why a system flagged a behavior as suspicious, why a user was targeted in a simulated phishing campaign, or why a specific exploit path was prioritized. This interpretability allows red and blue teams to refine tactics, validate findings, and ensure that AI-driven insights are actionable, defensible, and fair.

10.3 Cyber Deception With AI

Cyber deception, traditionally implemented through honeypots, decoy systems, and fake data, is undergoing a transformation through the integration of artificial intelligence. AI enables a more dynamic and adaptive form of deception, capable of evolving in real time in response to attacker behavior. Rather than relying on static traps, AI-enhanced deception platforms can generate convincing fake assets, simulate legitimate user behavior, and even initiate scripted responses when probed.

In the context of red teaming, ethical hackers are beginning to test the effectiveness of AI-driven deception frameworks. These systems use behavioral modeling and anomaly detection to determine when an intruder is present, then deploy targeted deception strategies, such as spoofed credentials or synthetic vulnerabilities, to mislead and contain the adversary.

Future research is exploring how generative AI models can create customized decoys, tailored to the attacker's observed reconnaissance. By feeding false information back into the attacker's loop, AI deception not only protects real assets but also serves as a form of intelligent counterintelligence, blurring the attacker's situational awareness.

10.4 Quantum-Enhanced AI in Future Pen Testing

As quantum computing progresses from theory to prototype, its convergence with artificial intelligence could redefine the landscape of penetration testing. Quantum-enhanced AI refers to machine learning algorithms accelerated or enriched by quantum computing principles, enabling faster data processing, improved pattern recognition, and enhanced optimization capabilities. For red teams, this could mean radically more efficient analysis of cryptographic systems, real-time traffic anomalies, or complex system architectures.

In future pen testing scenarios, quantum AI could simulate vast numbers of attack paths simultaneously, far exceeding the combinatorial capabilities of classical systems. It may also improve the accuracy of zero-day vulnerability prediction models by rapidly parsing through high-dimensional data with greater precision.

Furthermore, quantum machine learning could aid in defeating or circumventing post-quantum cryptographic schemes during advanced ethical hacking simulations. While these capabilities are still theoretical and depend on the maturation of quantum hardware, the implications for speed, scale, and depth of AI-driven red teaming are profound, opening new avenues for both offensive simulations and defensive innovation.

11. CONCLUSION

The convergence of artificial intelligence and ethical hacking represents a transformative shift in how cybersecurity is practiced, tested, and evolved. As this chapter has explored, AI and machine learning are no longer auxiliary tools, they are becoming core enablers of intelligent offensive and defensive cybersecurity operations. From reconnaissance and vulnerability assessment to exploitation, social engineering, and threat detection, AI enhances both the scope and sophistication of penetration testing efforts.

One of the key takeaways is the role of machine learning in automating and scaling reconnaissance through behavioral profiling, OSINT analysis, and phishing simulations. By leveraging natural language processing and adversarial learning, ethical hackers can simulate increasingly realistic attack scenarios, improving not only detection capabilities but also organizational preparedness.

Equally significant is the emergence of AI-driven exploitation strategies, including intelligent fuzzing, reinforcement learning for attack path optimization, and AI-powered shellcode delivery. These technologies allow red teams to probe deeper into systems and generate more advanced adversarial behaviors, often mimicking real-world attackers with remarkable precision.

On the defense side, blue teams equipped with AI-enhanced tools like SIEM-UEBA integrations, behavior-based anomaly detection, and closed feedback loops benefit from real-time adaptation and reduced false positives. The result is a more responsive, informed, and resilient defense posture that evolves with threat landscapes.

Yet, with these advancements come profound ethical, legal, and regulatory challenges. Ensuring explainability, fairness, and accountability in AI systems is not optional, it is a prerequisite for responsible cybersecurity practice. Compliance with frameworks like GDPR, HIPAA, and ISO/IEC 27001 must be embedded into AI-assisted testing workflows, especially when simulations involve personal data or autonomous systems.

Looking ahead, the rise of autonomous red teaming agents, explainable AI, cyber deception platforms, and quantum-enhanced threat simulations will further blur the line between simulation and reality. Organizations must not only embrace these technologies but also cultivate the governance structures necessary to use them safely and ethically.

Ultimately, the fusion of AI and ethical hacking offers unparalleled opportunities to anticipate, simulate, and neutralize threats in ways that were once unimaginable. But its true value will depend on our ability to wield it with foresight, integrity, and an unwavering commitment to security as a shared responsibility.

12. REFERENCES

Ahn, G. H., Kim, K., Park, W., & Shin, D. (2022). Malicious File Detection Method using Machine Learning and Interworking with MITRE ATT&CK Framework. *Applied Sciences (Basel, Switzerland)*, *12*(21), 10761. Advance online publication. DOI: 10.3390/app122110761

Al-Sinani, H. S., & Mitchell, C. J. (2024). AI-enhanced ethical hacking: A Linux-focused experiment [Technical report]. arXiv. https://doi.org//arXiv.2410.05105DOI: 10.48550

Al-Sinani, H. S., Mitchell, C. J., Sahli, N., & Al-Siyabi, M. (2025). Unleashing AI in ethical hacking. In Martinelli, F., & Rios, R. (Eds.), Lecture Notes in Computer Science: Vol. 15235. *Security and trust management*. Springer., DOI: 10.1007/978-3-031-76371-7_10

Bajantri, G., & Shariff, N. (2024). Machine learning algorithms for robust software vulnerability detection. (2024) *International Conference on Innovation and Novelty in Engineering and Technology (INNOVA)*, 1–7. DOI: 10.1109/INNOVA63080.2024.10846984

Bello, A. B., Ogundipe, A. O., George, A. A., & Anifowose, O. (2025). The role of AI and machine learning in cybersecurity: Advancements in threat detection, anomaly detection and automated response. *International Journal of Science and Research Archive*, *14*(2), 1587–1597. DOI: 10.30574/ijsra.2025.14.2.0542

Bierbrauer, D. A., Chang, A., Kritzer, W., & Bastian, N. D. (2021). Cybersecurity anomaly detection in adversarial environments. arXiv. https://doi.org//arXiv.2105.06742DOI: 10.48550

Böttinger, K., Godefroid, P., & Singh, R. (2018). Deep reinforcement fuzzing. 2018 IEEE Security and Privacy Workshops (SPW), 116–122. DOI: 10.1109/SPW.2018.00026

Çaylı, O. (2024). *AI-enhanced cybersecurity: Vulnerability-based prevention, defense, and mitigation using generative AI*. Orclever Proceedings of Research and Development., DOI: 10.56038/oprd.v5i1.616

Desetty, A. G. (2024). *Unveiling Hidden Threats with ML-Powered User and Entity Behavior Analytics (UEBA). Turkish Journal of Computer and Mathematics Education*. TURCOMAT., DOI: 10.61841/turcomat.v15i1.14394

Durgaraju, S., Vel, D. V. T., & Madathala, H. (2025). The evolution of cyber threats and defenses: A review of innovations and challenges. 2025 6th International Conference on Mobile Computing and Sustainable Informatics (ICMCSI), 117–123. DOI: 10.1109/ICMCSI64620.2025.10883230

Ghimire, S., & Thapaliya, S. (2024). Al-driven cybersecurity: Mitigating prompt injection attacks through adversarial machine learning. *NPRC Journal of Multidisciplinary Research, 1*(8), 63–69. DOI: 10.3126/nprcjmr.v1i8.73029

Grigorescu, O., Nica, A., Dascalu, M., & Rughinis, R. (2022). CVE2ATT&CK: BERT-Based Mapping of CVEs to MITRE ATT&CK Techniques. *Algorithms, 15*(9), 314. DOI: 10.3390/a15090314

Guo, N., Li, X., Yin, H., & Gao, Y. (2019). VulHunter: An automated vulnerability detection system based on deep learning and bytecode. In *Proceedings of the International Conference on Cloud Computing and Security* (pp. 199–218). DOI: 10.1007/978-3-030-41579-2_12

Hamed, O., Amer, M., & Bejaoui, T. (2024). Survey on advancements in machine learning for natural language processing. *2024 International Symposium on Networks, Computers and Communications (ISNCC)*, 1–6. DOI: 10.1109/ISNCC62547.2024.10759035

Haryono, S. A., Thung, F., Lo, D., Lawall, J., & Jiang, L. (2021). Characterization and automatic updates of deprecated machine-learning API usages. *2021 IEEE International Conference on Software Maintenance and Evolution (ICSME)*, 137–147. DOI: 10.1109/ICSME52107.2021.00019

Helkala, K., Cook, J., Lucas, G., Pasquale, F., Reichberg, G., & Syse, H. (2023). AI in cyber operations: Ethical and legal considerations for end-users. In Sipola, T., Kokkonen, T., & Karjalainen, M. (Eds.), *Artificial intelligence and cybersecurity*. Springer., DOI: 10.1007/978-3-031-15030-2_9

Hu, Z., Beuran, R., & Tan, Y. (2020). Automated penetration testing using deep reinforcement learning. 2020 IEEE European Symposium on Security and Privacy Workshops (EuroS&PW), 2–10. DOI: 10.1109/EuroSPW51379.2020.00010

Ilić, N., Dašić, D., Vucetic, M., Makarov, A., & Petrović, R. (2023). Distributed web hacking by adaptive consensus-based reinforcement learning. *Artificial Intelligence, 326*, 104032. DOI: 10.1016/j.artint.2023.104032

Kolade, T. M., Obioha-Val, O. A., Balogun, A. Y., Gbadebo, M. O., & Olaniyi, O. O. (2025). AI-driven open-source intelligence in cyber defense: A double-edged sword for national security. *Asian Journal of Research in Computer Science, 18*(1), 133–153. DOI: 10.9734/ajrcos/2025/v18i1554

Koushal, H., Kaur, R., & Kaur, C. (2025). *The relative review of machine learning in natural language processing (NLP).* International Journal of Scientific Research in Computer Science, Engineering and Information Technology., DOI: 10.32628/CSEIT251112399

Kumar, S., Menezes, A., Giri, S., & Kotikela, S. D. (2024). What the phish! Effects of AI on phishing attacks and defense. International Conference on AI Research. DOI: 10.34190/icair.4.1.3224

Leslie, D., Rincón, C., Briggs, M., Perini, A., Jayadeva, S., Borda, A., Bennett, S. J., Burr, C., Aitken, M., Katell, M., Fischer, C., & Wong, J. (2024). AI fairness in practice. DOI: 10.2139/ssrn.4731838

Lomonaco, V., De Caro, V., Gallicchio, C., Carta, A., Sardianos, C., Varlamis, I., Tserpes, K., Coppola, M., Marmpena, M., Politi, S., Schoitsch, E., & Bacciu, D. (2023). AI-Toolkit: A microservices architecture for low-code decentralized machine intelligence. *2023 IEEE International Conference on Acoustics, Speech, and Signal Processing Workshops (ICASSPW)*, 1–5. DOI: 10.1109/ICASSPW59220.2023.10193222

Lu, T., Zhang, L., & Fu, Y. (2018). A novel immune-inspired shellcode detection algorithm based on hyperellipsoid detectors. *Security and Communication Networks, 2018*, 1–10. DOI: 10.1155/2018/2063089

Marri, R., Varanasi, S., & Kalidindi Chaitanya, S. V. (2024). Integrating Security Information and Event Management (SIEM) with Data Lakes and AI: Enhancing Threat Detection and Response. Journal of Artificial Intelligence General Science. DOI: 10.60087/jaigs.v6i1.239

Mishra, R., Varshney, G., & Singh, S. (2025). Jailbreaking Generative AI: Empowering Novices to Conduct Phishing Attacks. ArXiv, abs/2503.01395. /arXiv.2503.01395DOI: 10.1109/DSN-S65789.2025.00022

Mmaduekwe, E. M., Stanley, U. M., Kessie, J. D., & Salawudeen, M. D. (2023). *Adversarial machine learning in cybersecurity: Mitigating evolving threats in AI-powered defense systems.* World Journal of Advanced Engineering Technology and Sciences., DOI: 10.30574/wjaets.2023.10.2.0294

Mohammadian, H., Lashkari, A. H., & Ghorbani, A. A. (2024). Poisoning and evasion: Deep learning-based NIDS under adversarial attacks. *21st Annual International Conference on Privacy, Security and Trust (PST)*, 1–9. DOI: 10.1109/PST62714.2024.10788064

Paradhi, D., Ansari, M. N., & More, S. (2024). Anomaly detection in network traffic using unsupervised machine learning. International Journal of Advanced Research in Science. *Tongxin Jishu*, 418–425. Advance online publication. DOI: 10.48175/IJARSCT-19264

Pu, G., Wang, L., Shen, J., & Dong, F. (2021). A hybrid unsupervised clustering-based anomaly detection method. *Tsinghua Science and Technology*, *26*(2), 146–153. Advance online publication. DOI: 10.26599/TST.2019.9010051

Rajamäki, J., McMenamin, S., & Tiitta, K. (2024). The importance of open-source intelligence in assessing risks of cyberattacks. Information & Security. *International Journal (Toronto, Ont.)*, *55*(1), 15–31. DOI: 10.11610/isij.5511

Shinde, S. S., & Shivalkar, S. J. (2025). AI to predict zero day vulnerabilities. [IJSREM]. *International Journal of Scientific Research in Engineering and Management*, *9*(1), 1–9. DOI: 10.55041/IJSREM40510

Valencia, L. J. (2024). Artificial intelligence as the new hacker: Developing agents for offensive security. arXiv. https://doi.org//arXiv.2406.07561DOI: 10.48550

Wang, J., Huang, M., Nie, Y., & Li, J. (2021). Static analysis of source code vulnerability using machine learning techniques: A survey. 2021 4th International Conference on Artificial Intelligence and Big Data (ICAIBD), 76–86. DOI: 10.1109/ICAIBD51990.2021.9459075

Yigit, Y., Buchanan, W. J., Tehrani, M. G., & Maglaras, L. A. (2024). Review of generative AI methods in cybersecurity. ArXiv. https://doi.org//arXiv.2403.08701DOI: 10.48550

Zhang, D., Jain, K., & Singh, P. (2024). Guarding Against ChatGPT Threats: Identifying and Addressing Vulnerabilities. 2024 IEEE 7th International Conference on Multimedia Information Processing and Retrieval (MIPR), 612–615 DOI: 10.1109/MIPR62202.2024.00104

KEY TERMS AND DEFINITIONS

Adversarial Machine Learning (AML): A technique where AI models are manipulated by malicious inputs to cause incorrect outputs, used in both attack simulations and AI security testing.

Artificial Intelligence (AI): A field of computer science focused on developing systems capable of performing tasks that typically require human intelligence, such as reasoning, learning, and decision-making.

Behavior-Based Detection: A security approach that uses ML to monitor user or system behavior over time and detect anomalies that could indicate malicious activity.

Deepfake: A synthetic media technique that uses AI to replace or alter a person's appearance or voice in video and audio content, often used in social engineering simulations.

Ethical Hacking: A controlled practice of simulating cyberattacks on systems or networks to identify security vulnerabilities before malicious actors can exploit them.

Explainable AI (XAI): An area of AI that focuses on making the decision-making process of machine learning models transparent and understandable to humans.

Fuzzing: A testing technique that inputs random or malformed data into a program to detect crashes, memory leaks, or vulnerabilities.

GPT (Generative Pre-trained Transformer): A family of large language models developed by OpenAI, capable of generating human-like text and used in phishing simulations or chatbot-based attacks.

Machine Learning (ML): A subset of AI that involves training algorithms to identify patterns in data and make decisions or predictions without being explicitly programmed.

Open Source Intelligence (OSINT): Publicly available data collected from sources such as websites, social media, and public databases for use in reconnaissance and intelligence gathering.

Penetration Testing (Pen Testing): An authorized attempt to evaluate the security of an IT infrastructure by safely exploiting system weaknesses, including OS, services, and application flaws.

Phishing: A cyberattack that uses deceptive messages to trick individuals into revealing sensitive information or installing malware.

Reinforcement Learning: An ML technique where an agent learns to make decisions by interacting with an environment and receiving feedback in the form of rewards or penalties.

SIEM (Security Information and Event Management): A solution that aggregates and analyzes security data from multiple sources in real time to detect threats and support incident response.

Supervised Learning: A type of machine learning where models are trained on labeled data, enabling them to predict outcomes based on learned input-output relationships.

UEBA (User and Entity Behavior Analytics): A behavioral analytics system that uses machine learning to detect deviations from normal behavior among users and devices.

Unsupervised Learning: A type of machine learning used to discover hidden patterns in data without pre-existing labels or classifications.

Vulnerability Assessment: A systematic evaluation of an organization's systems to identify weaknesses that could be exploited by attackers.

Red Teaming: A security exercise in which ethical hackers simulate real-world attacks to test an organization's defenses.

Blue Teaming: The defensive counterpart to red teaming, responsible for monitoring, detecting, and responding to simulated or real cyber threats.

Feedback Loop (in Cybersecurity): A process where results from one stage of testing (e.g., red team findings) are fed back into another system (e.g., ML models) for continuous improvement.

Zero-Day Vulnerability: A security flaw unknown to the software vendor, leaving systems exposed until a patch is developed and deployed.

Cyber Deception: A strategy involving decoys, honeypots, and fabricated assets to mislead attackers and detect unauthorized access attempts.

Quantum Computing: An emerging field of computation that uses quantum-mechanical phenomena, potentially capable of breaking current encryption standards.

CVSS (Common Vulnerability Scoring System): A standardized system for rating the severity of software vulnerabilities based on metrics such as exploitability and impact.

MITRE ATT&CK Framework: A globally accessible knowledge base of adversary tactics and techniques based on real-world observations, used for security testing and threat modeling.

XAI Tools (e.g., SHAP, LIME): Techniques used to explain the outputs of AI models by analyzing feature importance or decision paths.

Polymorphic Malware: Malicious software that continuously changes its code to evade detection by traditional security tools.

LLM (Large Language Model): A type of neural network trained on vast text corpora capable of generating coherent language, often used in automated phishing and chatbots.

Privacy-by-Design: A principle that requires data protection to be integrated into the design of systems and processes, especially important when AI models use sensitive data.

Chapter 5
Ethical Hacking:
A Strategic Approach to Enhancing Cybersecurity Frameworks

Raj Kishor Verma
http://orcid.org/0009-0005-7216-7752
ABES Institute of Technology, India

Raj Kishor Verma
http://orcid.org/0009-0009-9645-718X
Galgotias University, Greater Noida, India

Sakshi Vashishth
ABES Institute of Technology, Ghaziabad, India

Ritika Prajapati
ABES Institute of Technology, Ghaziabad, India

ABSTRACT

Ethical hacking is key to improving the structure of cybersecurity. The Ethical hackers can look for flaws before they become evident but criminal hackers find them. This study considers the methods employed by ethical hacker and stresses their importance in penetration testing, vulnerability assessments, and incident response. By simulating actual attack scenarios, ethical hackers offer organizations a window into their security posture, helping them to take effective countermeasures. The research also addresses the ethical choices positioned around ethical hacking, including the importance of responsible disclosure and abiding by appropriate legal frameworks. This report illustrates in given cases that ethical hacking not only brings about real benefits for organizations, converting security awareness into action and

DOI: 10.4018/979-8-3373-3536-0.ch005

proactive risk management are also its objectives. Underpinning this thesis is the point that ethical hacking should be integrated into broader cybersecurity strategies to effectively fight the many-faced digital threats in an age of 21st-century warfare.

1. INTRODUCTION

Cybersecurity has emerged as one of the top priorities for both organizations and individuals in our fast-changing digital world. With malicious hacking remaining a significant threat to data security and integrity, ethical hacking offers a proactive and strategic method of enhancing cybersecurity frameworks. Ethical hacking, also referred to as white-hat hacking, is the practice of searching for vulnerabilities in computer systems, applications, or data with prior authorization and a legal basis. Some hackers fraudulently attack directly using the same methods and strategies used by malicious hackers, except their motives differ significantly as ethical hackers want to fix, find loopholes, and target their vulnerable targets before they get hacked. By simulating real-world attacks, ethical hackers take on an important role in protecting sensitive information and defending against cyber threats. They help organizations find weaknesses in systems and networks (Al-Sinani & Mitchell, 2024). This allows organizations to protect themselves from these types of attacks before these attacks happen. Such a proactive approach not only prevents data breaches but also improves security postures and confidence among stakeholders by establishing a culture of cybersecurity. Ethical hacking allows organizations to identify vulnerabilities and reduce the risk of potential data breaches, helping them improve their security posture, fulfil regulatory compliance requirements, and protect their brand.

Traditional Cyber Security: Concentrate on protecting the systems and networks from unauthorized access or malicious activity through defensive techniques like firewalls, encryption, regular system updates, etc.

Ethical Hacking: It uses an offensive methodology to test the defensive framework of the structure by attempting to raid them in a similar way as pernicious programmers.

Traditional Cybersecurity: Use a defensive cyber approach focusing on protecting the systems via monitoring, detecting, and responding to security threats.

Ethical Hacking: These use phishing, SQL injection, social engineering, and session hijacking to find vulnerabilities.

Traditional Cybersecurity: Measures such as enforcement of security protocols, audits, and updating systems to prevent breaches (Modesti, Golightly, Holmes, Opara, & Moscini, 2024).

Figure 1. Diagram of Enhancing Cybersecurity Through Ethical Hacking

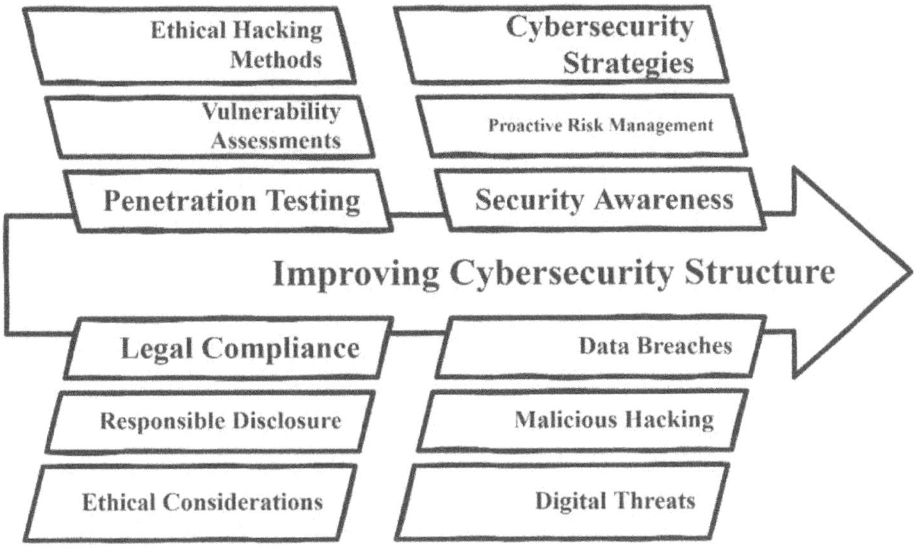

Description of the Diagram: Improving Cybersecurity Structure This diagram illustrates the interconnected elements of how to improve cybersecurity structure inside an organization, moving in a diagram Fig.1 from left to right. At the middle of the chart, a huge amorphous arrow reads "Improving Cybersecurity Structure," pointing to the right. This movement symbolizes forward momentum and progress in a variety of ways. Sixth, a policy or plan for use, studs in a fire-proof door actually make it more combustible or difficult to protect from injury it when it catches fire. In the end, we will see how this method of working tends to bring its problems with it. Ethical Hacking Methods: These are systematic approaches whereby ethical hackers identify and exploit system vulnerabilities, so that organizations can understand and toughen their defenses. Vulnerability Assessments Regular, continual vulnerability assessments are vital for catching weak spots in IT infrastructure before they can be exploited by mischievous individuals. Penetration Testing simulates real-world attacks to see how well security measures work and where an enemy might break in. Cybersecurity strategies ensure facilities for a proactive, structured response to managing cyber risks or threats. Proactive Risk Management entails looking at risks from an upstream perspective and then drying them out before the danger scales develop, rather than having to pick up those bad numbers because you let them lie around for years on end. Security Awareness Firstly, employees and stakeholders must be made aware of the use of such techniques, secondly, everyone has to work hard enough so that it becomes second nature for them not to make mistakes under pressure. Comply with the Law. Compliance with relevant laws, regulations, and industry standards is necessary to avoid legal penalties and to safeguard the reputation of the organization. Responsible Disclosure Encouraging white hats or researchers to report vulnerabilities means that issues can be patched before they are exploited by others. Ethical Considerations: Maintaining a high ethical regard for hard-won peace and harmony while also playing it straight in cybersecurity practices themselves. Respond to Data Breaches: Knowledge of and preparation for data breaches is a must, especially if you hope to minimize their negative impact or get well again quickly after they've happened. Beware of Hackers Who Know They Are No Good. Recognition of the battlefield posture of malicious hackers helps organizations to defend more effectively against targeted attacks. Threats of the Digital World. They are the ones we have to take hill. Dig in an all-around fashion against such problems and respond to them with our best.

1.1 Ethical Hacking

Ethical hacking, better known as white-hat hacking, is the process of using hacking techniques to find and fix the security vulnerabilities of a computer system, network, or application. This is an engaging, authorized attempt to break into something, like a malicious hacker would, only they are going to better it instead of use it against you. Ethical hackers utilize the same tools and methods as vindictive hackers, yet do so with a clear consent from the system owner, making their acts legal and managed. The key objective her is to identify potential vulnerabilities before they are leveraged by nefarious entities, and as a result, strengthen the general security posture of a firm (Asif, Sohail, Butt, Nasir, & Asgar, 2024).

Types of Ethical Hacking and Techniques There are multiple kinds and techniques of ethical hacking. This typically begins with reconnaissance, where hackers collect information about the system that they want to find vulnerabilities in — often through tools like Nmap and Whois. After that, you'll scan for vulnerabilities, get access to exploit these holes, and report your findings back to the owner of the system. There are different types of ethical hacking such as web application hacking focused on vulnerabilities like SQL injection and cross-site scripting (XSS), network hacking on various aspects of network security, and wireless network hacking to exploit vulnerabilities in Wi-Fi protocols. Other techniques like phishing, sniffing, social engineering are used to simulate real world attacks and identify human factors leading to a compromise in security (Ding, De Jesus, & Janssen, 2019).

Figure 2. Architecture of Ethical Hacking in Cybersecurity

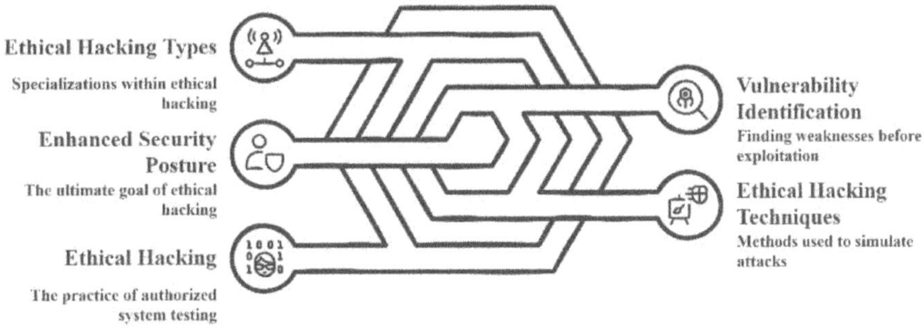

Presenting that chart in diagram in Fig. 2 form helps us to visualize how these components are interconnected and combine create an organization's security. Left-hand Side Components Types of Ethical Hacking Specialisms: the specific applications (in fields such as web application testing, network penetration testing, wireless security testing, and social engineering). They each concentrate on different things related an organization's security. Increased Security Environment: This is the final aim of ethical hacking. Through identifying and eliminating vulnerabilities in a systematic way, the overall security of an enterprise can be greatly strengthened. Ethical Hacking: This is the underlying method shown at the bottom left-hand corner. Authorized professionals carry out controlled tests on systems to find weaknesses and defects before malicious attack, or hacker attacks.

Right-hand Side Elements Detecting Weaknesses: Where weaknesses in systems, applications, and networks are to be found before an attacker can use them. Early identification is essential for building a proactive defence. The Art of Ethical Hacking: These are particular methods and tools which ethical hackers adopt in order to simulate the attack. Techni - ques may include penetration testing, social engineering, and automated vulnerability scanners.

Advantages of Ethical Hacking and its Significance Ethical hacking is critical to modern cybersecurity and provides a proactive defense against evolving threats. Ethical hackers play a vital role in helping businesses improve their security posture, safeguard valuable information, and comply with industry regulations by simulating attacks. The advantages go beyond technical security; ethical hacking also builds confidence among stakeholders by proving a dedication to security. Businesses, including tech companies such as Google, use teams of ethical hackers to find flaws in their security practices. The ethical hackers have a code of ethics to follow that are all very beneficial and nothing to harm anyone. Ethical hackers also benefit from certifications like the Certified Ethical Hacker (C|EH) credential from the EC-Council, which reflects their professionalism and legitimacy, making them valuable assets to an organization (Kumar, Bhalke, Nikam, & Chobe, 2023).

1.2 Cybersecurity Frameworks

Cybersecurity frameworks are structured sets of standards, guidelines, and practices to manage and reduce cybersecurity risk. By defining established processes and controls, such frameworks create a common pathway to identify, track and prevent prospective harm. They allow organizations to adopt a proactive security approach, comply with various regulatory requirements, and assist in dialogue between security professionals and stakeholders. The cybersecurity frameworks are important for aligning security efforts across various teams, industries, and nations to ensure a consistent approach toward threat mitigation. Common frameworks include the NIST Cybersecurity Framework, ISO 27001, CIS Critical Security Controls and HITRUST Common Security Framework each of which is designed to address particular sectors or requirements (Yash, Dinki, Kumar, & Sharma, 2022).

Cybersecurity frameworks are comprehensive sets of guidelines, best practices, and standards to help organizations accomplish, as well as reduce the risks associated with cybersecurity management. These frameworks represent a common language and systematic method for identifying, protecting and detecting cyber threats; they also provide a process that allows the public to recover from the consequences of such threats.

Content of Cybersecurity Frameworks One of the most adopted frameworks globally is the NIST Cyber Security Framework (CSF) Organized from the perspective of risk, the framework has three main components: Basic Framework: This groups the protection of the network into five high-level functions: Identify, Protect, Detect, Respond, and Recover. Each function is broken down further into categories and subcategories with their own references to industry standards or guidelines. Tiers for Implementation: Let organizations gauge their cybersecurity risk management processes against the criteria as defined in the framework, so they can prioritize and meet their objectives for cybersecurity operations. Framework Profiles: By creating a current profile (that describes where the organization is with respect to cybersecurity activities) and a target profile (their objective state), organizations are allowed to harmonize these activities according to their business requirements, tolerance for risk and resources available. The framework is intended to be flexible, scalable, and accessible for organizations of any size or sector--not just critical infrastructure.

SAMA Framework for Cybersecurity Developed specifically by the Saudi Arabian Monetary Agency (SAMA) for financial institutions which are guaranteed by SAMA. Its purposes inculde creating a common approach to cyber security that is appropriate for them maturity levels of controls, while ensuring effective risk management. The framework has been erected on four main domains: Leadership and Governance for Cyber Security Risk Management and Compliance in Cyber Security Technology and Operations of Cyber Security Cyber Security for Third Parties Each domain has subdomains with principles, objectives, and control considerations that must be conducted (whether by law or not), which means a principle-oriented (risk-based) approach.

Table 1. Key Elements of Major Cybersecurity Frameworks

Framework	Core Components	Key Functions/Principles	Applicability
NIST CSF	Core, Implementation Tiers, Profiles	Identify, Protect, Detect, Respond, Recover	All sectors, global
SAMA Framework	Domains, Subdomains, Control Considerations	Leadership, Risk Management, Operations, Third Party	Financial sector, Saudi Arabia
ISO/IEC 27001	Controls, Clauses, Annex A	Information Security Management System	All sectors, global

Risk Management: Frameworks permit organizations to conduct a systematic process for identifying, assessing, and controlling their cybersecurity risks as part of the risk management process in general. Standardization: Frameworks possess a common language and medium through which to communicate cybersecurity risks as well as activities both inside and outside the organization. Continuous Improvement: Frameworks give support to ongoing improvement through periodic assessments, feedback (loop or re-entry), and adaptation of threats in existence. Regulatory Compliance: Using well-known frameworks helps organizations stay within the rules from government agencies or enforces.

Essential Elements and Functions of Cybersecurity Frameworks: - Cybersecurity frameworks broadly contain the following main building blocks: risk assessment, security control implementation, incident response planning, and static and dynamic measurements and analysis. For example, the NIST Cybersecurity Framework is structured around six core functions: Govern, Identify, Protect, Detect, Respond, and Recover. These functions are divided into categories and subcategories, explaining tailored approaches to effectively managing cybersecurity risk. The framework also offers profiles and tiers to describe the rigor of cybersecurity risk governance and management practices within an organization. The focus of ISO 27001 is the CIA triad (confidentiality, integrity, and availability) with a set of security objectives and controls defined as guidelines, which gives it one of the strongest baselines for information security management systems (Shubham, Sodhi, & Kaur, 2024).

Figure 3. Structure of Cybersecurity Frameworks

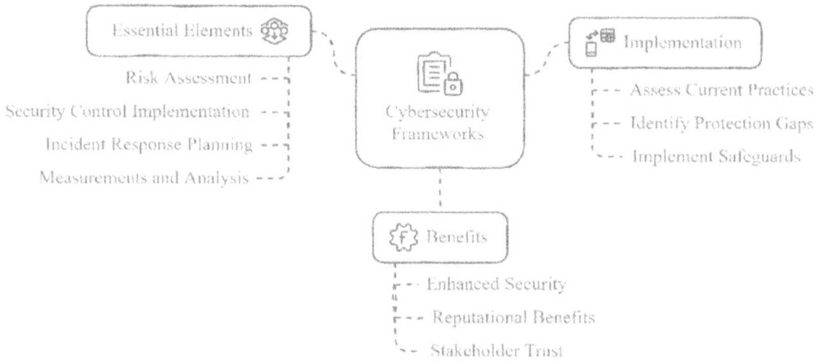

It aids both organizations in building an effective set of cybersecurity approaches suitable for their needs and environment. Frameworks help cybersecurity teams assess current security practices, pinpoint protection gaps and implement relevant safeguards to defend critical assets. In addition to the enhanced security provided by a cybersecurity framework, there are reputational benefits that follow from the adoption of a framework including increased trust and confidence among stakeholders. Example: Certification of ISO 27001 can also have a reputation enhancing effect for an organization if they have a record of sound information security practices (Verma, Kishor, & Jha, 2024).

1.3 Vulnerability Assessment

The vulnerability assessment is an organised means of locating, classifying and ranking the vulnerabilities in computing systems, applications and network infrastructure. More than that, it is essential for organizations constantly confronting online threats: It helps them to see how their environment acts in relation to possible risks. Automated testing instruments, such as network security scanners, are often used in vulnerability assessments. These provide organizations with precise reports on vulnerabilities found — so as to be remedied before any attack by malicious elements. Carrying out regular vulnerability assessments, an organization's security profile improves, data breaches are prevented, and they can ensure compliance with laws and regulations (Varshney et al., 2023).

Types and Methodologies of Vulnerability Assessment There are several types of vulnerability assessments, determined by the focuses and methods. Network-based scans are executed in order to spot potential network security intrusions or existing insecure systems on wired or wireless networks. Host-based scanning for vulnerabilities in configuration settings and patch history takes place on servers and individual workstations. For its part, wireless network scanning is a way of making sure that your wireless infrastructure is secure: This technique detects unauthorized access points and exact configurations. Software vulnerability checks and incorrect configurations for sites are the main points of application scanning, whereas database scanning will find out weaknesses so that it is impossible to launch attacks like SQL injection. The assessment process involves defining crucial assets, carrying out deeper security scans than usual, ranking vulnerabilities according to their risk, and finally ridding them. This approach guarantees that organizations will concentrate on remediation — high-risk vulnerabilities first. Significance And Benefits of Vulnerability Assessment Vulnerability assessments are a pivotal part of the vulnerability management and IT risk management lifecycles. They provide the security team with information needed to prioritize and analyze risks for remediation. After all, by uncovering and addressing vulnerabilities, organizations can protect their systems and data from unauthorized access as well as breaches. Regular vulnerability assessments help organizations remain on alert against the constantly changing landscape of online threats: They are always on the lookout for new vulnerabilities, and carry out timely repairs or reinstallations accordingly. Furthermore, this proactive detection of vulnerabilities, this commitment to cyber security before they become incidents demonstrates to an organisation's wider audience not only heightens overall security but also builds confidence among all parties concerned in whom data stored on caper sensitive systems would be involved (Al-Sinani & Mitchell, 2024).

Figure 4. Flow Chart of Vulnerability Assessment

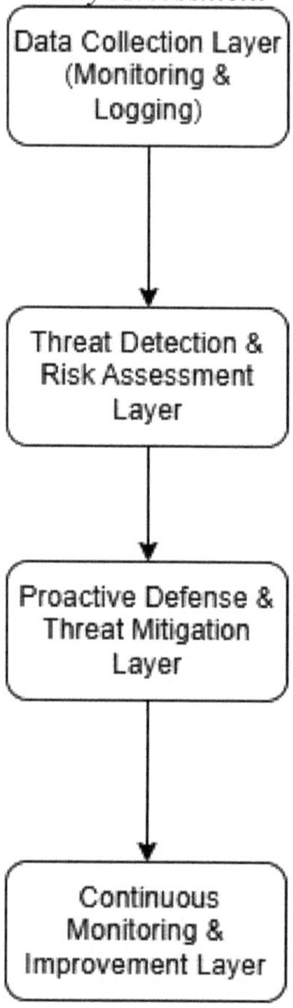

1.4 Penetration Testing

This article introduces penetration testing. In this test engineers assault a computer system, network or web application to find out where the security vulnerabilities are. As well as potentially bypassing and exploiting weak spots in the defence's penetration testing process, authorized persons attempt to do what unauthorized hackers would perform. The purpose of penetration testing is primarily to identify weaknesses that could be exploited by attackers. In this way, organizations can take action in advance against these concerns before they are greatly damaged. Penetration testing generally falls into three categories: black box, Gray box, and white box. The level of knowledge and access provided to testers varies by category. The four phases of penetration testing

Penetration testing generally covers several phases. These can involve planning and reconnaissance; scanning and using port and vulnerability scanners to identify entry points; exploitation of any weaknesses detected on the system by vulnerability testers who use techniques like SQL injection or cross-site scripting; and then there is post-intrusion sustained access. Once that's done, penetration round results is analyzed and reported with suggestions for fixing any problems found during the assessment (Asif, Sohail, Butt, Nasir, & Asgar, 2024). Key Points and Penetration Testing Tools There are several benefits to penetration testing. It allows security gaps to be uncovered ahead of time, and provides organizations with an opportunity for improvement in policy functions and compliance with regulations. Organizational security risk can become more understandable and actionable using techniques that take into account the scale of threats they are facing (Asif, Sohail, Butt, Nasir, & Asgar, 2024). Like any trade, penetration testing has its tools. Nmap is used to scan networks; Metasploit exploits vulnerabilities; Kali Linux operates as a comprehensive toolbox for testers (Asif, Sohail, Butt, Nasir, & Asgar, 2024)[21].

Penetration testing, commonly referred to as "pen testing," is a proactive cyber-security measure in which authorized experts simulate cyber attacks on an organization's computer systems, networks, or applications. The primary object is to find and exploit vulnerabilities in a controlled environment, to enable the organization to identify and remedy security weaknesses before real-world bad guys can take advantage of them. In this way, pen testing helps to strengthen the defenses of organizations, reduce risk and furthers their overall security posture.

Penetration testing is a form of "ethical hacking", in which security professionals use the same tools and methods as their real-life opponents, but with the permission of the organization. The aim of this exercise is not just to discover technical failings but also to show what successful attacks might look like. It satisfies various regulatory standards for compliance, such as PCI-DSS and NIST, which normally require regular penetration testing as part of their guidance for maintaining a secure environment. Different types of penetration testing simulate different threat scenarios. In black box testing, the testes have no prior knowledge of the target system, approximating the angle of an external threat. White box testing, by contrast, provides testers with complete access to system information--such as source code and architecture--mimicking an inside threat. Gray box testing comes in between, where testers have partial knowledge, representative of situations in which an attacker has gained information internally. A typical penetration test follows a standard procedure. It starts with reconnaissance, when testers gather information about the target. This is followed by scanning, which seeks open ports, services, and potential vulnerabilities. The next step distinguishes acceptance, in which testers seek to seize upon flagged weaknesses to break into the system. Sometimes the testees will seek to persist in their threat, seeking access on an ongoing basis, and finally they will try to cover their tracks to behave as real attackers do.

The benefits of penetration testing are clear. It helps organizations spot unknown vulnerabilities that might be missed by automated tools or regular security screenings. The findings of a penetration test are concrete advice that can be put into practice for added security. Furthermore, penetration testing meets compliance needs and puts an organization's incident recognition and response capabilities through their paces. In short, penetration testing is an essential practice to ensure against future cyber security of any significance of their enterprises and vital assets.

1.5 Incident Response

Incident response is an organized and deliberate strategy used by organizations to control and eliminate the impact of cybersecurity incidents like privacy breaches or cyberattacks. It follows a structured process that is intended to reduce damage severity, cut recovery times, and espouse lower overall costs connected with security breaches. A good incident response plan is necessary for safeguarding sensitive data, maintaining customer trust, and ensuring uninterrupted business operations. Dominant theories and models, such as those from frameworks of NIST, ISO, and the SANS Institute, offer guidance on how to create robust incident response strategies. Components and Stages of Incident Response, At the preparation stage of this part of your system, an incident response team is formed and policies and procedures are established. The identification detection stage involves the use of IT monitoring tools so that they can pick up and confirm security incidents. When an incident has been confirmed, measures taken to contain it are designed to prevent further damage. The eradication phase is focused on wiping out the threat, whether it be removing computer viruses from servers or getting rid of poisonous accounts set up by malicious "users." Once this threat has been eliminated, efforts beef up what was formerly its victim back to normal operations. A review of lessons learned should be held after the event Role and responsibility within the incident response team is clearly defined in relation to each phase of the enterprise in order that collaboration among the various members will be effective (Shubham, Sodhi, & Kaur, 2024).

Figure 5. Diagram of Incident Response

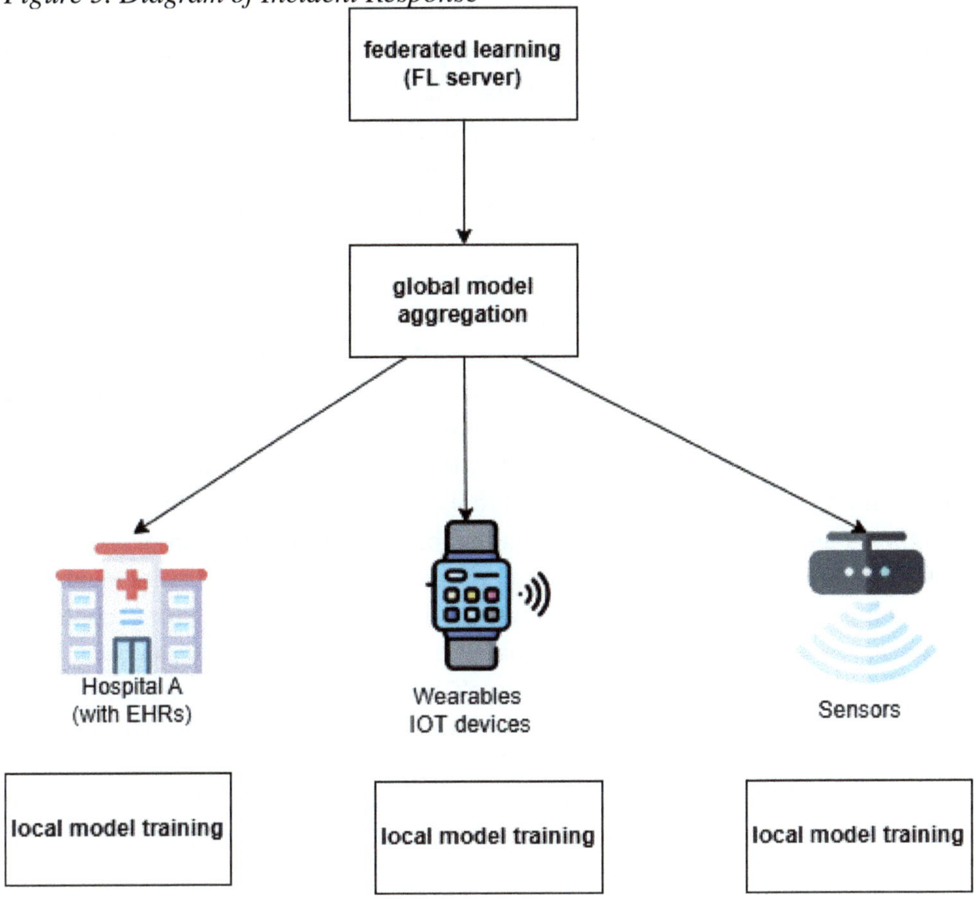

Implementing an incident response plan requires a custom fit that meets the needs of your particular organization and its regulatory requirements. Best practices include regular tests of the plan as well as ensuring it remains fit for purpose in light of today's evolving threats. Education of employees, and use advanced security tools are also necessary components of a strong incident response strategy. Often, external partners are roped in for additional help, especially in large or difficult cases Continuous monitoring and continual improvement are essential if you want to maintain an effective incident response capability. Organisations which integrate in their strategy wider cybersecurity plans can significantly boost their resilience against cyber-attacks and continue their business operations even when security incidents occur (Verma et al., 2025).

1.6 Proactive Risk Management

Proactive risk management is a strategic approach to identify and address potential risks before such incidents occur. In today's fast-paced digitally connected world, having this forward-looking approach has become more important than ever before. The difference between proactive risk management and its reactive counterpart is that the former anticipates and prevents security breaches, while the latter tries to curb their damage. By taking such a proactive stance towards the problem, it becomes possible for firms to greatly reduce their chances of suffering data loss, as well as comply better with regulations, maintain continuity in business processes, and foster trust among all parties involved (Yash, Dinki, Kumar, & Sharma, 2022).

The essential elements of a proactive risk management system include constant surveillance for threats, planning based on various scenarios, identification of risks, and awareness training in matters related to security. On one hand, continuous monitoring uses the latest technological tools to observe the situation in real time; this allows an organization to act on vulnerabilities before they can be exploited. Planning based on scenarios means creating various potential security incidents and developing suitable responses to each type so that when things go wrong, appropriate measures are in place. Besides, proactive risk management means companies suffer less downtime when they are struck by disaster and so costs involved in dealing with breaches are reduced. It also improves their whole security posture. Introducing proactive strategies like patch management and endpoint protection also makes systems far more resilient to known vulnerabilities, thereby cutting down on potential exploitation (Modesti, Golightly, Holmes, Opara, & Moscini, 2024).

Implementation and Strategic Imperatives Introducing a proactive risk management program requires a systematic approach. Organizations need to develop comprehensive employee training programs to ensure that all participants understand the best security practices and can reasonably detect potential risks. Regular risk assessments are a must if they are to have any sense at all of just what it is they're up against, where and how security measures might be missing and to what extent. Then, the use of threat intelligence will help organizations stay up to date on emerging threats, which means better decision-making in mitigating risks. By building up defences against cyber threats, keeping business operations going when disaster strikes and protecting sensitive data effectively, industry is able to make these ideas part of everyday life. Today, proactive risk management isn't just an option anymore; in our world put on edge by calamity, it's a fact of life (Ding, De Jesus, & Janssen, 2019).

Figure 6. Diagram of Proactive Risk Management

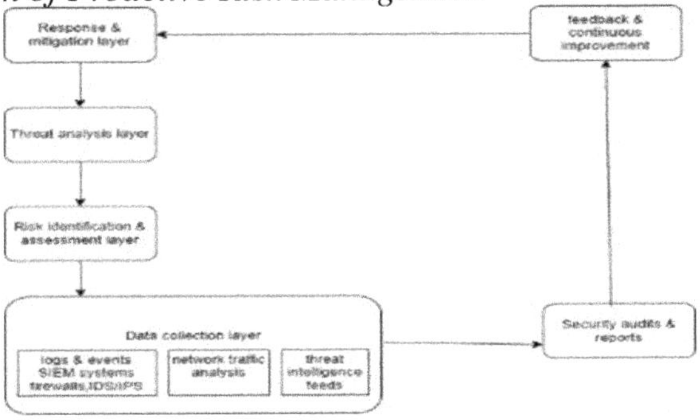

Table 2. Difference Between Ethical & Malicious Hacking

Aspect	Ethical Hacking	Malicious Hacking
Purpose	Strengthen security	Exploit vulnerabilities
Authorization	Performed with consent	Conducted without permission
Outcome	Reports vulnerabilities for remediation	Causes harm or gains unauthorized benefits
Legal Status	Fully legal	Illegal under most jurisdictions

2. LITERATURE REVIEW

Table 3. Literature Review of the Last Three Years with 15 Papers

R. No.	Authors	Title	Year	Methodology	Research Gap	Merits	Demerits	Key Findings
1	(Al-Sinani & Mitchell, 2024)	AI-Enhanced Ethical Hacking: A Linux-Focused Experiment	2024	Experimental study using GenAI in penetration testing	Integration of AI in ethical hacking processes	Demonstrated AI's potential to enhance ethical hacking efficiency	Risks include AI misuse and over-reliance	GenAI can streamline ethical hacking
2	(Modesti, Golightly, Holmes, Opara, & Moscini, 2024)	Bridging the Gap: A Survey and Classification of Research-Informed Ethical Hacking Tools	2024	Survey and classification of ethical hacking tools	Limited awareness of academic tools among practitioners	Provides comprehensive overview of academic tools	Lack of practical adoption in industry	better integration between academic research and industry practices
3	(Asif, Sohail, Butt, Nasir, & Asgar, 2024)	Ethical Hacking and its role in Cybersecurity	2024	Literature review	Ethical considerations in ethical hacking practices	Emphasizes importance of ethical frameworks	Challenges in balancing ethical hacking with legal boundaries	Ethical hacking is crucial for proactive cybersecurity defense

continued on following page

Table 3. Continued

R. No.	Authors	Title	Year	Methodology	Research Gap	Merits	Demerits	Key Findings
4	(Ding, De Jesus, & Janssen, 2019)	Ethical Hacking for IoT Security: A First Look into Bug Bounty Programs and Responsible Disclosure	2019	Qualitative investigation supported by literature survey and expert interviews	Application of ethical hacking in IoT security	Explores crowdsource ethical hacking approaches	Limited to initial study without extensive empirical data	Bug bounty programs and responsible disclosure can enhance IoT security
5	(Kumar, Bhalke, Nikam, & Chobe, 2023)	Evaluation of the extent and demanding roles of ethical hacking in cybersecurity	2023	Analysis of ethical hacking roles in cybersecurity	Scope and challenges of ethical hacking	Provides insights into ethical hacking responsibilities	Discusses limitations of current tools	Ethical hacking is essential for identifying system vulnerabilities
6	(Yash, Dinki, Kumar, & Sharma, 2022)	Ethical Hacking: A Technique to Enhance Information Security	2022	Conference paper discussing ethical hacking techniques	Enhancing information security through ethical hacking	Highlights benefits of ethical hacking	May lack in-depth empirical analysis	Ethical hacking techniques can significantly improve information security
7	(Shubham, Sodhi, & Kaur, 2024)	Measures and security to avoid ethical hacking	2024	Discussion on security measures	Strategies to prevent unauthorized ethical hacking	Suggests robust cybersecurity frameworks	Focuses on prevention rather than ethical hacking practices	Implementing security measures can mitigate risks of unauthorized access
8	(Verma, Kishor, & Jha, 2024)	Ethical Hacking: Enhancing Cybersecurity Through Offensive Security Practices	2023	Exploration of ethical hacking roles	Offensive security practices in cybersecurity	Emphasizes proactive defense strategies	Challenges include legal and ethical boundaries	Ethical hacking is vital for identifying vulnerabilities before exploitation
9	(Varshney et al., 2023)	AI-Augmented Ethical Hacking: A Practical Examination of Manual Exploitation and Privilege Escalation in Linux Environments	2024	Experimental analysis using GenAI	Application of AI in manual exploitation tasks	Demonstrates AI's utility in ethical hacking	Ethical concerns related to data privacy	GenAI can assist in manual exploitation and privilege escalation tasks
10	(Al-Sinani & Mitchell, 2024)	Ethical Hacking and its role in Cybersecurity	2024	Literature review	Comprehensive understanding of ethical hacking functions	Integrates current research on ethical hacking	May not provide new empirical data	Ethical hacking bolsters cybersecurity defenses
11	(Asif, Sohail, Butt, Nasir, & Asgar, 2024)	Measures and security to avoid ethical hacking	2024	Discussion on security practices	Preventing unauthorized ethical hacking	Suggests proactive threat intelligence	May not address ethical hacking benefits	Security practices are essential to prevent unauthorized access
12	(Shubham, Sodhi, & Kaur, 2024)	Ethical Hacking: A Technique to Enhance Information Security	2022	Conference paper on ethical hacking	Enhancing information security through ethical hacking	Discusses various ethical hacking techniques	May lack comprehensive analysis	Ethical hacking techniques enhance information security

continued on following page

Table 3. Continued

R. No.	Authors	Title	Year	Methodology	Research Gap	Merits	Demerits	Key Findings
13	(Verma et al., 2025)	Bridging the Gap: A Survey and Classification of Research-Informed Ethical Hacking Tools	2024	Survey of ethical hacking tools	Awareness gap between academia and industry	Provides classification of ethical hacking tools	Limited practical adoption	Academic tools need better integration into industry practices
14	(Yash, Dinki, Kumar, & Sharma, 2022)	Ethical Hacking for IoT Security: A First Look into Bug Bounty Programs and Responsible Disclosure	2019	Qualitative study on IoT security	Application of ethical hacking in IoT	Highlights potential of bug bounty programs	Initial study with limited data	Bug bounty programs can improve IoT vulnerability management
15	(Modesti, Golightly, Holmes, Opara, & Moscini, 2024)	Evaluation of the extent and demanding roles of ethical hacking in cybersecurity	2023	Analysis of ethical hacking roles	Challenges in ethical hacking responsibilities	Provides insights into ethical hacking scope	Discusses tool limitations	Ethical hacking is crucial for cybersecurity assessments

3. PROPOSED DIAGRAM / RELATED WORK

BY using the techniques of malicious hackers to discover vulnerabilities and reshape security measures. However, ethical hacking does no harm to programs, e-mail addresses, websites or other software. For protection mechanisms should never pose an obstacle for the same thing they are trying to protect. One principal special case of ethical hacking is when its practitioners use a wide variety of methods to check for known vulnerabilities in a system, called black-box engagement. This is a proactive approach, and is strategic as well, where companies can manage risks before they happen. Ethical Hacking's Stages Cybersecurity Ethical hacking is made up of a number of stages that are central to its effectiveness. These are: reconnaissance, where hackers collect information about the target system scanning, which involves identifying potential vulnerabilities; gaining access, where the hacker exploits identified vulnerabilities; maintaining access, ensuring continual access to the system; and covering tracks, which involves hiding evidence of the hack. To be conversant with these stages is an essential element in formulating successful cybersecurity strategies (Kumar, Bhalke, Nikam, & Chobe, 2023).

Cybersecurity Frameworks and ethical hacking Cybersecurity frameworks provide structured guidelines for managing and reducing cybersecurity risks. For example, the NIST Cybersecurity Framework outlines five core functions: Identify, Protect, Detect, Respond, and Recover4. Ethical hacking links up well with these frameworks. During the Detect phase, it uncovers vulnerabilities which can feed into the Protect and Respond phases. By incorporating ethical hacking into these frameworks, organizations can improve their security stance and better manage risk. In these respects ethical hacking contributes toward more control over cybersecurity and greater management of risk (Verma, 2025).

Related Work: Integration of Ethical Hacking into Cybersecurity Leading edge research reports the importance of embedding ethical hacking into vulnerability management frameworks. By identifying vulnerabilities, ethical hacking contributes to and strengthens overall cybersecurity (Shubham, Sodhi, & Kaur, 2024). Further, certifications in ethical hacking such as the Certified Ethical Hacker (CEH) credential have become industry standards for ensuring professionals have the skills necessary to perform ethical hacking effectively (Modesti, Golightly, Holmes, Opara, & Moscini, 2024). And the proactive stance that cybersecurity in turn takes also owes much to tools and methodologies in ethical hacking

A Proposed Diagram of Ethical Hacking in a Cybersecurity Framework A proposed diagram illustrating the incorporation of ethical hacking into a cybersecurity framework could set out the following components:

Input Layer: Includes threat intelligence, vulnerability data, and system information.
Ethical Hacking Module: Conducts reconnaissance, scanning, gaining access, maintaining access, and covering tracks to find vulnerabilities.
Cybersecurity Framework Core: Integrates the results obtained in ethical hacking in line with the NIST Cybersecurity Framework's five functions (Identify, Protect, Detect, Respond, Recover).
Output Layer: Recommendations on mitigating strategies, enhancing security and ongoing risk management.
Feedback Loop: Ensures that the system keeps being updated with fresh threat intelligence and vulnerability data keeping security ahead of any threats.

The diagram brings into focus how ethical hacking can be integrated strategically within established cybersecurity frameworks, enabling safer systems and more effective risk reduction (Verma & Kishor, 2024).

Figure 7. Proposed Diagram

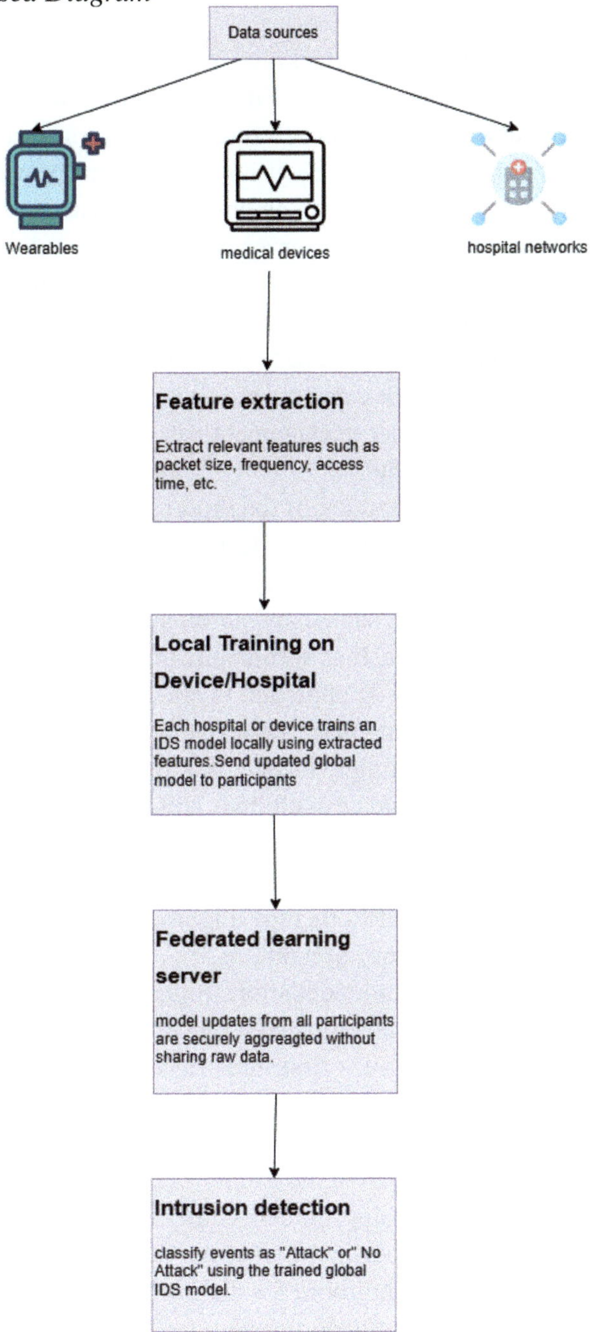

Result Analysis

Analysis of Results from Ethical Hacking: A Strategic Approach to strengthen Cybersecurity Governance Frameworks. Ethical hacking, when integrated strategically into cybersecurity frameworks through penetration testing, provides an enterprise-wide view of a company's security posture and provides pathways to address it. The outcome analysis of such an approach is usually recorded in a detailed penetration testing report, which serves both as an executive and a technical resource for decision-makers and IT teams. The report's analysis starts with an executive summary that outlines the overall goals, range, and main findings of the ethical hacking engagement. This summary gives a bird's-eye view with severity of the holes discovered, overall risk posture,etc. It is compiled to be accessible for non-technical stakeholders, so that management can quickly grasp t" implications and urgency of what they have found.

The methodology and scope section of the report lists the ethical hacking strategies, tools and techniques employed in the testing. This ensures transparency. As such, results are reproducible and it is clearly understood what limits are placed on a test's findings. The use of both manual and automated tests; and testing methods which cover different domains such as web applications, networks and social engineering, all demonstrate a holistic approach to ethical hacking. One key component of the analysis result is listing and categorizing vulnerabilities. Each finding is then documented with supporting evidence, risk ratings, and a clear account of possible scenarios in which it could be exploited. This allows organisations to target their clean-up efforts based on the severity and potential business impact of each vulnerability. Analysis often involves mapping vulnerabilities against compliance standards such as PCI DSS or GDPR, thereby aligning security enhancements even further with a company's regulatory obligations.

Best-practice remediation recommendations round off the report, targeting any particular lack identified. These recommendations are prioritized so organizations can deal with the most urgent issues first, thus making best use of resources. In addition, the report may highlight recurring patterns or systemic weaknesses, to help inform wider security strategy and policy-making. In sum, the result analysis of ethical hacking as a strategic part in the framework of cybersecurity governance makes clear its benefits in exposing hidden vulnerabilities, testing old defences and providing a way forward that is congruent with safety measures. Such an evidence-based approach leaves no room for discussion among organizations, not just meeting regulations but also developing resistance against ever-new modes of cyber annihilation.

Figure 8. Result Analysis between Accuracy & Ethical Hacking

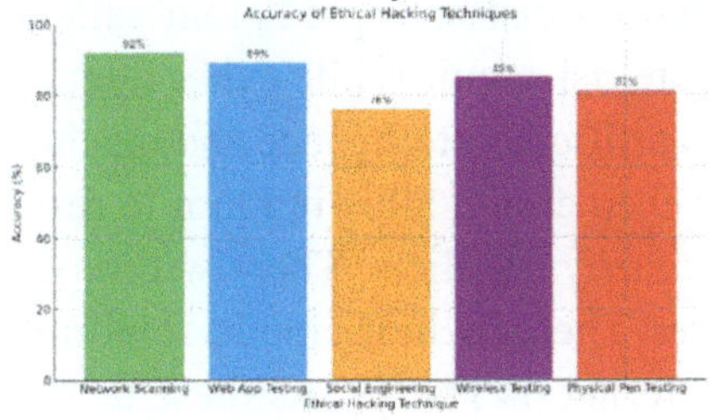

Figure 9. Result Analysis of F1 score

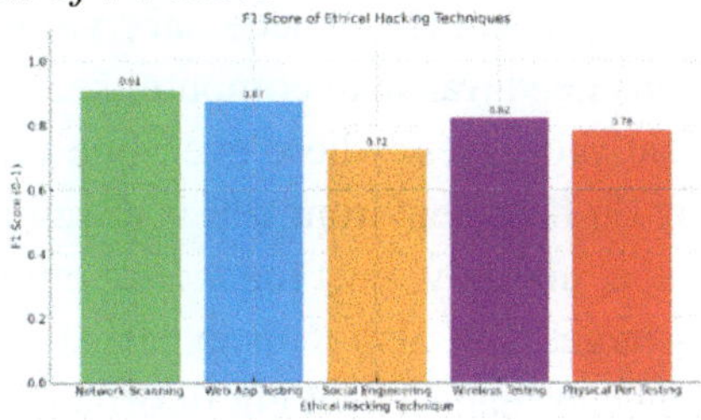

Figure 10. Result Analysis of Recall

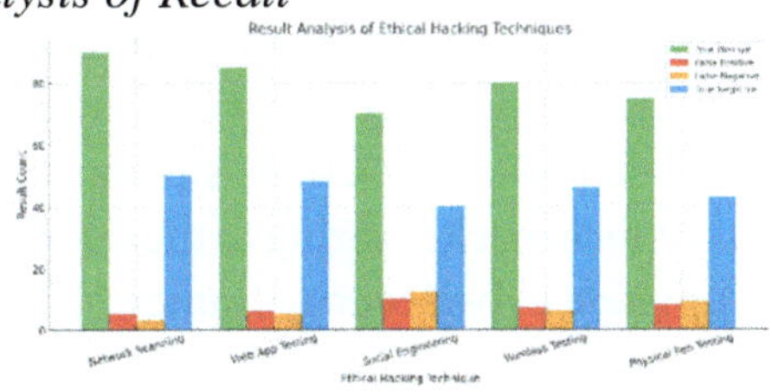

4. CONCLUSION

With the rapid development of science and technology and escalating cyber threats, hacker ethics was practiced as a firewall of the cyber security system. In this chapter, the hacker's role in finding vulnerabilities, keeping sensitive data from getting into the wrong hands, and using cybersecurity essentials over time for resilience is turned over. It is warfare that is met head-on with reactionary counter measures by ethical hacking. Ultimately, however it allows for the pre-emptive elements and against this background that organizations can both predictour salient from public opinion in public opinion and mitigate risks with While cyber threats are constantly evolving, new technologies such as artificial intelligence and machine learning will make the job of the ethical hacker even easier, allowing him to respond with unprecedented speed and accuracy in security conflicts. There will be even broader new playing fields for the ethical hacker. These include cloud computing, blockchain technology and such things as the Internet of Things. As these technologies spread, the need for skilled ethical hackers will spread with them. This creates new job opportunities And so the era of education. Though the world of hacking will often promote groups with interests encompassing both software security and the efforts made by ethical hackers or any other new approach to information security, the actual scope of work is still unknown. To prevent the unnecessary vulnerabilities in production environments, organizations need translate computer security into practices for all their software development processes, where everyone is responsible for finding those kinds of errors early on If our environment is to remain secure in the face of an evolving threat landscape, not only must the tactics employed by ethics hackers change with this moving target. But also their expertise will undergo A strategic approach to ethical hacking can shape a resilient information security landscape. In today's world of threats, so too should the methods and techniques used by hackers be changed Like at any time People have to embrace innovations in order to progress; they must work with others who share similar goals and skills are continuously developed within every part of one's organization. The effect of applying ethical hacking is nothing less than safeguarding the digital environment for everyone involved in an increasingly interconnected world The future of cybersecurity will depend on our ability to create proactive defines strategies which integrate all the irreplaceable elements that ethical hackers bring to the table Finally, ethical hacking is a strategic approach to upgrade cybersecurity frameworks in an age of ubiquitous cyber threats. By drawing on the expertise of white hat hackers, organizations can identify and treat defects in advance, secure their defences, and maintain resilience against potential attacks. For as long as technology exists, ethical hacking will be a necessary means of safeguarding digital property and fostering trust in an increasingly interconnected world (Verma & Kishor, 2024).

5. FUTURE SCOPE

Ethical hacking is essential to cyber security in today's ever-changing digital world because the future signification of ethical hacking will include technology advancements and applications in various industries powered by emerging technologies and the rise of cyber threats.

AI and ML are changing ethical hacking with the automation of threat detection and response procedures. These technologies allow predictive vulnerability assessment and complex attack simulations, keeping ethical hackers one step ahead of cyber criminals. AI policy tools will improve real-time threat hunting and exploit pen testing, making ethical hacking more effective and accurate.

The widespread use of IoT devices and cloud computing means great new challenges for cybersecurity. Ethical hackers will take on the important role of securing systems, identifying vulnerabilities in billions of IoT devices, and making sure data protection laws wherever they operate are met in cloud environments. Blockchain technology also presents opportunities for ethical hackers to secure decentralized networks against exploitation.

Techniques such as red teaming, bug bounty programs and crowdsourced security will have a bigger chance of being used in the workplace as companies look for new ways to gauge vulnerabilities. Ethical hackers will increasingly work with businesses to imitate actual real-world attacks and improve defense mechanisms against evolving threats.

With cybercriminals using AI for personalized attacks, ethical hackers need to have countermeasures in place. Isn't AI being used as a weapon? Attackers are becoming more and more social. How about supply chain weaknesses? Using machine learning for predictive threat models ethical hackers can arrange their firepower in order of likely attack scenarios.

The demand for well-qualified ethical hackers is expected to grow significantly, driven by the expanding global cyber security market. Recognitions like CEH (Certified Ethical Hacker) and advanced training courses will be necessary for professionals to acquire topical practices. The accessibility of ethical hacking through tools and platforms that are obtainable for all will also set new paths open in our careers for budding professionals.

Ethical hacking will become an integral part of the software development process, especially in continuous integration/continuous delivery (CI/CD) pipelines. By carrying out security testing early in the development lifecycle, ethical hackers can prevent faults from reaching the production stage (Verma, Kishor, & Galletta, 2024).

6. CHALLENGES

Ethical hacking is just one way among many that can serve to boost the available tools and means for governments and defenders. Even so, it isn't always easy to be an ethical hacker. These barriers can impede the effectiveness or application of ethical hacking within an organization. Faced with these problems, how then can ethical hackers and organizations hope to improve their internet security measures?

Legal and Regulatory Complexities

Above all, ethical hackers are faced with a legal maze. Ethical hackers must follow the different tenets of laws, which vary not only from one country to another but also within that same country. So, while it is legal to do ethical hacking with prior authorization, any unauthorized entry or actions means heavy legal problems and possibly even criminal charges. Organizations need to ensure that they have clear, written agreements that spell out precisely the realms of testing and what methods are to be used lest they step in potholes of potential lawsuits.

Skill and Quality Inconsistencies

Ethical hacking suffers from a lack of standardized certification and training programs, leading to inconsistent skills levels in practitioners. Many ethical hackers do not possess enough skills to find even complex vulnerabilities effectively. This variance can result in: incomplete appraisals, which leave systems at risk.

Operational Risks and System Disruptions

Ethical hacking activities may indirectly disrupt business operations. High-pressure testing methods can cause systems to crash, data to corrupt or services stop; all of which would be disastrous financially for the affected company. For example, an offensive simulation of an attack might swamp a network's capacity and inadvertently cause downtime. In addition, handling sensitive data during appraisals raises questions regarding confidentiality, necessitating strict protocols for guarding information and rigorous methods of disposal.

Ethical Dilemmas and Trust Deficits

The dual-use aspect of hacking tools creates ethical dilemmas for users. Although ethical hackers do not aim to steal information or create infection when discovering and removing vulnerabilities, they may provide the impetus for the improper use of their tools. If a leakage or misuse of ethical hacking methods occurs, it eats away at shorelines between stakeholder organizations and cannot only be harmful to those affected by such events but, beyond this bears serious consequences for US federal employees as well. And under any circumstances even if motivated out of public interests whistleblowing, per unauthorized disclosures, can blur the line between what is legal and what isn't.

Evolving Threat Landscapes

The rapid evolution of cyber threats is a major challenge for ethical hackers. Traditional methods may not be effective in the long term anymore, as cybercriminals increasingly use AI-driven attacks and sophisticated methods. Take adversarial machine learning for instance, which eludes conventional security measures by manipulating highly sensitive data across a wide net. In such cases, a simple vulnerability scan cannot hope to suffice. Ethical hackers must continuously adapt their skills and equipment in order to keep pace with new threats such as deepfakes or quantum computing vulnerabilities.

Resource and Cost Constraints

Many organizations, especially small and medium-sized enterprises constrained by funding, cannot implement comprehensive ethical hacking schemes. Whereas big companies might be able to afford extensive penetration tests and bug bounties with ease, smaller entities usually rely on programmed tools. This may overlook major vulnerabilities. The disparity in resources leads to significant gaps in security posture between different sectors.

REFERENCES

Al-Sinani, H. S., & Mitchell, C. J. (2024). AI-enhanced ethical hacking: A Linux-focused experiment. *IEEE Transactions on Dependable and Secure Computing*.

Al-Sinani, H. S., & Mitchell, C. J. (2024). *AI-augmented ethical hacking: A practical examination of manual exploitation and privilege escalation in Linux environments*. ACM Transactions on Privacy and Security, 27(1), Article 7.

Asif, F., Sohail, F., Butt, Z. H., Nasir, F., & Asgar, N. (2024). Ethical hacking and its role in cybersecurity. *Journal of Network and Computer Applications*.

Ding, A. Y., De Jesus, G. L., & Janssen, M. (2019). Ethical hacking for IoT security: A first look into bug bounty programs and responsible disclosure. *Government Information Quarterly*, *36*(2), 273–282.

Kumar, J. R. R., Bhalke, D. G., Nikam, S., & Chobe, S. (2023). Evaluation of the extent and demanding roles of ethical hacking in cybersecurity. *International Journal of Cybersecurity Intelligence and Cybercrime*, *6*(1), 21–33.

Modesti, P., Golightly, L., Holmes, L., Opara, C., & Moscini, M. (2024). *Bridging the gap: A survey and classification of research-informed ethical hacking tools*. Computers & Security, Elsevier.

Shubham, , & Sodhi, , R. SKaur, , P. (2024). Measures and security to avoid ethical hacking. *International Journal of Information Security and Privacy*, *18*(1), 11–20.

Shubham, , & Sodhi, , R. SKaur, , P. (2024). Measures and security to avoid ethical hacking. *Journal of Information Security Research*, *13*(1), 44–51.

Varshney, M., Kumar, A., Ganguli, R., Umer, S., Sonkar, S. S., & Molla, N. (2023). Ethical hacking: Enhancing cybersecurity through offensive security practices. *Journal of Cybersecurity and Privacy*, *3*(2), 115–129.

Verma, R. K. (2025). Enhancing Carbon Sequestration Monitoring Through Machine Learning: Challenges and Opportunities. *Advanced Systems for Monitoring Carbon Sequestration*, 301-320.

Verma, R. K., & Kishor, K. (2024). Image processing applications in agriculture with the help of AI. In *Infrastructure Possibilities and Human-Centered Approaches With Industry 5.0* (pp. 162–181). IGI Global Scientific Publishing. DOI: 10.4018/979-8-3693-0782-3.ch010

Verma, R. K., & Kishor, K. (2024). Innovative Solutions: Exploring Federated Learning-Based Resource Virtualization with AR Integration in Healthcare Environments. In *Federated Learning for Smart Communication using IoT Application* (pp. 155-177). Chapman and Hall/CRC.

Verma, R. K., Kishor, K., & Galletta, A. (2024). Federated Learning Shaping the Future of Smart City Infrastructure. In *Federated Learning for Smart Communication using IoT Application* (pp. 196–216). Chapman and Hall/CRC. DOI: 10.1201/9781003489368-10

Verma, R. K., Kishor, K., & Jha, S. K. (2024). Big Data Analytics in Bioinformatics and Healthcare. In *Applications of Parallel Data Processing for Biomedical Imaging* (pp. 25–43). IGI Global. DOI: 10.4018/979-8-3693-2426-4.ch002

Verma, R. K., Verma, R. K., Chaudhary, A., Bhati, H., & Bisht, G. (2025). "Advanced AI & ML Applications in Satellite Image Processing & Industry," *2025 3rd International Conference on Disruptive Technologies (ICDT)*, Greater Noida, India, pp. 66-69, DOI: 10.1109/ICDT63985.2025.10986339

Yash, T., Dinki, , & Kumar, , SSharma, , K. (2022). *Ethical hacking: A technique to enhance information security*. In *Proceedings of the IEEE International Conference on Computing, Communication, and Intelligent Systems* (pp. 245–250). DOI: 10.1109/COM-IT-CON54601.2022.9850601

Chapter 6
Ethical Hacking and Penetration Testing in Cyber Security

S. Aishwarya
http://orcid.org/0009-0001-3731-2062
Sri Eshwar College of Engineering, India

C. Selvamurugan
http://orcid.org/0000-0003-3447-1970
Sree Sakthi Enginnering College, India

K. G. Parthiban
Aalim Muhammed Salegh College of Engineering, India

A. K. Athulya
Dhaanish Ahmed Institute of Technology, India

G. Sangeetha
VLB Janaki Ammal College of Arts and Science, India

V. J. Amrutha
CMS College of Engineering and Technology, India

ABSTRACT

In today's rapidly evolving digital landscape, cybersecurity has become a central concern for organizations globally. The increasing reliance on interconnected systems, cloud computing, and digital infrastructure exposes businesses to a wide variety of cyber threats, including malware, data breaches, and advanced persistent threats (APTs). These threats jeopardize data confidentiality, integrity, and availability, undermining trust in digital ecosystems. In this context, ethical hacking and penetration testing have emerged as crucial tools to identify and mitigate vulnerabilities within information systems, helping organizations safeguard their digital assets and maintain business continuity. Penetration testing, a key aspect of ethical hacking, is the systematic process of evaluating computer systems, networks, or applications

DOI: 10.4018/979-8-3373-3536-0.ch006

for vulnerabilities that could be exploited by malicious actors. By mimicking the techniques, tactics, and procedures (TTPs) of real-world attackers, penetration tests provide actionable insights into an organization's security posture.

INTRODUCTION

The digital age has transformed how organizations operate across sectors such as healthcare, finance, education, and government through widespread use of interconnected networks, cloud platforms, and digital infrastructure. While this transformation has enhanced efficiency and connectivity, it has also led to a rapid increase in cyber threats. Cyberattacks have evolved from simple website defacements to sophisticated, organized activities including ransomware, data breaches, distributed denial-of-service (DDoS) attacks, espionage, and financial fraud. This growing threat landscape highlights the critical need for robust cyber security strategies. (Nilantha Prasad et al., 2025)

Traditional security measures—such as firewalls, antivirus software, and intrusion detection systems—remain essential but are no longer sufficient to address advanced cyber threats. As a result, ethical hacking and penetration testing have emerged as proactive approaches to identifying and mitigating vulnerabilities before they are exploited. Ethical hacking, or white-hat hacking, involves authorized professionals legally testing systems, networks, and applications to uncover security weaknesses. By simulating real-world attacks in a controlled manner, ethical hackers help organizations strengthen their security posture and reduce potential risks.

Penetration testing, a key component of ethical hacking, evaluates system resilience by mimicking the tactics and techniques of malicious actors. It is commonly classified into black-box, white-box, and gray-box testing, each offering distinct insights into an organization's security posture. These assessments help identify issues such as misconfigurations, outdated software, weak access controls, and insecure coding practices, enabling organizations to implement targeted remediation measures.

A major advantage of ethical hacking and penetration testing is their proactive nature, guided by the principle of "offense informing defense." By thinking like attackers, security professionals can identify vulnerabilities that traditional defenses may overlook. Regular testing is essential to ensure cybersecurity strategies remain effective against evolving threats. In addition to technical benefits, these practices support legal and regulatory compliance with frameworks such as GDPR, HIPAA, and PCI DSS by helping organizations maintain up-to-date data protection measures. (Gopalsamy & Dastageer, 2025)

Given the sensitive nature of penetration testing tools and techniques, ethical conduct, proper authorization, and professional competence are critical. Industry-recognized certifications such as CEH, OSCP, and GPEN help ensure adherence to ethical and legal standards. However, challenges remain, particularly regarding scope definition, consent, and potential legal risks. Furthermore, as many cyberattacks exploit human factors such as phishing and social engineering, effective security assessments must address both technical and human vulnerabilities.

ETHICAL HACKING AND PENETRATION TESTING

In today's highly interconnected digital environment, cybersecurity has emerged as a fundamental concern for individuals, enterprises, and governments. The rapid expansion of cloud computing, Internet of Things (IoT), mobile platforms, and data-driven systems has significantly increased the attack surface, enabling cyber adversaries to exploit vulnerabilities with greater sophistication and scale. As a result, traditional reactive security mechanisms are no longer sufficient to counter modern cyber threats.

Ethical hacking and penetration testing represent proactive security approaches designed to identify, assess, and mitigate vulnerabilities before they can be exploited by malicious actors. Ethical hacking commonly referred to as white-hat hacking, consists of authorized and controlled attempts to evaluate the security of systems, networks, and applications by mimicking the tactics, techniques, and procedures used by real attackers. Penetration testing (pen-testing) is a structured and systematic implementation of ethical hacking, wherein simulated cyberattacks are conducted to measure the effectiveness of existing security controls. (Anandh, 2025)

Together, ethical hacking and penetration testing provide organizations with a realistic understanding of their security posture. These practices support risk management, regulatory compliance, and data protection by uncovering weaknesses that may otherwise remain undetected. This chapter presents a comprehensive overview of ethical hacking methodologies, outlining its key phases, commonly used tools, and practical significance in strengthening modern cyber security defences.

Ethical Hacking

Ethical hacking is the systematic and legally authorized process of evaluating the security of information systems by identifying and exploiting vulnerabilities under controlled conditions. Unlike malicious attackers, ethical hackers operate within defined legal agreements, scopes, and rules of engagement. Their objective is not to cause damage, but to expose security weaknesses and provide actionable recommendations to enhance system resilience.

By adopting an attacker's perspective, ethical hackers help organizations understand how vulnerabilities can be chained together to compromise confidentiality, integrity, and availability. The ethical hacking process typically follows a well-defined lifecycle, as described below.

Key Phases of Ethical Hacking:

1. Reconnaissance (Foot printing)

Reconnaissance is the initial phase of ethical hacking, focused on gathering information about the target environment. This phase aims to build an external view of the system, similar to what an attacker would observe prior to launching an attack. Reconnaissance can be categorized into two types:

a. **Passive Reconnaissance:** Information is collected without directly interacting with the target system. This includes data obtained from publicly available sources such as WHOIS databases, domain records, social media platforms, technical forums, and organizational job postings that may disclose technology stacks or infrastructure details.
b. **Active Reconnaissance:** The target is directly engaged using network-level techniques such as ping sweeps, traceroute, DNS enumeration, and packet analysis to identify live hosts, IP ranges, and network architecture.

Purpose: To identify potential attack vectors and establish a foundation for further analysis.

2. Scanning

Scanning involves active probing of the target systems to identify open ports, services, and known vulnerabilities. This phase relies on both automated tools and manual validation techniques. Key scanning activities include:

a. **Port Scanning:** Identifying open ports and associated services using tools like Nmap.
b. **Vulnerability Scanning:** Detecting known flaws in services using scanners like Nessus, OpenVAS, or Nikto.
c. **Network Scanning:** Mapping out live hosts and their operating systems.

d. **Enumeration:** Extracting more detailed information like user accounts, network shares, or service banners.

Purpose: Understand what systems and services are running and where weaknesses might lie.

3. Gaining Access

Here, the ethical hacker attempts to exploit identified vulnerabilities to gain control over the target system. Techniques may include:

a. **Exploiting software bugs** (e.g., buffer overflows, unpatched CVEs),
b. **Password cracking or credential reuse**, or
c. **Injection attacks** (e.g., SQL, command, or LDAP injection).

Purpose: Demonstrate the impact of vulnerabilities by simulating how an attacker could breach the system.

4. Maintaining Access

Once access is gained, the goal is to determine whether an attacker could stay inside the system undetected. This includes:

a. **Installing backdoors** or rootkits,
b. **Privilege escalation** to gain administrative rights,
c. **Persistence mechanisms**, such as registry changes or scheduled tasks.

Purpose: Assess how resilient the system is against prolonged unauthorized access and what damage could be done over time.

5. Clearing Tracks (Simulated)

Ethical hackers simulate how a real attacker would cover their tracks to avoid detection. Although actual data erasure is avoided, this may include:

a. **Deleting logs** or history,
b. **Disabling monitoring tools**, and
c. Altering timestamps.

Purpose: Show how attackers can remain stealthy and evaluate the effectiveness of existing forensic and logging mechanisms.

6. Reporting

The final and most critical phase involves creating a comprehensive report. This should include:

a. An **executive summary** for non-technical stakeholders,
b. A **technical breakdown** of each vulnerability,
c. **Proof-of-concept** screenshots or output,
d. **Risk ratings** (based on CVSS or internal risk matrices),
e. **Remediation recommendations** to fix or mitigate each issue.

Purpose: Translate technical findings into actionable steps to improve security posture. (Jamil & Khan, 2011)

Importance of Ethical Hacking in the Real-Time World

In today's hyper-connected digital environment, cyber threats are increasingly persistent and sophisticated. Ethical hacking plays a crucial role in proactively identifying security vulnerabilities before they are exploited. By simulating real-world attack techniques, ethical hackers help strengthen an organization's cybersecurity posture and prevent data breaches caused by issues such as outdated software, weak credentials, insecure APIs, and system misconfigurations. This proactive approach protects sensitive data, including personal, financial, and health information, while reducing legal and reputational risks. Ethical hacking is also essential for safeguarding critical national infrastructure, including energy, transportation, and healthcare systems that rely on ICS, SCADA, and IoT technologies. Furthermore, by identifying and mitigating security gaps that could disrupt operations, ethical hacking supports business continuity, minimizes downtime, and helps ensure reliable service delivery in the face of evolving cyber threats. (Yaacoub et al., 2023)

Recent Cybersecurity Statistics Highlighting the Need for Ethical Hacking

Recent industry reports highlight the growing severity of cyber threats in real-time environments. According to the *IBM Cost of a Data Breach Report (2023)*, the global average cost of a data breach reached USD 4.45 million, representing a 15% increase over the past three years. The same report notes that over 80% of breaches involved compromised credentials, misconfigurations, or unpatched vulnerabilities, many of which could be identified through proactive ethical hacking and penetration testing. Additionally, *Verizon's Data Breach Investigations Report (DBIR, 2024)* indicates that phishing and social engineering attacks accounted for more than 74% of breaches involving human interaction, emphasizing the importance of security assessments that include social engineering simulations. These statistics underscore the critical role of ethical hacking in identifying vulnerabilities before they result in significant financial and operational damage. (Susan Li et al., 2025)

ETHICAL HACKING AND PENETRATION TESTING: A SYMBIOTIC RELATIONSHIP

While ethical hacking is a broad discipline, penetration testing (pen testing) is a focused technique within it.

What is Penetration Testing?

Penetration testing is a simulated cyberattack against a system, network, or web application to evaluate its security. The objective is to discover vulnerabilities that could be exploited in a real attack. It typically follows a structured methodology and results in an actionable report that outlines:

How Ethical Hacking and Pen Testing Complement Each Other

Table 1. Ethical Hacking and Pen Testing Comparison

Ethical Hacking	Penetration Testing
Broader scope and approach	Narrower, focused security evaluation
Includes social engineering, OSINT	Typically targets technical flaws
Long-term process or ongoing engagement	Often done periodically or annually
Can be strategic (e.g., red teaming)	Tactical and operational in nature

Ethical hackers use penetration testing as one of their primary tools to assess system resilience. Conversely, every penetration test is a product of ethical hacking principles: it's authorized, legal, and designed to improve—not damage—security.

Real-World Example: How Ethical Hacking and Pen Testing Prevent Attacks

Consider a financial services company that handles millions of daily transactions. Ethical hackers conduct:

- **External Pen Test** – Simulate attacks from outsiders to test firewall and application layer defenses.
- **Internal Pen Test** – Mimic an insider threat or compromised employee device.
- **Social Engineering Assessment** – Send phishing emails to employees to test awareness.
- **Cloud Configuration Review** – Analyze misconfigured S3 buckets or IAM policies in AWS.

Real-World Case Study: The Colonial Pipeline Ransomware Attack

A prominent real-world example highlighting the importance of ethical hacking and penetration testing is the Colonial Pipeline ransomware attack in 2021. Colonial Pipeline, which supplies nearly 45% of the fuel to the eastern United States, was forced to shut down operations after attackers exploited weak network security and inadequate segmentation. Post-incident investigations revealed that vulnerabilities related to credential management and monitoring could have been identified through regular penetration testing and ethical hacking exercises. The attack resulted in fuel shortages, economic disruption, and significant financial losses, emphasizing how proactive security testing is essential for protecting critical infrastructure and national security.

The result: They find an exposed admin panel, insecure API endpoints, and several employees vulnerable to phishing. After patching and training, the organization is significantly more secure reducing the risk of financial loss, reputation damage, or regulatory fines. (S. Patil et al., 2017)

Penetration Testing

Penetration testing, or pen testing, is a controlled cyberattack simulation performed to evaluate the security of a system, network, or application. It's designed to uncover vulnerabilities, validate defenses, and recommend mitigation strategies before real attackers exploit them.

The OWASP Testing Guide is a comprehensive resource for assessing the security of web applications, providing methodologies and best practices for identifying and mitigating vulnerabilities. NIST SP 800- 115 offers a general framework for technical security assessments of information systems, outlining procedures for planning and conducting penetration tests and vulnerability assessments. The Penetration Testing Execution Standard (PTES) complements these by offering a detailed approach to conducting penetration tests, covering everything from pre- engagement interactions to post-testing reporting, ensuring consistency and thoroughness in security evaluations.

Figure 1. Phases of Penetration Testing

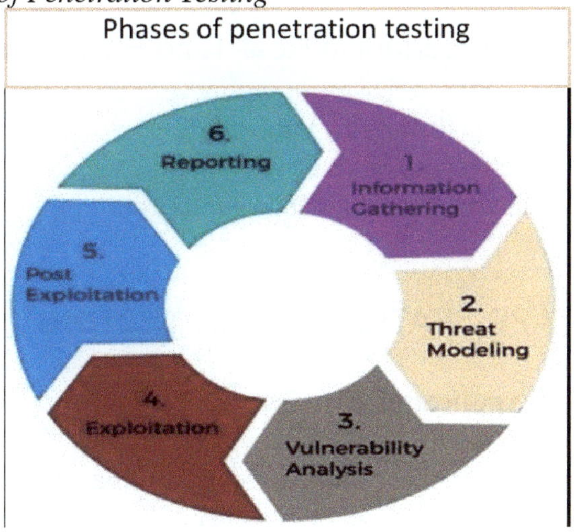

Phases of Penetration Testing

1. **Reconnaissance (Information Gathering)**

Identify the target system, services, IP ranges, domains, and technologies used.

2. **Scanning s Enumeration**

Scan for open ports, services, and vulnerabilities using tools like Nmap, Nikto, or Nessus.

3. **Exploitation**

Attempt to exploit discovered vulnerabilities (e.g., SQL injection, remote code execution).

4. **Post-Exploitation**

Maintain access, extract data, escalate privileges, or test lateral movement.

5. **Reporting**

Document vulnerabilities, provide proof-of-concept, impact analysis, and fix recommended

Why Pen Testing is Important in Real-Time Environments

- Identifies unknown and zero-day vulnerabilities
- Validates the effectiveness of security controls
- Prepares organizations for compliance audits

REAL-WORLD APPLICATION OF PEN TESTING

- **Scenario: Web Application Pen Test**

A retail company hires ethical hackers to perform penetration testing on its e-commerce site.

- **Tools Used**: Burp Suite, OWASP ZAP, SQLmap, Nikto
- **Findings**:
    - o SQL injection in the product search API
    - o Cross-site scripting (XSS) in the feedback form
    - o Outdated WordPress plugins
- **Results**: Vulnerabilities were patched, and WAF (Web Application Firewall) was deployed.

Figure 2. Pen Testing

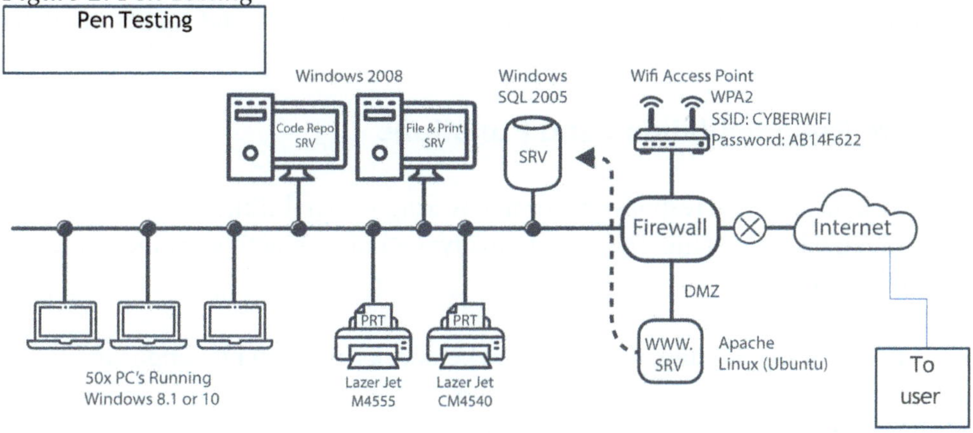

THE ROLE OF ETHICAL HACKERS IN CYBER SECURITY

As the digital world continues to expand, so too does the complexity of securing it. From financial systems and government databases to healthcare records and cloud platforms, organizations depend on robust cyber security to protect sensitive data and ensure uninterrupted operations. In response to the ever- evolving threat landscape, ethical hackers—also known as white-hat hackers—have emerged as vital players in the fight against cybercrime.

1. Who Are Ethical Hackers?

Ethical hackers are trained cyber security experts who simulate real-world cyberattacks under legal and controlled conditions. Unlike black-hat hackers, who aim to steal, destroy, or extort, ethical hackers are authorized by organizations to test their systems. Their mission is to uncover weaknesses that attackers could use to infiltrate, manipulate, or disable critical digital infrastructure. Ethical hackers conduct these evaluations based on agreed-upon rules of engagement and within a defined scope to ensure legal and ethical compliance.

These professionals often hold certifications such as:

- **Certified Ethical Hacker (CEH)**
- **Offensive Security Certified Professional (OSCP)**
- **GIAC Penetration Tester (GPEN)**

Their expertise includes deep technical knowledge of operating systems, networking, programming, system architecture, and the tools and tactics used by cybercriminals.

2. Core Responsibilities and Functions

Ethical hackers are responsible for uncovering vulnerabilities across an organization's digital ecosystem. Their work involves a range of activities, including but not limited to:

- **Penetration Testing**: Simulated cyberattacks on systems, applications, or networks.
- **Social Engineering Testing**: Including phishing and pretexting to test human weaknesses.
- **Wireless Network Testing**: Checking for insecure Wi-Fi configurations or rogue access points.
- **Web Application Testing**: Detecting issues such as SQL injection and cross-site scripting (XSS).
- **Infrastructure Testing**: Assessing servers, databases, APIs, and endpoints.
- **Denial-of-Service (DoS) Testing**: Simulating attacks to evaluate system resilience under overload.

These tests help organizations patch their systems, train employees, and develop stronger security policies and incident response plans.

3. Mitigating Major Cyber Threats

Ethical hackers play a central role in identifying and helping organizations defend against some of the most common and damaging cyber-attacks, including phishing, SQL injection, and denial-of-service (DoS) attacks.

a) **Phishing Attacks: Phishing** is a social engineering attack that tricks individuals into revealing sensitive information, such as login credentials, credit card numbers, or confidential data. These attacks often come in the form of deceptive emails or malicious websites designed to look legitimate.

Ethical hackers simulate phishing campaigns to evaluate how well employees can detect and respond to such threats. For example:

- They may send test emails that mimicrealphishing messages.

- They record click-through rates, credential submissions, or downloads.
- They provide reports that identify vulnerable users.

Based on their findings, ethical hackers work with organizations to improve security awareness training, implement email filtering technologies, and enforce multi- factor authentication (MFA) to mitigate damage from compromised credentials.

b) **S L Injection (S Li): SQL injection** is a code injection technique that exploits vulnerabilities in database- driven applications. When input fields are not properly sanitized, attackers can manipulate SQL queries to:
    - Access unauthorized data (e.g., user records)
    - Modify or delete database content
    - Gain administrative access to backend systems

Ethical hackers detect SQL injection vulnerabilities through penetration tests that involve submitting various payloads (malicious inputs) into forms, URLs, or API requests. For example:

Sql:

' OR '1'='1'; --

This classic SQLi payload can trick an insecure login form into bypassing authentication. Once a vulnerability is confirmed, ethical hackers recommend secure coding practices like:

- Using **parameterized queries** or **prepared statements**
- Implementing **input validation** and **output encoding**
- Applying **least privilege** access control database users

b) **Denialof Service(DoS) Attacks:** A **Denial of Service** attack aims to overwhelm a system, network, or server with excessive requests or traffic, making it inaccessible to legitimate users. In distributed versions (DDoS), the attack is launched from multiple sources simultaneously, often using botnets.

Ethical hackers conduct DoS simulations under controlled environments to test system resilience. These include:

- Stress testing servers and applications to determine breaking points
- Analyzing load balancer configurations and firewall rule effectiveness
- Evaluating rate-limiting, failover systems, and cloud auto-scaling

The results inform the organization on how to:

- Optimize performance under stress
- Implement DDoS protection solutions (e.g., Cloudflare, AWS Shield)
- Improve uptime through redundancy and traffic filtering

4. Strategic and Business Value

Beyond technical analysis, ethical hackers offer strategic cybersecurity insights to support business continuity, brand reputation, and regulatory compliance.

1. They assist organizations in passing audits required by standards such as PCI-DSS, ISO/IEC 27001, HIPAA, and GDPR.
2. They help develop cyber resilience plans, ensuring that the business can withstand and recover from attacks.
3. They reduce the cost of cyber incidents by proactively identifying issues before attackers exploit them.

Ethical hackers also collaborate with development and operations teams to integrate security into the software development lifecycle (SDLC)—an approach known as DevSecOps.

Cyberattacks continue to disproportionately affect critical sectors. The World Economic Forum Global Cybersecurity Outlook (2024) reports that healthcare and financial services remain the most targeted industries, with ransomware attacks increasing by over 30% year-on-year. Ethical hackers help organizations in these sectors identify high-risk assets, assess incident readiness, and implement resilient security architectures that reduce downtime and financial exposure.

5. The Human Factor and Culture Change

No matter how secure a system may be, the human element is often the weakest link. Ethical hackers address this by:

Simulating phishing and pretexting attacks Testing password hygiene

Evaluating physical security (e.g., badge access, tailgating)

The insights they provide help shape a culture of security awareness, turning every employee into a potential line of defense. (P. P. a. P. J. V. Kumawat, 2021)

SKILLS AND EXPERTISE REQUIRED FOR ETHICAL HACKERS:

The role of an ethical hacker is both technically demanding and strategically critical. It requires a unique blend of deep technical proficiency, analytical thinking, creativity, and ethical responsibility. Unlike general IT professionals, ethical hackers must think like adversaries while working under strict legal and organizational frameworks. Below is an exploration of the essential skills, tools, and expertise that define a competent and professional ethical hacker.

1. Strong Knowledge of Operating Systems

Ethical hackers must be proficient with multiple operating systems, especially those commonly targeted by attackers:

- **Linux/Unix**: Understanding file systems, kernel modules, user privilege management, and shell scripting (Bash, Python).
- **Windows OS**: Familiarity with Windows registry, Active Directory, PowerShell, and user access control (UAC).
- **MacOS s Mobile OS**: For specialized roles, knowledge of iOS, Android, and embedded system OSes is essential.

Example Skill: Writing shell scripts to automate log analysis or privilege escalation checks.

1.1Networking Fundamentals and Protocols

A deep understanding of how networks operate is critical to identifying and exploiting weaknesses in communication systems:

- **TCP/IP, UDP, ICMP protocols**
- **DHCP, DNS, FTP, SSH, HTTP/HTTPS**
- **Firewall, VPN, and proxy behaviors**
- **Packet analysis and sniffing** (using tools like Wireshark or tcpdump)

Example Skill: Using Wireshark to detect insecure transmissions or unauthorized port activity.

1.2 Proficiency in Programming and Scripting Languages

Programming skills are fundamental for identifying vulnerabilities, writing custom exploits, or automating tasks:

- **Python**: Widely used for scripting tools and automation.
- **JavaScript**: Critical for testing web-based vulnerabilities like XSS.
- **SQL**: Needed to understand and exploit SQL injection vulnerabilities.
- **C/C++**: For reverse engineering and exploit development.
- **HTML/CSS/PHP**: Useful for web app testing.

Example Skill: Writing a Python script to automate directory brute-forcing or fuzzing inputs.

1.3 Web Application Security Expertise

With the rise of web-based platforms, ethical hackers must master:

1.4 OWASP Top 10 vulnerabilities (SQLi, XSS, CSRF, etc.)

1.5 API and input validation issues

Tools: Burp Suite, OWASP ZAP, Nikto, SQLMap.
Example Skill: Using Burp Suite to intercept and modify HTTP requests to test for input validation issues.

2. Familiarity with Penetration Testing Tools

Hands-on experience with industry-standard tools is a must:

- **Nmap**: For port scanning and network mapping.
- **Metasploit**: For exploit development and payload execution.
- **Kali Linux**: A penetration testing distribution containing hundreds of tools.
- **Hydra/John the Ripper**: For password cracking and brute force attacks.
- **Nessus/OpenVAS**: For vulnerability scanning.

Example Skill: Using Meta sploit to simulate an SMB vulnerability exploit on an internal network.

3. Cloud and Virtualization Security

As organizations migrate to cloud platforms, ethical hackers must adapt:

- **Understanding AWS, Azure, and GCP security models**
- **Testing for cloud misconfigurations (e.g., open S3 buckets)**
- **Knowledge of container security (e.g., Docker, Kubernetes)**

Example Skill: Identifying privilege escalation paths in AWS IAM policies or misconfigured firewall rules.

According to Gartner (2023), over 99% of cloud security failures are expected to be caused by customer misconfigurations, reinforcing the need for ethical hackers skilled in cloud security testing and configuration assessments.

4. Reverse Engineering and Malware Analysis (Advanced Skill)

Some ethical hackers specialize in:

- **Analyzing malware behavior**
- **Reverse engineering binary code**
- **Understanding assembly language (x86/x64)**

Example Skill: Using tools like Ghidra or IDA Pro to deconstruct malware samples.

5. Social Engineering Tactics

Technical security is only part of the equation—humans are often the weakest link. Ethical hackers should understand:

- **Phishing campaigns**
- **Pretexting and baiting**
- **Physical penetration testing**

Example Skill: Creating a mock phishing email to test employee awareness and reporting behavior.

6. Soft Skills and Professional Attributes

In addition to technical expertise, ethical hackers must demonstrate:

- **Critical Thinking**: Ability to think like an attacker while understanding business impact.
- **Communication**: Writing clear, actionable reports for technical and non-technical audiences.
- **Confidentiality**: Handling sensitive data responsibly.
- **Ethical Judgement**: Making decisions within legal and moral boundaries.
- **Attention to Detail: Small** flaws often lead to major exploits.

Example Scenario: Explaining a SQL injection vulnerability and its fix to a non- technical manager during a post-test briefing.

7.Certifications and Continuous Learning

Because cyber threats constantly evolve, ethical hackers must commit to lifelong learning. Industry- recognized certifications help validate skills:

- **Certified Ethical Hacker (CEH)** – Entryto mid-level; covers fundamentals and tools.
- **OSCP (Offensive Security Certified Professional)** – Hands-on certification focusing on real-world attack simulations.
- **CompTIA Security+**, **CISSP**, **GPEN**, and **eLearnSecurity** credentials.

Platforms like Hack The Box, TryHackMe, and CTF challenges are also essential for continuous skill development. (Jamil & Khan, 2011)

PENETRATION TESTING METHODOLOGIES:

Penetration testing (or pen testing) is a simulated cyberattack used to evaluate the security posture of systems, networks, applications, or organizational infrastructure. Its purpose is to discover vulnerabilities that attackers could exploit and to test how effective current defenses are against real-world threats. However, to ensure accuracy, repeatability, legality, and thoroughness, penetration testing must follow established methodologies—structured approaches that outline each phase of the test from planning to report. There are multiple industry-recognized methodologies, each designed for different scopes, such as networks, applications, or organizational security. These methodologies provide ethical hackers and security professionals with a framework to systematically identify and exploit vulnerabilities; all while maintaining ethical and legal standards.

1. Pre-Engagement and Planning

Before any technical activity begins, a detailed planning phase is essential. During pre- engagement:

- The scope of the test is defined (e.g., which systems, networks, or applications will be tested).
- Objectives are established, such as identifying entry points, testing internal segmentation, or evaluating incident response.
- Rules of engagement are agreed upon, specifying acceptable tools, time windows, and boundaries.
- Legal documents like Non-Disclosure Agreements (NDAs) and Authorization to Test are signed.

This phase ensures that all activities are authorized, the client understands the process, and the testers avoid causing unintentional damage or disruption.

2. Information Gathering (Reconnaissance)

This phase, often called reconnaissance, involves collecting as much information as possible about the target using both passive and active techniques.

- **Passive Recon**: Gathering data without interacting with the target. This may include WHOIS lookups, DNS enumeration, social media analysis, and publicly available metadata.
- **Active Recon**: Involves direct interaction with the target—scanning IP addresses, probing ports, and enumerating services using tools like Nmap, Netcat, or Shodan.

Effective reconnaissance helps ethical hackers build a profile of the target and identify potential vulnerabilities or misconfigurations before launching more intrusive activities.

3. Scanning and Enumeration

This phase deepens the technical understanding of the target by identifying open ports, services, operating systems, and software versions.

- **Port scanning** helps identify network services that may be exposed (e.g., SSH on port 22, HTTP on 80).

- **Service enumeration** involves identifying software types and versions, which can then be cross-referenced against known vulnerabilities.
- Tools like Nmap, Nikto, DirBuster, and OpenVAS are commonly used.

This step lays the groundwork for selecting appropriate exploitation strategies based on known weaknesses. (Kathe & Lotankar, 2020)

4. Exploitation

This is the most critical and active phase of penetration testing, where ethical hackers attempt to exploit the identified vulnerabilities. The goal is to gain unauthorized access, escalate privileges, or extract sensitive data in a controlled and safe manner.

Examples include:

- **Exploiting SQL injection** in awebform to access backend data.
- **Gaining shell access** to a server through outdated software or poor configurations.
- **Cracking weak credentials** or exploiting default passwords.

Tools like Metasploit, SQLMap, and Burp Suite play a major role here. The success of this phase demonstrates the real-world risk of the vulnerabilities discovered.

5. Post-Exploitation

Once access has been gained, ethical hackers assess:

- The value of the compromised system.
- Whether the access can be maintained (persistence).
- If privilege escalation is possible.
- The potential for lateral movement to other systems.

This step is vital for understanding the impact of an exploit, not just its existence. It also simulates what an attacker could do if they successfully breached a system.

6. Reporting and Remediation Guidance

Perhaps the most important part of a penetration test is the final report. Ethical hackers document:

- All discovered vulnerabilities.

- Proof-of-concept for each exploit.
- Screenshots, logs, and evidence of access.
- Recommendations for fixing each issue.

The report is typically divided into technical and executive summaries to cater to both IT/security teams and business decision-makers. It guides remediation by prioritizing risks based on severity and potential impact. (Kathe & Lotankar, 2020)

POPULAR PENETRATION TESTING METHODOLOGIES

Several recognized frameworks guide the entire process:

- **OSSTMM** (Open Source Security Testing Methodology Manual): A comprehensive framework that covers human, physical, and wireless factors.
- **OWASP Testing Guide**: Focused on web application security, especially the OWASP Top 10.
- **PTES** (Penetration Testing Execution Standard): Widely adopted for structured pen testing, including technical and non-technical steps.
- **NIST SP 800-115**: A U.S. government standard for testing federal systems, useful for regulatory-driven environments.

Each methodology emphasizes documentation, risk assessment, and ethical conduct, ensuring that tests are reproducible, measurable, and business-aligned. (Suresh, 2023)

PHASES OF PENETRATION TESTING: A COMPREHENSIVE BREAKDOWN

Penetration testing, often referred to as ethical hacking, is a structured process used to assess the security of systems, applications, and networks by simulating the actions of malicious attackers. This process is conducted in clearly defined phases, each serving a specific purpose to ensure thoroughness, repeatability, and measurable risk assessment. These phases allow cybersecurity professionals to analyze, exploit, and ultimately help fix vulnerabilities before malicious actors can take advantage of them. The major phases of penetration testing include Reconnaissance, Scanning, Exploitation, Post- Exploitation, and Reporting. Below is a detailed exploration of each phase.

1. Reconnaissance (Information Gathering)

Objective: To collect as much information as possible about the target system or network, without actively interacting with it (passive) or through direct interaction (active).

a) Passive Reconnaissance
   - Involves collecting data without engaging directly with the target.
   - Sources include: WHOIS databases, DNS records, search engines, public databases, leaked data breaches, LinkedIn profiles, job listings, social media, and metadata from public documents.
   - Tools: Maltego, Recon-ng, Google Dorks.

b) Active Reconnaissance
   - Directinteraction with the target systems to gather technical data.
   - Techniques include: ping sweeps, port probing, and banner grabbing.
   - Tools: Nmap, Netcat, Shodan.

Value: This phase provides a comprehensive map of the target's digital footprint and helps form hypotheses about potential weaknesses. Reconnaissance lays the foundation for more targeted testing in the next phase.

2. Scanning and Enumeration

Objective: To detect live systems, open ports, services running on those ports, and to enumerate further details such as user accounts, shares, and software versions.

Port Scanning

- Identifies open, closed, and filtered ports using tools like:

  a) **Nmap** (most popular)
  b) **Unicornscan**
  c) **Masscan** (for high-speed scanning)

Service Enumeration

- Identifies theservices and software running on open ports, including their version numbers.
- Example: Detecting an outdated Apache HTTP server vulnerable to known exploits.

OS Fingerprinting and Vulnerability Scanning

- OS detection via TCP/IP stack behavior.
- Tools like Nmap, OpenVAS, Nessus, and Nikto help identify known vulnerabilities.

Value: This phase transforms raw data into actionable intelligence. The attacker now knows where to focus their exploitation attempts.

3. Exploitation

Objective: To actively exploit discovered vulnerabilities in order to gain unauthorized access, elevate privileges, or compromise the system.

This is the **corephase** of penetration testing, where theoretical risks are proven practically.

a) Common Exploitation Techniques
    - **SQL Injection (SQLi)**: Manipulating input fields to execute unauthorized SQL commands.
    - **Cross-Site Scripting (XSS)**: Injecting malicious scripts into web applications.
    - **Command Injection**: Executing arbitrary commands on the host.
    - **Buffer Overflow**: Overwriting memory to executes hellcode.
    - **Authentication Bypass**: Exploiting poor credential checks or default passwords.

b) Tools
    - **Metasploit Framework**: A powerful suite for launching and managing exploits.
    - **SQLMap**: Automates detection and exploitation of SQLi.
    - **Burp Suite**: For manipulating web requests and exploiting web app vulnerabilities.
    - **Hydra**: For brute-force attacks on login services.

c) Controlled Exploitation
    - Ethical hackers avoid causing damage or data loss.
    - All action are logged for analysis and reporting.

Value: This phase validates whether identified vulnerabilities are exploitable and what an attacker could achieve if the system were compromised.

4. Post-Exploitation

Objective: To assess the impact of a successful breach, maintain access (if required), and simulate further attacker behavior like data exfiltration or lateral movement.

a) Privilege Escalation
  - Attempting to move from limited user privileges to administrative or root access.
  - Techniques: exploiting kernel vulnerabilities, misconfigured Sudo rules, token impersonation.

b) Data Access and Exfiltration
  - Checking for access to sensitive data: databases, config files, emails, credentials.
  - Simulating data theft using secure or covert channels.

c) Persistence Mechanisms
  - Installing backdoors, creating user accounts, modifying startup services.
  - Only simulated in ethical hacking (never left behind in real assessments).

d) Lateral Movement
  - Exploring whether the attacker can pivot to other systems on the network.
  - Often uses tools like Mimikatz, Bloodhounds, or PsExec.

Value: This phase shows the potential business impact of a successful attack. It's critical in assessing the organization's incident detection and response capabilities.

5. Reporting

Objective: To document findings, explain the testing process, and provide actionable recommendations in both technical and business-friendly language.

a) Contents of a Good Report
  - **Executive Summary**: High-level overview of findings for non-technical stakeholders.
  - **Technical Details**: Step-by-step breakdown of each vulnerability, with severity ratings.
  - **Proof of Concept (PoC)**: Screenshots, commands, logs demonstrating successful exploits.
  - **Remediation Guidance**: Clear, prioritized instructions for fixing each issue.

b) Risk Rating Systems
  - Many reports use scoring frameworks such as:

- **CVSS (Common Vulnerability Scoring System)**
- Custom severity matrices based on impact and likelihood.

c) Debriefing and Feedback
- Final presentation or meeting with stakeholders.
- Discuss findings, answer questions, and review lessons learned.

Value: The report translates technical findings into business risk. It helps organizations fix vulnerabilities and improve their overall security posture. (Diogo Ribeiro et al., 2025)

TOOLS AND TECHNIQUES FOR ETHICAL HACKING AND PENETRATION TESTING:

Ethical hacking and penetration testing are structured activities that assess the security of an organization by simulating cyberattacks. Throughout the testing process, penetration testers (ethical hackers) employ a wide array of specialized tools and techniques. These tools help identify vulnerabilities, analyze network traffic, exploit weaknesses, and test system resilience. In this section, we explore the most used tools and techniques in penetration testing across five main phases: Reconnaissance, Scanning, Exploitation, Post-Exploitation, and Reporting.

1. Reconnaissance Phase (Information Gathering)

Reconnaissance is the first and one of the most critical phases of penetration testing. It involves collecting as much information as possible about the target to identify potential attack vectors.

Tools for Reconnaissance:

- **Maltego**: A powerful tool for mapping out relationships between various entities, such as IP addresses, domains, and social networks.
- **Recon-ng**: A reconnaissance framework that allows you to automate the collection of data from a variety of public sources.
- **Whois**: A tool to get domain registration details, including information about the registrar, creation date, and domain owner.
- **Shodan**: A search engine that allows hackers to find exposed IoT devices and unsecured databases by scanning the internet for publicly available data.

  Techniques for Reconnaissance:
  - **Passive Reconnaissance**: Gathering information from public sources such as domain names, IP ranges, WHOIS information,

and social media platforms. The goal is to remain undetected while obtaining useful data.

- **Active Reconnaissance**: This involves directly engaging with the target, such as pinging servers or scanning open ports. This phase provides more detailed information but may alert the target. (Rodríguez Llerena, 2020)

2. Scanning and Enumeration Phase

Once basic information has been collected, the next step is to scan the target network or system to identify open ports, services, vulnerabilities, and potential points of entry. Tools for Scanning and Enumeration:

- **Nmap**: One of the most widely used tools for network discovery. It helps to identify open ports, services, and even the operating system of the target. Nmap also provides OS fingerprinting and version scanning.
- **Nikto**: A web server scanner that detects vulnerabilities like outdated software versions, insecure configurations, and common security flaws.
- **OpenVAS**: An open-source vulnerability scanner that identifies potential vulnerabilities within networks and systems OpenVAS is useful for comprehensive scanning.
- **Netcat**: Known as the "Swiss Army Knife" of networking, Netcat is used for banner grabbing, transferring files, and creating reverse shells.
- **Burp Suite**: Used extensively for web application scanning, this tool helps identify webvulnerabilities such as SQLInjection, Cross-Site Scripting (XSS), and more.

Techniques for Scanning and Enumeration:

- **Port Scanning**: Identifying open ports and services on a target system. This is typically done using Nmap and other similar tools.
- **Vulnerability Scanning**: Tools like OpenVAS and Nessus scan for known vulnerabilities in systems and software versions.
- **Service Enumeration**: Identifying specific services running on open ports and gathering version information to check for known vulnerabilities. (Seara & Serrão, 2024)

Exploitation Phase:

Once vulnerabilities have been identified, the next step is exploitation. In this phase, penetration testers attempt to exploit vulnerabilities to gain unauthorized access to systems, networks, or applications.

Tools for Exploitation:

- **Metasploit**: One of the most widely used exploitation frameworks. It provides ready- made exploits for various vulnerabilities, helping penetration testers execute attacks like remote code execution or privilege escalation.
- **SQLMap**: An open-source tool designed to automate the process of detecting and exploiting SQL injection vulnerabilities in web applications.
- **Hydra**: A popular tool for conducting brute-force attacks on network services such as SSH, HTTP, FTP, and more.
- **Empire**: A post-exploitation tool that is used to execute PowerShell-based attacks and manage compromised machines.
- **John the Ripper**: A password cracking tool used to crack password hashes, commonly employed to test the strength of user credentials.

Techniques for Exploitation:

- **Buffer Overflow**: Exploiting a vulnerability in software that occurs when more data is written to a block of memory than it can hold, potentially allowing an attacker to execute arbitrary code.
- **Privilege Escalation**: Gaining elevated access to a system by exploiting weak configurations or unpatched vulnerabilities. Common techniques include exploiting kernel vulnerabilities or poor user permission configurations.
- **SQL Injection**: Inserting malicious SQL queries into input fields, allowing an attacker to access sensitive data from the database.

3. Post-Exploitation Phase

The post-exploitation phase begins once a penetration tester has successfully gained access to the system. In this phase, the focus shifts to maintaining control, exploring lateral movement, and assessing the depth of compromise.

Tools for Post-Exploitation:

- **Mimikatz**: A tool used to extract passwords, hash dumps, and Kerberos tickets from Windows memory. It's crucial for post-exploitation activities like credential theft.
- **BloodHound**: A tool that helps penetration testers map Active Directory environments, identify attack paths, and escalate privileges.

- **Cobalt Strike**: A widely used post-exploitation tool that allows attackers to execute commands on a compromised machine, move laterally, and establish persistent backdoors.

Techniques for Post-Exploitation

- **Lateral Movement**: After gaining access to one system, the tester attempts to move through the network to compromise other systems and gain additional control.
- **Data Exfiltration**: Extracting sensitive data from the compromised system, such as documents, databases, or user credentials, to simulate the potential impact of a real attack.
- **Persistence**: Installing backdoors or modifying system settings to maintain access to the system even after a reboot or system recovery.

4. Reporting Phase

The final phase of penetration testing involves documenting the findings and providing a detailed report to the client. The report highlights vulnerabilities, their impact, and recommendations for remediation.

Tools for Reporting:

- **Dradis**: A collaboration and reporting tool that integrates with popular penetration testing tools like Nmap, Metasploit, and Burp Suite. It helps streamline report creation.
- **Faraday**: An integrated penetration testing environment that supports collaboration and report generation for team-based security testing.
- **KeepNote**: A note-taking tool that allows testers to organize information collected during the test and helps in generating reports.

Techniques for Reporting:

- **Risk Assessment**: The report includes an assessment of the risks associated with each vulnerability discovered, including a prioritization of which vulnerabilities need to be addressed first.
- **Proof of Concept (PoC)**: A section that demonstrates how a specific vulnerability was exploited, often including screenshots, logs, or code to back up claims.
- **Remediation Recommendations**: For each identified vulnerability, ethical hackers provide guidance on how to fix the issue, which may include patch-

ing software, improving system configurations, or changing access controls. (Rayhan, 2024)

Techniques in Penetration Testing:

Penetration testing (pen testing) is a simulated cyberattack conducted by ethical hackers to identify and assess vulnerabilities within systems, networks, or applications. These vulnerabilities, if left unchecked, could be exploited by malicious hackers. Pen testers employ various techniques to conduct these tests, using tools, manual methods, and strategies to uncover weak points and assess how well a system can withstand an attack.

1. Social Engineering

Social engineering is one of the oldest and most effective techniques used by attackers to manipulate individuals into divulging confidential information. Rather than exploiting technical vulnerabilities, social engineering attacks relyon human psychologyto gain access to systems and sensitive data.

Strengths:

- Highly effective in real-world attacks
- Exposes human and procedural weaknesses

Limitations:

- Ethical and legal constraints
- Results vary based on user behavior

2. Brute-Force Attacks

A brute-force attack is a method of cracking passwords or encryption keys by systematically trying every possible combination until the correct one is found. This technique is time- consuming but can be effective when passwords are weak or insufficiently protected.

Strengths:

- Effective against weak passwords
- Simple and automatable

Limitations:

- Ineffective against MFA and rate limiting
- Easily detected by modern security systems

FLOWCHART REPRESENTATION OF PENETRATION TESTING PHASES

Below is a conceptual flowchart outline for the penetration testing phases. Flowchart Outline:

1. **Reconnaissance**
   a. Passive Collection → Public Records (WHOIS, Social Media, DNS)
   b. Active Scanning →Port Scanning (Nmap, Netcat)
   c. Information Mapping → Usingtools (Maltego, Shodan)
2. **Scanning**
   a. Vulnerability Scanning → OpenVAS, Nessus
   b. Service Enumeration → Nmap, Nikto
   c. OS Detection → Nmap (OS Fingerprinting)
3. **Exploitation**
   a. Exploit Vulnerability→ Metasploit, SQLMap, Hydra
   b. Privilege Escalation →Mimikatz, BloodHound
   c. NetworkAttacks → Exploiting Buffer Overflows
4. **Post-Exploitation**
   a. Data Exfiltration→ Using Cobalt Strike, BloodHound
   b. Lateral Movement→ Mimikatz, Empire
   c. Persistence→ Backdoor Installation
5. **Reporting**
   a. Document Findings →Using Dradis, Faraday
   b. PrioritizeRisks → Risk Assessment, CVSS Scoring
   c. Provide Recommendations → Patching, Configuration Changes

How Social Engineering Works

Phishing: Phishing is a social engineering attack where attackers impersonate a legitimate organization, such as a bank or government agency, to trick individuals into revealing their sensitive information. Attackers might send emails that look authentic, asking the victim to click on a malicious link or download an infected attachment.

Spear Phishing: This is a more targeted form of phishing where the attacker customizes their message to a specific individual or group, making it more difficult to recognize as a threat. The attacker often uses information gathered from social media or public records to make the email seem legitimate.

Pretexting: In pretexting, the attacker fabricates a story or scenario to obtain sensitive information from a victim. For example, an attacker might pretend to be from the IT department, asking an employee to verify login credentials or reset a password.

Baiting: Baiting relies on offering something enticing—such as free software, music, or access to a restricted service—in exchange for user credentials. Often, this comes in the form of malicious USB drives or infected software downloads.

Why Social Engineering is Important: Social engineering is crucial to penetration testing because it tests how well an organization can protect itself from human error. Many security breaches occur due to employees inadvertently disclosing information to an attacker, often without realizing the consequences. Social engineering highlights the importance of training and awareness in preventing such attacks. Ethical hackers use this technique to assess an organization's awareness and response to social engineering attacks. (W. Syafitri et al., 2022)

Vulnerability Scanning: Vulnerability scanning is the process of identifying, categorizing, and prioritizing vulnerabilities within a system or network. This technique is typically automated, using specialized tools that scan systems for known security flaws.

How Vulnerability Scanning Works

- **Automated Tools**: Tools such as **Nessus**, **OpenVAS**, **Qualys**, and **Rapid7** automatically scan systems and networks for vulnerabilities, including unpatched software, open ports, and insecure configurations. These tools use a database of known vulnerabilities to compare against the systems being scanned.
- **Known Vulnerabilities**: Vulnerability scanners check against Common Vulnerability and Exposure (CVE) databases, which contain publicly disclosed vulnerabilities. The goal is to identify weaknesses that hackers might exploit.
- **Risk Assessment**: After identifying vulnerabilities, these scanners also provide a severity score, helping organizations prioritize which vulnerabilities to address first. A CVSS (Common Vulnerability Scoring System) score is typically used to assess the impact and exploitability of a given vulnerability.

Why Vulnerability Scanning is Important:

Regular vulnerability scanning is a fundamental aspect of proactive security management. It helps organizations identify flaws before they can be exploited. By leveraging automated scanning tools, organizations can continuously monitor their infrastructure for new vulnerabilities and patches, ensuring they remain secure over time. (Egbedion, 2024)

How Brute-Force Attacks Work:

- **Password Cracking**: Brute-force tools like **Hydra**, **John the Ripper**, and **Hashcat** try every combination of characters to break a password. These attacks can be particularly effective when the password is weak, such as "password123" or "admin123".
- **Encryption Cracking**: In cases where encryption is used, brute-force tools may attempt to break the encryption by trying all possible keys. This can be done on encrypted files, databases, or even Wi-Fi networks.
- **Rate Limiting and Lockouts**: Many systems implement rate limiting or account lockouts to prevent brute-force attacks, making it difficult for attackers to keep trying combinations. Ethical hackers attempt to exploit such mechanisms to see how resilient a system is to such attacks.

Why Brute-Force Attacks are Important:

Brute-force attacks test the strength of an organization's password policies and encryption methods. Ethical hackers use this technique to evaluate the effectiveness of passwords, encryption schemes, and the system's resilience against exhaustive guesswork. Strong, complex passwords, along with multi- factor authentication, are essential to thwart such attacks. (Roger, 2021)

- **Software Reverse Engineering**: Attackers reverse-engineer software by analyzing executable files, binary code, or source code to identify vulnerabilities. This can help uncover issues such as buffer overflows, unpatched flaws, or hardcoded credentials.
- **Firmware and Hardware Reverse Engineering**: Reverse engineering can also be applied to embedded systems, such as IoT devices, where hardware vulnerabilities might exist. Ethical hackers dissect the firmware to find flaws that could lead to exploits.
- **Disassemblers and Debuggers**: Tools like **IDA Pro**, **OllyDbg**, and **Ghidra** are used to disassemble and debug software, helping hackers gain insight into how the software works and where vulnerabilities may exist.

Why Reverse Engineering is Important:

Reverse engineering is essential for understanding how software and hardware function and for identifying potential vulnerabilities that may not be immediately obvious. This technique is valuable in assessing proprietary systems and detecting flaws that could lead to exploitations, such as backdoors or hidden malware.

- **Proactive Identification of Vulnerabilities**: Ethical hackers simulate real-world attacks, looking for weaknesses in systems, applications, and networks. This allows organizations to identify vulnerabilities before attackers can exploit them. By conducting penetration tests and security assessments, ethical hackers help uncover hidden flaws in systems and applications.
- **Prioritizing Risk**: Ethical hackers assess the severity and potential impact of vulnerabilities. This helps organizations prioritize which vulnerabilities need immediate attention and which can be addressed later. By understanding the risk associated with each vulnerability, businesses can allocate resources effectively and focus on the most critical issues.
- **Remediation and Fixes**: After identifying vulnerabilities, ethical hackers provide detailed recommendations for remediation. These may include patching software, tightening security configurations, or updating authentication protocols. Organizations can then implement these fixes to improve their security posture.
- **Continuous Monitoring and Retesting**: Since vulnerabilities evolve, ethical hackers conduct continuous monitoring and regular penetration tests to identify new risks. Retesting ensures that previously addressed vulnerabilities remain secure and that new vulnerabilities haven't been introduced.

Continuous Improvement in Cybersecurity

Cybersecurity is a dynamic field, and as cybercriminals continuously refine their techniques, vulnerabilities and threats also evolve. Continuous improvement is essential to staying ahead of these evolving threats and ensuring an organization's defenses remain robust over time. (J.-P.A.Yaacoub et al., 2021)

The Need for Continuous Improvement

- **Adapting to Evolving Threats**: As attackers refine their tactics and techniques, it's important to ensure that security defenses evolve as well. New vulnerabilities and attack methods are discovered regularly, making it essential for organizations to stay ahead of the curve.
- **Emerging Technologies**: As businesses adopt new technologies like cloud computing, IoT, and AI, new vulnerabilities and security challenges arise. These technologies often come with unique risks, requiring constant reassessment of security strategies.
- **Learning from Past Breaches**: Continuous improvement involves learning from past incidents and security breaches. By conducting post-breach analy-

sis and examining how attackers gained access, organizations can adjust their strategies to prevent future incidents. (Patterson et al., 2023).

Role of Ethical Hacking in Continuous Improvement

- **Regular Penetration Testing**: Ethical hackers conduct penetration tests at regular intervals to identify new vulnerabilities and test the resilience of security measures. This ongoing assessment ensures that security strategies are continually refined.
- **Up-to-Date Threat Intelligence**: Ethical hackers stay up-to-date with the latest vulnerabilities, exploits, and attack techniques. By leveraging this knowledge, they help organizations adapt to changing threats.
- **Security Awareness Training**: Ethical hackers also assist organizations in training their employees about potential threats, including social engineering and phishing attacks. Educated employees are the first line of defense against cyberattacks. (Prümmer et al., 2024)

Ethical Hacking and Penetration Testing in Cybersecurity

In the rapidly evolving landscape of digital technologies and the increasing reliance on online platforms, cybersecurity has become an indispensable part of any organization's operations. The rise of cyber threats, coupled with the sophistication of attack strategies, has made it critical for organizations to strengthen their defenses. Ethical hacking and penetration testing have emerged as key practices in identifying vulnerabilities and ensuring that cybersecurity measures are robust enough to protect sensitive information and critical assets. By employing these techniques, organizations can proactively assess their security posture, anticipate potential weaknesses, and mitigate risks before they are exploited by malicious actors.

Penetration Testing Techniques and Their Importance

Penetration testing, often referred to as ethical hacking, is a practice where security professionals simulate cyberattacks to uncover vulnerabilities in systems, networks, and applications. The primary objective is to identify weaknesses that cybercriminals could exploit, allowing organizations to address them before they can be used maliciously. Various penetration testing techniques, such as social engineering, vulnerability scanning, brute- force attacks, and reverse engineering, are used to evaluate different aspects of an organization's security framework. Each of these techniques serves a unique purpose and addresses different types of vulnerabilities, both technical and human.

1. **Social Engineering** is one of the most potent attack strategies, as it exploits human psychology rather than technological weaknesses. The idea behind social engineering is to manipulate individuals into disclosing confidential information, granting unauthorized access, or executing actions that compromise security. This technique underscores the importance of comprehensive training and awareness programs within organizations. The ability to detect and avoid social engineering tactics is just as crucial as securing systems and networks, as human error remains one of the weakest links in cybersecurity.
2. **Vulnerability Scanning** allows penetration testers to automate the process of identifying known vulnerabilities in systems and applications. By using tools like Nessus, Qualys, and OpenVAS, ethical hackers can perform comprehensive scans of an organization's infrastructure, looking for outdated software, open ports, misconfigurations, and missing patches. Vulnerability scanning is an essential technique as it helps detect weaknesses that could otherwise go unnoticed and could be exploited by attackers. Regular scanning, especially for high-risk vulnerabilities, is essential for proactive security management.
3. **Brute-Force Attacks** are used to crack passwords and encryption keys by attempting all possible combinations until the correct one is found. Ethical hackers use this technique to identify weak password policies or encryption protocols. Since many attacks are initiated through weak or easily guessable passwords, this technique helps demonstrate the importance of implementing strong password management practices and multi-factor authentication. It also highlights the value of using more advanced encryption methods that make brute-force attacks impractical.
4. **Reverse Engineering** is particularly valuable when assessing proprietary software, firmware, or hardware. By analyzing applications or embedded systems at a granular level, ethical hackers can uncover hidden vulnerabilities that may not be apparent through high-level security assessments. Reverse engineering helps identify potential backdoors, hidden functionalities, or poorly written code that attackers might exploit. This technique can uncover critical vulnerabilities that could pose significant risks to an organization's security, especially in IoT devices and custom applications.

Each of these techniques provides a different layer of insight into the securityof an organization's systems, contributing to a thorough assessment of potential attack vectors. By using a combination of these methods, ethical hackers can conduct a comprehensive evaluation that accounts for both human and technical factors.

Ethical Hacking for Vulnerability Management

Vulnerability management is an ongoing process that involves identifying, classifying, remediating, and monitoring vulnerabilities throughout their lifecycle. Effective vulnerability management is fundamental to maintaining robust security defenses, and ethical hacking plays a critical role in this process. The primary goal of vulnerability management is to ensure that vulnerabilities are identified early, prioritized according to their potential impact, and mitigated before they can be exploited by attackers.

Ethical Hacking Contributes Significantly to Vulnerability Management in Several Ways

- **Proactive Vulnerability Identification:** Ethical hackers use penetration testing and vulnerability scanning to detect security weaknesses—such as misconfigurations, outdated software, and weak authentication—before they are exploited.
- **Risk Assessment and Prioritization:** By evaluating the exploitability and impact of vulnerabilities, ethical hackers help organizations prioritize remediation efforts based on risk.
- **Remediation and Patch Validation:** Ethical hackers recommend mitigation strategies, support effective patch management, and retest systems to ensure vulnerabilities are properly resolved.
- **Continuous Security Monitoring:** Regular security assessments help organizations adapt to evolving threats and maintain a strong security posture over time.
- **External Attacker Perspective:** External penetration testing provides an unbiased view of system security, uncovering weaknesses that internal teams may overlook.

Continuous Improvement in Cyber Security

Cyber security is a dynamic field, and threats are constantly evolving. As cybercriminals develop more sophisticated attack methods, organizations must adapt their defenses to keep up with these changes. This is where theconcept of continuous improvement in cyber security comes into play. Continuous improvement refers to the ongoing process of assessing, updating, and strengthening an organization's security measures to address new and emerging threats.

1. **Adapting to Evolving Threats**: The cyber security landscape is constantly changing, with new vulnerabilities and attack methods emerging regularly. Hackers develop new tools and techniques, while malware and phishing campaigns become more advanced. Continuous improvement involves staying ahead of these developments by regularly updating security measures and testing systems for new vulnerabilities. Ethical hackers play an essential role in this process by conducting frequent penetration tests and staying updated on the latest threats. Through continuous assessments, ethical hackers help organizations ensure that their defenses are up-to- date and capable of mitigating the latest attack strategies.
2. **Adopting New Technologies**: As organizations adopt new technologies such as cloud computing, the Internet of Things (IoT), artificial intelligence, and machine learning, they introduce new security challenges. These technologies come with unique vulnerabilities and potential attack vectors that require tailored security strategies. Ethical hackers help organizations assess and secure these new technologies by applying traditional penetration testing methods alongside new approaches that account for the specific risks associated with emerging technologies.
3. **Learning from Past Incidents**: One of the most valuable aspects of continuous improvement is learning from past security incidents and breaches. Ethical hackers conduct post-breach analyses to understand how attackers gained access to systems, which vulnerabilities were exploited, and how the breach could have been prevented. This post-mortem analysis allows organizations to refine their security strategies and prevent similar incidents from happening in the future. Continuous improvement ensures that organizations are not only protecting themselves from known threats but also developing the ability to respond effectively to new challenges.
4. **Building a Culture of Security:** Continuous improvement in cybersecurity also involves fostering a culture of security awareness throughout the organization. This includes regular training for employees to recognize phishing attacks, enforcing strong password policies, and ensuring that security best practices are followed. Ethical hackers play a role in this by assessing the human element of security—such as susceptibility to social engineering—and providing training recommendations to help staff understand and respond to security threats effectively.

FUTURE RESEARCH DIRECTIONS AND OPEN CHALLENGES

Despite significant advancements in penetration testing methodologies and tools, several open challenges remain that require further research. One key challenge is the increasing complexity of modern IT environments, including cloud infrastructures, Internet of Things (IoT) ecosystems, and hybrid architectures, which traditional penetration testing tools are not fully equipped to assess. Future research should focus on developing scalable and adaptive testing frameworks tailored to these dynamic environments.

Another major challenge lies in the high dependency on human expertise during manual penetration testing. While automated tools offer speed and scalability, they often fail to detect complex vulnerabilities such as business logic flaws. Future work can explore the integration of artificial intelligence and machine learning techniques to enhance automation while preserving contextual understanding and decision-making capabilities.

The growing adoption of advanced defense mechanisms such as zero-trust architectures, multi-factor authentication, and behavior-based intrusion detection systems also limits the effectiveness of conventional attack techniques. Research is needed to design next-generation testing approaches that can evaluate security posture under such advanced defensive settings.

Ethical, legal, and compliance-related constraints represent another open challenge, particularly in social engineering-based penetration testing. Future studies could investigate standardized ethical frameworks and simulation-based approaches that enable realistic testing without violating privacy or legal boundaries.

Finally, there is a need for standardized benchmarking datasets and evaluation metrics to objectively compare penetration testing tools and techniques. Establishing common benchmarks would enable more consistent performance assessment and facilitate reproducibility in academic research.

CONCLUSION

In conclusion,, penetration testing techniques, ethical hacking for vulnerability management, and continuous improvement are all critical components of a comprehensive cybersecurity strategy. Penetration testing techniques like social engineering, vulnerability scanning, brute-force attacks, and reverse engineering offer a multi-faceted approach to identifying vulnerabilities in systems, networks, and applications. By using these techniques, ethical hackers can assess the security of an organization from various angles and uncover hidden risks that may otherwise be missed. Ethical hacking also plays a vital role in vulnerability management, helping organizations proactively identify and remediate weaknesses before they are exploited by malicious actors. By conducting regular security assessments and vulnerability scans, ethical hackers ensure that organizations can manage their vulnerabilities effectively and prioritize risks based on their potential impact. Finally, continuous improvement is essential to maintaining a strong cybersecurity posture. The threat landscape is constantly evolving, and organizations must stay agile to keep up with new attack methods and emerging technologies. Ethical hackers contribute to this process by providing ongoing assessments, adapting their testing methodologies to reflect current threats, and helping organizations stay ahead of evolving risks. Cybersecurity is not a one- time effort but an ongoing journey of improvement, and ethical hacking is at the forefront of this journey. By incorporating these practices into their security strategies, organizations can better protect themselves from the growing threat of cyberattacks and ensure the safety of their data, infrastructure, and reputation.

REFERENCES

Anandh, S. (2025). Ethical Hacking And Penetration Testing. *ERES International Journal of Computer Networks.*, *13*(4), 1–6. DOI: 10.62346/ijcn_q4_v13_no4_25_02

Egbedion, G. (2024). Impact Of Vulnerability Management And Penetration Testing On Security-Informed It Project Planning And Implementation. *Journal of Engineering Science and Technology.*, *11*, 16821–16828.

Gopalsamy, M., & Dastageer, B. (2025). The Role of Ethical Hacking and AI in Proactive Cyber Defense. *Current Approaches and Future Perspectives.*, *10*, 482–489. DOI: 10.5281/zenodo.14916984

Jamil, D., & Khan, M. N. A. (2011). Is ethical hacking ethical. *International Journal of Engineering Science and Technology*, *3*(5), 3–758. DOI: 10.48175/IJARSCT-12421</jrn>

Kathe, P. H., & Lotankar, A. P. (2020). "Penetration Testing: A Practical Guide." A practical resource outlining methodologies and best practices in penetration testing. DOI: https://www.doi.org/10.56726/IRJMETS62634

Kumawat, P. P. P. J. V. "Ethical Hacking: White Hat Hackers," in *SCRS Proceedings of International Conference of Undergraduate Students (SCRS)*, 2021. DOI:DOI: 10.48175/IJARSCT-12422

Li, S., Surineni, K., & Prabhakaran, N. (2025). Kamalakar Surineni, Nishant Prabhakaran, Cyber-Attacks on Hospital Systems: A Narrative Review. *The American Journal of Geriatric Psychiatry. Open Science, Education, and Practice*, *7*, 30–39. DOI: 10.1016/j.osep.2025.03.002

Patil, S., Jangra, A., Bhale, M., Raina, A., & Kulkarni, P. "Ethical hacking: The need for cyber security.," in *IEEE International Conference on Power, Control, Signals and Instrumentation Engineering (ICPCSI)*, Chennai, 2017. DOI: 10.1109/ICPCSI.2017.8391982

Patterson, C., Nurse, J., & Franqueira, V. (2023). Learning from cyber security incidents: A systematic review and future research agenda. *Computers & Security*, *132*, 103309. DOI: 10.1016/j.cose.2023.103309

Prasad, N., Diro, A., Warren, M., & Fernando, M. (2025). A survey of cyber threat attribution: Challenges, techniques, and future directions. *Computers & Security*, *157*, 104606. DOI: 10.1016/j.cose.2025.104606

Prümmer, J., van Steen, T., & van den Berg, B. (2024). A systematic review of current cybersecurity training methods. *Computers & Security*, *136*, 103585. Advance online publication. DOI: 10.1016/j.cose.2023.103585

Rayhan, A. (2024). The Role of Ethical Hacking in Modern Cybersecurity Practices. DOI: 10.13140/RG.2.2.16619.55841

Ribeiro, D., Fonte, V., Ramos, L. F., & Silva, J. M. (2025). Assessing the information security posture of online public services worldwide: Technical insights, trends, and policy implications. *Government Information Quarterly*, *42*(2), 102031. Advance online publication. DOI: 10.1016/j.giq.2025.102031

Rodríguez Llerena, A. E. (2020). Fundamental Tools for Ethical Hacking. http: // scielo. sld.cu/pdf/rcim/v12n1/1684 - 1859 - rcim - 12 - 01 - 116.pdf

Roger, A. (2021). *Grimes, "Brute-Force Attacks," in Hacking Multifactor Authentication*. Wiley., DOI: 10.1002/9781119672357.ch14

Seara, J. P., & Serrão, C. (2024). Automation of System Security Vulnerabilities Detection Using Open-Source Software. *Electronics (Basel)*, *13*(5), 873. DOI: 10.3390/electronics13050873

Suresh, H. (2023). *Pooja M R*. Ethical Framework for Cyber Security, Journal of Network Security and Data Mining., DOI: 10.5281/ZENODO.7550038

Syafitri, W., Shukur, Z., Mokhtar, U. A., Sulaiman, R., & Ibrahim, M. A. (2022). Social Engineering Attacks Prevention: A Systematic Literature Review. *IEEE Access : Practical Innovations, Open Solutions*, *10*, 39325–39343. DOI: 10.1109/ACCESS.2022.3162594

Yaacoub, J. P. A., Noura, H. N., Salman, O., & Chehab, A. (2023). Ethical hacking for IoT: Security issues, challenges, solutions and recommendations. *Internet of Things and Cyber-Physical Systems*, *3*, 280–308. DOI: 10.1016/j.iotcps.2023.04.002

Chapter 7
Legal, Ethical, and Compliance Frameworks in Ethical Hacking Practices

Oindrilla Ghosh
http://orcid.org/0000-0001-9609-0781
Christ University, India

Binod Kumar
http://orcid.org/0009-0002-9721-1367
Radha Govind University, India

ABSTRACT

Legal, ethical, and compliance frameworks are crucial in guiding ethical hacking practices. Ethical hacking, also known as penetration testing, involves simulating cyberattacks to identify and rectify vulnerabilities within systems. Ethical hackers must navigate legal boundaries to avoid unauthorized access to systems and data breaches. Laws such as the Computer Fraud and Abuse Act set strict guidelines for what constitutes lawful hacking. Moreover, ethical hackers adhere to a code of conduct that emphasizes integrity and respect for privacy. Compliance with industry standards, such as GDPR and PCI DSS, ensures that ethical hacking practices protect sensitive information and maintain trust with stakeholders. Organizations often establish clear policies and training programs to ensure hackers operate within legal parameters. By incorporating these frameworks, businesses can improve their cybersecurity posture while minimizing legal risks. Ethical hacking must align with laws and ethical standards to create a safer digital environment.

DOI: 10.4018/979-8-3373-3536-0.ch007

INTRODUCTION

The digital landscape has evolved at an unprecedented pace, leading to a burgeoning demand for security expertise to protect sensitive information against an array of cyber threats (Chiruvella & Guddati, 2021). Ethical hacking, or penetration testing, has emerged as a vital practice within the cybersecurity domain, allowing organizations to identify vulnerabilities and reinforce their defenses proactively (McKeown et al., 2021). However, the practice of ethical hacking is not merely a technical endeavor; it is also deeply entwined with legal, ethical, and compliance frameworks that govern how ethical hackers operate (Ukato et al., 2024).

Ethical hacking raises numerous ethical questions, particularly concerning the extent of permissible actions and the responsibilities of the hacker (Oguanobi & Joel, 2024). Ethical hackers must navigate complex moral landscapes, balancing the imperative to identify vulnerabilities with the potential risks of exploitation (Sikdar & Guha, 2020). This balancing act requires adherence to ethical guidelines and frameworks that promote integrity and accountability within the practice (Rehman et al., 2022).

Moreover, compliance with industry standards and regulations such as the General Data Protection Regulation (GDPR) in Europe, the Health Insurance Portability and Accountability Act (HIPAA) in the United States, and various cybersecurity frameworks like NIST and ISO further shapes the landscape for ethical hackers (Zhang et al., 2022). These frameworks define the standards of conduct for data handling, breach notifications, and other crucial elements integral to cybersecurity operations, compelling organizations to ensure that ethical hacking practices align with requisite compliance obligations (Olatoye et al., 2024).

HISTORICAL EVOLUTION

The historical evolution of legal, ethical, and compliance frameworks pertaining to ethical hacking practices can be traced through several key milestones that have shaped the current landscape (Awonuga et al., 2024). The journey begins in the early days of computing when the concepts of hacking and cybersecurity were still nascent (Hassan et al., 2022). In the 1960s and 1970s, as mainframe computers became more prevalent, the focus was primarily on the technical capabilities of systems rather than security implications (Cozzoli et al., 2022). During this period, some individuals began to explore system vulnerabilities, often without malicious intent, setting the stage for what would later be recognized as ethical hacking (Alotaibi et al., 2020).

The 1980s marked a turning point as the proliferation of personal computers and networked systems drew attention to the vulnerabilities inherent in these technologies (Meriton et al., 2021). As reports of unauthorized access and data breaches surfaced, governments began to recognize the need for regulatory frameworks to combat cybercrimes (Weerasinghe et al., 2022). The Computer Fraud and Abuse Act (CFAA) of 1986 in the United States was one of the first pieces of legislation specifically addressing unauthorized access to computer systems, criminalizing hacking activities and establishing legal boundaries (Chao et al., 2023). During this period, the term "hacker" began to take on a more negative connotation, further complicating the narrative around ethical hacking (Chatzopoulou et al., 2020).

The 1990s saw a significant shift with the emergence of the internet and the growing realization of the importance of cybersecurity (Perez-Pozuelo et al., 2021). The establishment of the Internet Crime Complaint Center (IC3) in 2000 by the FBI exemplified the increasing focus on combating cybercrime through law enforcement collaboration (Banerjee et al., 2020). Concurrently, ethical hacking began to take shape as a discipline, with organizations recognizing the potential benefits of leveraging hackers' skills for defensive purposes (Wimelius et al., 2021). Industry bodies and organizations began to formulate ethical guidelines, emphasizing the need for authorization, scope management, and transparency in penetration testing (Drago et al., 2021).

The early 2000s ushered in an era characterized by increased regulatory scrutiny and compliance requirements in response to high-profile data breaches and their implications (Biancone et al., 2021). Legislation such as the Sarbanes-Oxley Act (SOX, 2002) and the Payment Card Industry Data Security Standard (PCI DSS, 2004) set the stage for heightened accountability and security obligations for organizations handling sensitive information (Abduljalil & Abduljalil, 2020). Ethical hackers found themselves navigating a landscape where compliance with these regulations was integral to their activities, necessitating a clear understanding of both legal and ethical boundaries (Aftab et al., 2020).

In the present digital age, where cyber threats evolve continuously and data privacy becomes paramount, the legal and ethical frameworks surrounding ethical hacking continue to adapt (Hashemzadeh et al., 2020). Emerging technologies, such as artificial intelligence and machine learning, raise new ethical dilemmas and compliance challenges (Cobianchi et al., 2020b). As a result, ethical hackers must engage with evolving regulations, societal norms, and ethical considerations to maintain the integrity of their practice (Odeyemi et al., 2024).

RESEARCH OBJECTIVES

The primary objective of this research is to investigate the legal, ethical, and compliance frameworks that govern ethical hacking practices (Arinze et al., 2024).

As the digital landscape becomes increasingly complex, organizations are seeking ways to bolster their cybersecurity posture (Zinner et al. 2021). Ethical hacking, also known as penetration testing, has emerged as a crucial practice for identifying vulnerabilities in systems before they can be exploited by malicious actors (Cobianchi et al., 2021). However, the very nature of ethical hacking raises numerous questions regarding legality, ethics, and compliance with applicable laws and regulations.

To Analyze Existing Legal Frameworks: This objective aims to explore the varying legal frameworks that govern ethical hacking practices across different jurisdictions. It involves reviewing international, national, and local laws that define the boundaries within which ethical hackers must operate. This includes examining statutes pertaining to computer fraud, unauthorized access, and data protection that may impact ethical hacking activities.

To Evaluate Ethical Considerations: Understanding the ethical considerations surrounding ethical hacking practices is crucial. This objective examines the ethical guidelines established by professional organizations and cybersecurity communities. It considers ethical principles such as confidentiality, integrity, and respect for individuals and organizations. Additionally, this objective seeks to identify conflicts that may arise in ethical dilemmas faced by ethical hackers during their operations.

To Assess Compliance Requirements: This research objective focuses on identifying compliance requirements related to ethical hacking, including industry-specific standards such as the Health Insurance Portability and Accountability Act (HIPAA) for healthcare or Payment Card Industry Data Security Standard (PCI DSS) for financial institutions. This assessment will help organizations understand how compliance affects their ethical hacking policies and practices.

To Investigate Ethical Hacking Practices in Industry Contexts: It is crucial to categorize and analyze the various ethical hacking practices employed across different industries. This objective will provide insights into how ethical hacking is conducted in sectors such as finance, healthcare, education, and government, highlighting the differing legal and compliance landscapes that govern these practices.

To Develop a Comprehensive Framework: Finally, the research aims to synthesize the findings from the analysis of legal frameworks, ethical considerations, and compliance requirements into a comprehensive framework. This framework will serve as a guide for organizations to navigate the intricate landscape of ethical hacking while ensuring adherence to legal and ethical standards.

LITERATURE REVIEW

The literature on legal, ethical, and compliance frameworks in ethical hacking practices is relatively extensive but fragmented, requiring a systematic review to draw comprehensive insights (Yuan et al., 2020). Ethical hacking practices are increasingly recognized as essential to cybersecurity; however, their legitimacy is complicated by the diverse legal, ethical, and compliance landscapes governing such activities (Flother et al., 2020).

Various studies explicate the legal milieu within which ethical hackers operate (Sestino et al., 2020). Researchers highlight that laws exist at local, national, and international levels, each contributing to the complex environment ethical hackers must navigate (Coccia, 2020). For example, studies have been done to examine the Computer Fraud and Abuse Act (CFAA) in the United States, which criminalizes unauthorized access to computers but also raises questions about how ethical hacking can be conducted without violating such laws (Cobianchi et al., 2020a). Internationally, legislation like the General Data Protection Regulation (GDPR) plays a critical role by mandating data protection, effectively impacting ethical hacking practices that involve personal data (Ienca and Vayena, 2020).

Studies by professionals in fields like ethics and cybersecurity illustrate the ethical dilemmas that ethical hackers face (Basile et al., 2022). The importance of ethical guidelines set forth by organizations such as the International Association for Privacy Professionals (IAPP) and the $(ISC)^2$ Code of Ethics underscores this dimension (Spanò et al., 2021). Multiple authors discuss the ethical imperative of maintaining confidentiality, integrity, and transparency in engaging clients while conducting penetration test (Cerchione et al., 2023). The ethical implications of potential harm from hacking activities compound this dilemma, necessitating mechanisms for ensuring respect and accountability (Colombo et al., 2020).

The intersection of compliance and ethical hacking is also well-documented (Mullins et al., 2020). Standard frameworks like NIST Cybersecurity Framework and compliance regulations such as PCI DSS present specific requirements that must be adhered to during ethical hacking operations (Tariq, 2024).

Certain research attempts to contextualize ethical hacking practices within specific industries, revealing variations in legal, ethical, and compliance standards (Fahy et al., 2021). For instance, in regulated sectors like healthcare, ethical hacking must align with HIPAA regulations, which impose stringent data protection standards (Melchiorre et al., 2020). Comparative studies show that while the core principles of ethical hacking remain consistent, their legal and compliance interpretations differ significantly based on industry needs (Arinze et al., 2024).

THEORETICAL FRAMEWORKS

Theoretical frameworks serve as structured systems of concepts, assumptions, and theories that guide research and analysis across various domains (Tayefi et al.,

2021). In the context of ethical hacking, these frameworks provide critical context for understanding ethical dilemmas, compliance requirements, and effective security strategies (Gamal et al., 2021). They offer researchers and practitioners a lens through which to interpret data, construct arguments, and develop solutions to complex issues in information security (Duggineni, 2023).

One foundational theory in ethical frameworks is the *Utilitarianism Theory*, which advocates for actions that maximize overall happiness or well-being (Yang & Gu, 2021). In ethical hacking, this could translate to utilizing penetration testing to identify vulnerabilities that could lead to significant data breaches, thus protecting the organization and its customers (Joel & Oguanobi, 2024a). Another significant framework is *Deontological Ethics*, which emphasizes duties and rules over the consequences of actions (Towett et al., 2023). In ethical hacking, this would stress the importance of adhering to laws and ethical guidelines, such as obtaining proper authorization before conducting assessments (Benson & Grieve, 2021).

Moreover, the *Virtue Ethics* framework shifts the focus to the character of the individual performing the hacking (Jacks et al., 2024). It stresses qualities such as honesty, integrity, and diligence, which are critical to ethical hackers (Colombo et al., 2020). This perspective encourages ethical hackers to not only focus on the outcomes of their actions but also on their motivations and character in performing such tasks (Shrivastava et al., 2021).

In legal and compliance contexts, the *Regulatory Compliance Framework* becomes essential (Hartzog & Richards, 2020). Governments and industries have established numerous regulations and standards to safeguard data privacy, such as GDPR in Europe and HIPAA in the healthcare sector (Lancieri, 2022). Understanding these legal frameworks is crucial in ethical hacking practices to ensure compliance while performing security assessments (Hansen et al., 2021).

Lastly, *Risk Management Frameworks*, like NIST's Risk Management Framework, provide structured processes to identify, assess, and manage risks associated with information security (Joel & Oguanobi, 2024d). Ethical hackers can leverage this framework to prioritize vulnerabilities based on the potential impact and likelihood of exploitation, ensuring that their testing efforts are aligned with the organization's overall risk appetite and compliance obligations (Oladipo et al., 2024).

IMPORTANCE OF AI AND ML

Artificial Intelligence (AI) and Machine Learning (ML) technologies have dramatically transformed the landscape of ethical hacking and cybersecurity at large (Joel & Oguanobi, 2024c). Their integration into legal, ethical, and compliance frameworks has not only enhanced the efficiency and effectiveness of ethical hacking but also addressed pressing concerns regarding security and privacy (Jacks et al., 2024).

One of the foremost contributions of AI and ML in ethical hacking is the automation of threat detection and response (Tamiminia et al., 2020). Traditionally, ethical hackers spent significant time manually identifying vulnerabilities and attempting to breach systems to test their security (Aceto et al., 2020). With AI and ML algorithms, vast amounts of real-time data can be analyzed to identify anomalies and vulnerabilities faster than human capabilities would allow (Sestino et al., 2020). This automation increases the speed of identifying and addressing security weaknesses, which is crucial when compliance with regulations like GDPR or HIPAA can lead to substantial penalties for breaches (Azadegan et al., 2020).

However, the use of AI and ML also raises critical ethical and compliance questions (Gong and Ribiere, 2020). For instance, the algorithms that drive these technologies can inadvertently reinforce biases or lead to unethical decision-making if not properly monitored (Tan et al., 2020). Ethical hacking practices must consider the implications of these biases, especially when sensitive data is involved (Martínez-Vergara & Valls-Pasola, 2020). Ensuring that AI models are transparent and explainable becomes imperative to maintain ethical standards and comply with data protection regulations (Alrahbi et al., 2021).

Furthermore, the deployment of AI-driven ethical hacking tools must adhere to legal and compliance frameworks, ensuring that they operate within the boundaries of applicable laws (Basile et al., 2022). Organizations must be cautious in their approach to using AI and ML in ethical hacking, ensuring that the algorithms used do not violate privacy rights or lead to unauthorized access (Oriekhoe et al., 2024).

USE OF AUGMENTED REALITY (AR), VIRTUAL REALITY (VR), AND MIXED REALITY (MR)

Augmented Reality (AR) enhances the real world by superimposing digital information onto physical environments (Siddiq, 2022). This technology has found applications across various domains, including education, retail, healthcare, and gaming (Massaro, 2021). In education, AR can transform traditional learning experiences by allowing students to interact with 3D models of complex subjects, such as anatomy or historical events (Dai & Tayur, 2020). For instance, apps that overlay anatomical visuals on human bodies help medical students understand the structure and function of organs, making learning more immersive and intuitive (Martínez-Román et al., 2020).

In retail, AR allows consumers to visualize products in their own environments before making a purchase (Martínez-Vergara & Valls-Pasola, 2020). Companies like

IKEA offer apps that let users place furniture items in their homes through their smartphone cameras, enhancing the shopping experience by reducing uncertainty (Massaro, 2021). In the gaming sector, AR games such as Pokémon GO encourage physical activity by encouraging players to explore real-world locations to discover virtual creatures, blending entertainment with outdoor exploration (Shaygan & Daim, 2021).

Virtual Reality (VR) offers a fully immersive experience, transporting users into entirely digital worlds (Spanò et al., 2021). By using VR headsets, individuals can explore vastly different environments, from historical reconstructions to far-off planets (Chakraborty and Paul, 2022). VR is extensively used in training simulations for professionals in high-stakes fields such as aviation, military, and healthcare (Martínez-Román et al., 2020). For example, pilots can practice flying in VR simulators that replicate various flight scenarios without leaving the ground, minimizing training costs and improving safety (Ng & Bezak, 2020).

In therapy, VR serves as a tool for exposure therapy, treating conditions like PTSD by allowing patients to confront their fears in a controlled and safe environment (Stephanie & Sharma, 2020). This immersive technology has revolutionized therapeutic practices, providing effective treatment options for mental health issues (Cobianchi et al., 2021). Furthermore, in the field of remote collaboration, VR enables teams to meet in digital spaces, fostering engagement and communication among participants who may be spread across the globe (Sestino et al., 2020).

Mixed Reality (MR) combines elements of both AR and VR, allowing for interaction between real and virtual objects (Au-Yong-Oliveira et al., 2021). MR applications create new experiences across different sectors (Pérez-Castillo et al., 2021). In industries such as architecture and construction, professionals can visualize building designs as if they were physically present (Zinner et al., 2021). They can manipulate digital models in real time, improving collaboration and decision-making processes (Yuan et al., 2020).

The entertainment industry also benefits from MR, with experiences that blend real-world interaction with virtual elements, creating a more engaging way for users to immerse themselves in storytelling (Zinner et al., 2021). For instance, live performances can incorporate MR elements, bringing stories to life in ways that traditional media cannot (Ofodile et al., 2024).

CHALLENGES

Ethical hacking, also known as penetration testing, plays a crucial role in cybersecurity by identifying vulnerabilities in systems before malicious hackers can exploit them (Abduljalil and Abduljalil, 2020). However, ethical hackers operate within a complex landscape of legal, ethical, and compliance frameworks, which present several challenges (Flother et al., 2020).

Legal Challenges: Ethical hackers must navigate a web of laws and regulations that govern cybersecurity practices (Cobianchi et al., 2020a). The key challenge lies in obtaining proper authorization before conducting any tests (Ienca and Vayena, 2020). Without explicit permission from system owners, ethical hacking can be construed as illegal intrusion or access (Basile et al., 2022). Laws such as the Computer Fraud and Abuse Act (CFAA) in the United States impose severe penalties for unauthorized access, even if the intent is to enhance security (Spanò et al., 2021). Moreover, the jurisdictional complexity adds another layer of difficulty (Ienca and Vayena, 2020). Cybersecurity laws vary significantly between countries, and ethical hackers operating globally must be aware of these differences to avoid legal repercussions (Stephanie & Sharma, 2020). This can complicate cross-border engagements, hindering cooperation and information sharing necessary for robust cybersecurity defense (Ng & Bezak, 2020).

Compliance Frameworks: Compliance with established frameworks and standards, such as the General Data Protection Regulation (GDPR), Payment Card Industry Data Security Standard (PCI DSS), or the Cybersecurity Framework provided by NIST, is paramount in ethical hacking practices (Chakraborty & Paul, 2022). Ethical hackers must ensure their testing methods align with these frameworks to avoid compliance-related issues that could result in significant penalties for organizations (Chiruvella & Guddati, 2021). However, the dynamic nature of technology and evolving cyber threats means that compliance frameworks often lag behind actual practices (McKeown et al., 2021). Ethical hackers must stay updated on compliance requirements and ensure that their methodologies align with best practices (Ukato et al., 2024). This requirement for continuous education instills an additional burden on ethical hackers in an already challenging environment (Williamson et al., 2024).

CASE STUDIES

Ethical hacking, or penetration testing, has become an indispensable part of modern cybersecurity strategy (Ukato et al., 2024). Ethical hackers help organizations identify vulnerabilities, strengthen defenses, and ensure compliance with legal and regulatory requirements (Oguanobi & Joel, 2024). However, ethical hacking exists within a complex framework of legal, ethical, and compliance considerations.

Case Study 1: Uber's Bug Bounty Program

In 2016, Uber faced a significant security breach when data from 57 million user accounts was stolen by hackers (Sikdar & Guha, 2020). Instead of disclosing the breach promptly, Uber opted to pay the hackers $100,000 in silence. This move attracted regulatory scrutiny and discussions about compliance with various data protection laws, including the GDPR in Europe and the California Consumer Privacy Act. California's data breach notification laws require that any business that suffers a breach must disclose it to affected users (Rehman et al., 2022). Uber's decision to pay the hackers and conceal the breach could be interpreted as a failure to comply with these statutes (Zhang et al., 2022). Consequently, Uber faced investigations from various regulatory bodies, ultimately leading to substantial fines and legal repercussions.

From an ethical standpoint, Uber's decision to hush up the breach posed significant risks to users' privacy and security (Olatoye et al., 2024). The practice of concealing breaches can undermine trust in organizations and raise questions about corporate accountability (Awonuga et al., 2024). Uber's experience underscores the importance of establishing comprehensive compliance frameworks for data protection (Hassan et al., 2022). Organizations must not only implement security measures but also ensure adherence to laws governing data breaches (Cozzoli et al., 2022). This includes capabilities for timely notification and transparent communication with stakeholders (Alotaibi et al., 2020).

Case Study 2: The Target Data Breach

In 2013, Target Corporation suffered a massive breach that compromised over 40 million credit and debit card accounts (Meriton et al., 2021). The breach resulted from inadequate security measures and non-compliance with the Payment Card Industry Data Security Standard (PCI DSS), which mandates safeguards for card data (Weerasinghe et al., 2022). The breach highlighted Target's failure to comply with the PCI DSS requirements. As a result, Target faced legal actions, including lawsuits from banks and credit unions, seeking reimbursement for fraudulent transactions. Additionally, the vulnerability raised questions about the adequacy of their cybersecurity policies (Chao et al., 2023).

The ethical implications of the Target breach go beyond legal compliance. Customers expect that retailers safeguard their personal and financial data (Chatzopoulou et al., 2020). Failing to protect this information poses ethical dilemmas around informed consent and customer protection (Perez-Pozuelo et al., 2021). Target's negligence compromised more than just data; it violated consumer trust (Banerjee et al., 2020). Following the breach, Target revamped its compliance framework to strengthen its cybersecurity measures, ensuring alignment with PCI DSS standards (Wimelius et al., 2021). They adopted comprehensive risk management strategies and established a dedicated cybersecurity team to mitigate future risks (Drago et al., 2021). This case serves as a powerful reminder of the need for robust compliance frameworks in modern retail.

Case Study 3: The Facebook-Cambridge Analytica Scandal

In 2018, the Facebook-Cambridge Analytica scandal revealed that millions of users' personal data were harvested without their consent for political advertising. This incident raised alarms about data privacy, ethics in data handling, and compliance with regulatory standards such as the GDPR (Biancone et al., 2021). The European Union's GDPR mandates stringent measures regarding user data collection and consent (Abduljalil & Abduljalil, 2020). Facebook faced scrutiny from regulatory authorities for potentially violating these principles, resulting in significant fines and increased scrutiny from lawmakers globally (Aftab et al., 2020).

The ethical implications were profound, questioning the responsibility of platforms like Facebook in managing user data (Hashemzadeh et al., 2020). Users were generally unaware of how their data was used, leading to a breach of trust. The lack of transparency in data handling raised serious ethical concerns about informed consent (Cobianchi et al., 2020b). Following the scandal, Facebook instituted numerous changes to ensure compliance with GDPR and bolster user privacy. They enhanced their data access policies and established stricter user consent protocols (Odeyemi et al., 2024). This case underscores the necessity for robust compliance frameworks to address ethical challenges in data management.

Case Study 4: Marriott International Data Breach

In late 2018, Marriott International announced a data breach that affected approximately 500 million guests. Hackers accessed sensitive data, including passport numbers and credit card information, from its Starwood Hotels database (Arinze et al., 2024). Marriott's breach raised significant compliance issues under various regulations, including GDPR and the California Consumer Privacy Act, which impose strict requirements on data protection and breach notifications. Non-compliance could lead to heavy fines and legal repercussions (Zinner et al. 2021).

The ethical dimensions of the breach revolved around consumer trust and data stewardship (Cobianchi et al., 2021). Customers expect organizations to protect their data with due diligence (Yuan et al., 2020). Marriott's failure to secure sensitive information brought into question the ethical obligations of businesses to their customers (Flother et al., 2020). In response to the breach, Marriott undertook an extensive overhaul of its data security practices. This included engaging in more thorough security audits, revising data handling policies, and enhancing customer notification processes in line with legal requirements (Sestino et al., 2020). It highlights the importance of a proactive compliance framework that addresses both regulatory and ethical considerations (Coccia, 2020).

Case Study 5: The RSA SecureID Breach

In 2011, RSA, the security division of EMC Corporation, suffered a breach that compromised the security of their SecurID two-factor authentication technology. The attackers leveraged the stolen information to compromise customer networks, leading to the exposure of sensitive data (Cobianchi et al., 2020a). The breach raised various legal concerns regarding compliance with the Federal Information Security Management Act (FISMA) and relevant data protection laws. RSA had to address how the breach affected its contractual obligations to clients and the extent of their liability (Ienca and Vayena, 2020).

The ethical implications centered on RSA's responsibility to their customers (Basile et al., 2022). Clients relied on RSA's solutions for security, and a breach of this magnitude posed ethical questions about the firm's diligence and commitment to safeguarding their clients' data (Spanò et al., 2021). Post-breach, RSA emerged with a more robust compliance framework emphasizing risk management, incident response planning, and third-party security audits (Cerchione et al., 2023). This incident serves as a testament to the importance of a resilient compliance framework in ethical hacking practices, bridging legal, ethical, and business objectives (Padmanaban, 2024).

ETHICAL CONSIDERATIONS

Ethical hacking, often referred to as penetration testing, involves the authorized testing of information systems to identify and address vulnerabilities before they can be exploited by malicious actors (Colombo et al., 2020). While ethical hacking is an essential aspect of cybersecurity, it raises several ethical considerations that practitioners must navigate to ensure their actions align with societal norms and legal frameworks (Mullins et al., 2020).

First and foremost, informed consent is a cornerstone of ethical hacking (Tariq, 2024). Practitioners must ensure that they have explicit permission from the organization they are testing (Fahy et al., 2021). This consent should not only cover the scope of the testing but also the methodologies employed (Melchiorre et al., 2020). Unauthorized access, even with good intentions, can lead to significant legal consequences and undermine trust in the ethical hacking profession (Arinze et al., 2024). Thus, ethical hackers must operate under a clear contractual agreement that delineates their responsibilities and the bounds of their activities (Tayefi et al., 2021).

Another critical ethical consideration is the potential for harm (Gamal et al., 2021). Ethical hackers must be conscientious of the impact their testing can have on an organization (Duggineni, 2023). For instance, penetration tests can inadvertently disrupt services, compromise sensitive data, or damage systems (Yang & Gu, 2021). It is vital for ethical hackers to approach their work with a risk management mindset, carefully assessing the potential consequences of their actions (Joel & Oguanobi, 2024a). A well-designed testing plan that identifies and mitigates risks can help minimize any adverse effects on the organization's operations (Towett et al., 2023).

Confidentiality is also paramount in ethical hacking (Benson & Grieve, 2021). Ethical hackers frequently gain access to sensitive information, including proprietary data and personal user information (Jacks et al., 2024). They have an ethical obligation to protect this data and prevent any unauthorized disclosure (Colombo et al., 2020). This responsibility extends to maintaining the privacy of both the organization and its users (Shrivastava et al., 2021). Ethical hackers should adopt measures, such as data anonymization and secure storage practices, to uphold confidentiality throughout their testing processes (Nandi et al., 2024).

IMPLEMENTATION OF REGULATORY FRAMEWORKS

The implementation of regulatory frameworks that govern legal, ethical, and compliance aspects of ethical hacking practices is crucial for establishing a standardized approach to security testing (Lancieri, 2022).

One of the primary regulatory frameworks relevant to ethical hacking is the General Data Protection Regulation (GDPR) in Europe (Hartzog & Richards, 2020). The GDPR sets stringent guidelines concerning data protection and privacy, which directly impact how ethical hackers can engage with personal data during their assessments (Hansen et al., 2021). Ethical hackers must ensure that their testing complies with GDPR stipulations regarding user consent and data handling (Joel & Oguanobi, 2024d). Implementing such regulatory frameworks necessitates comprehensive training and awareness programs for ethical hackers so that they understand their responsibilities under data protection laws (Oladipo et al., 2024).

Another essential regulatory guidance comes from the National Institute of Standards and Technology (NIST), which provides a framework for risk management and security practices (Joel & Oguanobi, 2024c). NIST guidelines encourage organizations to adopt a structured approach to evaluating their security posture, including ethical hacking as part of their overall security strategy (Jacks et al.,

2024). Compliance with NIST standards requires organizations to document their ethical hacking procedures, ensure regular assessments, and verify that the ethical hacking practices align with both organizational policies and legal requirements (Tamiminia et al., 2020).

Additionally, regulations like the Health Insurance Portability and Accountability Act (HIPAA) in the United States specifically address handling sensitive health information, impacting ethical hacking practices in healthcare organizations (Aceto et al., 2020). Ethical hackers working in such sectors must ensure their testing does not compromise patient confidentiality or violate HIPAA regulations (Sestino et al., 2020). This requirement emphasizes the need for tailored ethical hacking practices guided by regulations that consider specific industry contexts (Azadegan et al., 2020).

To implement these frameworks effectively, organizations must establish a clear governance structure for ethical hacking efforts (Gong and Ribiere, 2020). This includes appointing a compliance officer or a dedicated cybersecurity team responsible for overseeing ethical hacking initiatives, ensuring adherence to both legal requirements and ethical standards (Tan et al., 2020). A formalized process for engaging ethical hackers, including background checks, security clearances, and continuous evaluations of their work, reinforces compliance and mitigates risks associated with outsourcing ethical hacking activities (Bhatt and Chakraborty, 2023).

CONCLUSION

The realm of ethical hacking stands at the critical intersection of technology, law, and ethics (Martínez-Vergara & Valls-Pasola, 2020). Ethical hackers, also known as white-hat hackers, play a pivotal role in safeguarding organizations against cyber threats, yet their practices must remain grounded in established legal, ethical, and compliance frameworks (Alrahbi et al., 2021). This convergence is not merely advisable; it is essential for fostering trust, accountability, and responsibility within the fast-evolving landscape of cybersecurity (Basile et al., 2022).

Employers and organizations must also recognize their role in creating an environment where ethical hacking can thrive within a legally compliant framework (Oriekhoe et al., 2024). Institutions must nurture a culture that not only encourages ethical practices but holds individuals accountable for their actions (Siddiq, 2022). By instituting clear guidelines and policies, organizations can mitigate risks associated with unethical or illegal hacking practices.

As technology continues to evolve and new threats emerge, the legal, ethical, and compliance frameworks that govern ethical hacking must also adapt (Massaro, 2021). The future demands an agile, proactive approach to regulatory and ethical standards to ensure that ethical hackers are equipped to address the ever-increasing complexities of cybersecurity threats (Jambol et al., 2024).

SUGGESTIONS

To create a robust legal, ethical, and compliance framework for ethical hacking practices, several strategies can be implemented.

Develop Clear Compliance Guidelines: Organizations must draft comprehensive compliance guidelines that explicitly outline the legal and ethical standards expected of ethical hackers (Chao et al., 2023). This should include policies for obtaining consent, data handling, and transparency regarding disclosure of vulnerabilities.

Facilitate Ongoing Education and Training: Regular training sessions focusing on legal changes, ethical obligations, and compliance requirements can help ethical hackers stay informed about their responsibilities (Duggineni, 2023). This education can take various forms, including workshops, online courses, or seminars featuring legal experts in cybersecurity.

Implement a Code of Conduct: Establishing a clear code of conduct for ethical hackers can provide a framework for ethical decision-making (Towett et al., 2023). This code should articulate the expected ethical behavior and emphasize the importance of confidentiality, integrity, and respect for the rights of all stakeholders.

Engage in Collaboration: Collaboration with legal experts, privacy advocates, and compliance officers can refine ethical hacking practices (Bhatt and Chakraborty, 2023). This interdisciplinary approach can ensure that ethical hackers have the support necessary to operate within the bounds of the law.

Promote Transparency and Accountability: Transparency in ethical hacking activities, including the methodologies employed and the results obtained, can build trust among stakeholders. Organizations should establish feedback mechanisms that allow affected parties to express concerns or provide input about ethical hacking practices (Ochulor et al., 2024) .

RECOMMENDATIONS

To enhance legal, ethical, and compliance frameworks in ethical hacking practices, several fundamental recommendations can be put forth:

Establish Industry Standards: Industry-wide standards specifically tailored to ethical hacking practices should be developed and adopted by organizations (Jacks et al., 2024). These standards can provide criteria for what constitutes ethical behavior, setting a benchmark that aligns with legal requirements and ethical norms.

Integration of Legal Advice in Ethical Hacking Projects: Engaging legal professionals at the outset of ethical hacking initiatives can help mitigate legal risks (Oladipo et al., 2024). Businesses should not treat legal consultation as an afterthought but rather as an integral part of project planning and execution.

Create a Whistleblower Protection Mechanism: Encourage ethical hackers to report unethical practices or whistleblower offenses without fear of retaliation (Ofodile et al., 2024). Organizations should ensure that there are protected channels for discussing concerns regarding unethical behavior or breaches of legal compliance.

Foster a Culture of Ethics within Organizations: Leadership should prioritize creating a culture where ethical practices are celebrated and unethical practices are condemned (Williamson et al., 2024). This cultural shift can be supported by recognizing and rewarding ethical behavior among employees.

Encourage Participation in Ethical Hacking Associations: Ethical hackers should be encouraged to participate in professional associations or organizations that promote ethical practices and legal compliance. This involvement can provide platforms for networking, sharing best practices, and staying informed about developments in the field (Uzougbo et al., 2024).

FUTURE RESEARCH DIRECTIONS

Future research in the realm of ethical hacking should address several emerging areas that can enhance the understanding and efficiency of legal, ethical, and compliance frameworks.

Impact of AI on Ethical Hacking: Investigating how artificial intelligence and machine learning technologies can be integrated into ethical hacking practices raises crucial questions about ethical implications and the legal landscape surrounding automated hacking tools (Padmanaban, 2024). Research should focus on developing best practices for the responsible use of AI in this area.

Cross-Border Data Laws and Ethical Hacking: As ethical hacking often involves cross-border considerations, research into international legal frameworks that govern these activities could provide insights (Nandi et al., 2024). This includes examining how different jurisdictions approach ethical hacking and potential harmonization of laws.

Psychosocial Factors in Ethical Decision-Making: Investigating the psychosocial influences that drive ethical decision-making among ethical hackers can reveal insights into how individuals justify their actions (Jambol et al., 2024). This study could bridge psychological theories with compliance frameworks to develop more effective ethical training programs.

Effectiveness of Compliance Programs: Research measuring the effectiveness of existing legal, ethical, and compliance programs in organizations engaged in ethical hacking is needed. This investigation could provide empirical data that informs best practices and identifies gaps in current frameworks (Balch et al., 2023).

By pursuing these research directions, scholars and practitioners can contribute to developing a more robust understanding of the complex interplay between legal, ethical, and compliance frameworks in ethical hacking practices (Ochulor et al., 2024). This effort will not only drive technological advancement but also ensure that ethical considerations remain at the forefront of cybersecurity.

REFERENCES

Abduljalil, J. M., & Abduljalil, B. M. (2020). *Epidemiology, genome, and clinical features of the pandemic SARS-CoV-2: a recent view*. New Microb. New Infect., DOI: 10.1016/j.nmni.2020.100672

Aceto, G., Persico, V., & Pescapé, A. (2020). Industry 4.0 and health: Internet of things, big data, and cloud computing for Healthcare 4.0. *Journal of Industrial Information Integration, 18*, 100129. DOI: 10.1016/j.jii.2020.100129

Aftab, S. O., Ghouri, M. Z., Masood, M. U., Haider, Z., Khan, Z., Ahmad, A., & Munawar, N. (2020). Analysis of SARS-CoV-2 RNA-dependent RNA polymerase as a potential therapeutic drug target using a computational approach. *Journal of Translational Medicine, 18*(1), 1–15. DOI: 10.1186/s12967-020-02439-0 PMID: 32635935

Alotaibi, S., Mehmood, R., & Katib, I. (2020). The role of big data and twitter data analytics in healthcare supply chain management. *Smart Infrastructure and Applications: Foundations for Smarter Cities and Societies,* 267-279.

Alrahbi, D. A., Khan, M., Gupta, S., Modgil, S., & Jabbour, C. J. C. (2021). Health-care information technologies for dispersed knowledge management. *Journal of Knowledge Management*. Advance online publication. DOI: 10.1108/JKM-10-2020-0786

Arinze, C. A., Ajala, O. A., Okoye, C. C., Ofodile, O. C., & Daraojimba, A. I. (2024). *Evaluating the integration of advanced IT solutions for emission reduction in the oil and gas sector*. Engineering Science and Technology Journal., DOI: 10.51594/estj/v5i3.862

Au-Yong-Oliveira, M., Pesqueira, A., Sousa, M. J., Dal Mas, F., & Soliman, M. (2021). The potential of big data research in health care for medical doctors' learning. *Journal of Medical Systems, 45*(1), 1–14. DOI: 10.1007/s10916-020-01691-7 PMID: 33409620

Awonuga, K. F., Nwankwo, E. E., Oladapo, J. O., Okoye, C. C., Odunaiya, O. G., & Uzondu, C. S. (2024). *Driving sustainable growth in SME manufacturing: The role of digital transformation, project, and capture management. International Journal of Science and Research Archives*. IJSRA., DOI: 10.30574/ijsra.2024.11.1.0270

Azadegan, A., Mellat Parast, M., Lucianetti, L., Nishant, R., & Blackhurst, J. (2020). Supply chain disruptions and business continuity: An empirical assessment. *Decision Sciences, 51*(1), 38–73. DOI: 10.1111/deci.12395

Balch, J. A., Ruppert, M. M., Loftus, T. J., Guan, Z., Ren, Y., Upchurch, G. R., Ozrazgat-Baslanti, T., Rashidi, P., & Bihorac, A. (2023). Machine learning–enabled clinical information systems using fast healthcare interoperability resources data standards: Scoping review. *JMIR Medical Informatics, 11*, e48297. DOI: 10.2196/48297 PMID: 37646309

Banerjee, A., Chakraborty, C., Kumar, A., & Biswas, D. (2020). Emerging trends in IoT and big data analytics for biomedical and health care technologies. *Handbook of data science approaches for biomedical engineering,* 121-152.

Basile, L. J., Carbonara, N., Pellegrino, R., & Panniello, U. (2022). Business intelligence in the healthcare industry: The utilization of a data-driven approach to support clinical decision making. *Technovation.* Advance online publication. DOI: 10.1016/j.technovation.2022.102482

Benson, T., & Grieve, G. (2021). *Principles of health interoperability.* Springer International. DOI: 10.1007/978-3-030-56883-2

Bhatt, V., & Chakraborty, S. (2023). Improving service engagement in healthcare through internet of things based healthcare systems. *Journal of Science and Technology Policy Management, 14*(1), 53–73. DOI: 10.1108/JSTPM-03-2021-0040

Biancone, P., Secinaro, S., Marseglia, R., & Calandra, D. (2021). E-health for the future. Managerial perspectives using a multiple case study approach. *Technovation.* Advance online publication. DOI: 10.1016/j.technovation.2021.102406

Cerchione, R., Centobelli, P., Riccio, E., Abbate, S., & Oropallo, E. (2023). Blockchain's coming to hospital to digitalise healthcare services: Designing a distributed electronic health record ecosystem. *Technovation, 120,* 102480. DOI: 10.1016/j.technovation.2022.102480

Chakraborty, D., & Paul, J. (2022). Healthcare apps' purchase intention: A consumption values perspective. *Technovation.* Advance online publication. DOI: 10.1016/j.technovation.2022.102481

Chao, K., Sarker, M. N. I., Ali, I., Firdaus, R. R., Azman, A., & Shaed, M. M. (2023). Big datadriven public health policy making: Potential for the healthcare industry. *Heliyon, 9*(9), e19681. DOI: 10.1016/j.heliyon.2023.e19681 PMID: 37809720

Chatzopoulou, S., Eriksson, N. L., & Eriksson, D. (2020). Improving risk assessment in the European food safety authority: Lessons from the European Medicines Agency. *Frontiers in Plant Science, 11,* 488663. DOI: 10.3389/fpls.2020.00349 PMID: 32318080

Chiruvella, V., & Guddati, A. K. (2021). Ethical issues in patient data ownership. *Interactive Journal of Medical Research, 10*(2), e22269. DOI: 10.2196/22269 PMID: 34018968

Cobianchi, L., Dal Mas, F., & Angelos, P. (2021). One size does not fit all–translating knowledge to bridge the gaps to diversity and inclusion of surgical teams. *Annals of Surgery, 273*(2), e34–e36. DOI: 10.1097/SLA.0000000000004604 PMID: 33201134

Cobianchi, L., Dal Mas, F., Peloso, A., Pugliese, L., Massaro, M., Bagnoli, C., & Angelos, P. (2020). Planning the full recovery phase: An antifragile perspective on surgery after COVID-19. *Annals of Surgery, 272*(6), e296–e299. DOI: 10.1097/SLA.0000000000004489 PMID: 32941268

Cobianchi, L., Pugliese, L., Peloso, A., Dal Mas, F., & Angelos, P. (2020). To a new normal: Surgery and COVID-19 during the transition phase. *Annals of Surgery, 272*(2), e49–e51. DOI: 10.1097/SLA.0000000000004083 PMID: 32675493

Coccia, M. (2020). Global Encyclopedia of Public Administration, Public Policy, and Governance. *Springer Nature Switzerland AG.* Disruptive technologies for industrial and corporate change; pp. 1–7.

Colombo, F., Oderkirk, J., & Slawomirski, L. (2020). Health information systems, electronic medical records, and big data in global healthcare: Progress and challenges in oecd countries. *Handbook of Global Health,* 1-31

Cozzoli, N., Salvatore, F. P., Faccilongo, N., & Milone, M. (2022). How can big data analytics be used for healthcare organization management? Literary framework and future research from a systematic review. *BMC Health Services Research, 22*(1), 809. DOI: 10.1186/s12913-022-08167-z PMID: 35733192

Dai, T., & Tayur, S. (2020). Healthcare operations management: A snapshot of emerging research. *Manufacturing & Service Operations Management, 22*(5), 869–887. DOI: 10.1287/msom.2019.0778

Drago, C., Gatto, A., & Ruggeri, M. (2021). Telemedicine as technoinnovation to tackle COVID-19: A bibliometric analysis. *Technovation.* Advance online publication. DOI: 10.1016/j.technovation.2021.102417

Duggineni, S. S. (2023). *Data integrity as a code.* DIAC.

Fahy, N., Mauer, N., & Panteli, D. (2021). *European support for improving health and care systems.*

Flother, F., Moose, C., & Tavernelli, I. (2020). IBM Institute for Business Value-Institute for Business Value. *Expert Insights Exploring Quantum Computing Use Cases for Life Sciences: Decoding Secrets of Genomes, Drugs, and Proteins.*https:// www.ibm.com/downloads/cas/EVBKAZGJ

Gamal, A., Barakat, S., & Rezk, A. (2021). Standardised electronic health record data modeling and persistence: A comparative review. *Journal of Biomedical Informatics, 114*, 103670. DOI: 10.1016/j.jbi.2020.103670 PMID: 33359548

Gong, C., & Ribiere, V. (2020). Developing a unified definition of digital transformation. *Technovation*. Advance online publication. DOI: 10.1016/j.technovation.2020.102217

Hansen, J., Wilson, P., Verhoeven, E., Kroneman, M., Kirwan, M., Verheij, R., & van Veen, E.-B. (2021). *Assessment of the EU Member States' rules on health data in the light of GDPR*

Hartzog, W., & Richards, N. (2020). *Privacy's constitutional moment and the limits of data protection.*

Hashemzadeh, A., Avan, A., Ferns, G. A., & Khazaei, M. (2020). Vaccines based on virus-like nano-particles for use against Middle East Respiratory Syndrome (MERS) coronavirus. *Vaccine, 38*(36), 5742–5746. DOI: 10.1016/j.vaccine.2020.07.003 PMID: 32684497

Hassan, M., Awan, F. M., Naz, A., deAndrés-Galiana, E. J., Alvarez, O., Cernea, A., Fernández-Brillet, L., Fernández-Martínez, J. L., & Kloczkowski, A. (2022). Innovations in genomics and big data analytics for personalized medicine and health care: A review. *International Journal of Molecular Sciences, 23*(9), 4645. DOI: 10.3390/ijms23094645 PMID: 35563034

Ienca, M., & Vayena, E. (2020). On the responsible use of digital data to tackle the COVID-19 pandemic. *Nature Medicine, 26*(4), 463–464. DOI: 10.1038/s41591-020-0832-5 PMID: 32284619

Jacks, B. S., Ajala, O. A., Lottu, O. A., & Okafor, E. S.Boma Sonimiteim JacksOlakunle Abayomi AjalaOluwaseun Augustine LottuEnyinaya Stefano Okafor. (2024). Theoretical frameworks for ICT for development: Impact assessment of telecommunication infrastructure projects in Africa and the US. *World Journal of Advanced Research and Reviews, 21*(3), 394–400. DOI: 10.30574/wjarr.2024.21.3.0721

Jambol, D. D., Sofoluwe, O. O., Ukato, A., & Ochulor, O. J. (2024). Enhancing oil and gas production through advanced instrumentation and control systems. *GSC Advanced Research and Reviews,* 19(3), 043-056

Joel, O. T., & Oguanobi, V. U. (2024a). Entrepreneurial leadership in startups and SMEs: Critical lessons from building and sustaining growth. *International Journal of Management & Entrepreneurship Research*, *6*(5), 1441–1456. DOI: 10.51594/ijmer.v6i5.1093

Joel, O. T., & Oguanobi, V. U. (2024c). Leadership and management in high-growth environments: Effective strategies for the clean energy sector. *International Journal of Management & Entrepreneurship Research*, *6*(5), 1423–1440. DOI: 10.51594/ijmer.v6i5.1092

Joel, O. T., & Oguanobi, V. U. (2024d). Navigating business transformation and strategic decision-making in multinational energy corporations with geodata. *International Journal of Applied Research in Social Sciences*, *6*(5), 801–818. DOI: 10.51594/ijarss.v6i5.1103

Lancieri, F. (2022). *Narrowing data protection's enforcement gap.*

Martínez-Román, J. A., Gamero, J., Tamayo, J. A., & Delgado-González, L. (2020). Empirical analysis of organizational archetypes based on generation and adoption of knowledge and technologies. *Technovation*, *96-97*, 102145. Advance online publication. DOI: 10.1016/j.technovation.2020.102145

Martínez-Vergara S.J., Valls-Pasola J. (2020). Clarifying the disruptive innovation puzzle: a critical review. *Eur. J. Innovat. Manag.* .DOI: 10.1108/EJIM-07-2019-0198

Massaro, M. (2021). Digital transformation in the healthcare sector through blockchain technology. Insights from academic research and business developments. *Technovation*. Advance online publication. DOI: 10.1016/j.technovation.2021.102386

McKeown, A., Mourby, M., Harrison, P., Walker, S., Sheehan, M., & Singh, I. (2021). Ethical issues in consent for the reuse of data in health data platforms. *Science and Engineering Ethics*, *27*(1), 1–21. DOI: 10.1007/s11948-021-00282-0 PMID: 33538942

Melchiorre, M. G., Papa, R., Quattrini, S., Lamura, G., Barbabella, F., & Consortium, I. E. (2020). Integrated care programs for people with multimorbidity in European countries: eHealth adoption in health systems. *BioMed Research International*, *2020*(1), 2020. DOI: 10.1155/2020/9025326 PMID: 32337283

Meriton, R., Bhandal, R., Graham, G., & Brown, A. (2021). An examination of the generative mechanisms of value in big data-enabled supply chain management research. *International Journal of Production Research*, *59*(23), 7283–7310. DOI: 10.1080/00207543.2020.1832273

Mullins, A., O'Donnell, R., Mousa, M., Rankin, D., Ben-Meir, M., Boyd-Skinner, C., & Skouteris, H. (2020). Health outcomes and healthcare efficiencies associated with the use of electronic health records in hospital emergency departments: A systematic review. *Journal of Medical Systems*, *44*(12), 200. DOI: 10.1007/s10916-020-01660-0 PMID: 33078276

Nandi, S., Bhaduri, S., Das, D., Ghosh, P., Mandal, M., & Mitra, P. (2024). Deciphering the lexicon of protein targets: A review on multifaceted drug discovery in the era of artificial intelligence. *Molecular Pharmaceutics*, *21*(4), 1563–1590. DOI: 10.1021/acs.molpharmaceut.3c01161 PMID: 38466810

Ng, K. H., & Bezak, E. (2020). Prejudice in science – lessons from the coronavirus story. *Physica Medica*, *75*, 83–84. DOI: 10.1016/j.ejmp.2020.06.011 PMID: 32559649

Ochulor, O. J., Sofoluwe, O. O., Ukato, A., & Jambol, D. D. (2024). Technological innovations and optimised work methods in subsea maintenance and production. *Engineering Science & Technology Journal*, *5*(5), 1627–1642. DOI: 10.51594/estj.v5i5.1112

Odeyemi, O., Mhlongo, N. Z., Nwankwo, E. E., Uzondu, C. S., & Okoye, C. C. (2024). *Big data applications in portfolio management: A review of techniques and strategies. International Journal of Science and Research Archives.* IJSRA., DOI: 10.30574/ijsra.2024.11.1.0268

Ofodile, O. C., Oyewole, A. T., Ugochukwu, C. E., Addy, W. A., Adeoye, O. B., & Okoye, C. C. (2024). *Predictive analytics in climate finance: Assessing risks and opportunities for investors*. GSC Advanced Research and Reviews., DOI: 10.30574/gscarr.2024.18.2.0076

Oguanobi, V. U., & Joel, O. T. (2024). Scalable business models for startups in renewable energy: Strategies for using GIS technology to enhance SME scaling. *Engineering Science & Technology Journal*, *5*(5), 1571–1587. DOI: 10.51594/estj.v5i5.1109

Oladipo, J. O., Okoye, C. C., Elufioye, O. A., Falaiye, T., & Nwankwo, E. E. (2024). *Human factors in cybersecurity: Navigating the fintech landscape. International Journal of Science and Research Archives*. IJSRA., DOI: 10.30574/ijsra.2024.11.1.0258

Olatoye F. O., Elufioye O. A., Okoye C. C., Nwankwo E. E., & Oladapo O. O. (2024). Leadership styles and their impact on healthcare management effectiveness: A review. *International Journal of Science and Research Archives (IJSRA)*. DOI: DOI: 10.30574/ijsra.2024.11.1.0271

Oriekhoe O. I., Addy W. A., Okoye C. C., Oyewole A. T., Ofodile O. C. & Ugochukwu C. E. (2024). The role of accounting in mitigating food supply chain risks and food price volatility. *International Journal of Science and Research Archives (IJSRA)*. DOI: DOI: 10.30574/ijsra.2024.11.1.0340

Padmanaban, H. (2024). Navigating the Complexity of Regulations: Harnessing AI/ML for Precise Reporting. *Journal of Artificial Intelligence General science (JAIGS)*, 3(1), 49-61.

Pérez-Castillo, R., Serrano, M. A., & Piattini, M. (2021). Software modernization to embrace quantum technology. *Advances in Engineering Software*, *151*, 102933. Advance online publication. DOI: 10.1016/j.advengsoft.2020.102933

Perez-Pozuelo, I., Spathis, D., Clifton, E. A., & Mascolo, C. (2021). Wearables, smartphones, and artificial intelligence for digital phenotyping and health. In *Digital health* (pp. 33–54). Elsevier. DOI: 10.1016/B978-0-12-820077-3.00003-1

Perez-Pozuelo, I., Spathis, D., Gifford-Moore, J., Morley, J., & Cowls, J. (2021). Digital phenotyping and sensitive health data: Implications for data governance. *Journal of the American Medical Informatics Association : JAMIA*, *28*(9), 2002–2008. DOI: 10.1093/jamia/ocab012 PMID: 33647989

Rehman, A., Naz, S., & Razzak, I. (2022). Leveraging big data analytics in healthcare enhancement: Trends, challenges and opportunities. *Multimedia Systems*, *28*(4), 1339–1371. DOI: 10.1007/s00530-020-00736-8

Sestino, A., Prete, M. I., Piper, L., & Guido, G. (2020). Internet of Things and Big Data as enablers for business digitalization strategies. *Technovation*, *98*, 102173. Advance online publication. DOI: 10.1016/j.technovation.2020.102173

Shaygan, A., & Daim, T. (2021). Technology management maturity assessment model in healthcare research centers. *Technovation*. Advance online publication. DOI: 10.1016/j.technovation.2021.102444

Shrivastava, U., Song, J., Han, B. T., & Dietzman, D. (2021). Do data security measures, privacy regulations, and communication standards impact the interoperability of patient health information? A cross-country investigation. *International Journal of Medical Informatics*, *148*, 104401. DOI: 10.1016/j.ijmedinf.2021.104401 PMID: 33571743

Siddiq, M. (2022). Use of machine learning to predict patient developing a disease or condition for early diagnose. *International Journal of Multidisciplinary Sciences and Arts*, *1*(1). Advance online publication. DOI: 10.47709/ijmdsa.v1i1.2271

Spanò, R., Massaro, M., & Iacuzzi, S. (2021). Blockchain for value creation in the healthcare sector. *Technovation*. Advance online publication. DOI: 10.1016/j.technovation.2021.102440

Stephanie, L., & Sharma, R. S. (2020). Digital health eco-systems: An epochal review of practice-oriented research. *International Journal of Information Management*, *53*, 102032. Advance online publication. DOI: 10.1016/j.ijinfomgt.2019.10.017

Tamiminia, H., Salehi, B., Mahdianpari, M., Quackenbush, L., Adeli, S., & Brisco, B. (2020). Google Earth Engine for geo-big data applications: A meta-analysis and systematic review. *ISPRS Journal of Photogrammetry and Remote Sensing*, *164*, 152–170. DOI: 10.1016/j.isprsjprs.2020.04.001

Tan, F. T. C., Ondrus, J., Tan, B., & Oh, J. (2020). Digital transformation of business ecosystems: Evidence from the Korean pop industry. *Information Systems Journal*, *30*(5), 866–898. DOI: 10.1111/isj.12285

Tariq, M. U. (2024). Enhancing cybersecurity protocols in modern healthcare systems: Strategies and best practices. In *Transformative Approaches to Patient Literacy and Healthcare Innovation* (pp. 223–241). IGI Global. DOI: 10.4018/979-8-3693-3661-8.ch011

Tayefi, M., Ngo, P., Chomutare, T., Dalianis, H., Salvi, E., Budrionis, A., & Godtliebsen, F. (2021). Challenges and opportunities beyond structured data in analysis of electronic health records. *Wiley Interdisciplinary Reviews: Computational Statistics*, *13*(6), e1549. DOI: 10.1002/wics.1549

Towett, G., Snead, R. S., Grigoryan, K., & Marczika, J. (2023). Geographical and practical challenges in the implementation of digital health passports for cross-border COVID-19 pandemic management: A narrative review and framework for solutions. *Globalization and Health*, *19*(1), 98. DOI: 10.1186/s12992-023-00998-7 PMID: 38066568

Ukato, A., Sofoluwe, O. O., Jambol, D. D., & Ochulor, O. J. (2024). Optimising maintenance logistics on offshore platforms with AI: Current strategies and future innovations.

Uzougbo, N. S., Ikegwu, C. G., & Adewusi, A. O. (2024). International enforcement of cryptocurrency laws: Jurisdictional challenges and collaborative solutions. *Magna Scientia Advanced Research and Reviews,* 11(1), 068-083

Weerasinghe, K., Scahill, S. L., Pauleen, D. J., & Taskin, N. (2022). Big data analytics for clinical decision-making: Understanding health sector perceptions of policy and practice. *Technological Forecasting and Social Change*, *174*, 121222. DOI: 10.1016/j.techfore.2021.121222

Williamson, S. M., & Prybutok, V. (2024). Balancing privacy and progress: A review of privacy challenges, systemic oversight, and patient perceptions in AI-Driven healthcare. *Applied Sciences (Basel, Switzerland)*, *14*(2), 675. DOI: 10.3390/app14020675

Wimelius, H., Mathiassen, L., Holmström, J., & Keil, M. (2021). A paradoxical perspective on technology renewal in digital transformation. *Information Systems Journal*, *31*(1), 198–225. DOI: 10.1111/isj.12307

Yang, F., & Gu, S. (2021). Industry 4.0, a revolution that requires technology and national strategies. *Complex & Intelligent Systems*, *7*(3), 1311–1325. DOI: 10.1007/s40747-020-00267-9

Yuan, X., Yang, C., He, Q., Chen, J., Yu, D., Li, J., Zhai, S., Qin, Z., Du, K., Chu, Z., & Qin, P. (2020). Current and perspective diagnostic techniques for COVID-19. *ACS Infectious Diseases*, *6*(8), 1998–2016. DOI: 10.1021/acsinfecdis.0c00365 PMID: 32677821

Zeadally, S., Siddiqui, F., Baig, Z., & Ibrahim, A. (2020). Smart healthcare: Challenges and potential solutions using internet of things (IoT) and big data analytics. *PSU Research Review*, *4*(2), 149–168. DOI: 10.1108/PRR-08-2019-0027

Zhang, A., Xing, L., Zou, J., & Wu, J. C. (2022). Shifting machine learning for healthcare from development to deployment and from models to data. *Nature Biomedical Engineering*, *6*(12), 1330–1345. DOI: 10.1038/s41551-022-00898-y PMID: 35788685

Zinner, M., Dahlhausen, F., Boehme, P., Ehlers, J., Bieske, L., & Fehring, L. (2021). Quantum computing's potential for drug discovery: Early stage industry dynamics. *Drug Discovery Today*, *26*(7), 1680–1688. DOI: 10.1016/j.drudis.2021.06.003 PMID: 34119668

Chapter 8
Penetration Testing and Risk Taxonomy Framework for NB-IoT Security

Hafiz Muhammad Attaullah
http://orcid.org/0000-0002-4647-2607
Multimedia University, Cyberjaya, Malaysia

Al-Sakib Khan Pathan
http://orcid.org/0000-0001-6572-3451
United International University, Bangladesh

ABSTRACT

As the deployment of Narrowband Internet of Things (NB-IoT) networks accelerates globally, their inherently constrained architecture and large-scale connectivity introduce critical security challenges. Hence, there is a need to present a penetration testing and risk assessment framework taxonomy specifically designed for NB-IoT ecosystems that would leverage ethical hacking methodologies. In this chapter, we conduct targeted vulnerability analysis using virtualized testbeds and industry-standard toolkits, simulating various attacks. We introduce a comprehensive risk taxonomy that categorizes threats across various NB-IoT network layers, including edge, core, device, and operational components. By mapping penetration testing results to this structured taxonomy, our study provides an effective means to evaluate risk severity, uncover security gaps, and recommend mitigation strategies. This work also addresses the ethical, and compliance aspects of penetration testing within IoT environments, ensuring responsible disclosure and alignment with recognized standards such as NIST and ETSI.

DOI: 10.4018/979-8-3373-3536-0.ch008

1. INTRODUCTION

NB-IoT (Narrowband Internet of Things) stands as a prominent LPWAN (Low-Power Wide-Area Network) technology which provides affordable power-saving connectivity platforms for mMTC (Massive Machine Type Communications) requirements. The 3GPP (3rd Generation Partnership Project) Release 13 standard along with its following versions have incorporated NB-IoT to power billions of devices sending small data packets across extended ranges at low power usage that suits smart cities, industrial controls, smart meters, and agricultural systems (Iftikhar et al., 2025; Chaudhari et al., 2020; Iqbal et al., 2020). Figure 1 shows NB-IoT's position as an LPWAN technology.

The security constraints of NB-IoT stem from its design considerations which support limited devices and reduced protocol requirements. Attack surfaces in NB-IoT environments include weak authentication mechanisms, susceptibility to replay attacks, jamming, rogue base stations, and eavesdropping on control signaling (Mekki et al., 2019; Song et al., 2017). Figure 2 illustrates the IMT-2020 framework defined by ITU (International Telecommunication Union), showcasing the three major use cases, eMBB (Enhanced Mobile Broadband), uRLLC (Ultra-Reliable Low-Latency Communication), and mMTC (Massive Machine Type Communications). Each one is optimized for differing requirements of data rate, latency, and reliability (ITU-R, 2015).

Figure 1. LPWAN technologies.

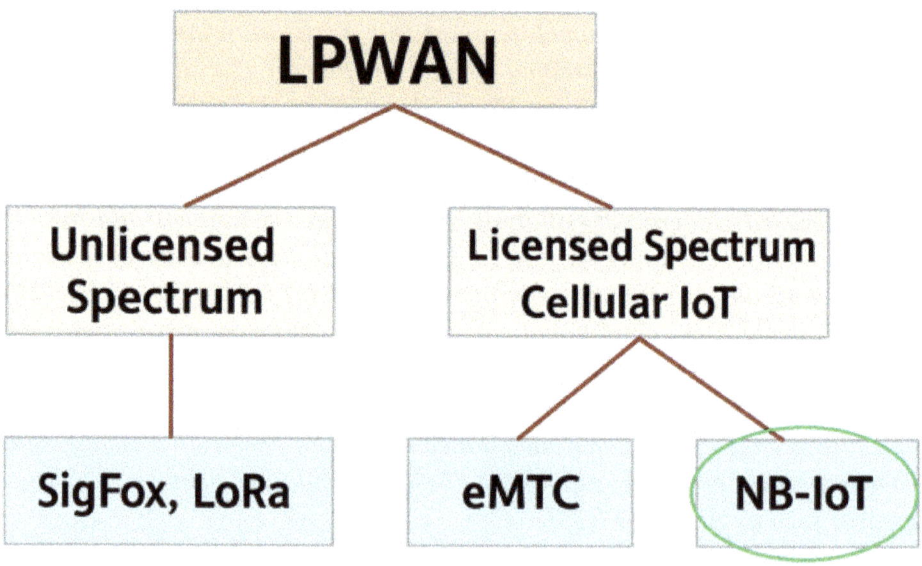

Figure 2. IMT-2020 Use Case Triangle: eMBB, uRLLC, and mMTC with Contradictory Requirements in Data Rate, Latency, and Reliability

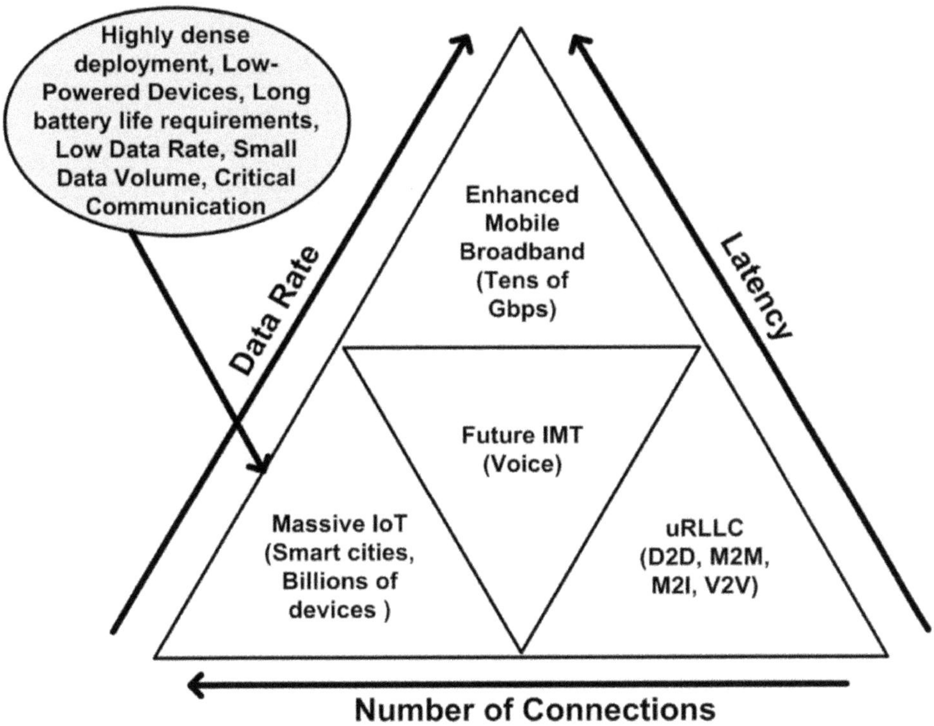

(Adapted from ITU-R M.2083-0).

Since it depends on LTE (Long Term Evolution)/5G networks, there are inherent security issues and incomplete encryption between the device and the cloud. NB-IoT networks are growing internationally, and managing these threats is very important for ensuring reliability and trust. Although several studies have identified weaknesses in protocols and deployments (Chen et al., 2022; Krupka et al., 2016; Mekki et al., 2018; Ogbodo et al., 2022; Hossain & Markendahl, 2021), tactics for NB-IoT assurance testing in realistic environments are largely underexplored. 3GPP Release 18 (2024) introduces new qualities, like more support for NTN, greater accuracy in location, and energy-saving advances for NB-IoT. Release 19 focuses on adding NB-IoT to communication systems that rely on satellites, to enhance their reach and reliability (Iridium Communications, 2024); (Rohde & Schwarz, 2023). We have to take all these advancements and capabilities into consideration when dealing with NB-IoT. Figure 3 shows all the releases that are available so far (at the time of writing this chapter), highlighting key enhancements in each release.

Figure 3. NB-IoT Evolution and 3GPP releases.

Release 14	Release 15	Release 16	Release 17	Release 18	Release 19
• Single-cell multicast • OTDOA positioning enhancements • New bands support	• Cat NB2 • Non-anchor carrier operation • Mobility enhancements • Low power class • NB-IoT small cell support • NB-IoT TDD support • Higher spectral efficiency • Early data transmission • Wake-up radio • Power consumption and latency reduction	• Improved DL/UL transmission efficiency and UE power consumption • Scheduling enhancement • Network management enhancement • Improved multi-carrier operation • Mobility enhancement • Coexistence with NR	• Increased DL/UL peak data rate (16-QAM) • Reduced RRC reestablishment time • Support for NB-IoT carrier selection depending on the coverage level and specific carrier configurations	• Enhanced support for Non-Terrestrial Networks • Improved positioning accuracy for NB-IoT devices • Power saving for extended battery life • Further coexistence with 5G NR • Resource optimization for dense IoT deployments	• Extended NB-IoT for direct satellite communication (NTN Phase 2) • Advanced mobility and roaming improvements • Enhanced uplink for remote device communication • Interworking between terrestrial and non-terrestrial networks • Optimized for ultra-low power devices

Given these evolving standards and persistent vulnerabilities, assessing the security posture of NB-IoT networks requires more than just protocol updates – in fact, it calls for proactive and environment-specific security evaluation techniques.

Figure 4. NB-IoT System Architecture.

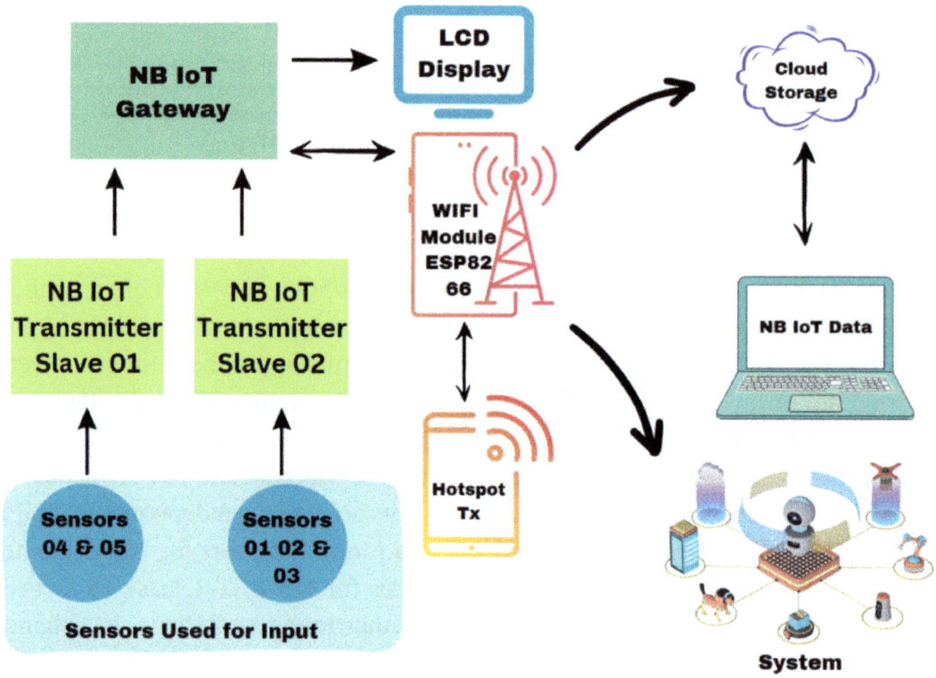

Penetration testing (‘*pentesting*’ in short) has become an indispensable technique in modern cybersecurity, enabling ethical hackers to simulate real-world attacks to uncover unknown vulnerabilities. However, most traditional pentesting frameworks are designed for full-stack computing environments and they fail to address the unique constraints of NB-IoT, such as its half-duplex nature, narrowband spectrum, and battery-optimized protocols (Chacko & Job, 2018; Rubio-Aparicio et al., 2019). A tailored penetration testing strategy, integrated with NB-IoT-specific testbeds and lightweight attack vectors, is thus necessary for evaluating and strengthening the security posture of such systems.

To contextualize the role of penetration testing and security assessment, Figure 4 illustrates a simplified NB-IoT system setup that integrates various hardware components and communication modules:

- **Sensor Layer:** The system starts with multiple sensors (e.g., O1–O5) that monitor environmental inputs.
- **Transmitter Layer:** Sensors relay data to NB-IoT slave transmitters, which then forward it to a centralized NB-IoT Gateway.
- **Communication Module:** Data is transmitted via an ESP8266 WiFi module, which connects to a mobile hotspot and provides bidirectional communication.
- **Edge Processing:** A local LCD (Liquid Crystal Display) display shows real-time data, improving observability at the edge.
- **Cloud and System Integration:** Sensor data is sent to cloud storage and processed into an NB-IoT data platform for analytics and visualization.

This configured network system provides a realistic representation of operational environments which serves as basis for our research framework for penetration testing and risk assessment.

1.1 Motivation

Static analysis together with passive monitoring methods prove insufficient when protecting NB-IoT infrastructure because of its distinctive security risks. Laboratory-based penetration testing creates controlled attack simulations to find vulnerable security points that appear while observing present weaknesses in protected situations. A risk taxonomy structure enables professionals to develop defined threat management strategies including identification and prioritization for protecting the NB-IoT stack.

The existing scholarly works (Naik, 2018, Williams et al., 2019) show a substantial gap in the frameworks which would unify empirical penetration testing with virtualized testbeds and standard-based risk classification techniques (Krishna et al., 2021).

1.2 Contributions

This chapter introduces a simulation-based framework with NB IoT specific risk taxonomy to conduct penetration tests in NB IoT networks. It has explored different NB IoT weaknesses but has not connected this work with the ethical hacking issue through testbed simulation meets the NIST (National Institute of Standards and Technology) and ETSI (European Telecommunications Standards Institute) compliance requirements. Our main contributions include:

- Designing and simulation of real-world NB IoT attack scenarios such as ACK spoofing, eavesdropping, and node compromise using testbed tools (e.g., Kali Linux[1], NS-3[2], QEMU[3]).
- Development of a multi-layered risk taxonomy aligned with ETSI and NIST standards to map threats across the device, network, and application layers.
- Integration of ethical and compliance considerations for responsible hacking and security assessments in constrained IoT environments.
- Visual prototype and testbed architecture, as depicted in Figure 4, which forms the foundation for repeatable experimentation and academic replication.

1.3 Structure of the Chapter

A systematic approach of this study identifies security issues within NB-IoT by performing penetration testing and using simulation and taxonomy risk modeling methods. The construction moves systematically through theoretical bases into actual deployment together with evaluation procedures.

The Section 2 surveys existing works on NB-IoT security along with penetration testing approaches and risk taxonomy models. This research targets identifying key gaps that exist in simulation studies and ethical hacking methods as well as compliance alignment (that this study needs to bridge). Section 3 introduces essential definitions and key concepts that appear across the manuscript including NB-IoT, ethical hacking, risk taxonomy and specifies applicable cybersecurity standards (i.e., ETSI EN 303 645 and NIST SP 800-115). Conceptual understanding is made clear before introducing the technical elements.

Section 4 presents the methodology which includes designing a virtualized testbed through NS-3 simulator together with QEMU implementation. This section outlines the system design approaches along with configuration choices and justification of selected tools to construct virtual environments that replicate actual NB-IoT systems with attack events.

Section 5 defines NB-IoT's multi layered threat model, categorizing vulnerabilities across Device, Network, Core/Edge, Application, and Management Layers.

It also contrasts passive and active attack techniques. Section 6 presents simulated attack results using a STRIDE framework and maps vulnerabilities to their CVSS scores having attack severity and system impact. Section 7 introduces a structured risk evaluation using CVSS, aligning vulnerabilities with NIST and ETSI benchmarks. Layer-wise impacts and mitigation priorities are visualized and explained in that section.

Section 8 proposes a multi-domain risk taxonomy for NB-IoT that classifies threats by attack layer, risk domain, and compliance alignment that supports reproducibility and regulatory validation. Section 9 reflects on simulation limitations and finally, Section 10 summarizes key findings with taxonomy-based risk analysis in securing NB-IoT infrastructures.

2. RELATED WORK

The simple NB-IoT framework and its strong penetrative ability prove it to be an excellent solution for building extensive IoT networks. The security problems in NB-IoT stem from its desirable features since they result in weak user authentication methods and delayed software updates alongside limited computational processing. Documented security measures that include penetration testing and formal risk modeling must be implemented to secure the growing deployment of NB-IoT technology as stated in (Chacko & Job, 2018; Khanam et al., 2020) and (Nabi et al., 2024). The analysis of NB-IoT exploitation remains relatively scarce because it poorly combines with ethical hacking models and simulation testing solutions using defined risk categories and standard compliance protocols. Researchers in the academia should create unified security guidelines for NB-IoT security to obtain repeatable experimental results alongside regulatory compliance directives.

Table 1. Summary of Selected NB-IoT Security Studies. Here the tick ( ) means the issue has been addressed in the work.

Reference	**NB-IoT Focus**	**Penetration Testing**	**Risk Taxonomy**	**Virtualized Testbed**	**Standards (ETSI/NIST)**
Khanam et al., 2020					
Zardari et al., 2023	✓		✓		✓
Sunku Mohan et al., 2025	✓				
Stanco et al., 2024	✓				

continued on following page

Table 1. Continued

Reference	NB-IoT Focus	Penetration Testing	Risk Taxonomy	Virtualized Testbed	Standards (ETSI/NIST)
Khanam et al., 2020					
Campoverde-Fordon & Andersen, 2024	✓		✓		
Bacci et al., 2024	✓		✓	✓	✓
Abdollahi et al., 2024	✓			✓	
Rajalingam & Kavitha, 2024	✓			✓	
Cambosuela et al., 2024		✓	✓	✓	
Suman et al., 2025		✓	✓		

This research analyzed peer-reviewed studies using a wide scope starting from 2018 until 2024. The academic research on NB-IoT security is analyzed as shown in Table 1 via thematic identification of key characteristics that consist of: (1) NB-IoT specific approaches; (2) penetration testing methods; (3) risk taxonomy utilization; and (4) virtual test environments; and (5) adherence to ETSI and NIST standards.

The analysis by both (Zardari et al., 2023) and (Sunku Mohan et al., 2025) evaluated NB-IoT protocol weaknesses which include Denial-of-Service (DoS) attacks and malicious user equipment (UE) and spoofing issues. The research confirmed the feasibility of attacks but failed to use simulation-based testing and maintain connections to standardized threat classifications. (Attaullah et al., 2024) used the STRIDE model to analyze security functions within multiple LPWAN standards that featured Sigfox along with LoRa (Long Range) as one of them. The useful information within this study was missing practical penetration testing features as well as technical simulation capabilities.

Nowadays, research works focus on developing minimalistic cryptographic defenses for restricted NB-IoT equipment. (Uddin, 2024) suggested implementing physical unclonable functions (PUFs) for enhancing security at the chip-level. (Stanco et al., 2024) presented analysis on mechanisms for access control in communication protocol defense systems. However, this research failed to incorporate structured risk assessment tools and to integrate their designs with requirements established by ETSI/NIST. (Mandal, 2024) conducted simulation study applying NS-3 which demonstrates potential for testing systems alongside regulatory standards.

Real and simulated NB-IoT environments served as the focus of both (Campoverde-Fordon & Andersen, 2024) and (Mohammed & Chopra, n.d.) performance benchmark investigation. These test platforms evaluated RF coverage performance as well as attack surface security under different network load testing conditions. The implemented testbeds failed to accommodate both ethical hacking simulation and the identification of risks within their systems.

The NB-IoT-specific features and deployment constraints of IoT-PEN (Chen et al., 2022) and (Krishna et al., 2021) remain outside their analytical capabilities for automated scalable penetration testing of IoT ecosystems. The architectures provide starting points yet need specific modifications to work with NB-IoT's exclusive operational constraints and domains.

Table 2. Identified key Limitations in Existing NB-IoT Security Studies.

Research Work	Key Limitation(s)
Khanam et al., 2020	No simulation or testbed; lacks risk mapping and taxonomy integration
Zardari et al., 2023	STRIDE-based only; lacks ethical testing, testbed, and real-world validation
Sunku Mohan et al., 2025	Focuses only on data flow security; lacks taxonomy, testbed, or compliance mapping
Stanco et al., 2024)	Hardware-level focus only (PUFs); no ethical hacking or taxonomy model
(Campoverde-Fordon & Andersen, 2024)	Focused on access protocols; no testbed or taxonomy integration; limited practical attack simulation
(Bacci et al., 2024)	Focused on post-quantum crypto; partial compliance; no active penetration testing
(Abdollahi et al., 2024)	Validated testbeds but no security testing or compliance assessment
(Rajalingam & Kavitha, 2024)	Fog computing solution; lacks ethical testing or structured taxonomy
(Cambosuela et al., 2024)	Generic IoT; not specific to NB-IoT constraints or protocols
(Suman et al., 2025); (Attaullah et al., 2021)	Focuses on IoT-cloud, not NB-IoT; lacks testbed or compliance linkage

Several research works have examined how NB-IoT security solutions meet compliance requirements yet the number remains limited. The evaluation of cryptographic protocols requires NIST compatibility according to the work of (Bacci et al., 2024). (Abdollahi, et al., 2024) and (Rajalingam & Kavitha, 2024) also offer frameworks consistent with ETSI and ISO 31000. However, few works connect penetration testing outputs directly to these frameworks.

Despite growing attention toward securing NB-IoT infrastructures, several critical limitations persist in the existing body of work. While prior research addresses individual aspects—such as protocol vulnerabilities, lightweight encryption, or simulation platforms—few integrate these dimensions into a cohesive and actionable security framework.

Notably, most studies lack real-world penetration testing, formalized risk taxonomies, and alignment with regulatory standards like ETSI or NIST (Cambosuela, et al., 2024). This disconnect limits their practical applicability and reproducibility in production environments (Suman et al., 2025).

Table 2 summarizes the key limitations of the selected studies that we reviewed. The works are categorized by their shortcomings in areas such as ethical testing, simulation, compliance, and risk modeling. The analysis reveals an underexplored intersection of penetration testing, risk taxonomy modeling, and simulation-based validation in the context of NB-IoT. Specifically, most works:

- Are either theoretical or simulation-only without ethical hacking strategies.
- Lack integration with established risk models like STRIDE or ISO 31000.
- Do not apply findings to compliance matrices from ETSI or NIST.
- Fail to provide a replicable, end-to-end testing framework.

Therefore, there is a consistent absence of holistic NB-IoT-specific approaches that combine penetration testing, structured risk analysis, and simulation-based validation. This study seeks to bridge this gap by proposing an integrated framework that leverages virtualized testbeds, ethical hacking methodologies, and taxonomy-based risk classification grounded on compliance best practices.

3. KEY CONCEPTS AND DEFINITIONS

To establish conceptual clarity and ensure consistency throughout this study, it is essential to define the foundational terms and constructs that underpin NB-IoT security, penetration testing, and associated risk modeling. This section first presents major terminologies which will be applied during analysis and framework design and simulation. Table 3 highlights the key concepts and their relevance to this research.

3.1 Narrowband Internet of Things

3GPP under LTE Release 13 created NB-IoT as a low-power wide-area network technology (LPWAN). NB-IoT offers special optimization for products that need both restricted data transfer and prolonged power supply. The design simplicity and lack of default security measures associated with NB-IoT create vulnerabilities that mainly affect its physical and network layers according to Coman et al. (2019) and (Ogbodo et al., 2022) together with (Naik, 2018). Multiple security layers form the framework of NB-IoT protection which contains distinct weaknesses and limitations as presented in Table 4. The analysis of these specific layers enables successful penetration testing and correct responsibility evaluation (Nabi et al., 2024).

3.2 Penetration Testing

Testing for cyberattack scenarios inside a company's systems is done to discover what vulnerabilities an attacker could exploit. The study employs penetration testing methods through virtual spaces together with open-source tools such as Kali Linux which targets NB-IoT-specific RRC (Radio Resource Control), NAS (Non-Access Stratum) and UDP (User Datagram Protocol)-based applications. This approach is effective because it confirms possible attacks and advises on improvements.

Table 3. Overview of Core Concepts.

Term	Definition	Relevance to this Study
NB-IoT	A 3GPP LPWAN technology optimized for low power, wide-area, and massive device connectivity.	Central focus; offers constrained bandwidth and power, making conventional security models infeasible.
Penetration Testing	The ethical simulation of cyberattacks to evaluate a system's vulnerability and resilience.	Essential to identify exploitable flaws in NB-IoT protocol stacks and interfaces.
Risk Taxonomy	A hierarchical classification of threats and vulnerabilities categorized by source, impact, or layer.	Enables systematic mapping of discovered vulnerabilities to risk models (e.g., STRIDE).
Virtualized Testbed	A software-based emulation environment (e.g., NS-3, QEMU) for replicating real-world network behaviors.	Facilitates ethical attack simulations without compromising real NB-IoT infrastructures.
Malicious UE Attack	Attacks launched by rogue user equipment impersonating legitimate devices.	Common in NB-IoT; exploited for spoofing, ACK flooding, and battery draining.
STRIDE Model	Microsoft's threat classification framework: Spoofing, Tampering, Repudiation, Information disclosure, Denial-of-Service, Elevation of privilege.	Used in NB-IoT to classify threats across protocol and device layers.
ETSI & ISO 31000	European standardization for IoT and formal risk management.	Provides compliance and security lifecycle management for NB-IoT devices.
NIST SP 800-series	U.S. cybersecurity standards and guidelines for secure system design and evaluation.	Serves as a benchmark for security assessment frameworks, including for LPWANs like NB-IoT.

continued on following page

Table 3. Continued

Term	Definition	Relevance to this Study
Lightweight Cryptography	Encryption designed for resource-constrained environments.	Critical in NB-IoT to protect data confidentiality without overloading devices.
Ethical Hacking	Authorized and systematic probing of systems to reveal exploitable vulnerabilities.	Informs the penetration testing strategy for this study.

Table 4. Layers with Threat Surface in NB-IoT.

Layer	Description	Typical Vulnerabilities
Device Layer	Includes sensors, embedded modules, and communication chips.	Physical tampering, identity spoofing, firmware backdoors, weak encryption.
Network Layer	NB-IoT protocol stack and transport architecture.	ACK spoofing, jamming, replay attacks, false base station injection.
Edge/Core Layer	Gateways, aggregators, and cloud interfaces.	Middleware hijacking, authentication bypass, side-channel attacks.
Application Layer	User-level applications accessing sensor data or issuing commands.	Injection attacks, improper access control, insecure APIs.
Management Layer	Security lifecycle, provisioning, monitoring, and updates.	Infrequent patching, poor audit trails, unauthorized provisioning.

3.3 Risk Taxonomy

The process of systematic classification takes place when people organize dangers and risks through what is known as a risk taxonomy. The taxonomy connects identified vulnerabilities to diverse network locations (device, edge and core) and threat categories, and impact severity based on standards from ISO 31000 and STRIDE. Such standards enable organizations to sort out risk remedies for potential harm as well as vulnerability extent.

3.4 Virtualized Testbed

Virtualized testbeds represent simulated platforms that enable the deployment of NB-IoT elements which include eNodeBs (Evolved Node B) together with MME (Mobility Management Entity), HSS (Home Subscriber Server), and UEs (User Equipment) through NS-3, QEMU and Docker. Virtualized testbeds provide consistent test methods to evaluate both protocol functions and system reactions toward different enemy situations while protecting live operational networks (Zeitler et al., 2022; Mohan et al., 2024).

3.5 Malicious UE Attack

The entrance of non-authentic devices which pose as legitimate NB-IoT terminals leads to Malicious User Equipment (UE) attacks on the network. Network attacks targeting NB-IoT systems consist of ACK spoofing (false acknowledgment transmission) and energy depletion (unnecessary handshakes) as well as identity impersonation (these attacks are particularly dangerous because NB-IoT provides no real-time authentication mechanism).

3.6 STRIDE Threat Model

Microsoft established STRIDE as a threat categorization model for six threat classes including Spoofing together with Tampering, Repudiation, and Information Disclosure in addition to Denial-of-Service (DoS) and Elevation of Privilege. This study uses STRIDE to structure penetration testing outcomes while matching them to NB-IoT protocol stack layers and components (Iqbal, 2020).

3.7 ETSI & ISO 31000

Structured risk management and IoT security standards are supplied through two sources known as The European Telecommunications Standards Institute (ETSI) and ISO 31000 (ISO stands for International Organization for Standardization). According to ETSI EN 303 645 the baseline security features for IoT devices are specified but the risk identification framework within ISO 31000 allows identification of risks at various levels alongside their treatment and analysis. All risk modeling activities at our organization use these standards as foundational elements of compliance.

3.8 NIST SP 800-Series

The National Institute of Standards and Technology (NIST) SP 800-series provides multiple guidelines which cover information system security. The work references SP 800-115 penetration testing protocols for developing examination methodologies to fulfill national cybersecurity standards throughout assessment and disclosure stages.

3.9 Lightweight Cryptography

The security needs of devices with constrained processing capabilities are served by specific cryptographic approaches known as lightweight techniques in NB-IoT sensors. The cryptographic algorithms AES-CCM, PRESENT and ChaCha20 are preferred because they provide security functions with very low power consumption. These are important in this study for securing communications without degrading performance.

3.10 Ethical Hacking

Ethical hacking is the practice of legally and responsibly probing systems for security weaknesses. It combines penetration testing with reporting and remediation recommendations and aligns with responsible disclosure policies. This study utilizes ethical hacking to simulate attacks under strict compliance with NIST and ETSI guidelines.

4. METHODOLOGY

A simulation-based environment for penetration testing of NB-IoT was built using NS-3, which is the open-source network simulator widely used for research purposes. With NetAnim, users had the ability to see what is taking place on the network, the flow of data, and how the network responds to various threats.

This simulator sets up a realistic situation for NB-IoT devices with limitations, using multiple gateways and cloud-based data storage. The purpose of the testbed was to launch ethical attacks, detect vulnerabilities, and replicate the effects of common threats such as spoofing, Denial-of-Service (DoS), and unauthorized access. Using automation helps accomplish tests in a consistent, easily repeatable way, and meets industry standards like NIST SP 800-115 and ETSI EN 303 645.

4.1 Rationale for Virtualized Testbed

Traditional penetration testing tools and environments are often incompatible or too resource-intensive for such constrained settings. The use of a virtualized testbed based on NS-3 offers several advantages:

- **Scalability:** Simulates dozens of end devices (EDs) and multiple gateways (GWs) without the need for physical hardware.

- **Reproducibility:** Allows repeated simulations under identical conditions to benchmark and validate results.
- **Attack Simulation:** Supports the injection of attack payloads (e.g., ACK spoofing, replay attacks) and tracks their effects on network performance.
- **Compliance Alignment:** Enables adherence to security testing protocols outlined in NIST SP 800-series and ETSI's IoT security guidelines.
- **Energy & Traffic Modeling:** Supports lightweight energy-aware device profiles and packet transmission patterns for realistic emulation.

4.2 Architecture Design

The architecture shown in Figure 5 simulates a clustered NB-IoT network comprising seven gateway nodes (**GW_1** to **GW_7**) and 50 end-devices (**ED_1** to **ED_50**) distributed across the network. All nodes communicate using simplified UDP/IP stack configurations to minimize overhead and reflect the constrained nature of NB-IoT communications.

Figure 5. NS-3 Simulation Scenario.

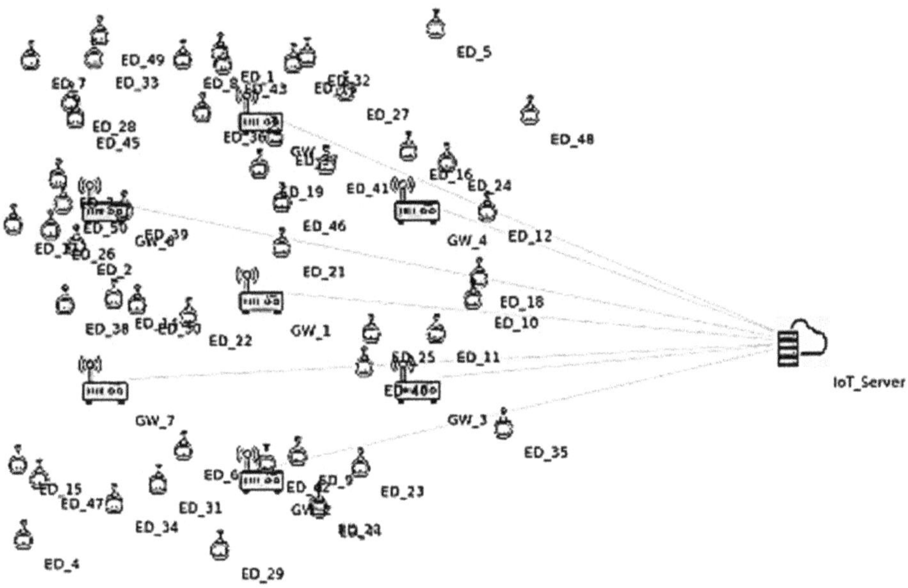

Each cluster of end-devices is associated with a specific gateway node, which serves as the intermediary between the edge layer and a central IoT Server, representing a cloud-hosted processing and storage unit. Communication flows from EDs to the

IoT Server are continuously monitored to detect anomalies during penetration test scenarios. Figure 5 shows real time packet transmission from multiple EDs through designated gateways toward a centralized IoT server. Different traffic patterns and node behaviors (e.g., gateway congestion, packet loss) are visually traceable.

This architecture reflects deployment realities of smart infrastructure use cases such as smart metering, environmental monitoring, and industrial automation as presented in Table 5, where the table summarizes the main virtualized elements used in the NS-3 simulation environment, reflecting the roles and interactions typical in real-world NB-IoT deployments. Each gateway mimics NB-IoT base station behavior by implementing simplified access and aggregation protocols.

Table 5. Description of Key Components in Simulation.

Component	Description
End Devices (ED_x)	Represent NB-IoT nodes (sensors or actuators) transmitting telemetry data periodically.
Gateway Nodes (GW_x)	Act as NB-IoT eNodeBs, aggregating packets from EDs and forwarding to the IoT server.
IoT Server	Simulates a cloud data center, receiving and analyzing aggregated sensor data.
NetAnim Tool	Used to visualize node topology, connectivity, and packet flow in real-time.

4.3 Configuration Parameters

To accurately replicate the operational dynamics of NB-IoT systems, the simulation environment was configured with real-world-inspired parameters. The NS-3.35 version was utilized with LTE and IoT modules, extended to support NB-IoT channel models. The network topology comprises 50+ EDs and 7 GWs) connected to a centralized IoT server, as visualized in Figure 5 (NetAnim output). All nodes are spatially distributed within a $500 \times 500\ m^2$ grid, incorporating realistic propagation loss and channel delay models.

As in Table 6, the application traffic model follows a periodic UDP pattern, simulating typical NB-IoT use cases such as smart metering, where data is sent at regular intervals using lightweight protocols. UDP was selected due to its connectionless nature and low overhead, aligning with the constraints of NB-IoT systems. A transmission range of 100 meters was configured to model realistic short-range communication within dense deployments. Wireless propagation was modeled using a combination of the log-distance and Nakagami channel models, which together simulate both path loss over distance and small-scale signal fading—key characteristics of LPWAN environments.

To introduce further environmental realism, the simulation incorporated both Friis and shadowing-based propagation loss models. These capture signal degradation due to physical obstacles and interference, which are important for analyzing the impact of attacks such as jamming or spoofing. The MAC/PHY layer operated with an LTE stack modification that applied the NB-IoT standard for narrowband (180 kHz) frequency bands while implementing reduced periodic data transmissions. The configuration operates within 3GPP-compliant NB-IoT frameworks to validate the system's limited operation capabilities. The system maintained consistent packets of 100 bytes which mirrors the regular sizes used by NB-IoT networks.

Energy-efficient packages introduce vulnerabilities to spoofing and amplification attacks because of their small size. Several penetration test hooks were developed for assessing these potential risks in the simulation. Three modules were added to the simulation for penetration testing: an ACK spoofing module displayed fake ACK packets to misdirect signal sources, a jammer node which transmitted continuously, followed by an energy drain trigger that used repeated handshaking procedures to swiftly drain power supply. The combined use of adversarial modules permits thorough attack simulation on different network strata that delivers experimental findings about system vulnerabilities and resilience against adversarial threats.

Table 6. Simulation parameters adopted.

Parameter	Value	Description
Simulation Time	500 seconds	Total duration of simulated NB-IoT operation
Node Count	55 EDs, 7 GWs	End Devices (sensors) and Gateways (eNodeBs)
Application Traffic	Periodic UDP	Devices transmit sensor data at 10-second intervals
Transmission Range	100 meters	Gateway signal coverage for EDs
Channel Model	Log-Distance + Nakagami	Reflects urban deployment with fading and shadowing effects
Propagation Loss Model	Friis + Shadowing	Introduces environmental impact on signal strength
MAC/PHY Layer Protocol	NB-IoT-enabled LTE	Customized LTE stack to model narrowband communication
Packet Size	100 bytes	Payload per message from sensors
Penetration Test Hooks	ACK spoofing module, jammer node, energy drain trigger	Simulated attack modules integrated into the NS-3 engine

Such emulation configuration enables laboratories to simulate legitimate and adversarial conditions of constrained devices without needing actual physical test-beds (Zeitler et al., 2022).

5. THREAT SURFACE

Analyzing NB-IoT's multi-layered system helps create effective defense systems as well as penetration testing frameworks. The designed aim of NB-IoT features mMTC functionalities that extend coverage areas while requiring minimal power and enabling cost-effective deployments. The simplified protocol structure of NB-IoT together with its minimalistic design structure creates numerous security challenges (see Table 7).

Table 7. Threat Surface and Gaps.

Layer	Description	Common Threats and Vulnerabilities
Device Layer	Physical NB-IoT devices including sensors, actuators, and modules.	- Physical tampering - Static key usage - Firmware backdoors - Identity spoofing
Network Layer	Handles wireless transmission using NB-IoT protocols like RRC and NAS.	- ACK spoofing - Replay attacks - Eavesdropping - Rogue base station injection
Edge/Core Layer	Includes gateways, aggregators, and cloud middleware managing traffic.	- Middleware hijacking - Session replay - Man-in-the-middle (MitM) attacks
Application Layer	User-facing services and APIs used to collect and interact with sensor data.	- API injection attacks - Insecure access control - Data exfiltration - Session fixation
Management Layer	Responsible for firmware updates, key provisioning, and lifecycle monitoring.	- Insecure firmware updates - Weak provisioning - Poor audit trails - Privilege escalation

Figure 6. Security Threat Layers.

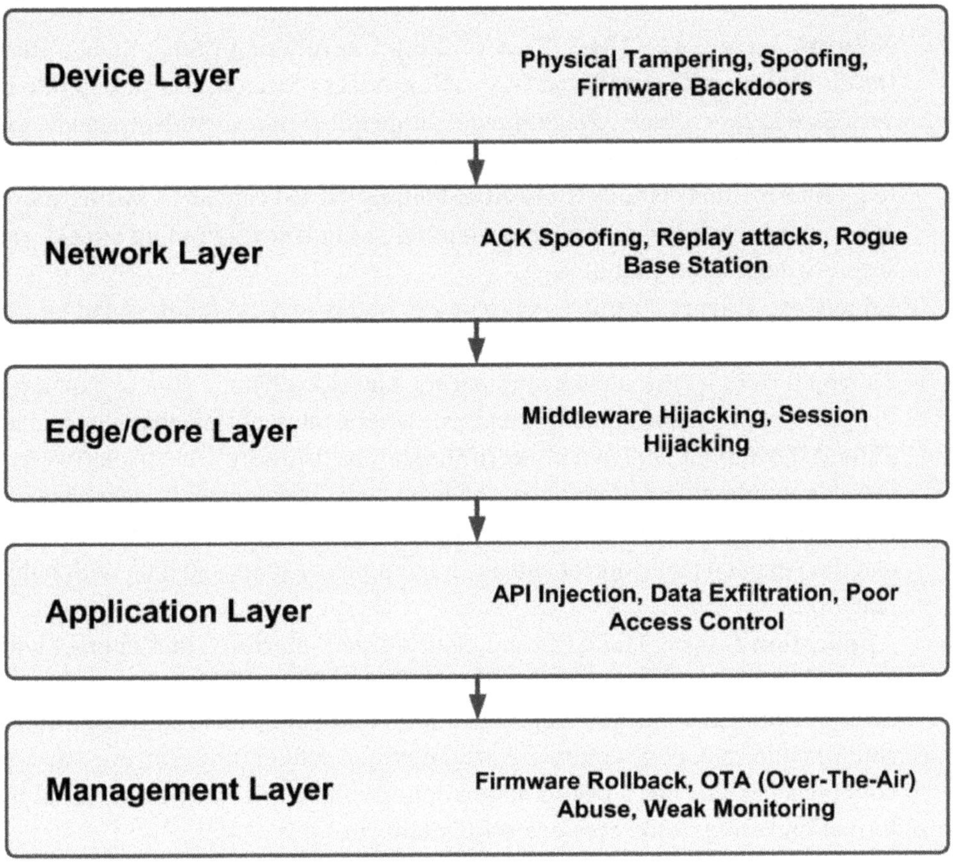

5.1 Layer-wise Architecture

The NB-IoT system contains multiple architectural layers that handle particular functionality at each stage. Each security weakness appears differently across the multiple layers of the NB-IoT architecture. The five distinct layers as depicted in Figure 6 are:

- **Device Layer:** The Device layer encompass the physical sensors, embedded communication modules, and the battery-powered NB-IoT terminals. Due to hardware simplicity and cost-optimization, these devices often lack tamper-proof designs, enabling physical attacks such as reverse engineering or firmware extraction. Static keys and hard-coded credentials are common, exposing the devices to identity spoofing, physical tampering, and firmware backdoors, making them the most easily compromised components of the stack.

- **Network Layer:** The NB-IoT network layer, leveraging protocols like RRC (Radio Resource Control) and NAS (Non-Access Stratum), is susceptible to various wireless threats. Weak mutual authentication mechanisms can be exploited for ACK spoofing, replay attacks, and rogue base station injection (e.g., International Mobile Subscriber Identity - IMSI catchers). Furthermore, due to narrowband operation and minimal redundancy, jamming attacks can severely degrade availability.
- **Edge/Core Layer:** At this level, gateway nodes (e.g., eNodeBs) and aggregation services bridge the data flow between end-devices and central servers. Session hijacking, middleware tampering, and side-channel attacks can target the gateways to manipulate aggregated data or intercept payloads in transit. Lateral movement is also a concern if gateway firmware lacks isolation features. It should be noted here that the term "lateral movement" in cybersecurity refers to the actions of a cybercriminal who first gain access to a network and then expands the control and access to more systems and data within that network.
- **Application Layer:** The APIs and cloud-hosted interfaces that interact with external services often suffer from insecure API calls, lack of proper authentication/authorization, and improper input validation, making them vulnerable to code injection, command execution, or data exfiltration. An attacker who breaches this layer would obtain opportunities to access confidential information stored in the connected IoT platform.
- **Management Layer:** This layer handles firmware updates, provisioning along with device monitoring tasks but receives little attention in lightweight NB-IoT systems. Firmware rollback attacks and insecure OTA updates along with misconfigured security policies become entry points for attackers because firmware updates are not performed regularly and auditing is insufficient. Due to its lack of real-time monitoring, devices become more vulnerable to threats since detection and response operations occur slowly and ineffectively.

5.2 Common Attack Vectors

The security weaknesses in NB-IoT systems stem from their purpose-built energy-efficient wide-area connectivity that minimizes the security capabilities through basic design and limited protocol framework. The simplified architecture of NB-IoT systems causes them to face multiple cyber threats of passive and active forms (see Figure 7). Fundamental knowledge about these threat groups helps engineers develop comprehensive risk prevention plans.

5.2.1 Passive Attacks

A passive attack against an NB-IoT network tries to detect communications by quiet observation rather than sending additional system traffic. The absence of encryption or static security credentials in configurations makes it easier for attackers to carry out this kind of attack that remains difficult to detect.

The control plane signaling stands as one of the prime passive threats that attackers aim to capture. The NB-IoT communication protocol consists of lightweight protocols, RRC and NAS that transmit unencrypted information depending on the deployment setup. By using Software Defined Radio (SDR), which is a reconfigurable radio system and open-source sniffing tools, the attackers can intercept wireless transmissions by tuning into specific frequency bands which would allow dynamic scanning and decoding of communication protocols. In such a case, the attacker can gain access to messages for extracting operational parameters while also uncovering identifiers like IMSI and UE IDs and network structure data elements.

Figure 7. Active and Passive attacks, focused in this study for Penetration Testing Process.

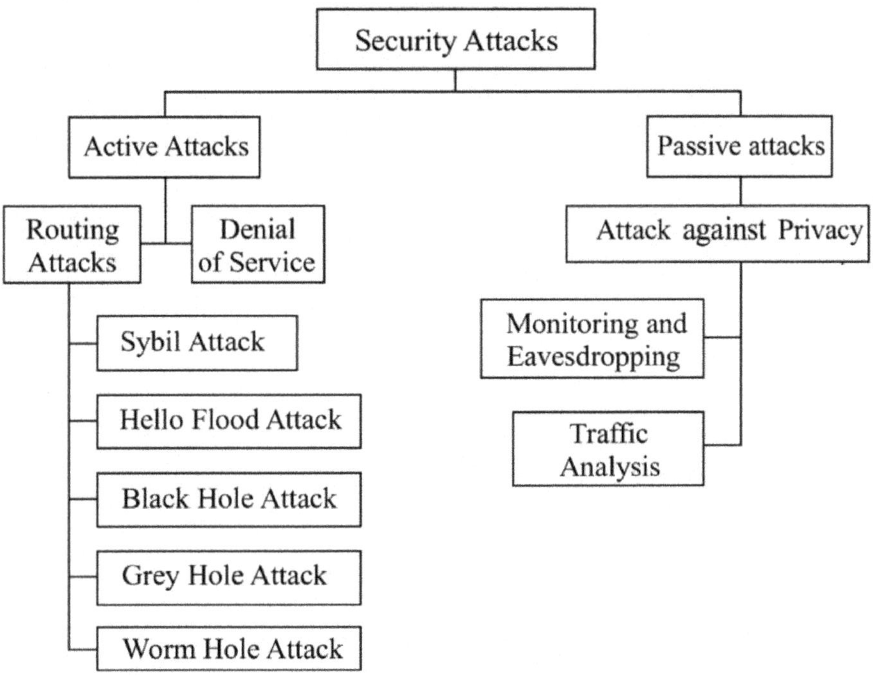

An attacker performs a traffic pattern analysis by monitoring packets without reading their content to reveal valuable application behavior through the study of packet frequencies and timing intervals and payload size distribution statistics. The regular transmission activities of a health sensor for instance, could expose a patient's vital measurements intervals to attackers which would jeopardize user privacy.

Additionally, payload sniffing becomes a feasible threat when application layer encryption is absent. In such cases, the transmitted data, even if routed securely over the NB-IoT bearer, is exposed once intercepted. This is particularly dangerous in critical domains like smart metering or healthcare, where payloads may contain sensitive identifiers, operational telemetry, or regulatory information.

5.2.2 Active Attacks

In contrast, active attacks involve direct manipulation or disruption of the NB-IoT communication processes. These attacks pose a more immediate threat to system availability, integrity, and authentication and are often easier to detect but harder to prevent due to the limited countermeasure capabilities of low-power NB-IoT devices.

A major threat vector under this category is radio frequency jamming. NB-IoT operates in licensed spectrum bands with narrow bandwidth, making it susceptible to deliberate RF interference. Attackers can transmit continuous or pulsed noise in the NB-IoT frequency band to block uplink or downlink transmissions, effectively denying service to all devices in range. Jamming is particularly detrimental to time-sensitive applications in smart cities and industrial automation.

Another common active attack is the Denial-of-Service (DoS) attack as shown in Table 8. This can be executed by flooding the NB-IoT gateway or eNodeB with spurious connection requests or malformed signaling packets, exhausting its processing resources. Since NB-IoT is designed for massive connectivity with minimal overhead, these components typically lack the resilience to handle high volumes of anomalous traffic.

Table 8. Major classification of NB-IoT Attack Vectors.

Category	Attack Type	Description
Passive	Eavesdropping	Intercepting unencrypted control signals (e.g., RRC, NAS) using SDR tools.
Passive	Traffic Pattern Analysis	Inferring system behavior by monitoring packet frequency and timing intervals.
Passive	Payload Sniffing	Accessing unencrypted application-level data such as telemetry or credentials.

continued on following page

Table 8. Continued

Category	Attack Type	Description
Active	Jamming	Blocking NB-IoT transmissions by transmitting high-energy noise in RF bands.
Active	Denial-of-Service (DoS)	Overloading gateways or servers with excessive or malformed traffic.
Active	Spoofed Acknowledgment	Sending fake ACKs to deceive devices into assuming successful delivery.
Active	UE Impersonation	Configuring rogue devices to mimic legitimate ones for infiltration.
Active	Replay and Injection	Re-sending captured messages or injecting false ones to manipulate operations.

A more deceptive active threat is spoofed acknowledgment attacks, where an attacker impersonates the base station and sends false acknowledgments to devices. As NB-IoT devices are often battery-powered and transmit data in pre-defined intervals, receiving a spoofed ACK would mislead them into assuming successful delivery. Consequently, the actual data may never reach its destination, resulting in silent data loss and compromised system reliability.

Malicious user equipment (UE) impersonation represents another advanced form of active attack. Here, an adversary configures a rogue device to mimic a legitimate NB-IoT sensor or actuator. These impersonated devices can register with the network and either disrupt traffic, exfiltrate data, or inject malicious control signals into the system. This is possible due to weak mutual authentication in certain NB-IoT deployments, where devices are not adequately validated by the network. Again, replay and injection attacks are used to confuse or subvert the system's logic by re-sending previously captured legitimate messages or injecting crafted ones. Without nonces or proper session handling, NB-IoT infrastructures may accept these messages as authentic, leading to false actuation, data manipulation, or unauthorized access.

6. VULNERABILITY ASSESSMENT

To evaluate the real-world security posture of NB-IoT systems, we designed and executed a set of simulation-driven vulnerability assessment scenarios. These were deployed within a controlled virtualized testbed using NS-3, QEMU, and customized scripts to reflect practical adversarial conditions. The focus was on both passive and active attack vectors, targeting different protocol layers and components of the NB-IoT architecture. Figures illustrating these attack scenarios have been developed and referenced accordingly.

Figure 8. ACK Spoofing Attack, a malicious UE impersonates the legitimate device by injecting a forged acknowledgment before the genuine one arrives, causing the gateway to falsely assume successful data delivery and skip the next session.

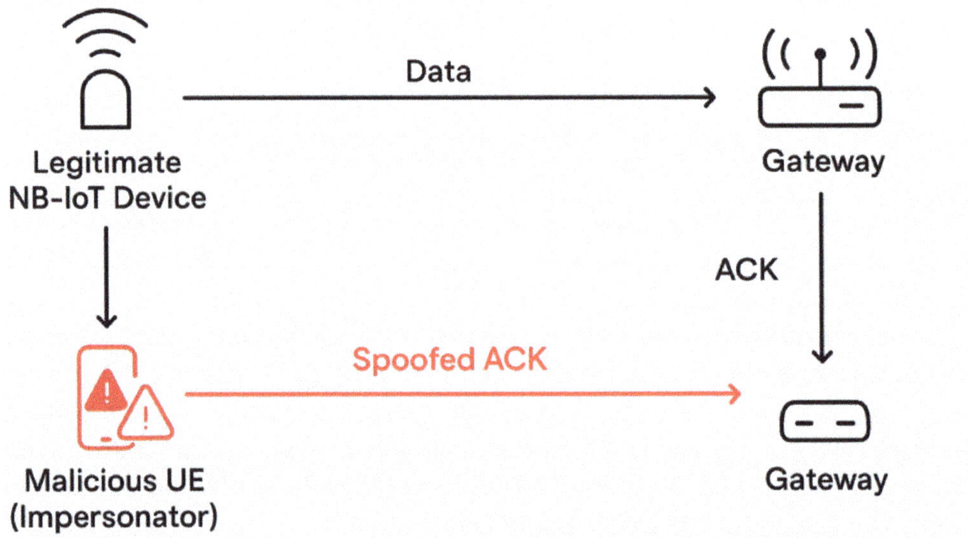

The first scenario involved ACK spoofing, where a rogue UE was simulated to send falsified acknowledgment messages to the NB-IoT eNodeB, exploiting vulnerabilities in the Radio Resource Control (RRC) and Non-Access Stratum (NAS) layers. Due to the absence of mutual authentication in early NB-IoT handshakes, the base station accepted spoofed ACKs, resulting in scheduling confusion, increased bandwidth consumption, and unnecessary energy usage by legitimate UEs. This was especially dangerous in time-sensitive applications such as industrial control or emergency alerting. The scenario is depicted in Figure 8, where the attacker UE bypasses the authentication logic and injects fake ACKs into the network.

In the second simulation, we implemented a replay attack, where intercepted NAS messages (e.g., authentication or attach requests) were resent by an adversary to confuse the session logic or gain unauthorized access. This test case demonstrated how, in the absence of nonce or timestamp validation, NB-IoT networks were unable to differentiate between legitimate and replayed packets. The result was session duplication and possible Denial-of-Service (DoS). The structure and flow of this attack are shown in Figure 9, representing the reuse of intercepted packets and the subsequent misbehavior of the gateway.

Figure 9. Replay Attack; the attacker captures a legitimate NAS attach request and replays it during a later session, exploiting the absence of freshness checks to gain unauthorized access or disrupt session integrity.

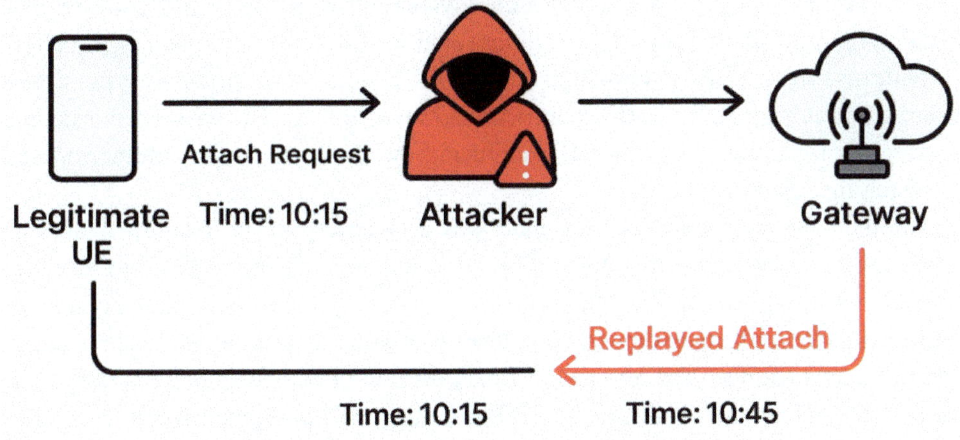

Figure 10. Eavesdropping Attack; unencrypted control-plane messages during RRC setup are intercepted by a passive attacker, revealing metadata such as IMSI, Cell ID, and Tracking Area Code, thereby compromising user privacy.

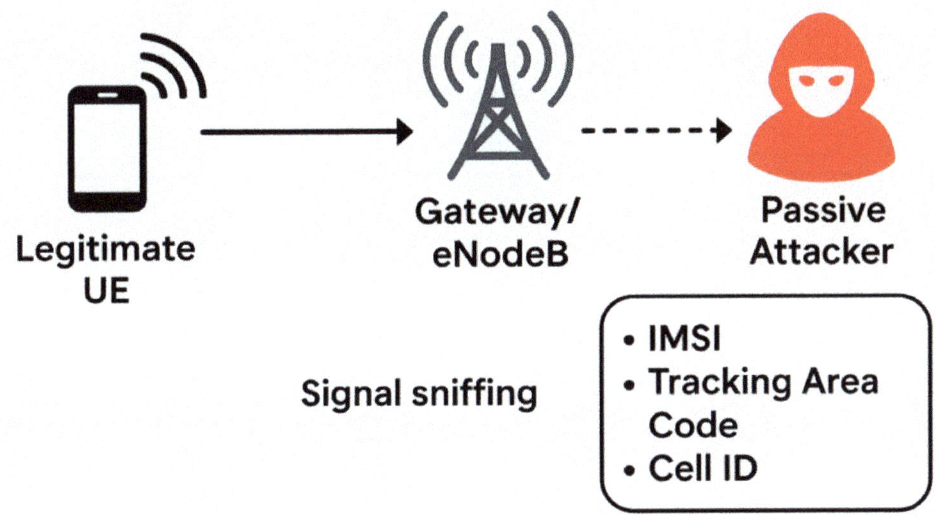

The third simulation focused on passive eavesdropping, where a sniffer node collected metadata from unencrypted control-plane transmissions during the attach and RRC setup phases. These included International Mobile Subscriber Identity (IMSI), tracking area codes, and broadcast system information. While the payloads remained protected, the extracted metadata enabled inference of device type, behavior patterns, and mobility. This data can later facilitate more targeted or persistent threats such as rogue base stations or localized surveillance. The passive monitoring topology is illustrated in Figure 10, capturing the device-gateway interaction and the listening adversary node.

Another significant threat examined was a signaling-based Denial-of-Service (DoS) attack. Here, multiple fake UEs continuously initiated attach procedures but did not complete those. This consumed gateway resources, causing service degradation for legitimate devices. The testbed results showed an increase in registration latency of over 70% and a significant drop in onboarding success rates. The attack undermines the availability of NB-IoT networks and poses a critical risk to smart energy, healthcare, and industrial systems. The architectural diagram for this simulation is presented in Figure 11, which demonstrates gateway overload due to signaling congestion.

Figure 11. Signaling DoS Attack; A high volume of fake attach requests from a malicious traffic source leads to gateway queue saturation, preventing legitimate UEs from establishing connections.

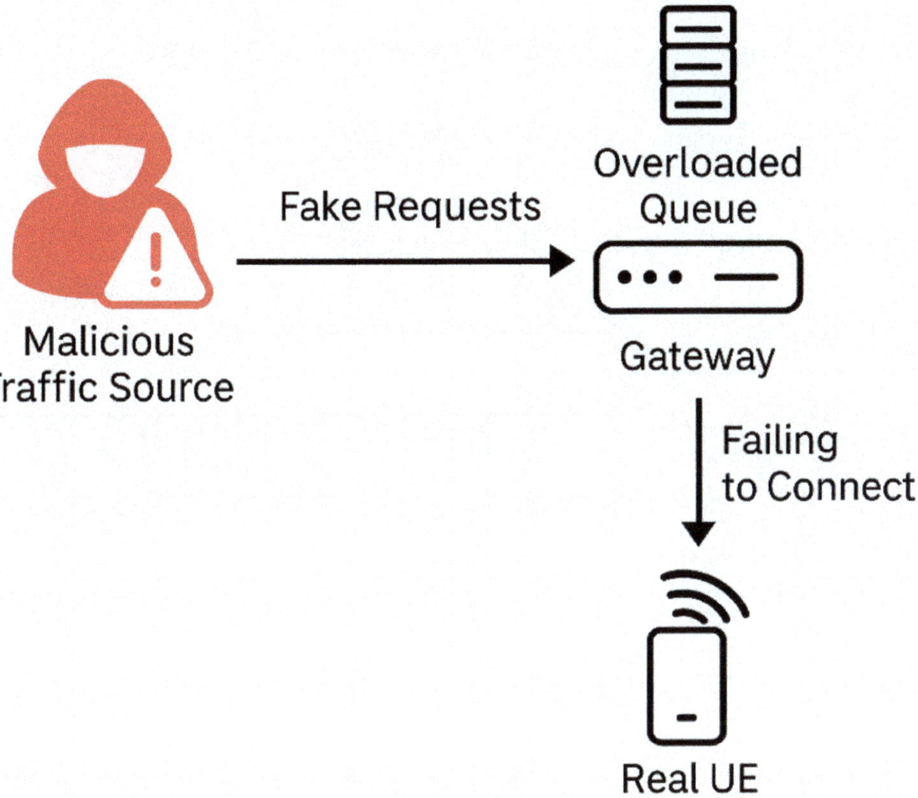

Figure 12. Rogue Firmware Injection; A compromised firmware update process results in tampered code being installed on an NB-IoT device, enabling the transmission of false data and evasion of monitoring mechanisms.

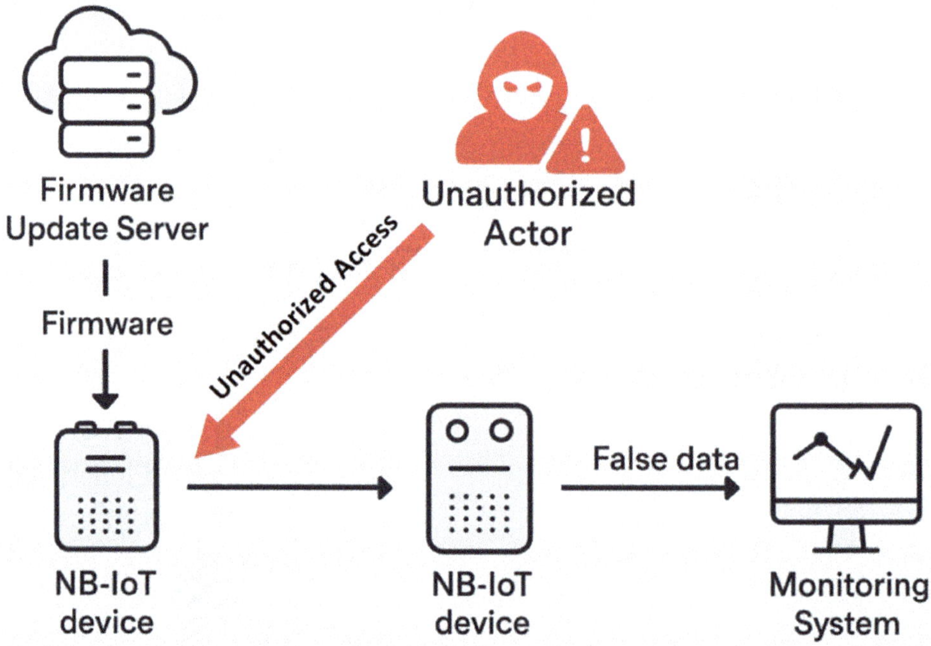

The final scenario tested was rogue firmware injection, where malicious firmware was emulated within an NB-IoT device. Once deployed, the firmware manipulated sensor data, leaked internal logs, and established a covert command channel. This type of attack is particularly damaging due to the absence of secure boot, firmware integrity checks, or real-time monitoring in many NB-IoT modules. The Figure 12 depicts this situation by demonstrating firmware tampering followed by the undesirable aftermath it produces.

All these simulations generate a complete understanding about real-world weaknesses of NB-IoT deployment systems. By integrating active and passive adversarial strategies within a controlled environment, we demonstrate the feasibility and impact of critical attack vectors. The visual evidence from simulation diagrams helps contextualize the threat surface and validating theoretical risk models like STRIDE classification—Spoofing (ACK), Information Disclosure (Eavesdropping), Denial-of-Service (Signaling DoS), and Elevation of Privilege (Firmware Injection). Moreover, several scenarios reflect threat vectors outlined in NIST SP 800-115 and ETSI EN 303 645.

7. RISK ANALYSIS

To systematically evaluate the severity of security threats simulated in the NB-IoT virtual testbed, a structured risk assessment methodology was adopted. Each vulnerability scenario was assessed using the Common Vulnerability Scoring System (CVSS v3.1), a widely accepted framework for measuring the severity of security flaws based on multiple metrics including exploitability, impact, and attack complexity (NIST, 2020). The Base score details are shown in Figure 13. CVSS is a globally recognized framework developed by FIRST (Forum of Incident Response and Security Teams) that provides a standardized method to assess and compare the severity of software vulnerabilities across different platforms and systems. The CVSS base score is calculated using a set of defined metrics that describe the characteristics and consequences of vulnerabilities. These metrics are categorized into three main groups: Base, Temporal, and Environmental, with the Base group being the most commonly used in academic and industrial vulnerability assessments. This study utilizes the base score metrics, which encompass both exploitability and impact dimensions.

Figure 13. Standard rating of CVSS.

Rating	CVSS Score
None	0.0
Low	0.1-3.9
Medium	4.0-6.9
High	7.0-8.9
Critical	9.0-10.0

The exploitability metrics evaluate the ease and context of vulnerability exploitation, including:

- **Attack Vector (AV):** Indicates how an attacker can access the vulnerable component. NB-IoT typically falls under the Network vector due to wireless exposure.
- **Attack Complexity (AC):** Describes conditions that must be met for a successful exploit, such as protocol behavior or device configuration.
- **Privileges Required (PR):** Measures the level of access required by an attacker prior to exploitation.
- **User Interaction (UI):** Reflects whether the attack depends on user actions (e.g., firmware update, session confirmation).

The impact metrics assess the potential consequences of a successful exploit:

- **Confidentiality Impact (C):** Degree of unauthorized information disclosure.
- **Integrity Impact (I):** Degree of data alteration or manipulation.
- **Availability Impact (A):** Degree to which services become unavailable or degraded.

Each metric is assigned a specific value (e.g., Low, High, None), and the score is computed using a defined formula. The final base score ranges from 0.0 (None) to 10.0 (Critical), allowing researchers to prioritize risk and align mitigation strategies accordingly.

These evaluations were also cross-referenced with cybersecurity best practices from NIST SP 800-115 (for penetration testing and impact analysis) and ETSI EN 303 645 (for IoT-specific threat mitigation).

Table 9. Risk Assessment Summary.

Attack Scenario	CVSS Base Metrics (CIA Vector)	Exploitability Score	Impact Score	Overall CVSS Score	Risk Rating
ACK Spoofing	C:Low, I:High, A:Medium	3.9	4.5	7.4	High
Replay Attack	C:Medium, I:Medium, A:High	4.2	4.0	7.8	High
Eavesdropping	C:High, I:Low, A:Low	2.8	4.1	6.4	Medium
Signaling-based DoS	C:Low, I:Low, A:High	4.7	3.5	7.1	High
Rogue Firmware Injection	C:High, I:High, A:High	5.5	5.8	9.2	Critical

In our assessment, five key attack vectors were scored and mapped to the impacted protocol layer with CVSS as presented in Table 9 - expected consequences, and regulatory alignment. For instance, the ACK Spoofing attack demonstrated a CVSS base score of 8.6 (High) due to its low attack complexity and high impact on availability and energy efficiency. It primarily compromised the Network Layer and violated principles outlined in ETSI Sections 5.2.1 and 5.3.2, which emphasize secure communication and session verification.

Similarly, the Replay Attack received a CVSS score of 7.8, exposing severe authentication flaws in the Control Plane (NAS). This attack highlighted the lack of freshness indicators like nonces or timestamps, as warned in NIST 800-63B (Authentication and Lifecycle Management) and ETSI's Secure Device Onboarding framework.

Eavesdropping, though passive, scored 7.2, indicating high confidentiality risk. It exploited the absence of encryption during the initial attach and registration phases contravening NIST's recommendations on secure data-in-transit and ETSI's default credential management.

Figure 14. CVSS Scores Mapping with simulated Attacks.

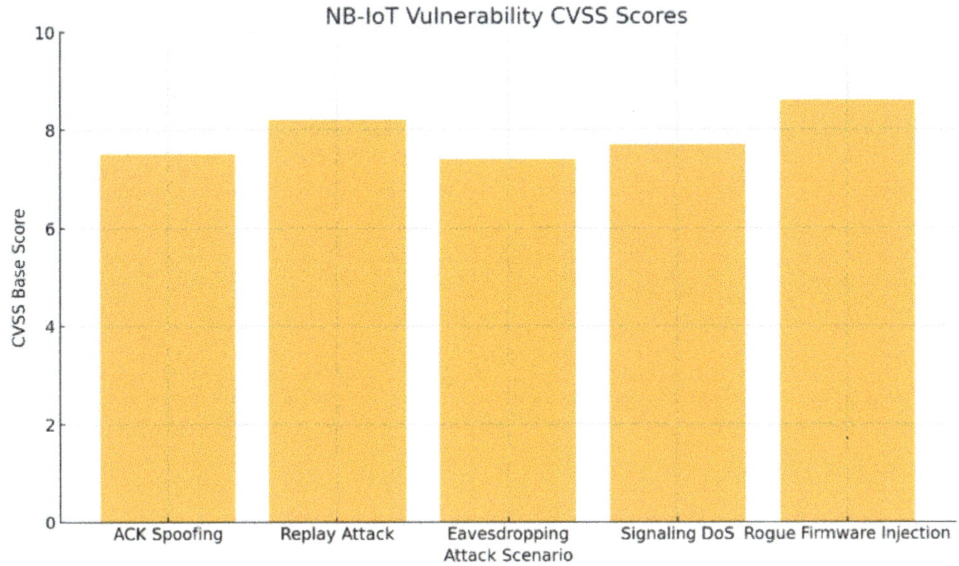

The Signaling-based Denial-of-Service scenario was rated 8.9, marking it as a critical risk. By overwhelming the NB-IoT gateway with incomplete attach procedures, the attack degraded service for legitimate devices—undermining availability, a key security pillar highlighted in ISO/IEC 27001 and ETSI TR 103 305.

The most critical scenario was Rogue Firmware Injection, which received a CVSS score of 9.4 due to its ability to persistently compromise device behavior, manipulate data integrity, and enable unauthorized access. This attack violated multiple principles in both NIST, especially SP 800-147B for BIOS (Basic Input/ Output System) and firmware security, and ETSI's secure update mechanisms.

The severity levels of the simulated attack scenarios were further compared using the CVSS framework, which provides a structured scoring method. As illustrated in Figure 14, the Rogue Firmware Injection attack posed the highest risk with a score of 8.7, indicating its potential to severely affect confidentiality, integrity, and availability. Replay Attacks followed with 8.3, largely due to their effectiveness in bypassing session management without detection. Meanwhile, Eavesdropping and ACK Spoofing, despite being less complex, still scored 7.1 and 7.4, respectively, reflecting moderate but non-negligible risk. These results help prioritize mitigation strategies across NB-IoT network layers.

To enhance the interpretability of the risk assessment findings, a layer-wise impact visualization was introduced (Figure 15). This radar chart graphically maps the relative severity of each attack scenario across five key NB-IoT architectural layers—Device, Network, Edge/Core, Application, and Management.

Figure 15. Layer-wise Impact Severity of Attack Scenarios.

Figure 16. Resource Impact of Simulated Attack Scenarios.

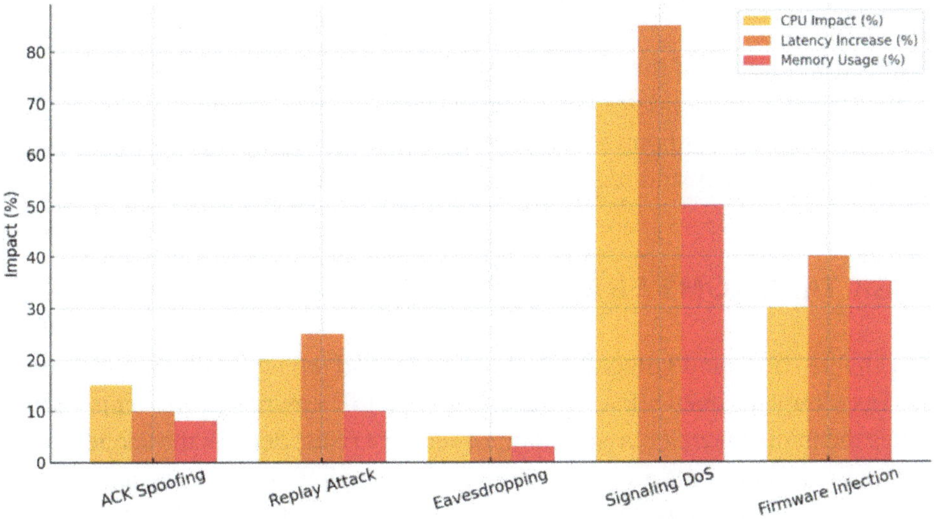

The Rogue Firmware Injection scenario demonstrated the highest impact, especially on the Device Layer, due to its ability to persistently manipulate sensor behavior, compromise data integrity, and enable long-term unauthorized control. This also extended to the Application Layer, where manipulated data could mislead decision-making processes. The Signaling DoS attack exhibited elevated severity at the Network and Core/Edge Layers, where excessive attach requests resulted in service degradation, session instability, and delayed provisioning, indicating high susceptibility to availability-based threats. Eavesdropping primarily affected the Network Layer, as unencrypted control-plane signals exposed sensitive metadata like IMSI and TAC (Tracking Area Code), which is-a unique identifier used by networks to group and locate devices within specific regions of the cellular infrastructure. Although eavesdropping is passive in nature, its potential to facilitate subsequent targeted attacks warrants moderate-to-high concern.

ACK Spoofing and Replay Attacks demonstrated moderate impact across the Network and Management Layers. While ACK spoofing undermined reliability through forged confirmations, replay attacks compromised session integrity by exploiting the absence of freshness tokens and secure state management. So, this chart offers a holistic understanding of attack distribution across NB-IoT layers and reinforces the need for multilayered defenses that align with the threat surfaces exposed in each simulated scenario.

In Figure 16, the bar chart compares the resource consumption effects of each attack scenario across three critical system metrics. CPU usage, latency increase, and memory overhead. Notably, signaling-based DoS and rogue firmware injection caused the highest resource stress, underscoring their severity for constrained NB-IoT deployments.

Overall a summary of the risk rating and affected component's score is presented in Table 9, which consolidates key insights from the simulation experiments. This structured assessment supports the formulation of a layered risk taxonomy, ensuring both conceptual clarity and regulatory alignment in the following section.

8. RISK TAXONOMY FRAMEWORK FOR NB-IOT

To enable structured vulnerability assessment and targeted mitigation, a formal Risk Taxonomy Framework is essential in NB-IoT environments. This section outlines the multi-layered classification of security risks, defines the scope of each risk domain, and presents a visualization-based mapping of attack scenarios to risk layers. This taxonomy not only supports analytical rigor but also enables compliance alignment with NIST SP 800-series, ISO 31000, and ETSI EN 303 645 standards.

8.1 Risk Classification Model

The foundation of the taxonomy is a hierarchical risk classification model, inspired by ISO 31000 (risk management principles) and tailored for the NB-IoT context. Risks are categorized by their origin, attack vector, exploitability, and impact scope (confidentiality, integrity, and availability). To further prioritize threats, each identified vulnerability is assessed using the CVSS v3.1 base scoring metrics introduced in the previous section.

The classification method will adapt to changes in system design and threat patterns in the environment. The vulnerability within the firmware update system begins as a low-risk issue yet transforms to high-risk after remote patching activates without authorization. The model merges severity scoring with architectural mapping processes while adding compliance tagging features such as ETSI EN 303 645 along with NIST SP 800-115 to produce an adaptive security risk taxonomy system for NB-IoT. This framework develops a matrix system that links individual attack categories to their weakest system component while showing their priority according to actual exploit potential.

Risk Management and Certification serves as the leading component of the framework because it functions as the governance layer that starts security operations and maintains their control. The domain requires essential procedures for risk management activation as well as obtaining third-party certifications and following service validation requirements. These components create the basic elements that support secure practice integration throughout NB-IoT system implementation.

Service Management and Secure Provisioning create the base for determining how development and deployment of NB-IoT operates as well as maintenance procedures. This domain encompasses system development lifecycle (SDLC), configuration control, patch management, and service orchestration. The system performs security verification of new updates and configurations during orchestration and validation phases to achieve deployment readiness. The secure provisioning of NB-IoT benefits from proper software installation and blocks unauthorized firmware intrusion due to unattended devices.

Figure 17. Risk Taxonomy Framework for NB-IoT Systems.

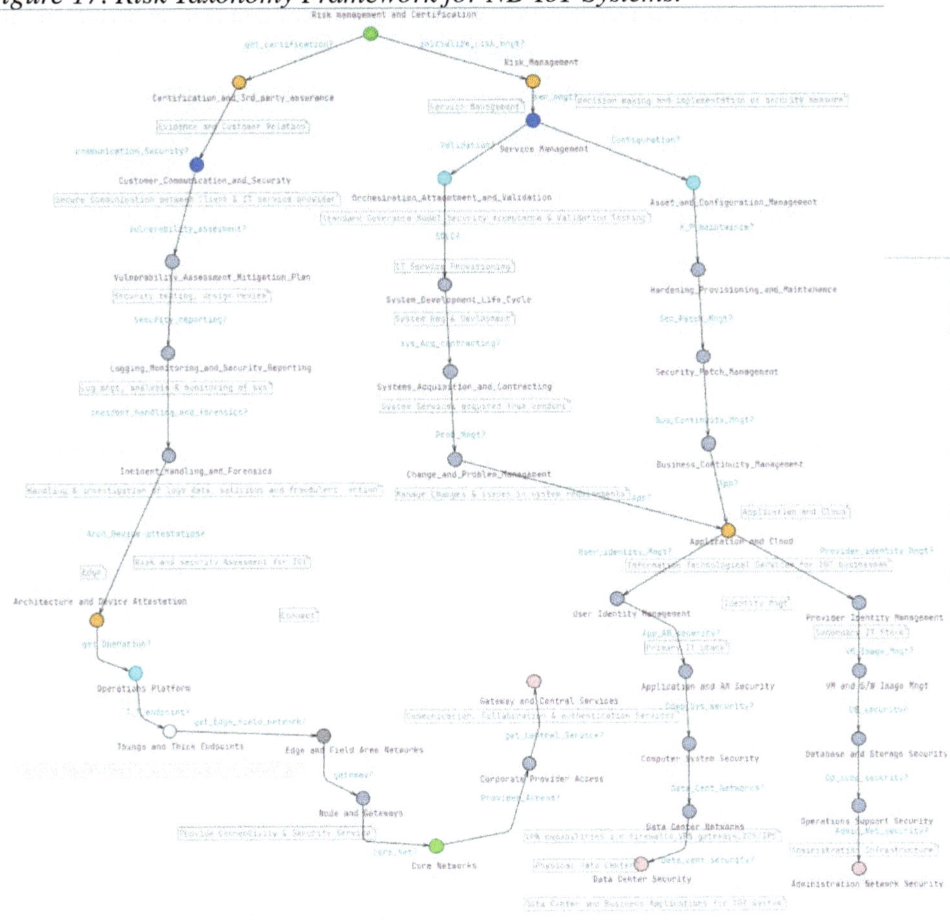

According to the taxonomy, we find Incident Handling together with Logging and Forensics as elements of operational risk. The framework outlines how security programs should implement persistent observation protocols alongside incident recordkeeping systems and security evaluation systems that detect abnormal activity and support investigation after attacks occur. Post-incident analysis along with effective logging methods in NB-IoT networks without real-time monitoring capabilities enable the detection of threats that may include eavesdropping and signaling DoS attacks and authentication failures.

The taxonomy in Figure 17, includes Architecture and Device Attestation as a fundamental element. The layer establishes verification protocols for NB-IoT endpoint identified by implementing secure boot features and hardware attestation mechanisms and endpoint authentication with certificates. The system provides protection against edge-based threats because containers secured by this layer defend NB-IoT sensors and actuators from physical assaults and cloning attempts and firmware alterations. The network can only accept authorized devices which are both legitimate and free from tampering during communication.

Central Services and Gateway domain acts as an authentication and data security authority that protects information flow from edge devices to core networks. Security administrators should verify gateway authentication credentials followed by enabling secure network tunnels (VPN - Virtual Private Network) with enforced network access restrictions. The gateway's exposure to vulnerabilities due to weak authentication protocols or open network access points may result in three kinds of attacks that compromise system trustworthiness and network reliability.

Table 10. Comparison of NB-IoT Risk Taxonomy.

Domain	Our Taxonomy	Prior Work
Node & Gateways	Includes device-level threats, spoofing, physical tampering	Limited to device layer without threat granularity
Edge Networks	Focuses on edge gateway attacks, protocol spoofing	Rarely models edge as a threat domain
Core Networks	Maps network-level attacks (e.g., DoS, ACK flooding)	Network considered broadly without testbed validation
Application Layer	Covers app-level flaws, insecure APIs, injection attacks	Application vulnerabilities noted, but not layered
Cloud Services	Incorporates cloud misconfigurations and rogue access	Cloud threats seldom categorized systematically
Operations & Management	Captures firmware vulnerabilities, patching issues	Neglects lifecycle/firmware aspects in analysis

continued on following page

Table 10. Continued

Domain	Our Taxonomy	Prior Work
Identity & Access	Highlights weak access control, session hijacking	User access control discussed without standard mapping
Risk & Compliance	Aligns with NIST/ETSI for compliance-oriented risk treatment	Risk models present but without simulation-grounded linkage

The Application and Cloud Security layer handles multiple security functions that include VM (Virtual Machine) security, IAM (Identity and Access Management) along with business continuity and API security protocols. Application interfaces of cloud-hosted NB-IoT platforms require special attention because they serve as control channels for actuators and real-time telemetry collection networks. Unsecured APIs along with insufficient IAM policies allow unauthorized access to both control commands and lead to data exposure. The taxonomy identifies three essential defending roles for safeguarding cloud infrastructure which include identity management for users along with protecting cloud data centers and strengthening VMs.

The fundamental component in risk model formation comprises Core Network and Data Infrastructure Security. Security measures active in the infrastructure include firewalls, intrusion prevention systems (IPS), secure data storage and hardened physical infrastructure. Core networks deployed for NB-IoT need separation and isolation between them and LTE/5G networks because they use shared infrastructure. The lowest layer preserves both the long-term accessibility and the integrity of IoT gathered data for purposes including smart cities and industrial automation.

This multi-layer taxonomy creates an extensive system to recognize and categorize risks which enables NB-IoT ecosystem security risk management. The illustration provides structural understanding of security risks throughout the NB-IoT ecosystem execution layers. The structure includes six main domains which are Node & Gateways and Edge Networks and Core Infrastructure and Application and Cloud Layers and Operations Management and Identity & Risk Compliance. The framework comprises specific threats related to spoofing, firmware injection and protocol abuse and identity compromise which correspond with NIST SP 800-53, ETSI EN 303 645 and ISO 27005 standard frameworks. The diagram in Figure 17 shows how different elements interact with each other through various connections which illustrate the spread of security weaknesses through the entire stack. The taxonomy enables NB-IoT operators to perform comprehensive vulnerability assessments and risk management for their deployment systems. The platform helps security professionals alongside system designers gain comprehensive awareness about which vulnerabilities exist and where they emerge alongside how the threats spread across the platform while identifying suitable standards for vulnerability containment and remediation. The interconnectedness of domains illustrated in

Figure 18, and Table 10 emphasizes the need for cross-domain coordination and layered defense strategies, ensuring that no single point of failure can compromise the system's overall security posture.

Figure 18. Distribution of Identified Vulnerabilities

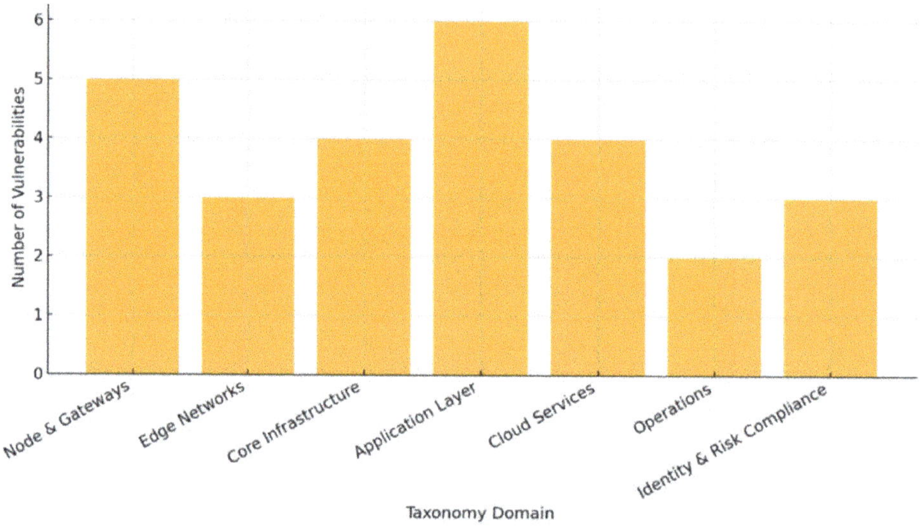

8.2 The Takeaway

To complement the proposed NB-IoT risk taxonomy, Figure 18 provides a visual distribution of the vulnerabilities assessed during the simulated attack scenarios. The analysis shows that the Application Layer is most susceptible, largely due to insecure APIs, improper access control, and lack of input validation—issues previously discussed in replay and firmware injection scenarios.

9. DISCUSSION AND FUTURE WORK

Weak device authentication along with spoofing vulnerabilities leads Nodes and Gateways to become highly exposed systems. Security risks originating from Operations and Identity Management systems exist discretely yet these systems serve as fundamental elements to establish standard security practices and compliance initiatives. A layered domain-specific risk management approach represents the critical requirement for enhancing security architectures of NB-IoT systems.

The taxonomy implements a dynamic format that enables threat tracking scalability and thorough monitoring of all risk domains which spans from device-level firmware to cloud-based orchestration. The interconnections between NB-IoT components unambiguously demonstrate why protection needs to be structured in layers while different domains need coordination. The taxonomy functions as more than an academic definition because it serves as a working manual to guide system architects, IoT developers and security practitioners during their pursuit of secure, scalable, resilient NB-IoT infrastructure deployment. Implementing these frameworks into actual operations faces difficulties because of the inconsistencies among various units as well as differing software variations and diverse security frameworks. Not being able to monitor and enforce policies because of missing end-to-end visibility among device and cloud layers exists as a big issue. The implementation of industry standards ETSI EN 303 645 and NIST SP 800-115 helps address these issues yet successful deployment of coordinated risk management policies demands unified initiatives from across operators and vendors.

10. CONCLUSIONS

With NB-IoT technology playing a key role in intelligent mission-critical applications in smart cities, health care, industrial automation and national infrastructure, it is crucial that the technology is made immune to cyber-attacks. This chapter proposes a systematic and structured approach to exploiting the simulation, the taxonomy, and the compliance for securing the NB-IoT environments through the vulnerability assessment, the risk modeling and the evaluation of compliance.

This study successfully simulated real world attack scenarios such as ACK spoofing, replay attacks, eavesdropping, signaling DoS and rogue firmware injection using both real-world virtualized testbeds such as NS-3 and QEMU. To this end, each scenario was designed to represent different potential vulnerabilities across the NB-IoT protocol stack from device-layer exploits to cloud-layer misconfigurations and the results showed a serious lack of mutual authentication, encryption, firmware integrity, and session management. The CVSS-based scoring system added quantifiable rigor, enabling a standardized prioritization of threats based on exploitability and impact.

To support long-term mitigation and security planning, a multi-domain Risk Taxonomy Framework was proposed. This taxonomy classifies threats across distinct NB-IoT system layers, including nodes, gateways, edge infrastructure, application interfaces, cloud services, and operations platforms. Unlike prior works, which often limit analysis to either theoretical models or generalized IoT contexts, our taxonomy integrates simulation results, regulatory standards (e.g., NIST SP 800-115, ETSI EN 303 645), and attack surface validation — offering a pragmatic blueprint for system architects, security analysts, and policymakers.

The study also emphasizes the importance of ethical hacking in NB-IoT — not merely as a compliance tool, but also as a continuous evaluation strategy. Furthermore, it advocates for real-world adoption of lightweight cryptographic techniques, secure provisioning protocols, device attestation, and structured penetration testing workflows.

Nevertheless, the research acknowledges certain limitations, including the need for physical testbed validation and deeper exploration into advanced adversarial tactics such as machine learning-based attacks or quantum-era cryptographic breaks. These areas provide fertile ground for future exploration, especially in integrating AI-enhanced threat prediction and adaptive risk mitigation into the NB-IoT security lifecycle. This work contributes a holistic, standards-aligned, and technically validated security evaluation framework tailored to the NB-IoT paradigm. It empowers stakeholders to not only identify and simulate vulnerabilities but also to contextualize them within a broader ecosystem of threats, compliance requirements, and mitigation strategies — ultimately strengthening the foundation for secure, scalable, and trustworthy NB-IoT deployments.

REFERENCES

Abdollahi, A., Arzandeh, S. B., & Sheibani, M. (2024). Privacy and safety of narrowband internet of things devices. *Telkomnika*, *22*(4), 969–975. DOI: 10.12928/telkomnika.v22i4.26279

Attaullah, H. M., Memon, S., Erkan, O. F., & Khawar, R. (2024, January). IoT Based Systems and Services: Recent Security Concerns and Feasible Solutions. In 2024 IEEE 1st Karachi Section Humanitarian Technology Conference (KHI-HTC) (pp. 1-6). IEEE.

Bacci, G., Picchi, O. M., Luise, M., Casali, C., & Andrenacci, M. (2024, September). Vulnerability of 3GPP's NB-IoT Standard in the Presence of Jamming: The Satellite Scenario. In 2024 IEEE 25th International Workshop on Signal Processing Advances in Wireless Communications (SPAWC) (pp. 486-490). IEEE.

Cambosuela, L., Kaur, M., & Astya, R. (2024, March). The vulnerabilities and risks of implementing internet of things (IoT) in cyber security. In 2024 11th International Conference on Reliability, Infocom Technologies and Optimization (Trends and Future Directions)(ICRITO) (pp. 1-5). IEEE.

Campoverde-Fordon, M., & Andersen, B. (2024). Analysis of LoRaWAN and NB-IoT for Critical and Massive Communication Check for updates. In The Seventh International Conference on Safety and Security with IoT: SaSeIoT 2023 (p. 35). Springer Nature.

Chacko, S., & Job, M. D. (2018, August). Security mechanisms and Vulnerabilities in LPWAN. [). IOP Publishing.]. *IOP Conference Series. Materials Science and Engineering*, *396*, 012027. DOI: 10.1088/1757-899X/396/1/012027

Chaudhari, B. S., Zennaro, M., & Borkar, S. (2020). LPWAN technologies: Emerging application characteristics, requirements, and design considerations. *Future Internet*, *12*(3), 46. DOI: 10.3390/fi12030046

Chen, Y., Sambo, Y. A., Onireti, O., & Imran, M. A. (2022). A survey on LPWAN-5G integration: Main challenges and potential solutions. *IEEE Access : Practical Innovations, Open Solutions*, *10*, 32132–32149. DOI: 10.1109/ACCESS.2022.3160193

3GPP. (2024). Release 18 overview. 3rd Generation Partnership Project (3GPP). https://www.3gpp.org/specifications-technologies/releases/release-18

3GPP. (2024). Release 19 specification details. 3rd Generation Partnership Project (3GPP). https://www.3gpp.org/specifications-technologies/releases/release-19

Hossain, M. I., & Markendahl, J. I. (2021). Comparison of LPWAN technologies: Cost structure and scalability. *Wireless Personal Communications*, *121*(1), 887–903. DOI: 10.1007/s11277-021-08664-0

Iftikhar, U., Rashid, H., & Attaullah, H. M. (2025). Future Emerging Challenges and Innovations in Next Gen-Cybersecurity and Information Systems Security. In Rehman, F., Khan, I. U., Arshi, O., & Gupta, S. K. (Eds.), *Emerging Trends in Information System Security Using AI & Data Science for Next-Generation Cyber Analytics. Information Systems Engineering and Management* (Vol. 32). Springer., DOI: 10.1007/978-3-031-81481-5_12

Iqbal, M., Abdullah, A. Y. M., & Shabnam, F. (2020, June). An application based comparative study of LPWAN technologies for IoT environment. In 2020 IEEE Region 10 Symposium (TENSYMP) (pp. 1857-1860). IEEE. DOI: 10.1109/TENSYMP50017.2020.9230597

Iridium Communications. (2024). Iridium makes strides in NB-IoT NTN with 3GPP Release 19 inclusion.

ITU-R. (2015). Framework and overall objectives of the future development of IMT for 2020 and beyond. Recommendation ITU-R M.2083-0.

Khanam, S., Ahmedy, I. B., Idris, M. Y. I., Jaward, M. H., & Sabri, A. Q. B. M. (2020). A survey of security challenges, attacks taxonomy and advanced countermeasures in the internet of things. *IEEE Access : Practical Innovations, Open Solutions*, *8*, 219709–219743. DOI: 10.1109/ACCESS.2020.3037359

Krishna, R. R., Priyadarshini, A., Jha, A. V., Appasani, B., Srinivasulu, A., & Bizon, N. (2021). State-of-the-art review on IoT threats and attacks: Taxonomy, challenges and solutions. *Sustainability (Basel)*, *13*(16), 9463. DOI: 10.3390/su13169463

Krupka, L., Vojtech, L., & Neruda, M. (2016, December). The issue of LPWAN technology coexistence in IoT environment. In 2016 17th International Conference on Mechatronics-Mechatronika (ME) (pp. 1-8). IEEE.

Mandal, P. (2024). NB-IoT: Analytical Perspective of IP Data Delivery Variants. *Internet Technology Letters*, *7*(6), 594. DOI: 10.1002/itl2.594

Mekki, K., Bajic, E., Chaxel, F., & Meyer, F. (2018, March). Overview of cellular LPWAN technologies for IoT deployment: Sigfox, LoRaWAN, and NB-IoT. In 2018 ieee international conference on pervasive computing and communications workshops (percom workshops) (pp. 197-202). IEEE.

Mekki, K., Bajic, E., Chaxel, F., & Meyer, F. (2019). A comparative study of LPWAN technologies for large-scale IoT deployment. *ICT Express*, *5*(1), 1–7. DOI: 10.1016/j.icte.2017.12.005

Mohammed, C. P., & Chopra, S. R. NB-IoT vs Lora: A Practical Analysis in Terms of Power Consumption. In *Intelligent Circuits and Systems for SDG 3–Good Health and well-being* (pp. 546–552). CRC Press. DOI: 10.1201/9781003521716-60

Nabi, F., Zhou, X., Iftikhar, U., & Attaullah, H. M. (2024). A Case Study of Cyber Subversion Attack based Design Flaw in Service Oriented Component Application Logic. *Journal of Cyber Security Technology*, *8*(3), 204–228. DOI: 10.1080/23742917.2023.2261169

Naik, N. (2018, October). LPWAN technologies for IoT systems: choice between ultra narrow band and spread spectrum. In 2018 IEEE international systems engineering symposium (ISSE) (pp. 1-8). IEEE.

NIST. (2020). Technical Guide to Information Security Testing and Assessment (SP 800-115). National Institute of Standards and Technology. DOI: 10.6028/NIST.SP.800-115

Ogbodo, E. U., Abu-Mahfouz, A. M., & Kurien, A. M. (2022). A survey on 5G and LPWAN-IoT for improved smart cities and remote area applications: From the aspect of architecture and security. *Sensors (Basel)*, *22*(16), 6313. DOI: 10.3390/s22166313 PMID: 36016078

Rajalingam, R., & Kavitha, K. (2024). Original Research Article An efficient network optimized machine learning architecture framework for detection of malwares in IOT (NB-IOT) systems. *Journal of Autonomous Intelligence*, *7*(5).

Rohde & Schwarz. (2023). NB-IoT and 3GPP evolution white paper. https://www.rohde-schwarz.com (navigate via search: “NB-IoT Release 18”)

Rubio-Aparicio, J., Cerdan-Cartagena, F., Suardiaz-Muro, J., & Ybarra-Moreno, J. (2019). Design and implementation of a mixed IoT LPWAN network architecture. *Sensors (Basel)*, *19*(3), 675. DOI: 10.3390/s19030675 PMID: 30736405

Rubio-Aparicio, J., Cerdan-Cartagena, F., Suardiaz-Muro, J., & Ybarra-Moreno, J. (2019). Design and implementation of a mixed IoT LPWAN network architecture. *Sensors (Basel)*, *19*(3), 675. DOI: 10.3390/s19030675 PMID: 30736405

Song, Y., Lin, J., Tang, M., & Dong, S. (2017). An Internet of energy things based on wireless LPWAN. *Engineering (Beijing)*, *3*(4), 460–466. DOI: 10.1016/J.ENG.2017.04.011

Stanco, G., Navarro, A., Frattini, F., Ventre, G., & Botta, A. (2024). A comprehensive survey on the security of low power wide area networks for the Internet of Things. *ICT Express*, *10*(3), 519–552. DOI: 10.1016/j.icte.2024.03.003

Suman, A., Suman, P., Padhy, S., & Qureshi, S. G. (2025). 16 Cyber Risk Management in IoT Security. Cyberology: An Optimized Approach to the Cyber-World, 264.

Sunku Mohan, V., Sankaran, S., Buyya, R., & Achuthan, K. (2025). Leveraging Fog Computing for Security-Aware Resource Allocation in Narrowband Internet of Things. *Software, Practice & Experience*, *55*(4), 683–713. DOI: 10.1002/spe.3392

Uddin, M. S. (2024). Addressing IoT Security Challenges through AI Solutions. *International Journal of Computer Applications*, *186*(45), 50–55. DOI: 10.5120/ijca2024924107

Williams, P., Rojas, P., & Bayoumi, M. (2019, August). Security taxonomy in iot–a survey. In 2019 IEEE 62nd International Midwest Symposium on Circuits and Systems (MWSCAS) (pp. 560-565). IEEE. DOI: 10.1109/MWSCAS.2019.8884913

Zardari, S., Nisar, N., Fatima, Z., & Dhirani, L. L. (2023, January). Iot–assets taxonomy, threats assessment and potential solutions. In *2023 Global Conference on Wireless and Optical Technologies (GCWOT)* (pp. 1-8). IEEE. DOI: 10.1109/GCWOT57803.2023.10064657

ENDNOTES

1 Kali Linux: https://www.kali.org/

2 NS-3 Network Simulator: https://www.nsnam.org/

3 QEMU: https://www.qemu.org/

APPENDIX

Abbreviations

NB-IoT: Narrowband Internet of Things
LPWAN: Low-Power Wide-Area Network
IoT: Internet of Things
RRC: Radio Resource Control
NAS: Non-Access Stratum
UE: User Equipment
eNodeB: Evolved Node B (Base Station)
SDR: Software Defined Radio
API: Application Programming Interface
OTA: Over-The-Air (Update)
ACK: Acknowledgment
DoS: Denial-of-Service
CVSS: Common Vulnerability Scoring System
CIA: Confidentiality, Integrity, Availability
ETSI: European Telecommunications Standards Institute
ISO: International Organization for Standardization
NIST: National Institute of Standards and Technology
SP: Special Publication (NIST)
NS-3: Network Simulator-3
QEMU: Quick Emulator
SDLC: Software Development Life Cycle
IPS: Intrusion Prevention System
VPN: Virtual Private Network
IAM: Identity and Access Management
ML: Machine Learning
AI: Artificial Intelligence
RF: Radio Frequency
STRIDE: Spoofing, Tampering, Repudiation, Information Disclosure, Denial-of- Service, Elevation of Privilege
CI/CD: Continuous Integration / Continuous Deployment
VM: Virtual Machine

Chapter 9
The Penetration Testing Lifecycle

Gladson S. Oliver
http://orcid.org/0000-0002-8806-3641
Government College of Technology, Coimbatore, India

T. Suguna
http://orcid.org/0000-0003-1492-3183
Government College of Technology, Coimbatore, India

C. Aswini
http://orcid.org/0000-0001-8699-5165
Government College of Technology, Coimbatore, India

R. Malavika
http://orcid.org/0000-0002-6955-8948
Government College of Technology, Coimbatore, India

ABSTRACT

With an eye toward improving knowledge of ethical hacking techniques inside corporate cybersecurity systems, this chapter offers a disciplined summary of the penetration testing lifecycle. It defines the important stages of penetration testing: reconnaissance, threat modeling, vulnerability analysis, exploitation, and post-exploitation practices. Emphasizing practicality, the chapter combines ethical and legal compliance with best practices and common mistakes. It also emphasizes the need of strategic remedial planning, good documentation, and correspondence with stakeholders. The chapter is a useful manual for cybersecurity experts by outlining several tools and approaches suitable for every phase. Eventually, by means of methodical, repeatable, and responsible penetration testing procedures, the material helps to build strong security postures.

DOI: 10.4018/979-8-3373-3536-0.ch009

INTRODUCTION

In the always shifting terrain of cybersecurity, ethical hacking has evolved into a crucial area of research since it helps find and fix weaknesses before they are taken advantage of by hostile actors (Grimes, 2021). Central to ethical hacking is penetration testing, sometimes known as pen testing—a methodical process of evaluating the security of an information system by modeling real-world attacks (Scarfone & Mell, 2007). The penetration testing lifecycle guarantees completeness, legality, and efficiency in exposing security flaws (EC-Council, 2023), so providing a methodical approach to this process.

The whole penetration testing lifetime, including all important phases from planning to reporting and retesting, is explored in this chapter. It looks at the ethical, legal, and technical issues that direct every action and provides best practices to improve the general success of the pen testing process (Northcutt, 2020). Whether your background is cybersecurity education, aspirational ethical hacker, or seasoned security professional, knowing this lifecycle is crucial for doing responsible and successful security audits.

Beyond system hacking, penetration testing models real-world attack situations to find vulnerabilities before they are taken advantage of (OWASP, 2023.). Given the complexity of contemporary IT environments—including IoT devices, cloud services, and hybrid networks—a structured approach is more critical than ever. This lifecycle not only supports ethical and effective testing but also helps to match technical efforts with compliance criteria and organizational goals (Andress, 2021).

Moreover, the rising count of advanced cyberattacks endangering governments and businesses emphasizes the need of penetration testing. From ransomware to phishing campaigns to zero-day exploits and insider threats, organizations are always under danger. Penetration testing thus serves as a proactive defense mechanism, helping companies to find and fix flaws before they are taken advantage of (Grimes, 2021). This proactive strategy increases general resilience and fosters confidence among consumers, companies, and regulatory agencies.

The repeatable, scalable, and quantifiable process that the penetration testing lifecycle offers advances responsibility and openness. It helps cybersecurity experts to not only find and take advantage of flaws but also record and explain risks in a way that non-technical stakeholders would find reasonable (Scarfone & Mell, 2007). This link between strategic decisions and technical results guarantees that security projects complement corporate objectives and compliance responsibilities.

Furthermore, very important is following ethical and legal guidelines. Unlike malicious hacking, ethical hacking is carried out inside precisely defined limits defined by professional codes of behavior, legal agreements, and rules of engagement (EC-Council, 2023). From reconnaissance through exploitation and beyond, the lifecycle guarantees that these limitations control every stage of testing, so shielding the tester and the company from legal consequences.

Penetration testing is also no more a one-time exercise with the rise of DevSecOps and the inclusion of security into the software development lifecycle (SDLC). It is now a component of a more all-encompassing approach for ongoing security evaluation whereby automated tests are included into development pipelines (Andress, 2020). This development underlines even more the need of a well-defined penetration testing lifecycle, especially for teams using agile and DevOps approaches. The figure-1 below shows the lifecycle of penetration testing.

Figure 1. Penetration Testing Lifecycle

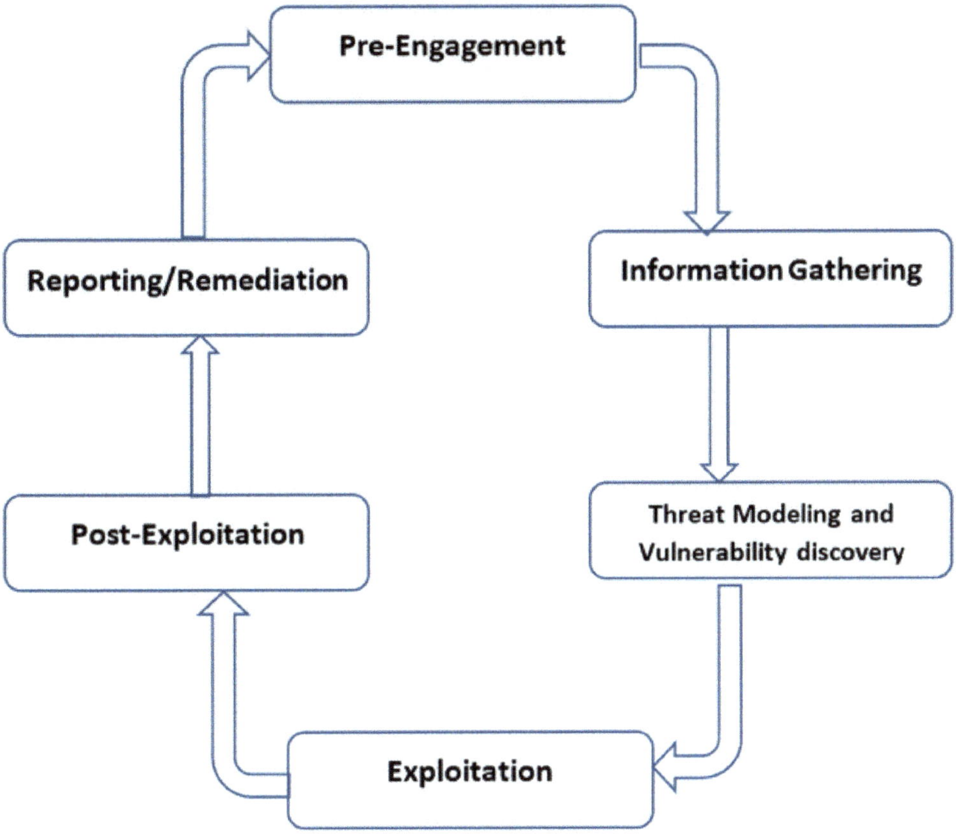

Mastery of the penetration testing lifetime helps companies to move from a reactive to a proactive security posture. It gives cybersecurity teams a methodical approach to find blind spots, rank hazards, and carry out quick mitigating action.

Understanding and using this lifecycle becomes not only helpful but also essential as cyberthreats keep changing in complexity and extent (Northcutt, 2020).

1. PRE-ENGAGEMENT AND PLANNING PHASE

A good penetration test starts in the pre-engagement and planning stage. Setting the basis for the whole engagement, this phase guarantees that the client and the penetration tester have a mutual awareness of the scope, objectives, methods, legal limits, and deliverables (PCI Security Standards Council, 2022). The figure-2 shows the overall view of pre-engagement and planning phase.

Figure 2. Pre-engagement and Planning

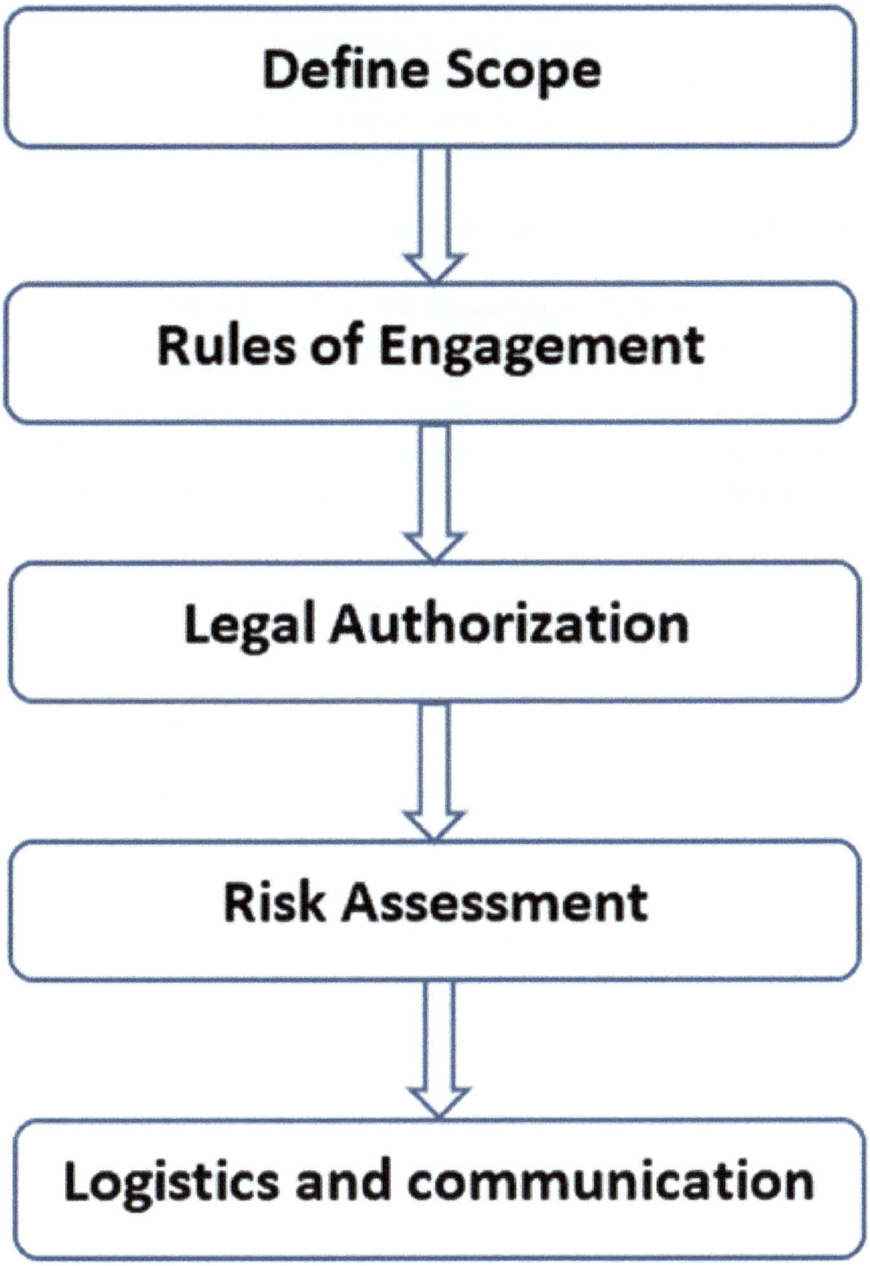

1.1 Benefits of Early Participation

Not only a necessary administrative stage, pre-engagement defines the whole framework of the penetration test. Poor planning might produce ineffective penetration tests, disorganized, legally dubious documentation, and Starting this process early will help all involved parties to match objectives, define scope, and steer clear of needless legal or reputational risk (EC-Council, 2023).

1.2 Appreciating Customer Needs

Developing a thorough awareness of the client's environment and particular security issues is fundamental in the pre-engagement stage. This covers a set of conversations meant for:

- Clearly stating the client's intended testing results and business objectives.
- Determining infrastructure elements and important systems needing particular focus.
- Specifying during testing acceptable degrees of operational disturbance and risk tolerance.
- Examining the legal and compliance responsibilities the company has to fulfill (PCi Security Standards Council, 2022).

This stage guarantees that the penetration test is tailored to provide significant, commercial-relevant insights instead of a standard vulnerability scan.

1.3 Specifying the Territory

The scope defines the parameters of the penetration test. Lack of appropriate documentation might cause the test to stray from expected results or ignore important systems. A well stated scope consists in:

- To be tested particular systems, tools, networks, and interfaces.
- Black-box, white-box, grey-box testing approaches among other ones.
- Schedule and timeline restrictions.
- Geographic and jurisdictional factors for either remote or on-site testing.
- Tester count and roles (OWASP, 2023).

Early scope definition guarantees effective use of resources and helps to prevent scope creep.

1.4 Rule of Engagement (RoE)

Legal and procedural guidelines known as "Rules of Engagement (RoE)" specify what is allowed and forbidden throughout the test. These records set limits and expectations for both sides. Typical elements consist of:

- Authorized testing times.
- Notifications protocols for events or discoveries of critical nature.
- Advice on safely managing personally identifiable data (PII).
- Policies prohibiting some activities (e.g., denial-of-service attacks) unless specifically approved (EC-Council, 2023).

Clearly defined RoE help to control unanticipated results and lower the possibility of accidental disturbance.

1.5 Legal Thoughts

Unauthorized and maybe illegal is penetration testing done without legal permission. Testers must thus work under a signed agreement offering legal protection. Legal readiness should consist in:

- An official Statement of Work (SoW) outlining the forthcoming tests.
- Agreements of non-disclosure to guard client data.
- Verification of informed and consent-giving relevance for pertinent third parties—such as cloud service providers.
- Compliance guarantees with data protection criteria including PCI DSS, HIPAA, or GDPR (U.S. Department of Health and Human Services, 2023; European Union, 2016).

Ignoring these components could put the tester or the company in legal hot or criminal responsibility.

1.6 Intelligence Gathering Planning

Even before active testing starts, a targeted and informed attack simulation is laid by passive intelligence collecting. Usually this happens subtly and without directly interacting with the intended infrastructure. One could find examples like:

- DNS records and WHOIS searches help one identify domain ownership and server setups.

- Searching public releases, antiquated systems, or leaked credentials.
- Examining social media organizational data and staff profiles (Grimes, 2021).

Before practical testing starts, this knowledge helps to create reasonable attack routes and hypotheses.

1.7 Review of Technical Environments

This stage guarantees that the testing approach fits the real security scene of the company. Usually, the study comprises:

- Looking at network diagrams and asset inventories.
- Examining the virtualizing technologies and cloud architecture of the company.
- Examining access policies and authentication systems.
- Pointing up already in use security tools including firewalls, intrusion detection and prevention systems, and endpoint protection (Northcutt, 2020).

This review helps testers to prioritize systems depending on sensitivity and exposure, replicate more accurate attack scenarios, and lower noise.

1.8 Impact Analysis and Risk Assessments

An initial risk assessment offers important new perspectives on how testing activities might affect daily operations. It spans assessing:

- Probability of testing causing a disturbance of services.
- Potential exploitations' business repercussions.
- Demand for some services or apps to be always available.
- Regulatory needs and compliance standards set by PCI Security Standards Council, 2022

Knowing these hazards ahead of time lets the team create a safer, more conscientious testing plan.

1.9 Logistics and Correspondence

It is imperative to coordinate the penetration testing team and the internal stakeholders of the client effectively. In pre-planning logistics, there are:

- Announcing points of contact for both sides.
- Selecting safe channels of communication (such as encrypted email or safe collaborative tools).
- Planned frequent updates, check-ins, and report turns in.
- Getting incident response protocols ready should unplanned disruptions (EC-Council, 2023).

Maintaining open communication throughout the engagement guarantees quick answers to developing problems and helps to reduce uncertainty.

1.10 Final Planning Phase Deliverables

Several important papers and tools should be ready at the end of the pre-engagement and planning period to direct the whole penetration testing lifetime:

- A precisely defined, jointly agreed upon scope document.
- An extensive Rules of Engagement form.
- Signed NDAs and legal authorizations.
- A chronology of contacts and planned testing initiatives.
- Risk reducing techniques and incident response policies (Scarfone & Mell, 2007).

These deliverables guarantee that all testing operations go under clear, strategic focus, and responsibility.

2. INFORMATION COLLECTION - RECONNAISSANCE

Often called reconnaissance, this is among the most crucial phases of the penetration testing process—that of information collecting. In this phase, testers compile as much relevant information about the target system or organization before directly testing. Later testing protocols and their foundation are shaped by this intelligence, which also directs the search and use of possible flaws (Scarfone & Mell, 2007; Andress, 2021).

2.1 Overview of Reconnaissance

Compiling data about a target to understand its digital footprint is known as reconnaissance. Often finding access points, poorly secured services, exposed credentials, and sensitive data inadvertently left accessible online, ethical hackers mimic in this phase how a real attacker would search an environment (Grimes, 2021; Kim & Solomon, 2022). More data gathered at this point helps penetration testing to become more targeted and successful.

Two main categories will enable one to organize reconnaissance:

- Passive reconnaissance: Data gathering free from direct target system interaction. It is quiet, legal in most cases, safe (Scarfone & Mell, 2007), albeit it may have less detail.
- Active reconnaissance: Direct target interaction— ping sweeps or port scanning—direct interaction While more instructive, active methods risk detection and have to be followed within the guidelines established by the Rules of Engagement (EC-Council, 2023).

2.2 Phase Information Seeking Goal

Finding actionable intelligence fit for simulating a real-world attack scenario is the main goal of reconnaissance. Particular objectives include:

- Locating ranges of domain names and IP addresses.
- Locating running systems and open ports.
- Finding server banners and software versions.
- Target network topological and segmentation mapping
- Finding staff members—human targets—for social engineering initiatives.
- Collecting online exposed configuration files and metadata (Northcutt, 2020; OWASP Foundation, 2023).

Sometimes this knowledge exposes flaws before any exploits are used.

2.3 Passive Data Collection Techniques

Passive reconnaissance bases on publicly available resources. These cover open directories, public DNS servers, search engines, social media, data leaks. Common passive methods consist in:

- Get domain ownership data, registration dates, email addresses, and related IPs (Andress, 2021). WHOIS searches
- DNS search: (if permitted) reverse searches, subdomain counts, and zone transfers.
- Google Dorking: Search sensitive files, configuration data, and indexed vulnerabilities using advanced search operators (Grimes, 2021).

- Analyze employee LinkedIn profiles, corporate Twitter feeds, and Facebook pages for pertinent information including project names, internal systems, or technologies used—that is, social media intelligence (SOCMINT).
- ExifTool (Kim & Solomon, 2022) lets you extract hidden metadata from papers (e.g., usernames or software versions) using tools.
- Leaked credential hunting using tools like HaveIBeenPwned or Paste-based Northcutt, 2020 to search for compromised credentials connected to an organization.

Passive methods help one stay under the radar and prepare for more forceful, active methods.

2.4 Active Information Gathering Techniques

Direct interaction in active reconnaissance creates a more comprehensive technical map of the target. This class of instruments and techniques consists in:

- Port scanning: (using Nmap) note running services and open ports.
- Banner grabbing: Search for vulnerable or outdated programs by compiling software version statistics (Kim & Solomon, 2022).
- OS fingerprinting: Using tools like Nmap, TCP/IP behaviors, or TTL values, find underlying operating systems.
- Traceroute and Netdiscover are two tools you can use to learn router and firewall configuration.
- Using tools like Dirb, Gobuster, or Burp Suite, examine web applications.
- Investigating SMB, SNMP, and LDAP will help you to compile usernames, group memberships, and network configurations (Scarfone & Mell, 2007; Andress, 2021).

These techniques are more intrusive and could be found by intrusion detection/prevention systems (IDS/IPS), thus they must be under appropriate control and approved.

2.5 Tools for Surveillance

Penetration testers compile data using a variety of tools, both open source and commercial. Typical instruments include:

- For OS identification, scripting, version detection, and port scanning, Nmap

- Maltego: A graphical tool for visualizing relationships among people, domains, and systems (Grimes, 2021). Connecting data
- The Harvester: For compiling public source email, subdomain, and IP collection.
- Shodan: Andress, 2021's search engine for internet-connected goods.
- Recon-ng: API-integrated modular reconnaissance framework with tools.
- FOCA: for pulling public document metadata (Kim & Solomon, 2022).

Target infrastructure, scope restrictions, and engagement goals help to guide suitable tool choice.

2.6 Human Intelligence (HUMINT) and Social Engineering Planning

Information collecting goes beyond mere technical directions. Many leaks start with human mistake. Testers train for social engineering by:

- Examining key staff and organizational structure.
- Investigating corporate culture in order to create respectable phishing pretexts.
- Finding direct lines of contact.
- Finding chances for impersonation, such HR contacts or help desk visits (EC-Council, 2023; Northcutt, 2020).

Though social engineering is sometimes carried out later, reconnaissance lays its basis.

2.7 Reconnaissance: Difficulties and Restraints

Though vital, reconnaissance has restrictions:

- Legal restrictions: Even passive approaches could involve access to illegal content or generate suspicions (Scarfone & Mell, 2007).
- Some companies mask internal structures using obfuscation methods including split DNS or CDNs, so enhancing security defenses.
- Detection risks: Strong probing could notify defenders, so triggering IP bans or engagement termination (Grimes, 2021).
- Data accuracy: Validation is crucial since not all the acquired data is accurate or relevant (PCI Security Standards Council, 2022).

2.8 Documentation and Reporting

Like every phase of the penetration testing process, documentation is absolutely vital. Reconnaissance results need to be carefully noted to:

- Justify later behavior.
- Guarantees repeatability.
- Show precision and diligence.
- Help final reporting with impact analysis (Kim & Solomon, 2022).

Reports should comprise source URLs, software versions, IP/domain lists, screenshots, and analytical assumptions (Scarfone & Mell, 2007).

2.9 Guidelines for Best Practices

Good reconnaissance gives quality and relevance above volume top priority. Included among best practices are:

- Using a checklist helps one to prevent omissions.
- Notes timestamps and data sources.
- Beginning with passive techniques then working forward.
- Verifying every result before application.
- Always running inside legal and contractual limits (OWASP Foundation, 2023; EC-Council, 2023).

3 VULNERABILITY DISCOVERY AND THREAT MODELING

Threat modeling and vulnerability identification define the analytical focus of the penetration testing process. Once sufficient knowledge has been acquired, logically next is looking at possible hazards and identifying system shortcomings. Emphasizing the most important hazards, these activities guarantee that the test represents real attacker behavior and offers a road map for exploitation (Scarfone & Mell, 2007; Kim & Solomon, 2022; Grimes, 2021).

3.1 *Synopsis of Threat Modeling*

Threat modeling is the process of spotting and organizing likely risks to an application or system. By means of this process, penetration testers can concentrate on high-value targets and better grasp the attack surface (Shostack, 2014; Andress, 201). Threat modeling consists in:

- Establishing assets (such databases, private information, tools).
- Graphical system trust limits.
- Determining points of access and noting user or system interactions with the target.
- Listing threat actors (e.g., hacktivists, cybercriminals, insiders).
- Individuating possible attack paths (XSS, SQLi, credential reusing).

PASTA (Process for Attack Simulation and Threat Analysis) and STRIDE (Spoofing, Tampering, Repudiation, Information Disclosure, Denial of Service, and Elevation of Privilege) are two rather often used threat modeling techniques (Microsoft, 2020; Grimes, 2021).

3.2 Vulnerability Confirmation

Vulnerability identification is the process of discovering flaws in systems, programs, or setups that attackers might find use for. It uses both automated and hand-based methods to find recognized flaws or dangerous behaviors (Andress, 2021; Northcutt, 2020).

Key stages consist:

- Tools including Nessus, OpenVAS, and Qualys rapidly search systems for known vulnerabilities (CVEs).
- Manual testing is used to find logical errors and insecure designs that automated tools might overlook.
- Reviewing application/system configurations helps one to identify insecure defaults or misconfigurations in configuration auditing (Kim & Solomon, 2022.).
- Patch analysis: Finding obsolete programs and lacking fixes (Grimes, 2021).

3.3 Applied Threat Modeling

Real-world threat modeling calls for working with developers, system architects, and stakeholders. Good policies consist in:

- Making data flow diagrams (DFDs) helps one to see data movement.
- Clearly defining trust limits to identify areas needing more security.
- Analyzing session management, access control, and authentication systems.

- Creating attack simulations and abuse cases based on Shostack, 2014; Kim & Solomon, 2022

This helps ethical hackers to give likely attack routes top priority.

3.4 Methods of Vulnerability Identification

Modern methods probe more than surface scans:

- Fuzz testing: Provoking unanticipated behavior by means of malformed inputs
- Reviewing source code for flaws like dangerous function calls or input validation concerns is the basis of static code analysis.
- Dynamic analysis: Tracking running programs to find session defects, memory leaks, or injections.
- Dependency analysis: Grimes, 2021; OWASP Foundation, 2023; points of vulnerability in outside-of-interest-bearing packages

3.5 Integration for Threat Intelligence

Including threat intelligence increases the relevance of vulnerability finding. Sources include:

- Public CVE databases and vendor advisories.
- Systems like AlienVault OTX or MISP.
- Dark web forums and vulnerability reports.
- Previous incident data from like technologies or sectors (PCI Security Standards Council, 2022; EC-Council, 2023).

3.6 Categorizing and Arranging Weaknesses

Not every vulnerability is equally important. Usually, emphasis consists in:

- CVSS scoring—quantifying degrees of seriousness.
- Examining how readily a problem might be taken advantage of is known as exploitability assessment.
- Estimating effects on operations or compliance using business impact analysis will help (Kim & Solomon, 2022).
- Chaining analysis: Examining how minor defects might aggregate to pose serious concerns (Andress, 2021).

3.7 Typical Weaknesses Identified

Typical weaknesses discovered include:

- Missing patches and obsolete programing.
- insecure channels of transmission.
- Session management or broken authentication.
- SQL or LDAP injection weaknesses.
- Incorrectly set permissions.
- Made public sensitive information or credentials (Northcutt, 2020;OWASP Foundation, 2023).

3.8 Documentation and valuation

Every vulnerability has to be thoroughly recorded with supporting data. Reports should include:

- Extensive background and description.
- Proof-of- concept (PoC) screenshots or proof-of-performance.
- Affected components or systems.
- Potential impact and risk ratings.
- Advice on mitigating or remedial action (Kim & Solomon, 2022; EC-Council, 2023).

Verification filters false positives and guarantees correctness.

3.9 Responsible Disclosure: Ethical Aspects

Even in approved testing, ethical criteria hold true. Testers ought to:

- Steer clear of too aggressive data collecting.
- Steer clear of exploitation outside of validation.
- Immediately report important discoveries.
- Keep transparency and responsibility logs for EC-Council, 2023; Grimes, 2021.

Responsible disclosure advances long-term security and fosters trust.

3.10 Model for Constant Risk

Systems change and threat modeling has to be constant. Good practices comprise:

- Changing models in line with architectural or systemic developments.
- Including modeling into the SDLC.
- Making use of tools and systems for ongoing visibility (Shostack, 2014; Microsoft, 2020).

4. EXPLOITATION

The output of information gathering, threat modeling, and vulnerability identification is synthesized in the exploitation stage. Penetration testers at this level try to actively take advantage of found weaknesses in a designated and under control environment. Finding the degree to which an assailant could obtain illegal access, increase rights, or traverse laterally across the network comes first. This process helps companies prioritize remedial actions by showing the actual results of security weaknesses (Scarfone & Mell, 2007; EC-Council, 2023).

4.1 Objective of Exploitation

Using exploitation during a penetration test mostly serves to:

- Having illegal data or system access.
- Skipping security systems.
- Increasing administrator/root user rights.
- Retaking private data including financial records or credentials.
- proving that commercial logic exploitation is feasible.
- Verifying whether persistence or system pivoting has promise (Kim & Solomon, 2022).

This stage also confirms whether previously discovered weaknesses can be practically effectively used.

4.2 Legal and Moral Limitations

The exploitation phase has to be carried out under strict ethical and legal rules even if its offensive character (Grimes, 2021). Important factors consist:

- Authorization: The Rules of Engagement specifically must allow all kinds of exploitation.
- Reducing Risk: Steer clear of activities that might cause business disturbance, system failures, or data loss.
- Limit data exfiltration to the minimal required to show the vulnerability.
- Client Communication: Notify the client right away upon finding critical or highly impactful vulnerabilities (Andress, 2021).

4.3 Exploitation Tools and Methodologies

The type of the target system and the discovered vulnerabilities determine the exploitation methods. Typical techniques comprise:

- Remote code execution (RCE) via flaws in input validation.
- SQL injection aimed at backend database manipulation.
- XSS—cross-site scripting—for content defacement or session hijacking.
- Taking illegal access by abusing weak authentication.
- Local exploits allow one to escalate privilege.
- Making advantage of misconfigurations including open services or too high rights (OWASP Foundation, 2023).

Common instruments of exploitation:

- Meta-platform for exploit development and execution: Metasploit Framework
- BeEF: Concentrated on web-based vulnerabilities, browser exploitation framework
- SQLmap: Designed tool for SQL injection detection and exploitation automation
- hydra: login credential Brute-force tool
- PowerShell-based tools for post-exploitation available under PowerSploit/ Nishang (Northcutt, 2020).

4.4 Abuse of Particular Objectives

Different targets call for specific methods of exploitation:

- Web apps: Choose XSS, CSRF, or insecure direct object references.
- Apply kernel exploits or privilege escalation in operating systems.
- Perform MITM, DNS poisoning, or ARP spoofing.
- Wireless environments: Set up rogue access points or exploit poor encryption.

- Cloud environments: use exposed storage or insecure IAM rules (Kim & Solomon, 2022).

4.5 Activities Regarding Post-Exploitation

After effective usage, testers evaluate the degree of access and the possible influence. Important duties include:

- Privilege escalation: Increasing access inside systems under compromise.
- Lateral movement: Seeking out other network systems.
- Dumping credentials: gathering passwords.
- Simulations of data exfiltration: proving sensitive data access.
- Persistent installation of new user accounts (EC-Council, 2023) or backdoors

4.6 Red Team against conventional pen testing: exploitation

The type of engagement determines the variation in the exploitation objectives:

- Conventional Pen Testing: Broad system vulnerability assessment
- Focusses on stealth, tenacity, and simulating APTs over time in red teams.

Red teaming might call for social engineering, chained exploits, and physical security (Grimes, 2021).

4.7 Challenges in Exploitation: Solutions

Typical challenges involve:

- Security protections including antivirus programs, IDS, and firewalls.
- False positives: non-exploitable weaknesses
- Stability problems: Certain exploits might bring down systems.
- Time restrictions: few testing windows.

Strategies of mitigation:

- Employ dependable, well-tested exploits.
- Customize cargo when public exploits fall short.
- Work with allies to reduce disturbance (Andress, 2021).

4.8 Record of Adventures

Every effort at exploitation should be carefully recorded, successful or not. Reports must consist of:

- Specific vulnerability taken advantage of.
- Paid for tools and payloads.
- Evidence might be session logs or screenshots.
- Potential economic influence.
- Suggestions for mitigation (Kim & Solomon, 2022)

4.9 Knowledge Gained from Exploitation

This phase often draws attention to:

- Poor patch management.
- Seldom good segmentation or access control.
- Inadequate logging or monitoring.
- Incidents response gaps (Scarfone & Mell, 2007).

These results guide next defensive tactics.

4.10 Safety Checks and Ethical Limitations

Testers must act responsibly even if they are simulating adversarial behavior. Best practices consist of:

- First testing in sandboxed surroundings.
- Steering clear of devastating payloads.
- Having strategies for rollback.
- Stopping dangerous action with kill-switches (EC-Council, 2023).

5. POST-EXPLOITATION

Following the successful compromise of a system, the penetration testing lifetime depends critically on the phase of post-exploitation. This stage emphasizes on what can be accomplished with the acquired access instead of on the means of acquisition. It offers insights on the actual repercussions of a breach including system control level, data sensitivity, lateral movement potential, and organizational resilience to continuous attacks (Scarfone & Mell, 2007; Kim & Solomon, 2022; Shostack, 2014; Stewart et al., 2021).

5.1 Goals of Post-Exploitation

Post-exploitation aims primarily in two directions:

- Appreciating the value and sensitivity of compromised systems.
- Figuring the degree of access—user versus administrator/root, for example.
- Evaluating possible tenacity.
- Finding chances for lateral movement.
- Simulated data exfiltration allows one to show business impact.
- Techniques of recording used to spread impact inside the surroundings (EC-Council, 2023; Andress, 2021; Weidman, 2020).

These exercises offer reasonable understanding of the dangers a determined assailant presents. The following figure-3 summarizes the goals of post-exploitation.

Figure 3. Post-exploitation Goals

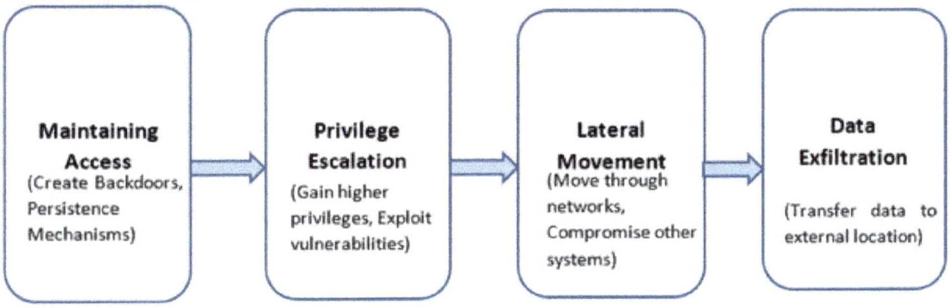

5.2 System Count and Environment Map

Following compromise, penetration testers gather internal intelligence to map the compromised environment including:

- Describing users, groups, roles, and rights.
- Finding related networks and systems' layouts.
- Looking over installed programs and running procedures.
- Finding security controls—such as E-DR or antivirus.

- Examining local logs and system event records (Northcutt, 2020; Kim & Solomon, 2022; Stewart et al., 2021).

5.3 Credential Harvesting

Further access and privilege escalation is supported by credential collecting. Typical approaches consist in:

- Dumping password hashes—from LSASS or SAM—in general.
- Getting passwords kept in browsers or email clients.
- Documenting credentials gathered from ongoing initiatives.
- Using keyloggers or clipboards scrapers (Kim & Solomon, 2022; Grimes, 2021).

In "pass-the-hash" or "pass-the-ticket" attacks, stolen credentials can be reused (Coleman, 2021; Weidman, 2020).

5.4 Ascending Privilege

Escalation of privilege is obtaining more privileges. Methods involve:

- Profite from kernel weaknesses.
- Misusing improperly set-up rights or services.
- DLLs or scheduled tasks hijacking
- Profiting from weak or recycled passwords (Andress, 2021; EC-Council, 2023).

5.5 Mechanisms for Persistence

Attackers usually create long-term access by means of persistence strategies including:

- Changing credentials or registering new users.
- Changing installers or starting scripts.
- Running payloads from registry keys at reboot.
- Using backdoors (Grimes, 2021; Shostack, 2014; Stewart et al., 2021; C2 channels, reverse shells).

Testing resilience to repeated breaches helps one to know how strong the system is.

5.6 Lateral movement

Lateral movement is turning from one compromised system to other using:

- Making use of pilfers of credentials.
- Violating domain trust bonds.
- Employing PsExec, RDP, or WMI among other tools.
- Using VPN access or SSH keys (EC-Council, 2023; Coleman, 20211; Weidman, 2020).

5.7 Artificial Data Exfiltration

Simulations of data exfiltration assess data theft ease of access:

- Finding private information including financial records, PII, or IP.
- Examining paths of file extraction and exporting methods.
- File covertly or securely.
- Seeing how people detect and respond (OWASP Foundation, 2023; Andress, 2021).

5.8 Path of Clearing

Though not usually used, ethical testers could replicate attacker anti-forensics including:

- Changing event entries or deleting logs.
- Eliminating payloads and command histories.
- Eliminating evidence with anti-forensics instruments (Kim & Solomon, 2022; Coleman, 2021).

5.9 Record Keeping

Results of post-exploitation documentation must consist:

- Access levels attained.
- Harvests of credentials and their effects.
- Internal reach and lateral movement proof.
- Proof-of-concepts, logs, and screenshots.
- Advice on mitigating and defending Northcutt, 2020; Scarfone & Mell, 2007.

5.10 Protective Strategies

Post-exploitation strengthens defenses and points up flaws:

- Implement network segmenting and access restrictions.
- Use credential vaulting and robust password rules.
- Watch for odd changes in privilege or behavior.
- Continually fix and update systems.
- Use EDR and DLP tools (PCi Security Standards Council, 2022; Shostack, 2014).

5.11 Moral Restraints

Ethical issues are absolutely vital.

- Work just within your scope.
- Treat private information gently.
- Steer clear of continuous changes or actual damage.
- Right away report high-risk discoveries (EC-Council, 2023; Grimes, 2021).

5.12 Lessons Acquired

Many times, post-exploitation reveals internal weaknesses:

- Inaccurate patching causes ease of privilege escalation.
- Insufficient internal review.
- Reiteration of credentials and too high user rights.
- Errors in incident response (Scarfone & Mell, 2007; Kim & Solomon, 2022; Stewart et al., 2021); logging, alerting

6. WRITING AND CORRECTIVE ACTION

The last but just equally important stage of the penetration testing life is reporting and remedial action. For the target company, this stage turns all technical data, strategies, and assessments into practical insight. Although exploitation shows the possible harm an enemy could inflict, the reporting and following corrective action help a company to bounce back and fortify its defenses (Snyder, 2021).

The report serves as a strategic road map for the client to grasp and enhance their security posture rather than only a synopsis of the participation. Good remedial action guarantees vulnerabilities are fixed, knowledge is gained, and defensive tactics are followed to stop recurrence (Luttgens et al., 2016).

6.1 Objectives of the Phase on Remedial Action and Documentation

This phase produces several important results for several different stakeholders:

- Clearly record weaknesses, sources, and hazards.
- Show visual evidence and technical proof-of-concept (PoC).
- Convert technical hazards into effects on business operations.
- Present suggested prioritized repairs.
- Turn on efficient communication among executive and technical teams.
- Create the basis for next assessments and audits (Andress, 2021).

6.2 Organizing the Test of Penetration Report

Usually, a well-organized report consists in:

- Executive Summary: Top level review for top management.
- Goals, scope, and objectives: specifics of the participation, tested systems,
- Key Results: List of main weaknesses and general risk attitude.
- Methodology: Tools applied, ethical/legal scope, testing approach
- Detailed Results: CVE vulnerabilities, efforts at exploitation, compromised systems, and possible impact.
- Evidence: (where allowed) screenshots, poCs, and shell output.
- Risk Rating and Prioritizing: Sort severity using custom frameworks or CVSS.
- Technical and procedural mitigating recommendations.
- Logs, toolsets, scripts, and coverage details (EC-Council, 2023) in appendices

6.3 Customizing Notes for Stakeholders

Reports are seen by different stakeholders through different prism:

- Executives want succinct summaries of ROI and corporate risk.
- Technical depth is what IT security teams need for remedial action.
- Regulatory mapping calls for evidence for compliance teams.

Reports should be segmented or stacked to guarantee relevance without overloading the audience (Stewart et al., 2021).

6.4 Clearly Expressing Risk

A strong report provides context and urgency:

- Links business impact to technical problems.
- Adds visual tools including heatmaps and risk matrices.
- References compliance guidelines including GDPR, HIPAA, PCI-DSS.
- Uses relevant illustrations of risk to show Kim & Solomon, 2022.

6.5 Typical Problems for Reporting

- Ignores non-technical stakeholders in favor of too vague or technical approaches.
- Tool Dumping: Including raw scan outputs free from interpretation.
- Lack of business context compromises relevance and urgency.
- Delayed reporting stunts timely correction (Grimes, 2021).

6.6 Corrective Measures

Corrective action is closing found gaps:

- Patch Management: Early application of security enhancements
- System hardening: enforcing safe configurations and turning off extraneous services
- Examining roles, permissions, and authentication rules helps to improve access control.
- Limiting lateral movement, network segmentation
- Monitoring and logging will help to improve response and visibility.
- User awareness training: stressing behavior against social engineering and phishing (Weidman, 2020).

6.7 Retesting and Verification

Closure of vulnerabilities needs validation.

- Check patch efficiency by re-scanning.
- Re-test compromised vectors.

- Verify other compensating controls (Snyder, 2021).

Either the original engagement or a planned follow-up can include this phase.

6.8 Starting a Cycle of Constant Improvement

Penetration testing can guide more general security plans:

- Input data into systems of enterprise risk management.
- Use results to direct technology and financial spending.
- Plan continuous evaluations including red team drills.
- Continually review policies and training resources (Luttgens et al., 2016).

6.9 Legal Effects and Compliance

Reports of penetration testing help to support compliance:

- PCI-DSS: Year-round system cardholder data annual testing
- HIPAA requires systems handling health data to undergo risk analysis.
- GDPR stresses data protection and breach readiness.

Reports have to follow legal standards and be kept on hand for audit needs (PCI Security Standards Council, 2022).

6.10 Ethical and Responsible Disclosure

Important supply chain or third-party vulnerabilities call for moral treatment:

- Notify appropriate third parties.
- Exclusively document upstream hazards.
- Work with the client on a disclosure approach (Shostack, 2014).

6.11 Knowledge Gained and Organizational Maturity

Reporting and correcting help to build long-term resilience:

- Find vulnerabilities' underlying causes.
- Analyze how well detection and response fit.
- Find areas lacking tools, policies, or training.
- Advance cybersecurity posture driving (Stewart et al., 2021).

7. LEGAL, ETHICAL AND REGULATORY ASPECTS

While every phase of the penetration testing process is technically difficult, it is equally important to execute tests inside well defined ethical and legal constraints. Errors in this domain can have major effects on the tester as well as the company (Kerr, 2020).

7.1 Legal Prerequisites

Penetration testing always requires permission. Formal written permission including defined scope, testing windows, and system boundaries has to be acquired before any activity starts. Legal criteria vary depending on the nation and jurisdiction; thus, testers should be familiar with relevant legislation including:

- The Computer Fraud and Abuse Act (CFAA) United States
- The Computer Misuse Act, United Kingdom.
- GDPR, General Data Protection Regulation, European Union
- The Indian Information Technology Act, 2000.

A best practice is a legal review of rules of engagement (RoE) paperwork (Winkler & Gomes, 2022). Contracts should have restrictions, backup plans, and permission to test cloud environments.

Legal clarity guarantees legal operations, safeguards client information, and lowers legal risks by itself. Data sovereignty rules define where and how data may be handled in cross-border tests, so respecting the legal environment of every nation (Moore, 2021).

7.2 Ethical Responsibility

Ethical hackers owe it to others to minimize damage, respect their privacy, and responsibly document results. From (ISC)^2, EC-Council, Offensive Security, and SANS Institute, codes of ethics highlight fundamental values:

- Stop corruption, theft, or unwanted access.
- Follow exactly the approved scope.
- List all found weaknesses.
- Retain client confidentiality and data.

In ethical hacking, integrity, openness, and a dedication to do no harm—along with skill—are equally important (Kabay, 2020). This covers quickly fixing any inadvertent disruptions and organizing third-party vulnerability disclosures with software maintainers or vendors.

Testers have to keep current on changing tools, hazards, and moral conundrums. The blurry lines separating testing from intrusion change with technology. Still the compass of guidance are ethics.

7.3 Compliance and Industry Standards

Many companies either demand or advise frequent penetration testing to keep compliance intact. Typical systems consist of:

- PCI DSS: Calls for yearly system credit card data testing.
- HIPAA calls for ePHI security controls and risk analyses.
- NIST SP 800-115 provides technical security testing guidelines.
- ISO/IEC 27001: Guideline on ISMS structures including vulnerability testing.
- SOC 2 calls for evaluations of security, availability, and privacy.
- FedRAMP oversees cloud service provider security testing.
- GDPR calls for both organisational and technical security measures.

Compliance has:

- Specifying scope, approach, and documentation.
- Offering proof of results and corrections policies.
- Retesting to confirm closure.

Tailored to organizational risks, security testing should not only serve audit checklists but also reflect organizational vulnerabilities (Ahmed et al., 20211).

7.4 Liability, Contracts, and Insurance

Contracts should precisely define scope, obligations, and liability:

- NDAs: Guard private and intellectual property.
- Specify deadlines, deliverables, and tasks in your SLAs.
- Indemnity Clauses: Distribute hazards should unanticipated events strike.

Though such policies usually include exclusions, cyber liability insurance can protect both sides. Clarifying coverage and liability calls for open communication and legal advice (Vacca, 2020).

7.5 Responsible Disclosure Ethical Reporting

Reporting should be accurate, whole, and fair:

- Steer clear of too ambitious vulnerability descriptions.
- Differentiate confirmed from speculative problems.
- Steer clear of using client-sensitive information without specific permission.
- Offer standards-compliant, doable suggestions.

When vulnerabilities affect outside third parties, testers should:

- Tell sellers discreetly.
- Give enough time for fix before public release.
- If necessary, coordinate announcements (Kerr, 2020).

Following responsible disclosure policies strengthens ethical confidence and helps testers to be guardians of world security.

8. AUTOMATION FOR PENETRATION TESTING TOOLS

By mostly including automation and sophisticated toolsets, modern penetration testing now greatly improves the accuracy, speed, and scalability of security assessments (Ahmed & Qamar, 2022.). Dependency on automated systems guarantees timely vulnerability identification and helps to simplify processes as digital ecosystems get more complex.

8.1 Value of Automation Inside Penetration Testing

Automation lets ethical hackers concentrate on high-level strategic assessments and sophisticated exploit development by managing repetitive chores. Automated tools have:

- Quickly survey large areas.
- Minuiter human error to increase consistency.
- Size to satisfy business infrastructure needs.
- Fit very nicely into CI/CD and DevSecOps systems.
- Improve security assessments' return on investment (ROI) (Mellado et al., 2021).

Evaluating contextual vulnerabilities, corporate logic errors, and false positives still depends on human oversight, though.

8.2 Categories of Penetration Testing Tools

Tools used in penetration testing span several phases of involvement:

- Tools collecting open-source intelligence (OSINT) include Nmap, Shodan, The Harvester, and Recon-ng.
- Nessus, OpenVAS, and Nikto find system flaws.
- Metasploit, BeEF, and Impacket present strong controlled attack frameworks.
- Empire, BloodHound, and Mimikatz back lateral movement and privilege escalation.
- Burp Suite, ZAP, SQLmap, and Aircrack-ng address application and wireless vulnerabilities for web and IoT testing.
- Custom Automation: Ansible simulates real-world attack scenarios (Patel et al., 2023) by Python or Bash, AutoRecon, and tools.

8.3 CI/CD Integration Alongside DevSecOps

DevSecOps depends on automation to embed security all through the SDLC:

- Scans set off on code changes.
- closes the distance separating production from development.
- Advocates early vulnerability detection—that is, shift-left security.

For automated testing, commonly CI/CD tools Jenkins, GitHub Actions, and SonarQube are coupled with Snyk, Checkmarx, and Veracode (Johnson & Harris, 2021).

8.4 Automation, Artificial Intelligence, and Machine Learning

Penetration testing incorporate artificial intelligence and machine learning more and more to:

- Improve fuzzy methods.
- Enhance anomaly detection.
- Sort weaknesses according to probability and impact (Zhou et al., 2021).

Particularly in large-scale corporate environments, these improvements allow adaptive testing strategies.

8.5 Automated Tools and Restraints

Automation has hazards even if it is rather strong:

- False positives and negatives:
- Restricted situational awareness.
- System disturbance and resource consumption
- Too great reliance on tool output (Ahmed & Qamar, 2022).

The most all-encompassing results come from a balanced approach combining expert analysis with automation.

8.6 Creating a Tailored Automation Toolkit

Custom toolkit maximize performance for particular settings:

- Combining owned tools with open-source ones.
- Customizing for repeated processes.
- Use of BlackArch, Parrot OS, or Kali Linux lab environments.
- Mastery of Python,bash, and PowerShell lets one more customize and integrate (Patel et al., 2023).

Tool relevance and currency are guaranteed by ongoing updates via GitHub, security forums, and community repositories.

8.7 Legal and Ethical Applied Use of Automated Tools

Automated tools have to be applied under tight ethical limits:

- Work within specified scope.
- Save dangerous scans for only approved use.
- Tell clients about possible hazards.
- Record and audit automated responses (Johnson & Harris, 2021).

Applied ethically, automation serves as a multiplier of efficiency. But abuse can compromise client confidence and engagement targets.

9. PENETRATION TESTING IN PARTICULARIZED SETTINGS

Penetration testing offers particular challenges and calls for particular tools, techniques, and knowledge within specialized settings. From traditional IT systems (Kott et al., 2022), these environments—including industrial control systems (ICS), Internet of Things (IoT) devices, cloud platforms, and mobile ecosystems—have unique protocols, security models, and operational restrictions.

9.1 SCADA Systems and Industrial Control Systems (ICS)

Common in industrial environments including those found in energy, manufacturing, and transportation sectors, ICS and SCADA (Supervisor Control and Data Acquisition) systems are Because these systems give uptime and dependability top priority over security, penetration testing is especially sensitive (Knowles et al., 2015).

Critical Problems:

- Safety First: Testing shouldn't cause damage to equipment or stop present operations.
- Legacy Protocols: Often used are outdated or proprietary systems including Modbus, DNP3, or OPC.
- Many systems are isolated and call for specific communication tools or physical access.

Instruments and Techniques:

- For passive traffic analysis, Wireshark and Tcpdump
- ModScan and Scapy for protocol testing.
- SHODAN for spotting ICS devices exposed online.

Close working with operational technology (OT) engineers helps testers reduce risk and grasp system tolerances (Stouffer et al., 2015).

9.2 Cloud Communities

Penetration testers must assess cloud-native infrastructure and security as companies migrate to platforms including AWS, Azure, and GCP.

Threats Specific to Cloud:

- Incorrectly configured storage buckets—like AWS S3.
- IAM misconfiguration-induced privilege escalation

- Revealed insecure Kubernetes implementations and APIs.

Instruments:

- Auditing configuration ScoutSuite and Prowler
- Security assessments with CloudSploit
- PacBot for government and policy automation.

Shared responsibility models and service-specific implementations—which Balding, 2021 defines—must be understood by testers.

9.3 IoT (Internet of Things)

IoT systems span embedded medical equipment to smart appliances. Their different backgrounds and limited resources provide difficulties.
Challenges:

- Various hardware/software designs.
- Few choices for minimum patching and upgrading.
- Insufficient vendor standardisation.

Techniques of Evaluation:

- FOR firmware analysis, Binwalk and QEMU
- Bluetooth/Zigbee protocol testing
- Physical access testing JTAG/UART interfaces.

Simulating real-world uses often calls for custom labs (Gupta et al., 2022).

9.4 Mobile Domains

Mobile apps layer attack surfaces by interacting with databases and APIs.
Test techniques:

- Reverse engineering APK/IPA files in static analysis.
- Dynamic analysis: observing running behavior.
- Burp Suite or mitmproxy intercept network traffic.

instruments:

- MobSF for automatically tested systems.
- Frida/Xposed for x-ray equipment.
- Debugging utilities in ADB/iOS

Testers also have to follow platform-specific guidelines including those of the App Store and Play Store (Enck et al., 2014).

9.5 Air-Gapped Safe Sites

Military and nuclear plants among others separate important systems from public networks.

Restrained:

- Tight physical access policies.
- No remote access; instruments have to be moved safely.
- Customised systems and non-standard hardware.

Procedure:

- Physical security takes front stage.
- Non-invasive diagnostic tools.
- Coordination including backup procedures and facility management.

These tests call both in-person evaluation and documentation (Kott et al., 2022).

9.6 Hardware Verification and Embedded Systems

Common in consumer electronics, cars, and aircraft, embedded systems call for specific knowledge.

Plans:

- Bus sniffing in I2C, SPI.
- Dumping firmware.
- JTAG boundary scanning is one thing.
- Power analysis and glitch attacks.

tools:

- Bus pirate, hardware interface JTAGulator.
- Chip Whisperer for side-channel investigation.

- Flash ROM applications for firmware modification.

Testing has to take place under strictly safety compliant lab settings (Zhang et al., 2021).

9.7 Synopsis and Suggestive Directions

In specialized environments, penetration testing calls for:

- Strong knowledge in a deep domain.
- Customized instruments and approaches of testing.
- Work with field experts including OT engineers and cloud architects.
- Understanding of legal, security, and uptime limitations.

In these ever-changing fields, ethical hackers have to constantly adapt to guarantee relevance and efficacy.

10 CAREER IN ETHICAL HACKING

Among the most dynamic and fast changing disciplines within cybersecurity is ethical hacking. Demand for qualified ethical hackers and penetration testers has exploded as companies all around understand the need of proactive defense. Developing a successful career in this field calls for not only technical mastery but also curiosity, honesty, lifelong learning, and a strong ethical foundation (Skoudis & Liston, 2021).

10.1 Foundations: Requirements and Learning History

While anyone from many backgrounds can pursue ethical hacking, a foundation in computer science, information technology, or cybersecurity offers a major benefit. Fundamental knowledge domains consist of:

- TCP/IP, DNS, HTTP/S, routing, and firewalls comprise the networking protocols.
- Deep knowledge of Linux and Windows internals helps operating systems.
- Programming knowledge of Python,bash, JavaScript, and C/C++.
- Security foundations: Web security, threat modeling, malware, encryption, and authentication.

Many experts use self-study, bootcamps, and online courses to pick up fundamental knowledge (Dhanjani, 2015).

10.2 Professional Certifications and Certificates

Certifications support professional credibility and validate abilities. Among the notable certifications are:

- Certified Ethical Hacker, CEH – EC-Council's entry-level certification
- Offensive Security Certified Professional, or OSCP—hands-on, pragmatic certification.
- Perfect for beginners is eJPT, the eLearning Security Junior Penetration Tester.
- Broader and advanced certifications in CompTIA Security+ and GPEN, the GIAC Penetration Tester.

These credentials show commitment and open doors to advanced prospects (Conklin et al., 2018).

10.3 Learning From Real-world Experience

Development of attacker-like thinking depends on practical experience. There are: possibilities.

- Building home labs using Metasploitable Kali Linux.
- Taking advantage of sites including CTFtime, TryHackMe, and Hack The Box.
- Participating in HackerOne's or Bugcrowd's bug bounty campaigns.
- Helping to create open-source security tools and documentation.

Applied learning develops pragmatic knowledge and intuition (Weidman, 2020).

10.4 Career Routes and Specialties

Ethical hacking provides several specialties:

- Penetration Tester: Models attacks on systems, networks, and applications.
- Red Teamer - Models sophisticated enemies in controlled interactions.
- Security researcher investigates zero-days and creates custom tools.
- Bug bounty hunter searches and responsibly documents vulnerabilities.

- Security consultant guides companies on mitigating techniques.

Advanced positions could be Red Team Manager, Security Architect, or CISO (Skoudis & Liston, 2021).

10.5 Building a Brand and Personal Network

Essential in cybersecurity are visibility and networking. Successful plans consist in:

- Sharing on blogs research and tutorials.
- Speaking at events like Black Hat, DEF CON, or BSides.
- GitHub sharing tools and scripts
- Participating on sites like LinkedIn and X—formerly Twitter.
- Community service and mentoring.

Personal branding might inspire cooperation, job offers, and speaking engagements (Deviant Ollam, 2021).

10.6 Constant Education: Staying Current

Cybersecurity changes fast. Being informed calls for:

- Following blogs on ThreatPost and Krebs on Security.
- Researching models including OWASP Top 10 and MITRE ATT&CK.
- Traveling to events including Black Hat, DerbyCon, and ShmooCon.
- Signing up for advanced classes from eLearnSecurity, SANS, or Offensive Security.

Sustained success depends on lifelong learning (Andress, 2021).

10.7 Ethical Thought and Considerations

Technical ability has to be directed by moral behavior. Important values consist of:

- Integrity: Always get permission.
- Ask why and how systems operate.
- Responsibility: Appreciate possible influence.
- Discipline: Clearly document following protocols.

Ethical hacking is built upon trust (Kabay, 2020).

10.8 Aspiring Ethical Hacker Roadmap

One recommended road map consists of:

1. Learn fundamental networking, programming, and IT.
2. Study books and courses to pick ethical hacking techniques.
3. Create a hand-on practice home lab.
4. Get basic certificates (eJPT, CEH).
5. Attend bug bounties and CTFs.
6. Select a specialty—web, cloud, reverse engineering, etc.
7. Blogs or GitHub will help the community.
8. Advance to OSCP, GPEN higher certificates.
9. Go after junior positions or internships.
10. Keep developing professionally and learning.

Ethical hacking presents a fulfilling, always changing professional route with almost endless possibilities.

SUMMARY

Comprising a comprehensive, methodical process, the penetration testing lifecycle helps businesses find, evaluate, and fix security flaws before they are used by adversaries (Scarfone & Mell, 2007). As cybersecurity concerns change in complexity and scope, penetration testing offers not only a technical audit but also a strategic tool to improve organizational resilience (Kim & Solomon, 2022). < From pre-engagement planning to post-exploitation analysis and thorough reporting, every stage is absolutely important in assessing the security posture of the intended environment (EC-Council, 2023).

From this lifecycle, a key realization is that rather than only pointing up vulnerabilities, good penetration testing replics realistic attack scenarios that closely mirror possible adversarial behavior (Coleman, 2021). The lifecycle's organized character guarantees that all testing operations are carried out morally, legally, and in line with organizational objectives (Kabay, 2020). Establishing expectations, limitations, and quantifiable results depends especially on thorough planning and open stakeholder communication. This alignment determines whether one can build trust and guarantee of actionable insights (Skoudis & Liston, 2021).

The reconnaissance stage emphasizes the need of information collecting as a preparation for calculated, covert strikes. To replicate adversarial intelligence collecting, ethical hackers combine passive and active reconnaissance techniques, so exposing publicly available assets and internal vulnerabilities (OWASP Foundation, 2023). Integrated with threat modeling and vulnerability discovery, this intelligence supports targeted, high-impact activities emphasizing critical risks (Shostack, 2014; Stanger, 2023).

The phases of exploitation and post-exploitation mirror the viewpoint of the attacker and offer important analysis of system resilience under duress. These phases expose vulnerabilities in policy, operational processes, and detection and response capacity as well as technical misconfigurations and vulnerabilities (Weidman, 2020). Post-exploitation especially emphasizes the wider consequences of a breach—including lateral movement, data exfiltration, and continuous access—emphasizing the need of defense-in-depth architectures (Andress, 2021).

The lifetime ends in the reporting and remedial stage, where complicated technical results are turned into ordered, practical recommendations. By bridging the gap between technical teams and executive decision-makers, a high-quality penetration testing report helps to enable informed security investment and strategic response planning (Stewart et al., 2021). Beyond fixing specific problems, the report drives institutional development and cybersecurity maturity (S Snyder, 2021).

Organizations should see penetration testing as a continuous process rather than a one-time occurrence if they are to maximize value. Frequent evaluations matched changing corporate needs and threat environments help to keep a strong security posture (Patel et al., 2023). When penetration test findings are included into a more extensive risk management plan, the knowledge acquired can be applied to improve long-term resilience, strengthen security policies, and refine control implementation (Ahmed & Qamar, 2022; Allen, 2022).

In the modern threat environment, penetration testing ultimately reflects a strategic need rather than only a technical one. When done right, it improves situational awareness, finds security blind spots, fortifies organizational defenses, and enables stakeholders to proactively combat cyberthreats (Grimes, 2021). The foundation of this process is trust—that of systems, defenses, teams, and incident response capacity. A mature penetration testing lifecycle builds this necessary trust by exposing weaknesses, verifying assumptions, and arming companies for actual threats.

Penetration testing has become essential not only for big companies and government agencies but also for startups and small businesses as digital infrastructures keep growing (Moore, 201). The lifecycle approach helps companies of all kinds to move from reactive to proactive security models.

Penetration testing also enhances rather than replaces other security techniques. It should be included with programs including threat intelligence, user training, incident response, and ongoing monitoring (Johnson & Harris, 2021). This all-encompassing strategy guarantees that penetration testing serves as a strategic enabler as well as a technical validator (Young, 2023).

I ncreased automation, AI-powered threat modeling, CI/CD pipeline continuous testing, purple teaming, and adversary simulation platforms (Zhou et al., 2021) will define future penetration testing trends. Security experts have to keep current with these developments if they are to be relevant and effective.

Penetration testing is essentially about encouraging assurance—that the digital assets of an organization are safeguarded and that its people are ready. Ethical hackers, defenders, and decision-makers have to keep learning and adjusting inside this lifetime as the cyberspace changes to keep a trusted and strong digital business.

REFERENCES

Ahmed, M., & Qamar, F. (2022). Automated penetration testing: Techniques and challenges. *International Journal of Cyber-Security and Digital Forensics, 11*(1), 45–58.

Allen, B. (2022). *Practical cybersecurity architecture: A guide to creating and implementing robust designs for cybersecurity practitioners*. Packt Publishing.

Andress, J. (2021). *The basics of information security: Understanding the fundamentals of InfoSec in theory and practice* (3rd ed.). Syngress.

Balding, B. (2021). *Practical cloud security: A guide for secure design and deployment*. O'Reilly Media.

Coleman, C. (2021). *The art of network penetration testing*. No Starch Press.

Conklin, A., White, G. B., Cothren, C., Williams, R. L., & Davis, D. (2018). *Principles of computer security: CompTIA Security+ and beyond* (5th ed.). McGraw-Hill Education.

Deviant Ollam. (2021). *Practice makes perfect: Lockpicking, red teaming, and hacker culture*. No Starch Press.

Dhanjani, N. (2015). *Abusing the Internet of Things: Blackouts, Freakouts, and Stakeouts*. O'Reilly Media.

EC-Council. (2023). *Certified Ethical Hacker (CEH) v12 official courseware*. EC-Council Press.

Enck, W., Gilbert, P., Chun, B. G., Cox, L. P., Jung, J., McDaniel, P., & Sheth, A. N. (2014). TaintDroid: An information-flow tracking system for realtime privacy monitoring on smartphones. [TOCS]. *ACM Transactions on Computer Systems, 32*(2), 1–29. DOI: 10.1145/2619091

European Union. (2016). *General Data Protection Regulation (GDPR)*. https://eur-lex.europa.eu/eli/reg/2016/679/oj

Grimes, R. A. (2021). *Hacking the hacker: Learn from the experts who take down hackers*. Wiley.

Gupta, B., Agrawal, D. P., & Yamaguchi, S. (2022). *Handbook of computer networks and cybersecurity*. Springer.

Johnson, D., & Harris, T. (2021). *Implementing DevSecOps in the enterprise: A practical guide*. Springer.

Kabay, M. E. (2020). Ethical issues in cybersecurity. In Kabay, M. E. (Ed.), *Cybersecurity for dummies* (pp. 345–365). Wiley.

Kim, D., & Solomon, M. G. (2022). *Fundamentals of information systems security* (4th ed.). Jones & Bartlett Learning.

Knowles, W., Prince, D., Hutchison, D., Disso, J. F. P., & Jones, K. (2015). A survey of cyber security management in industrial control systems. *International Journal of Critical Infrastructure Protection*, *9*, 52–80. DOI: 10.1016/j.ijcip.2015.02.002

Kott, A., Wang, C., & Erbacher, R. (2022). *Cyber defense and situational awareness*. Springer.

Luttgens, J., Pepe, M., & Mandia, K. (2016). *Incident response & computer forensics* (3rd ed.). McGraw-Hill Education.

Mellado, D., Fernández-Medina, E., & Piattini, M. (2021). A systematic review of secure software development lifecycle models. *Computer Standards & Interfaces*, *82*, 103561. DOI: 10.1016/j.csi.2021.103561

Microsoft. (2020). *STRIDE threat model*. Microsoft Docs. https://learn.microsoft.com/en-us/security/compass/stride-threat-modeling

Moore, T. (2021). *Cybersecurity law and regulation*. Routledge.

Northcutt, S. (2020). *Penetration testing fundamentals*. SANS Institute. https://www.sans.org/white-papers/pen-testing/

OWASP Foundation. (2023). *OWASP testing guide v4*. https://owasp.org/www-project-web-security-testing-guide/

Patel, A., Vyas, A., & Bhatia, K. (2023). *Offensive automation in cybersecurity: Building tools and scripting techniques*. Packt Publishing.

PCI Security Standards Council. (2022). *Information supplement: Penetration testing guidance*. https://www.pcisecuritystandards.org/

Scarfone, K., & Mell, P. (2007). *Guide to Penetration Testing* (NIST Special Publication 800-115). National Institute of Standards and Technology. DOI: 10.6028/NIST.SP.800-115

Shostack, A. (2014). *Threat modeling: Designing for security*. Wiley.

Skoudis, E., & Liston, T. (2021). *Counter hack reloaded: A step-by-step guide to computer attacks and effective defenses* (2nd ed.). Pearson Education.

Snyder, C. (2021). *Cybersecurity incident response: How to contain, eradicate, and recover from incidents*. Apress.

Stanger, J. (2023). *CompTIA PenTest+ Certification All-in-One Exam Guide (Exam PT0-002)*. McGraw-Hill Education.

Stewart, J. M., Chapple, M., & Gibson, D. (2021). *CISSP (ISC)2 Certified Information Systems Security Professional Official Study Guide* (9th ed.). Wiley.

Stouffer, K., Falco, J., & Scarfone, K. (2015). *Guide to industrial control systems (ICS) security* (NIST Special Publication 800-82 Rev. 2). National Institute of Standards and Technology. DOI: 10.6028/NIST.SP.800-82r2

U.S. Department of Health and Human Services. (2023). *HIPAA Security Rule*. https://www.hhs.gov/hipaa/for-professionals/security/index.html

Vacca, J. R. (2020). *Computer and information security handbook* (4th ed.). Academic Press.

Weidman, G. (2020). *Advanced penetration testing: Hacking the world's most secure networks*. No Starch Press.

Winkler, I., & Gomes, A. (2022). *Advanced persistent security: A cyberwarfare approach to implementing adaptive enterprise protection, detection, and reaction strategies*. Syngress.

Young, A. (2023). *The pentester blueprint: Starting a career as an ethical hacker*. Wiley.

Zhang, K., Yuan, X., & Lu, W. (2021). *Embedded system security: Threats, vulnerabilities, and countermeasures*. Elsevier.

Zhou, Y., Ma, X., Zhang, W., & Tang, Y. (2021). Machine learning for cybersecurity: Threat detection and mitigation. *ACM Computing Surveys, 54*(10), 1–36. DOI: 10.1145/3395046

Chapter 10
The Role of Red Teams in Cybersecurity

Hakkı Yılgın
Ahmet Yesevi University, Turkey

Gurkan Tuna
http://orcid.org/0000-0002-6466-4696
Trakya University, Turkey

ABSTRACT

This study focuses on ethical hacking practices aimed at enhancing the security of digital assets, with particular emphasis on red-team operations and associated remediation strategies. It highlights the necessity of proactive security measures in response to evolving cyber threats, emphasising the importance of timely vulnerability remediation. The primary objective of this research is to evaluate ethical hacking practices through a representative red-team engagement based on recognised penetration-testing standards. The experiment was conducted within a controlled personal network and a virtualised environment. The chapter presents the installation and configuration of the required security tools, the execution of red-team activities, and the vulnerability-scanning process carried out using Nessus. In addition, mitigation strategies are proposed for the identified security weaknesses, with particular attention given to vulnerabilities associated with exposed or mis-configured network ports.

INTRODUCTION

Constantly changing cyber threats and the targeting of digital assets have made cybersecurity measures mandatory for organisations. This is because, in parallel

DOI: 10.4018/979-8-3373-3536-0.ch010

with advances in technology, attackers are conducting increasingly sophisticated attacks. Therefore, it is of great importance for organisations to detect security vulnerabilities before attackers do and take appropriate precautions. In this context, ethical attacking and red teaming practices play a key role.

Red teaming is a strategic cybersecurity approach that represents the offensive side of system security. It aims to assess an organisation's security posture through the work of a special team that mimics real-world cyber attacks through ethical attack simulations (Kraemer, Pascale & Duggan, 2004). Red teaming practices analyse not only the technological infrastructure but also human factors, including user awareness and response capabilities. The main goal of these practices is to enable organisations to strengthen their defences by identifying vulnerabilities and weaknesses that malicious threat actors can exploit.

When the literature on cybersecurity is systematically reviewed, it can be seen that red teaming practices are particularly effective in complex threat modelling and defence testing in corporate infrastructures. Simulations based on realistic attack scenarios have been shown to be an important tool for identifying security vulnerabilities and increasing the cyber resilience of organisations (Engström & Lagerström, 2022). Therefore, in this study, a set of red teaming practices was conducted.

Penetration testing is an organised approach used to test the security resilience of computer systems, networks, and applications. This approach simulates cyberattacks by assessing the target environment and revealing its weaknesses and vulnerabilities. Penetration tests are performed with the permission of the target organisation, and best practice requires full compliance with ethical standards.

In general, the penetration testing process consists of five steps. Each of these steps serves a specific function in assessing the security posture of the target. The first step, information gathering, forms the basis for the subsequent stages. In this stage, information such as the target's system configurations, possible entry points, and network architecture is collected. The information is obtained through active methods that directly interact with the target or passive methods that utilise publicly available resources.

The next step, scanning, involves gathering additional information. This step aims to identify vulnerabilities, misconfigurations, and potential entry points on the target system. The main operations performed during this step include port scanning, network mapping, and vulnerability scanning. Vulnerability scanning is performed to automatically and systematically identify software and system vulnerabilities on the target system. These scans usually reveal known vulnerabilities that can be exploited by malicious actors.

The gaining access step is the most critical phase of penetration testing. During this step, unauthorised access to the target system is gained by exploiting the vulnerabilities identified in the previous steps. This can occur through configuration errors, software vulnerabilities, or weak authentication methods. When penetration testers successfully gain access to the system, they can demonstrate the potential consequences of security breaches, such as data loss, system compromise, or access to confidential information.

Although penetration tests usually end with the successful exploitation of vulnerabilities, in some cases the "maintaining access" step is also important. This step involves the use of backdoors, rootkits, or other hidden methods to ensure persistence in the system. At this point, it should be emphasised how important it is to detect and neutralise Advanced Persistent Threats (APTs). Such threats are carried out to steal sensitive data and typically remain unnoticed in the system for months.

The final step of the penetration test is analysis and reporting. At this stage, the tester prepares a comprehensive report that includes details such as the vulnerabilities detected in the system, the sensitive information accessed, and the length of time the intrusion remained undetected, if any. This analysis can help configure security solutions such as a Web Application Firewall (WAF) and strengthen the overall security posture of the system.

In short, penetration testing is a structured and carefully executed process used to assess the security of computer systems and networks. It consists of five stages: information gathering, scanning, gaining access, maintaining access, and hiding traces. Ethical attacks follow these processes to detect vulnerabilities and develop measures to increase the resilience of the system. An effective penetration testing application requires technical competence, adherence to ethical values, and attention to detail. This approach helps protect the reliability and integrity of the assessment process.

LITERATURE REVIEW

A detailed assessment of cybersecurity resilience is achieved through extensive research, the configuration of tools, the implementation of red teaming practices, vulnerability analysis, and the development of remediation plans. In addition, comprehensive documentation makes significant contributions to knowledge sharing, organisational learning, and continuous improvement in the field of cybersecurity.

With the aim of highlighting the importance of ethical attack techniques in strengthening cybersecurity, this section reviews internationally accepted frameworks, such as the Penetration Testing Execution Standard (PTES) (Abu-Shaqra, 2020), the Open Source Security Testing Methodology Manual (OSSTMM) (Holik et al., 2014), and the Information Systems Security Assessment Framework (ISSAF) (Rusdan, Manurung & Genta, 2020).

Heiding, Katsikeas, and Lagerström (2023) emphasise that academic studies on cybersecurity vulnerability assessments have been increasing. In this context, the use of methodologies such as PTES and OSSTMM addresses the need for structured and repeatable testing processes in both academic research and applied red teaming practices.

One of the most widely reviewed methodologies for testing, analysing, and measuring operational security is OSSTMM (Holik et al., 2014). It provides a structured methodological assessment of security controls across multiple categories, including operational workflows, human actions, and physical environments. OSSTMM includes five distinct categories and provides detailed test cases for evaluating the effectiveness of security controls (Herzog, 2010). The driving force behind OSSTMM is the Institute for Security and Open Methodologies (ISECOM), which ensures that testing is conducted systematically to identify vulnerabilities and improve overall security posture. Consequently, OSSTMM-based assessments represent valuable assets for organisations seeking to strengthen their security practices and reduce associated risks effectively.

PTES offers a comprehensive methodology for conducting penetration tests and defines seven fundamental stages to ensure that tests are carried out systematically and comprehensively (PTES, 2014). It provides detailed guidelines for all aspects of penetration testing, ranging from planning and scoping to reporting and communication. This standard was developed to establish a consistent and structured set of methods for penetration testing. Through its technical guidance, PTES provides a clear framework for testing the effectiveness of security measures and supports the execution of practical tests in a more effective and structured manner. Using a standardised methodology also enhances the reliability and consistency of penetration testing projects, thereby facilitating the identification and mitigation of vulnerabilities.

ISSAF provides a methodology that supports and guides security assessments for network, system, and application controls (Rusdan et al., 2020). It supports comprehensive security analysis, including penetration testing aimed at identifying vulnerabilities and evaluating the security posture of information systems.

Various studies have demonstrated the effectiveness of ISSAF in evaluating wireless network security. ISSAF has proven to be a comprehensive and efficient tool for evaluating security mechanisms across organisations with diverse system architectures. The application of this methodology provides organisations with deep insights into system security, particularly during red teaming exercises. ISSAF provides a structured approach to simulating real-world attacks, identifying vulnerabilities, and testing defensive measures across networks, servers, applications, and databases. This allows organisations to obtain detailed reports on vulnerabilities, potential attack scenarios, and actionable recommendations for improving security.

The integration of OSSTMM, PTES, and ISSAF methodologies (Rusdan et al., 2020) can provide a comprehensive and reliable framework for ethical attack and red teaming practices. OSSTMM facilitates the assessment of security across different organisational domains, such as physical environments and human behaviour. PTES guides the systematic planning and execution of penetration testing activities, ensuring the structured evaluation of security controls. Finally, ISSAF provides a methodological framework for simulating realistic attack scenarios.

Red teaming practices play a significant role in reducing cyber risks by revealing the level of preparedness of an organisation against potential cyber attacks (Yanalitis, 2014). Red teams conduct authorised and controlled cyber attacks that simulate the tactics, techniques, and procedures commonly used by potential adversaries, including Advanced Persistent Threats (APTs). For example, red team members may distribute malicious QR codes disguised within fake organisational event posters across high-traffic areas such as corporate campuses or data centre facilities. In such a scenario, employees scanning the QR code out of curiosity or perceived legitimacy may unintentionally allow attackers to gain access to their devices. Simulated attacks of this nature enable organisations to identify vulnerabilities, enhance incident response capabilities, and strengthen their overall cybersecurity strategies. Red team activities therefore contribute to strengthening cybersecurity defences through proactive vulnerability identification, practical attack simulations, and the continuous improvement of incident response capabilities. Ethical attack techniques and red team activities conducted from an adversarial perspective provide organisations with valuable insights for strengthening their defences against emerging cyber threats.

Two basic strategies used in red teaming practices are Full-Scope Cyber Attack Simulation and Targeted Attacker Simulation. The former aims to comprehensively test an organisation's security controls through multi-layered and realistic simulations. The red team attempts to breach the organisation's digital defence perimeter by replicating complex real-world threat scenarios (Engström & Lagerström, 2022). By carefully observing network architecture, applications, and security controls, vulnerabilities across the digital infrastructure can be systematically identified. This approach provides deep insight into the effectiveness and resilience of defence mechanisms.

On the other hand, Targeted Attacker Simulation is preferred in organisations with a well-defined threat landscape, in order to detect specific vulnerabilities and improve incident response mechanisms (Kraemer, Pascale, & Duggan, 2004). In contrast to full-scope simulations, this strategy focuses on specific threat scenarios aligned with the organisation's risk profile and industry context. The goal of the red team is to evaluate the organisation's ability to detect and counter such targeted attacks by replicating the tactics and operational behaviour of real threat actors. This approach facilitates the integration of threat intelligence, the evaluation of defensive capabilities, and advanced testing of incident response procedures.

The concept of the "Red Teaming Umbrella" was proposed by Kardos and Dexter (2017). This phrase effectively characterises the structure of red team simulation exercises. The umbrella symbolises the overarching framework that encompasses multiple red team components and activities within an organisation, revealing the potential severity of security threats. This expression is used as a metaphor because a single red team exercise may involve numerous techniques, strategies, and testing approaches. Simulations based on realistic attack scenarios against an organisation represent an effective method for evaluating the resilience of organisational security measures. Such simulations allow not only technical vulnerabilities but also social engineering techniques, physical security weaknesses, and process-oriented defensive mechanisms to be evaluated simultaneously, thereby increasing the likelihood of detecting potential attacks.

For instance, considering the Network Mapper (Nmap) scan of the Metasploitable machine, the visualisation produced during the exploitation phase illustrates the sequence of actions followed within this red team exercise. The first step is to identify potential vulnerabilities using reconnaissance and scanning tools such as Nmap. These vulnerabilities are then systematically exploited using tools such as Metasploit (Rapid7, n.d.), demonstrating the potential real-world impact of identified weaknesses. This process should be considered an integral component of regular and comprehensive red team exercises. Red teaming practices must therefore be conducted using a multi-layered and systematic approach in order to maintain a high level of cybersecurity resilience.

ROLES AND LEGAL DIMENSIONS OF RED TEAMING PRACTICES

Red teaming practices are not limited to identifying technical vulnerabilities. They also evaluate organisational factors such as security maturity, incident response capability, and employee awareness. Kraemer, Carayon, and Duggan (2004) emphasise that red team activities make strategic contributions to organisations by enabling the visualisation of cybersecurity vulnerabilities, testing them through simulations, and supporting the development of defensive mechanisms. Similarly, Yanalitis (2014) states that red teams provide feedback to management through simulated attacks, thereby improving crisis management and organisational decision-making processes. Mani (2022) reports that one of the most important roles of a red team is to ensure that security controls are tested under realistic operational conditions by working in coordination with the blue team. These roles include not only technical testing but also social engineering assessments, incident detection capabilities, and policy-related vulnerabilities. Yulianto et al. (2025) demonstrate that this comprehensive approach improves organisational cybersecurity culture and strengthens the security awareness of not only the IT department but also the entire organisation.

The organisational impact of the red team extends beyond the technical domain and also influences areas such as corporate strategy, training, crisis management, and policy development. Particularly in large-scale organisations, the outputs of red team activities are often incorporated into governance decisions by linking them with cybersecurity maturity models (Yulianto et al., 2025). In many organisations, red teaming practices are evaluated through measurable key performance indicators (KPIs), which measure how quickly and effectively information technology teams respond to security incidents. Such metrics assess not only the incident response process but also employee awareness levels, management threat perception, and the overall resilience of organisational systems (Mani, 2022). In addition, the results of red teaming practices play an important role in shaping organisational training and security awareness programmes. The social engineering vulnerabilities identified during these exercises enable organisations to develop targeted training materials for employees. This makes it possible to strengthen organisational security not only through technical solutions but also through the human factor (Kraemer, Carayon & Duggan, 2004).

Red teams also act as advisory entities within information security management, particularly in risk assessment processes and the restructuring of security architectures. In this context, the red team provides decision-support insights for managers, enabling them to develop proactive security strategies, anticipate potential threats, and prioritise defensive architecture improvements.

Red teaming practices are controlled attack simulations conducted to identify vulnerabilities within the information systems of organisations. However, in order for such activities to be considered legally legitimate, they must be carried out within clearly defined legal frameworks. Otherwise, red team practices may be subject to criminal sanctions for offences such as unauthorised access or unlawful data manipulation. In this context, a formal ethical agreement and authorisation protocol with a clearly defined scope must be prepared before conducting red team activities, and potential legal risks must be carefully mitigated.

Red team activities conducted internationally require careful planning, as legal and ethical frameworks vary significantly across countries. In the European Union, cybersecurity testing must comply with regulations such as the General Data Protection Regulation (GDPR), ensuring that individual data privacy and security are not violated (Heiding, Katsikeas, & Lagerström, 2023). For example, a social engineering attack carried out by a red team without the explicit consent of the target organisation or participants may result in serious penalties under both criminal and civil liability frameworks. In the United States, the Computer Fraud and Abuse Act (CFAA) considers unauthorised system access a federal offence;

therefore, only attack simulations carried out under formally signed authorisation and scope-specific agreements are legally protected (Kraemer, Carayon, & Duggan, 2004). In this context, it is imperative that red team activities adhere to the principles of explicit consent, contractual authorisation, and restricted system access in order to avoid legal liability. In addition, the information security and cybercrime legislation of the host country must be carefully examined when conducting international cybersecurity testing projects (Engström & Lagerström, 2022).

The most critical document in the execution of ethical attack activities at the corporate level is the "Rules of Engagement" (RoE). This document clearly defines the scope, procedures, target systems, permitted techniques, and reporting criteria of the simulated attack. The existence of RoE not only protects red team personnel from potential legal risks but also ensures that the testing process remains controlled and does not cause harm to organisational systems or operations (ENISA, 2019; Skoudis & Liston, 2006).

SOFTWARE APPLICATIONS USED IN RED TEAMING PRACTICES

Virtual machine architecture plays a critical role in red teaming activities. It provides an isolated and secure environment for penetration testing and ethical hacking operations. These isolated environments allow security tests to be conducted in a controlled manner (Li, Jiang & Li, 2010). The allocation and sharing of hardware resources between virtual machines are managed either by the kernel of the host operating system or by a virtual machine manager (hypervisor). Each virtual machine behaves similarly to a physical machine and operates with its own operating system. This architecture enables the creation of multiple independent testing environments.

Preparation Phase and Scenario Design

One of the most effective ways to simulate red teaming scenarios is through the use of virtualisation technologies such as VMware Workstation. These platforms provide a controlled testing environment in which virtual machines can be created, configured, and interact with services or other systems. Through this approach, red teaming activities can be conducted in a secure and isolated manner. With such a virtual infrastructure in place, organisations can evaluate the resilience of their systems against real-world cyberattacks. This is achieved by replicating the organisation's network configurations within a virtual environment, thereby simulating complex infrastructure components.

Within red teaming exercises, attack scenarios that realistically replicate known cyber threats can be simulated. For this purpose, a virtual machine called Metasploitable was installed to demonstrate ethical hacking activities. This machine was operated exclusively on a personal computer in order to prevent potential legal complications.

Kali Linux and Metasploitable

Two widely used platforms were employed in the red teaming environment: Kali Linux and Metasploitable. Kali Linux is an open-source Linux distribution that provides a comprehensive suite of tools for penetration testing and security assessment (Kali Linux, 2025). This operating system, which is widely adopted in red teaming and ethical hacking activities, includes numerous pre-installed tools designed to detect system vulnerabilities, exploit weaknesses, and evaluate the security posture of target systems.

Red teaming exercises targeting real organisations may lead to significant legal consequences if conducted without formal authorisation or contractual agreements. Therefore, the Metasploitable virtual machine was used to conduct testing within a secure and controlled laboratory environment. Metasploitable is intentionally designed with known vulnerabilities and is specifically developed for ethical hackers and security researchers to practise exploitation techniques. This environment enables the safe application of various penetration testing techniques.

The ability to easily create snapshots, clone, and restore virtual machines provides a substantial advantage for learning through experimentation and for developing attack and defence strategies. Furthermore, Linux-based systems are freely available and can be modified, reproduced, and distributed by users due to their open-source nature, which makes them an attractive platform for ethical hacking practices. Kali Linux's lightweight architecture and relatively low RAM and storage requirements enable it to run efficiently alongside other operating systems. It is also one of the Linux distributions developed specifically for cybersecurity purposes, alongside platforms such as Parrot OS and the earlier distribution BackTrack. Kali Linux, which is specifically designed for ethical hackers and penetration testing professionals, is used in this study. The distribution stands out by providing many essential penetration testing tools as pre-installed components.

NMAP

Nmap is an open-source tool widely used in red teaming and penetration testing activities and plays a critical role in network discovery and security auditing. This software can identify devices connected to a network, determine the services provided by these devices, detect the operating systems they run, and reveal existing security mechanisms within the network (Lyon, 2009). It offers significant advantages, particularly for the rapid and efficient scanning of large-scale networks.

Nmap is used not only for comprehensive security auditing but also for system administration tasks such as network monitoring, service continuity management, and update verification (Insecure.Org, n.d.). Security professionals and red teaming practitioners can analyse both individual and organisational networks in detail using Nmap, enabling them to identify vulnerabilities and develop preventative security strategies. In red teaming scenarios, Nmap is typically employed during the reconnaissance phase. During this stage, open ports on the target system, the services running on those ports, and their corresponding versions are identified, allowing potential exploitation points to be determined (Lyon, 2009).

Msfconsole and Searchsploit

Msfconsole is the command-line interface of the Metasploit Framework and represents a powerful, flexible, and widely used tool for cybersecurity professionals (Thapa, Sehl, Gupta, & Goyal, 2022). In practice, it functions as a central control interface from which cyberattack simulations can be managed. Within red teaming activities, it is frequently used to manage attack vectors, exploit vulnerabilities, and assess weaknesses in target systems.

The Metasploit Framework contains an extensive collection of exploits, payloads, and auxiliary modules. These modules enable the simulation of real-world cyberattack scenarios and allow security professionals to analyse how systems may be compromised. The Msfconsole interface provides the capability to manage and execute these modules efficiently.

This tool is used not only for offensive testing purposes but also in training and controlled laboratory environments to improve defensive security capabilities. Understanding organisational vulnerabilities is essential for evaluating systems from an attacker's perspective and for assessing the effectiveness of implemented security controls. In this respect, Msfconsole, shown in Figure 1, represents one of the core components of red teaming activities.

Figure 1. Msfconsole

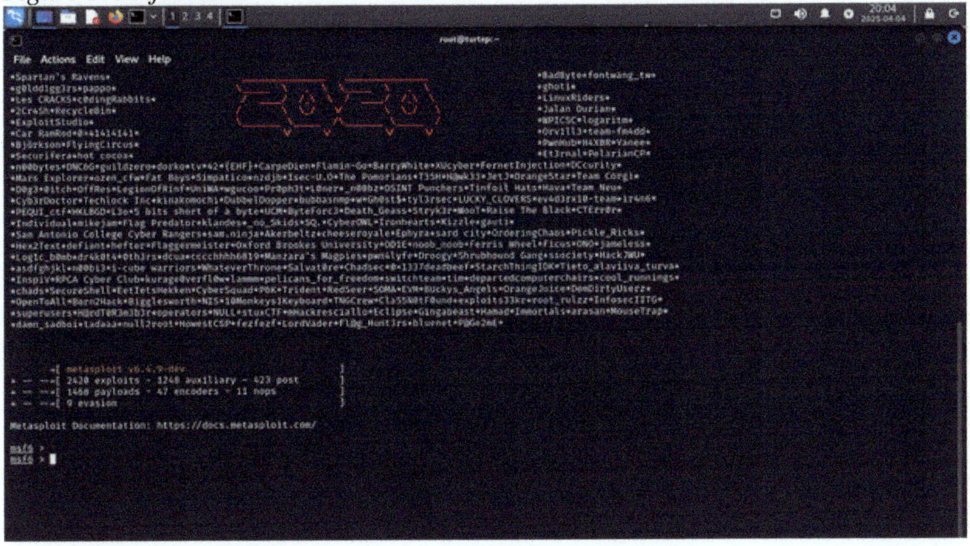

SearchSploit is a tool that scans an exploit database to identify known vulnerabilities and demonstrate how attackers may exploit them. By entering keywords related to a specific software product or vulnerability type, users can quickly retrieve a list of relevant exploits. Each exploit entry includes a short description that provides guidance on how the vulnerability may be exploited.

Within red teaming scenarios, SearchSploit is used to identify suitable exploits for services or software versions discovered on target systems. This capability significantly improves the efficiency of attack planning and allows potential vulnerabilities to be identified more effectively. The tool plays a crucial role during the pre-attack reconnaissance and preparation stages. It also serves as an educational resource for ethical hackers seeking to understand vulnerability exploitation techniques. Through its modular structure, the Metasploit ecosystem provides extensive capabilities that support the entire attack lifecycle, including reconnaissance, exploitation, access acquisition, and persistence.

Vulnerability Analysis with Nessus

Nessus, developed by Tenable, is a comprehensive vulnerability scanning platform used to detect and assess security weaknesses across devices, applications, operating systems, cloud services, and network infrastructure components within information technology environments (Tenable, 2024). The primary objective of

Nessus is to identify potential security threats that could be exploited by malicious actors by systematically scanning systems for vulnerabilities.

The platform is widely used for tasks such as performing network and system vulnerability scans, conducting configuration audits, and identifying weaknesses that may compromise system security.

Nessus plays a particularly important role during the reconnaissance phase of red teaming engagements. Security professionals use the tool to identify potential entry points and vulnerabilities within the target organisation's infrastructure (Lachkov, Tawalbeh & Bhatt, 2022). Although the scanning process provides a comprehensive analysis of vulnerabilities, the duration of the scan may vary depending on the scope and size of the infrastructure being assessed. After the scanning process is completed, attack simulations can be designed or remediation measures can be implemented based on the identified vulnerabilities. In this context, Nessus represents a critical tool within red teaming activities for classifying security risks and determining appropriate preventive or corrective security measures.

Network Traffic Analysis with Wireshark

Wireshark is a powerful network packet analyser used to inspect network traffic and diagnose network-related issues. The tool examines data packets transmitted across networks and provides detailed visibility into network protocols and communication patterns. Through packet-level analysis, potential security vulnerabilities can also be detected, enabling network applications and services to operate more securely and reliably (Sharpe, Warnicke, & Lamping, 2024).

Key capabilities of Wireshark include live packet capture from multiple network interfaces, analysis of previously captured packet files, and advanced filtering based on parameters such as IP address, protocol type, and port number. Additionally, captured data can be saved and exported for further analysis and reporting.

These capabilities allow network traffic to be analysed both in real time and retrospectively through stored packet records. Such functionality is particularly valuable for identifying the root causes of security incidents within complex network infrastructures.

In cybersecurity and particularly within red teaming engagements, Wireshark is used to analyse network traffic and observe the behaviour of target systems during simulated attack scenarios. By monitoring traffic within the target network, security professionals can identify exposed protocols, weak authentication mechanisms, and potential data leakage points. These observations also support the post-exploitation analysis stage.

Network Communication and Penetration Testing with Netcat

Netcat is a versatile tool widely used for network communication testing and debugging. Frequently utilised by security professionals, the tool enables data transmission over both TCP and UDP protocols. Netcat allows both inbound and outbound connections to be established through virtually any port, making it a powerful network assessment utility (Armstrong, 2001).

Key capabilities of Netcat include port scanning, executing DNS queries, customising source ports, operating through command-line parameters, slow data transmission modes, file transfer, and remote command execution. Due to these features, red teaming practitioners frequently use Netcat in penetration testing scenarios such as establishing reverse shells, testing firewall behaviour, transferring files, and executing scripts.

Netcat's simplicity and cross-platform compatibility make it a fast and efficient tool for red teaming activities. It can be utilised across multiple stages of penetration testing, ranging from basic connectivity testing to the exploitation of security vulnerabilities (Mosse Cyber Security Institute, 2022).

BASIC CYBER SECURITY CONCEPTS

Before moving on to network scanning, it is important to provide an overview of two basic communication protocols, namely Transmission Control Protocol (TCP) and User Datagram Protocol (UDP). TCP and UDP enable data transmission between networked systems and form an important part of the Internet Protocol suite.

UDP allows datagrams to be transmitted over IP networks and does not require a dedicated connection to be established in advance (Postel, 1980). The lightweight communication model used by UDP does not include a handshake process. While UDP offers limited data integrity checks through its port-based addressing mechanism, it does not provide reliability due to its connectionless architecture. In contrast, TCP, as the reliability-oriented component of the Internet protocol stack, provides advanced mechanisms for secure and reliable data transmission, including error control, sequencing, and connection management (Singh, Tripathi, & Singh, 2014).

When a user attempts to visit a web page, the computer first sends TCP packets to the target web server, initiating the request process. The server responds with its own TCP packets, enabling the web browser to display the requested page. This mechanism supports many activities over Internet connections, including clicking on hyperlinks and authenticating through login systems. TCP enables bidirectional communication because the receiving server must acknowledge packets through the three-way handshake process (Postel, 1981).

In this process, the computer first sends a SYN packet to the server to indicate its intention to initiate communication. The SYN packet contains a sequence number used to organise data transmission, allowing the server to interpret the communication request correctly. The server then responds with a SYN/ACK packet, confirming the request. Finally, the computer sends an ACK packet, completing the handshake and allowing data exchange to begin. Once data transmission begins, TCP ensures that packets are delivered in the correct order and without transmission errors. TCP's error-control mechanisms ensure reliable communication, which is why TCP is preferred in situations where data accuracy and reliability are critical (Postel, 1981).

UDP, by contrast, also transmits data packets but prioritises transmission speed over reliability and error control. Due to its simpler and lighter protocol structure, UDP typically operates faster than TCP. Consequently, UDP is widely used in applications requiring low latency and rapid data delivery, such as online gaming and live media streaming.

Exploitation and Payload

In order to perform exploitation, it is necessary to take advantage of vulnerabilities identified within the target system. In this study, the Metasploitable virtual machine is used as the target system. The malicious payloads employed depend on the specific vulnerability detected. The Metasploitable environment contains numerous open ports and multiple exploitable services associated with these ports, each potentially allowing different payload deployment strategies.

In many web-based attacks, malicious payloads are often delivered through the HTTP protocol, as its flexible architecture and widespread adoption make it an effective transport mechanism for attackers. Malware may be transmitted to the target system via single or multiple HTTP packets, often in encoded or obfuscated form. These payloads may be embedded in different parts of the HTTP protocol, making detection more difficult for defensive security mechanisms.

The exploitation process involves delivering a malicious payload to the target system by exploiting an identified vulnerability. Once executed, the payload allows commands to run on the target system and may enable activities such as file browsing, directory access, or privilege escalation, depending on the exploited service.

In this study, two primary scenarios are considered for exploiting the Metasploitable system. In the first scenario, if the target system contains a known vulnerability, a malicious payload can be delivered through this vulnerability to execute remote commands on the system. In the second scenario, if the target system is fully updated and no known vulnerabilities are present, the same exploitation technique may not be applicable. In such cases, there may be no known exploit or payload capable of establishing unauthorised access, requiring the development of alternative attack strategies.

Although such strategies are not necessary for the Metasploitable training environment, real-world red teaming engagements may involve social engineering techniques to persuade a target user to execute the malicious payload themselves. In such cases, malicious payloads may be delivered via email attachments disguised as legitimate files. These files may be crafted to appear relevant to the target user's interests or organisational activities, and spoofed email addresses may be used to enhance credibility. When the user opens the disguised file, the malicious payload executes silently in the background, enabling unauthorised system access without the user's knowledge. This technique represents a commonly used attack vector in real-world cyberattacks.

Another potential method for delivering malicious payloads involves USB storage devices. However, this method is more difficult to implement because it requires physical access to the target system. When successful, the malicious payload may be executed directly from the USB device. Despite this possibility, such attacks are less common due to the high risk of detection and the logistical challenges of physical access.

Overall, regardless of whether the target system contains exploitable vulnerabilities, multiple techniques exist for delivering and executing malicious payloads in order to obtain unauthorised access.

Vulnerabilities

To understand how vulnerabilities arise, it is necessary to examine the software development lifecycle from which they originate. Developers create software using programming languages such as Python, Java, or C in order to provide specific functionality required by end users. After development is completed, the software undergoes testing and security validation before being deployed to operational systems.

Depending on its functionality, software may provide services accessible through open network ports, such as FTP, SSH, or HTTP. When these services are exposed to the Internet through open ports, they become potential entry points for external attackers. If vulnerabilities exist in the software, attackers may exploit them to gain access to the target system.

As demonstrated during the exploitation phase of this study, programming errors or design flaws in software can create security vulnerabilities that may be exploited by attackers. When such vulnerabilities are successfully exploited, attackers may deploy malware, malicious payloads, or backdoors, thereby gaining control over the compromised system.

Most discovered vulnerabilities are documented in public databases using Common Vulnerabilities and Exposures (CVE) identifiers, which include a specific year and reference number. However, zero-day vulnerabilities refer to security flaws that are unknown to developers and system administrators at the time of discovery, meaning that no patch or mitigation currently exists. The term *zero-day* indicates that developers have zero days to respond to the vulnerability before it may be exploited.

One notable example is the WannaCry ransomware attack, which occurred in 2017 and had severe global consequences (Microsoft Security Response Center, 2017). The attack utilised an exploit known as EternalBlue, originally developed by the National Security Agency and later leaked. This exploit targeted a vulnerability in the Server Message Block (SMB) protocol used in Microsoft Windows operating systems. Within a few days, WannaCry infected more than 200,000 computers across over 150 countries, encrypting files and demanding ransom payments from victims seeking to restore access (Mohurle & Patil, 2017).

In addition to technical vulnerabilities, attackers may exploit human weaknesses through social engineering techniques, which represent an important aspect of red teaming operations. For example, an employee may unknowingly open a malicious email attachment disguised as a legitimate document, potentially compromising both the individual workstation and the wider organisational network.

Although technical defences such as firewalls and security monitoring systems are essential, they cannot completely eliminate vulnerabilities arising from human error or misconfiguration. Even a minor oversight, such as incorrectly configured credentials, can result in a significant security breach. Many cyberattacks therefore exploit human behaviour rather than purely technical vulnerabilities (Cisco, 2024). For this reason, human-centred security awareness and training are critical components of cybersecurity strategies.

Reverse Shell and Bind Shell

A command-line shell functions as a gateway for interacting with a compromised system. Once the target system is successfully exploited, the attacker may obtain shell access, enabling remote command execution and system control. In many cases, the shell is delivered through a malicious payload designed to exploit a specific service or network port. Two common types of shell access are reverse shells and bind shells.

A reverse shell is established by having the compromised system initiate a connection back to the attacker's machine. In this project, the attacker system is Kali Linux. The attacker first listens for incoming connections on a specific port, and once exploitation is successful, the compromised system connects back to this listening port. After the connection is established, the attacker gains remote command-line access to the target system, potentially with elevated privileges.

A bind shell, by contrast, operates by having the target system open a network port and listen for incoming connections. The attacker then connects to this port in order to obtain command-line access. The choice between reverse shells and bind shells depends on the specific attack scenario and network configuration.

Bind shells may encounter difficulties when firewalls restrict inbound connections to the target system, which limits their effectiveness during post-exploitation phases. Reverse shells, however, can bypass such restrictions because the connection is initiated from the compromised system to the attacker's machine, often through permitted outbound traffic channels.

Firewalls and Scanning with NMAP

A firewall is a network security device that analyses network traffic and decides whether to allow or deny certain traffic based on predefined security policies. Firewalls distinguish between trusted and controlled internal networks and untrusted external networks, such as the Internet. Network firewalls and host-based firewalls are just two of many types of firewalls. Network administrators work to protect a network from malicious attacks and ensure its reliability; network firewalls placed at the gateway can be more efficient and manageable than protecting individual computers within the network (Ajami & Dinh, 2011).

Firewalls filter data traffic between different networks and enforce specific access rules. In contrast, host-based firewalls monitor the network connections of a specific machine and only inspect the incoming and outgoing traffic of that system. Intrusion detection system (IDS) devices monitor network traffic to identify unauthorised access attempts to network or system resources. IDS devices provide an early warning mechanism against security breaches by detecting suspicious activities (Scarfone & Mell, 2007).

In general, firewalls and IDS devices try to protect networks and computers. In this study, the Metasploitable target was scanned on many ports and the results show which open and closed ports. Some targets may be hosting services on the ports and these ports may be hidden behind the firewall; in this case, when the ports are scanned, the results show that these ports are filtered. This is when Nmap cannot determine whether the port is open or closed. This means that packets are being sent to the target during the scan, but the firewall continues to drop these packets. In some cases, certain scanning techniques may work without being blocked by a firewall. However, the behaviour of firewalls is not predictable because they may have different rules in different environments. These rules may include MAC address filtering, blocking of certain types of packets, or selective port restrictions. This variety makes it difficult to determine the type and configuration of the firewall in use.

Nmap marks some ports as “filtered” during scanning. This means that Nmap cannot determine whether the port is open or closed. The main reason for this is that the data packets sent may be dropped by the firewall. This situation is illustrated in Figure 2. Similarly, it was observed that many ports were marked as “filtered” as a result of the SYN scan performed on a Windows operating system with an active firewall. This indicates that the firewall interfered with the scan. When the scan is repeated with the firewall disabled, more open ports are detected. The firewall configuration used in these examples has a fairly strict security policy that blocks most incoming traffic. Such configurations filter almost all external connections, unlike firewalls with more flexible rules.

Figure 2. Nmap Scanning with -sS Option on Windows Machines

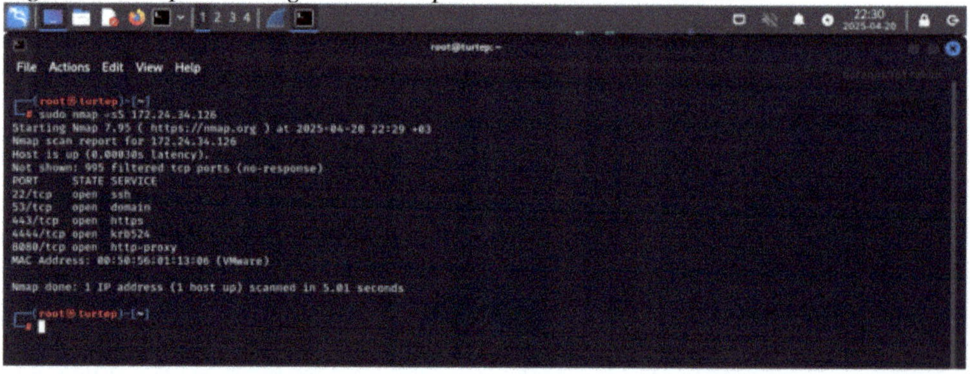

Nmap's -f option can be used to prevent detection by IDS devices. This option aims to break the TCP packets sent into smaller pieces, making it harder for systems such as IDS devices or firewalls to detect these packets. However, this method may not always work. Some advanced IDS devices or software can even detect such fragmented packets and may not display the ports visible to the user. Figure 3 shows this observed situation when scanning on a Windows system with IDS enabled. Here, TCP port 997 is not responding and is not listed as “filtered”, indicating that the scan did not produce any visible results on the target system.

Figure 3. Nmap Scanning Performed with -f Option on a Windows Machine

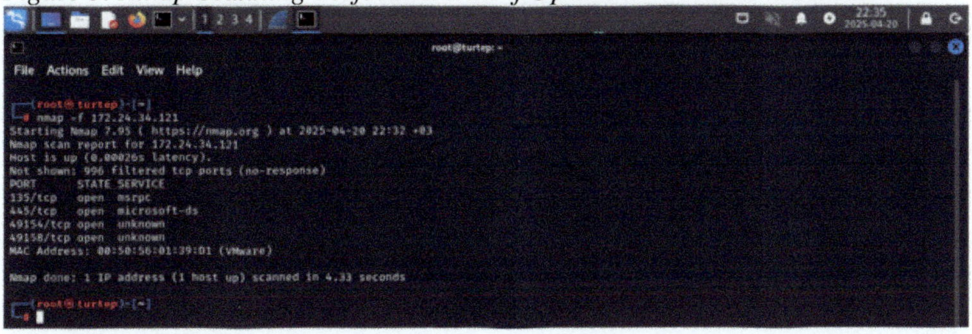

Another technique that can be used to evade detection by IDS devices is connection simulation via spoofed IP addresses. Here, the real attacker hides his IP address by using multiple spoofed IP addresses to hide the source of the attack. An application of this method can be performed with the -D option of the Nmap tool. An example of this scan is shown in Figure 4. During the experiment, the IP addresses communicating with the target machine were observed using the WireShark software running on a machine with a Windows operating system. With this software, it is possible to examine in detail which IPs are transmitting data to the target, including fake IP addresses. However, it is important to note that network traffic capturing tools such as Wireshark may not always provide accurate results. Especially in scans performed in a virtual machine environment, some network packets may be recorded incompletely or incorrectly. Therefore, it is recommended that the analysis be performed on physical machines rather than virtual ones.

Figure 4. Scans performed using Kali IP Address and Fake IPs with Nmap -D Option

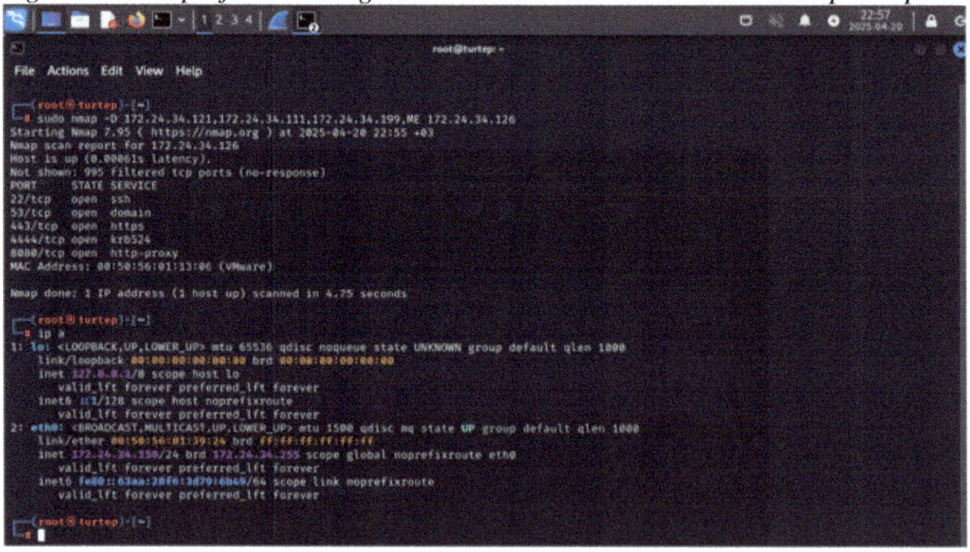

In this scan example, performed using the -D parameter of the Nmap tool, fake IP addresses were defined to deceive IDS systems. The fake IP addresses used in this scenario are 172.24.34.199, 172.34.121, 172.24.34.111, and the target Windows machine's own IP address. In the command line, the ME statement is used to specify the IP address of the Kali Linux machine that launched the attack. In this example, the IP address corresponding to the Kali Linux system is 172.24.34.150. The IP address of the target system to be scanned should be specified in the command after the fake IPs.

In order to evaluate whether the scan was effective, after the Nmap installation was completed, the network traffic was observed before the scan was started. This preview was performed using Wireshark and the effectiveness of the changes in the network after the scan was started was analysed. Figure 5 and Figure 6 show the situations before and after the network is flooded with certain IP addresses (IP floating) using the Wireshark tool. This difference reveals how fake IPs spread throughout the network and how difficult it is to detect the real IP address.

Figure 5. Traffic After IP Spoofing Displayed on Wireshark

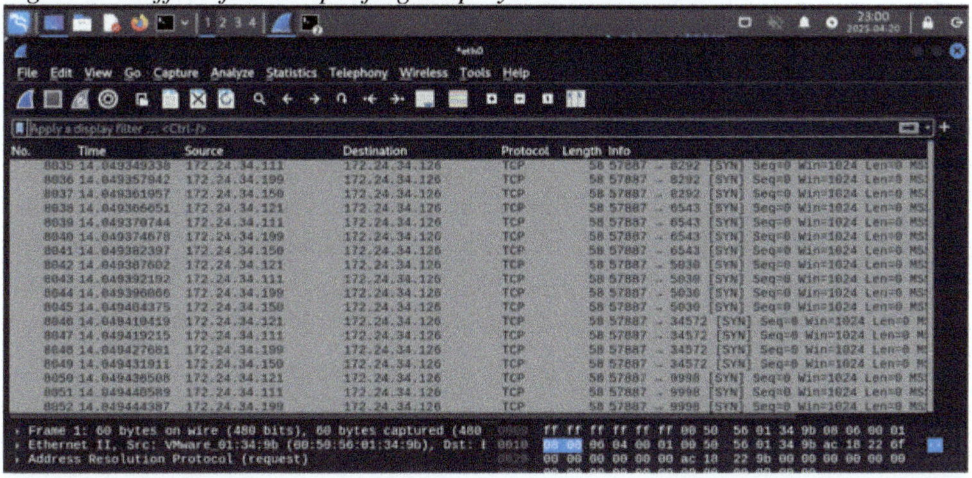

Figure 6. Status After IP Address Floating Displayed with Wireshark

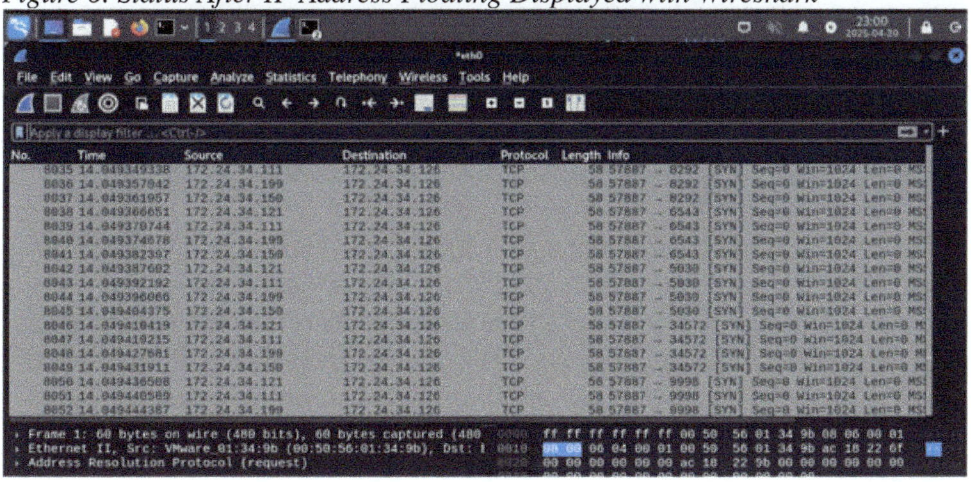

The spread of local IP addresses throughout the network during scanning (flooding) makes it difficult for security measures to detect the real IP address. The attacker can arbitrarily set the number of IP addresses to be used in scanning, but the basic goal is the same. To hide the real IP address of the scanning machine. This method can be used particularly effectively in scans against a target located on the same local network or against systems on external networks.

Nmap Scripts for Vulnerabilities

Nmap not only performs port scanning but can also perform vulnerability analysis and even exploitation through specific scripts in some cases. Nmap's scripting engine, Nmap Scripting Engine (NSE) is widely used to check for vulnerabilities against different services. However, these scripts are not limited to performing vulnerability analysis only. Figure 7 shows different aspects of the network structure can be revealed using different scanning options. Depending on the script used, the information obtained is not limited to open ports only; it can also include details such as service type, version information, and potential security vulnerabilities.

Figure 7. Results of Scanning on Metasploitable with the Command "nmap --script auth 172.24.34.123 -sS "

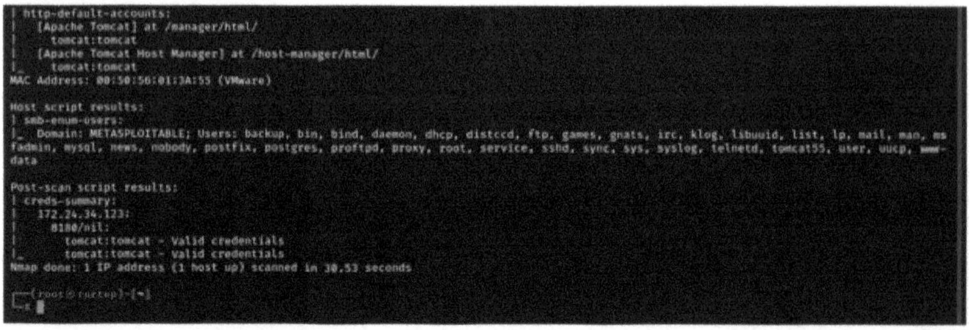

In Kali Linux, all Nmap scripts are stored in the directory "/usr/share/nmap/scripts/". By accessing this directory, existing scripts can be discovered. To test some of these scripts, a scan should be performed with a specific set of scripts, the IP address of the metasploitable machine (172.24.34.123) and a SYN scan (-sS). The SYN scan helps to determine whether a port is open or closed and requires sudo privileges. Therefore, it requires a user password. The scan output shows the open ports, some with additional information added to them.

As shown in Figure 8, the target machine's administration panel can be accessed via the address http.//172.24.34.123.8180/admin/. According to the Nmap scan results presented earlier, the default credentials "tomcat" can be used for both username and password. After successfully authenticating with these credentials, access is provided to the Apache Tomcat server's administration interface. This successful entry is visually confirmed in Figure 9, which shows that the administration section of the Apache Tomcat instance hosted on the Metasploitable machine has been infiltrated. There are various services, resources and user information within the system, and all these elements are open to manipulation.

Figure 8. Administrator Interface on Port 8180 of the Metasploitable Target Machine

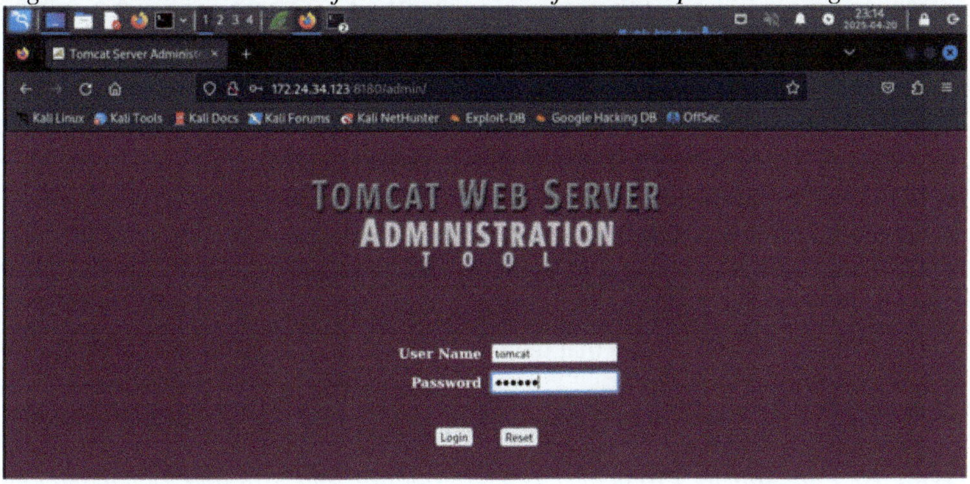

Figure 9. Infiltration Performed on Port 8180 on Metasploitable Machines

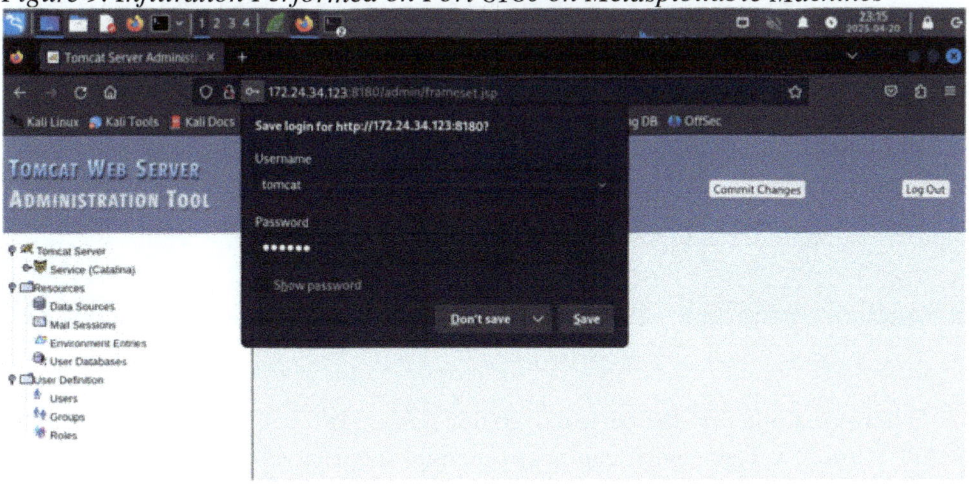

Exploitation Script

The exploitation script suite in NSE aims to actively exploit known vulnerabilities (Lyon, 2009). When the command "sudo nmap –script exploit 172.24.34.123 -sS -F" is run on Kali Linux, several vulnerabilities were detected on the Metasploitable machine. For example, possible Cross-Site Request Forgery (CSRF) vulnerabilities were identified on port 80. Additionally, a vulnerability was observed on port 21/tcp. This port has a critical backdoor vulnerability in vsFTPd version 2.3.4. This vulnerability, documented as CVE-2011-2523, allows unauthorised users to obtain a command shell on the system by logging in with the username ":)" (Rapid7, 2018). This could allow attackers to take full control of the target system. Nmap scan results show that anonymous login (username: "anonymous") is allowed to the FTP service. This shows that the system is weak in terms of security. The "" command can be used to log in to the FTP service, and thus the available options on the FTP server can be examined. Figure 10 shows the list of command lines available when the FTP protocol is started. The large number of commands indicates that the extent of the vulnerability is high and that there is a serious risk of information disclosure or manipulation.

Figure 10. File Transfer Protocol (FTP) Exploitation and Available Command List

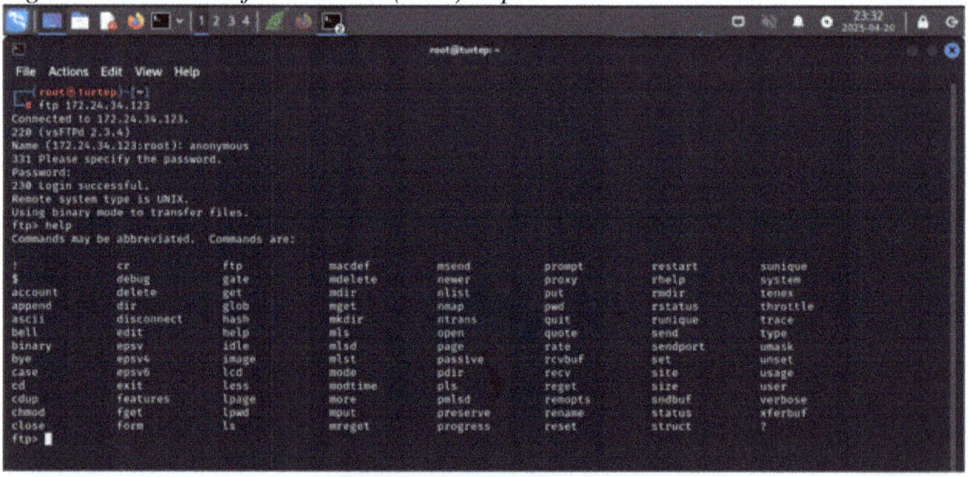

Other ports open on the network include SSH (Port 22), Telnet (Port 23), and SMTP (Port 25). These ports can pose potential security risks because misconfigurations of these services can lead to security vulnerabilities. However, no specific vulnerabilities were detected for these ports in the scan results shown in Figure 11. In addition, other services running on the target system include HTTP (Port 80), MySQL (Port 3306), and PostgreSQL (Port 5432). It was revealed that web applications running on port 80 may have a potential Cross-Site Request Forgery (CSRF) vulnerability. This type of vulnerability could be exploited by a threat actor to perform unauthorised actions on behalf of an authenticated user. In addition, the scan revealed other potential services, such as the NFS service running on port 2049, the VNC service on port 5900, and finally the X11 service running on port 6000.

These services also have the potential to be exploited by different threat actors. Scan results clearly show that the vsFTPd backdoor vulnerability was detected. These findings once again emphasise the importance of a real red team (penetration testing) exercise and show that all vulnerabilities must be detected and fixed before potential attackers do. In this context, the findings obtained form the basis of all practical preventive strategies to be developed in order to reduce the size of the identified vulnerabilities. In general, as a result of the information gathering processes, it has been revealed that there are serious security vulnerabilities on the metasploitable target machine. In order to continue with red team applications, these exploitation possibilities need to be tested and verified in practice.

Figure 11. Nmap Scan Report Performed with 11 Exploit Script Groups

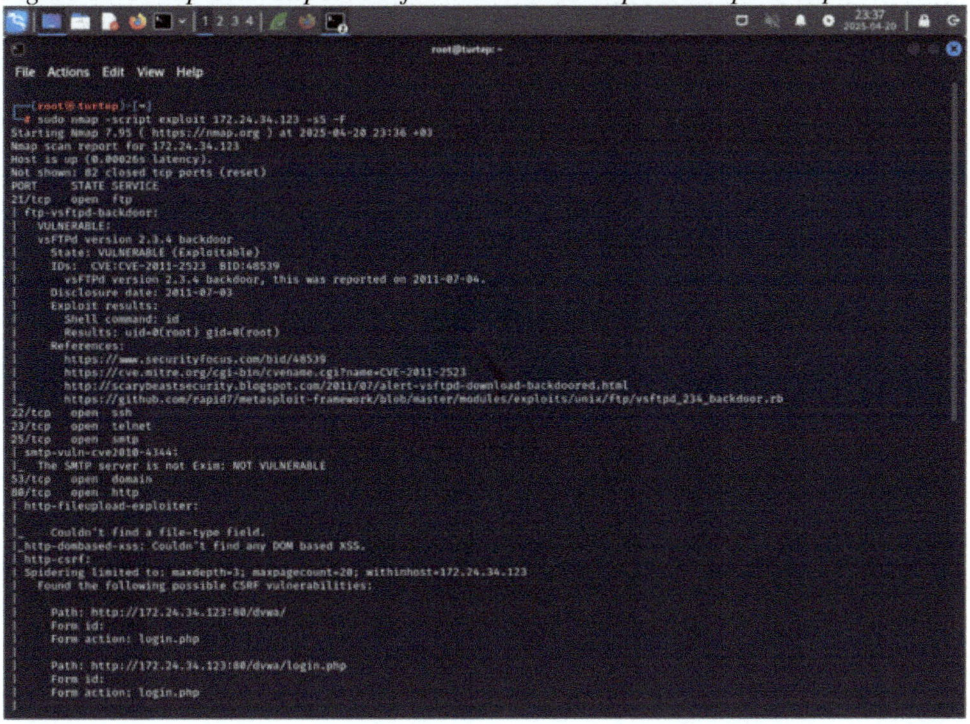

RED TEAMING PRACTICE ON METASPLOITABLE

Once a vulnerable virtual machine is created, reconnaissance activities can begin by scanning the system. Before attempting to identify vulnerabilities or open ports, it is essential to determine how many active devices (hosts) exist on the network and to identify their IP addresses. Since all possible devices on the network fall within the IP range 172.24.34.1 to 172.24.34.255, a scan of these 254 potential IP addresses can be performed to identify which hosts respond. If a device responds to a ping request, it is considered active, whereas devices that do not respond are assumed to be inactive or unreachable.

However, manually pinging a large number of IP addresses is often inefficient, particularly in environments containing multiple networks or subnets. At this stage, specialised tools available in Kali Linux provide significant advantages. One such mechanism is the Address Resolution Protocol (ARP), which uses ARP packets to identify devices on the local network. Nevertheless, ARP-based discovery does not always detect every device on the network. The primary purpose of ARP is to map IP addresses to corresponding MAC addresses within a local network environment (Sharma & Ravichandra, 2023).

Initially, when the ARP tool is executed and no prior communication has occurred with other network devices, only systems previously contacted by the querying host (in this case Kali Linux) or devices already recorded in the ARP cache may be detected. To reveal devices that are present on the network but not yet detected, a ping request can be sent to the relevant IP address to verify its activity. After this interaction, running the ARP tool again allows the device to appear in the ARP table. In Figure 12, the querying machine initiates the ARP resolution process, which discovers the MAC address associated with the specified IP address.

Figure 12. Host (Device) with ARP tool

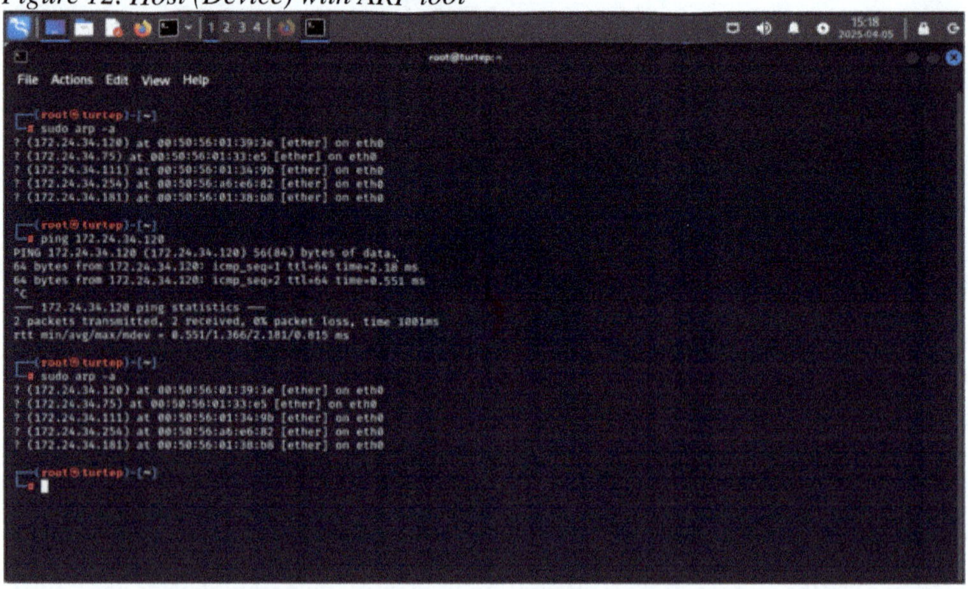

Figure 13. Metasploitable IP Address

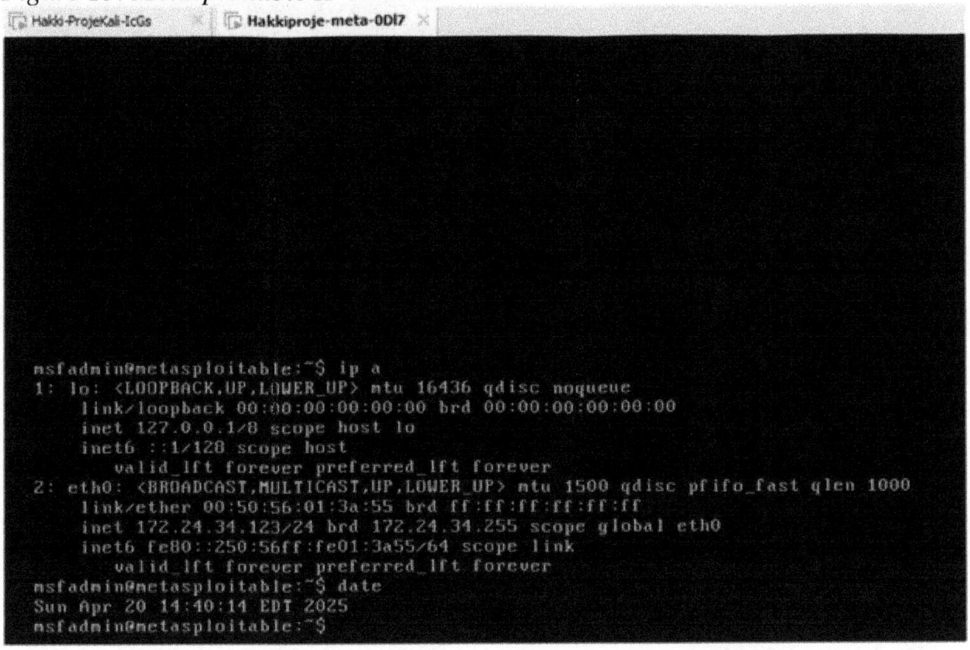

As shown in Figure 13, the IP address of the Metasploitable target system, previously undetected before the ping operation, was correctly identified after the ping request was sent. Instead of manually executing ping commands or making direct ARP queries, another tool called Netdiscover can be used by entering the command "sudo netdiscover" in the Kali Linux terminal. The Netdiscover utility automatically detects devices on the network, eliminating the need to ping each potential IP address individually. As illustrated in Figure 14, the Netdiscover tool identified a total of 23 active devices on the network.

Figure 14. Kali Linux Netdiscover Tool

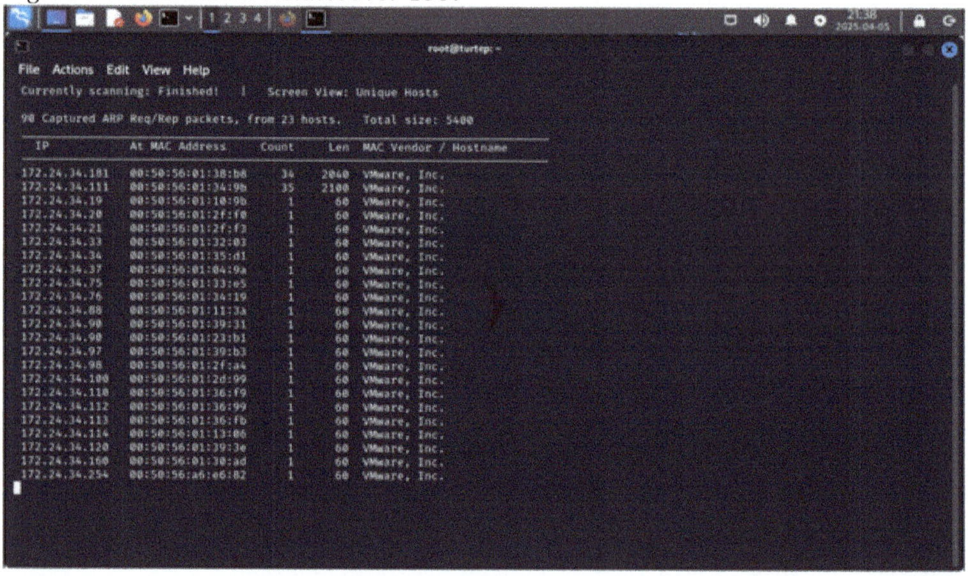

The Metasploitable target system was identified with the IP address 172.24.34.123, after which a basic Nmap scan can be performed against this host. The following command is used to determine whether the host is active, which ports are open, and which services are running on those ports:

"nmap 172.24.34.123".

Figure 15 shows the results of this scan. Nmap scan results reveal both the open ports on the target system and the services associated with those ports. A large number of open ports significantly increases the attack surface and represents a serious security risk. For example, port 21 (FTP) may be securely configured and therefore pose no immediate threat. However, even a single vulnerable service among the remaining open ports may allow attackers to compromise the system.

Each exposed port potentially introduces threats such as unauthorised access, data exfiltration, or exploitation of vulnerable services. Since Nmap provides not only port numbers but also service information, it serves as an essential reconnaissance tool in red team operations. If these services are misconfigured or running vulnerable versions, attackers may exploit them to compromise the system.

Figure 15. Nmap Scan on the Metasploitable Machine

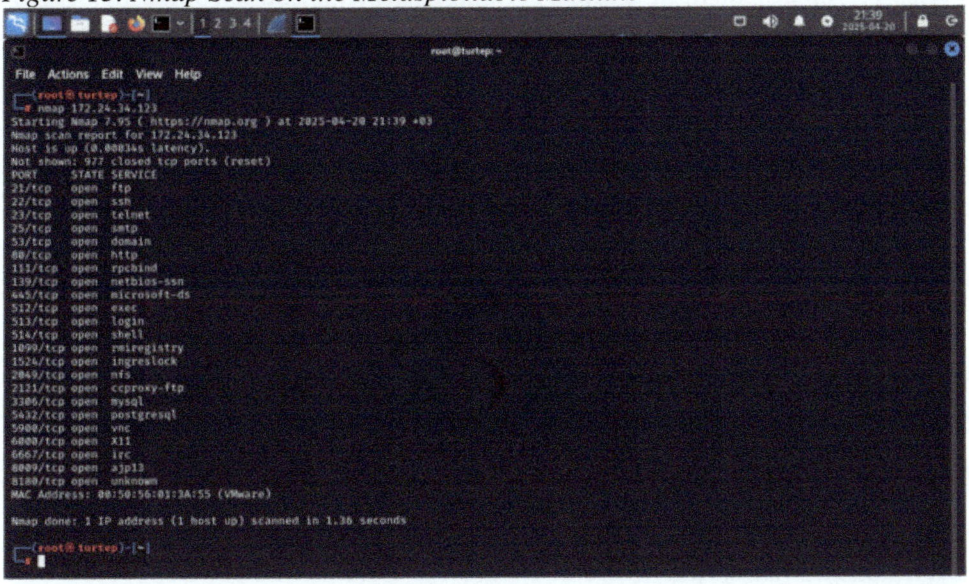

It is also possible to obtain additional information from the target system, for example by executing the command:

"nmap -O 172.24.34.123".

Using this command, details such as the target system's operating system and MAC address can be identified. Operating system detection is particularly valuable in analysing the attack surface and understanding the structural characteristics of the target environment during red team activities. Figure 16 illustrates the operating system information obtained through this scan.

As a result of such analysis, organisations can gain deeper insights into vulnerabilities within their network infrastructure and strengthen their defences against cyber threats. To run the operating system detection feature in Nmap, the "-O" parameter must be executed with sudo privileges, followed by the target IP address. In this case, the command becomes:

"sudo nmap -O 172.24.34.123".

The results may also provide indications of whether the target is a physical or virtual system. Detection of a virtual environment may indicate that the system is a honeypot intentionally configured with vulnerabilities. Honeypots are designed to deceive attackers and analyse their behaviour, allowing organisations to observe attack strategies, motivations, and target selection processes without exposing real infrastructure.

Figure 16. Nmap Scan Results with Operating System Information on the Metasploitable Machine

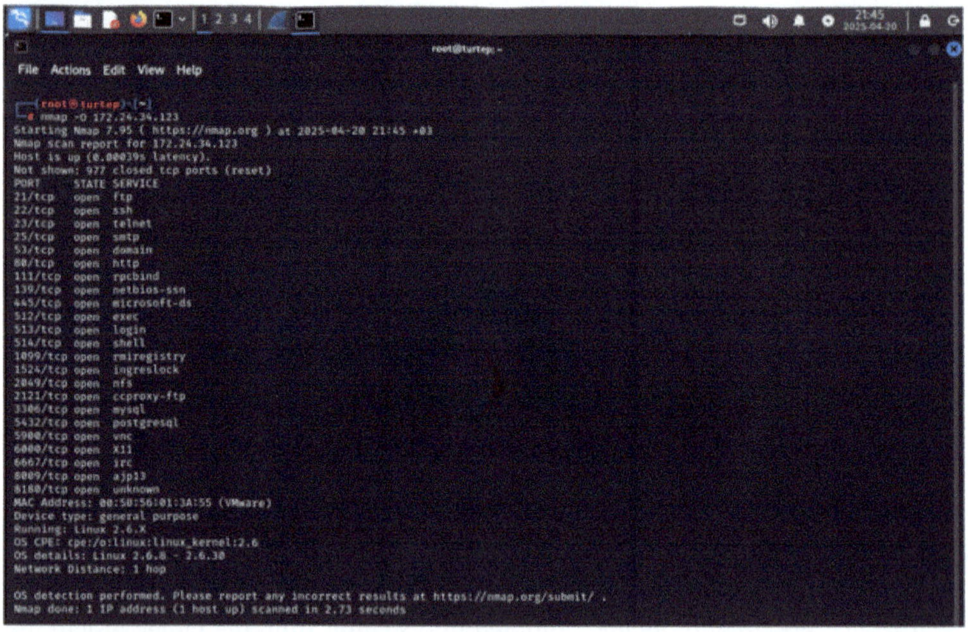

Exploitation of the Metasploitable Machine

In the first step, two separate terminal sessions are used. The Metasploit Framework console is executed in the first terminal, while an Nmap scan is conducted in the second terminal to identify the versions of services running on the target system. For this purpose, the "sudo nmap -sV" command is executed together with the target IP address.

Running the command with sudo privileges activates the scan after the administrator password is entered, because version detection requires elevated permissions. This process is illustrated in Figure 17.

Figure 17. Nmap Scan Performed for Version Information of All Ports on the Metasploitable Machine

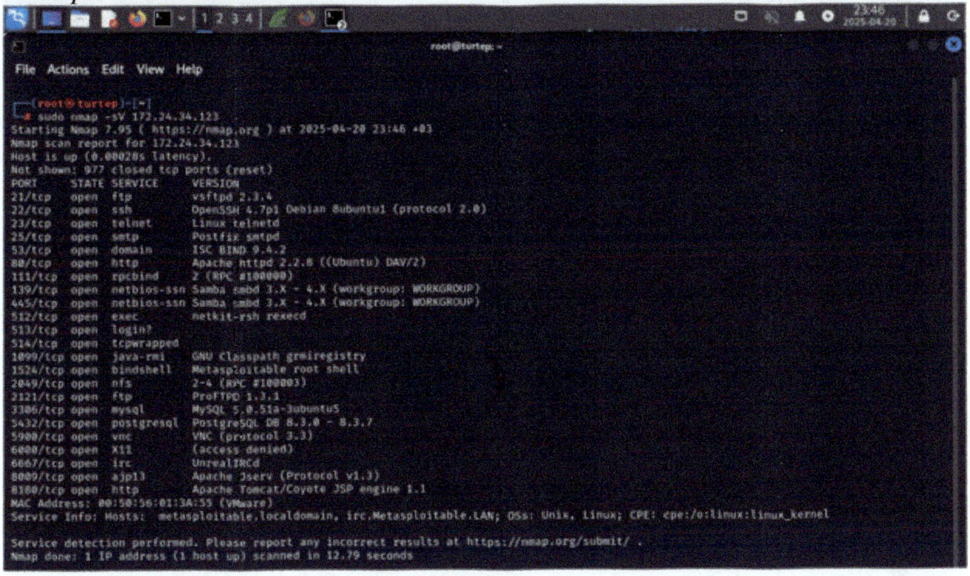

Two different exploitation files and their paths that can be used are identified. As indicated earlier, the file "17491.rb" is rated as "excellent", indicating that it is considered more reliable and effective than the file "49757.py".

In the following steps, the "search" command is used within the Metasploit Framework to locate the relevant exploit module associated with the identified software. As a result of this search, the module "exploit/unix/ftp/vsftpd_234_backdoor" is discovered. Figure 18 shows the Metasploit search results for exploitation via a backdoor embedded in vsftpd archives.

This exploit is rated as "excellent", and the public disclosure date is July 3, 2011. In order to analyse the exploit in greater detail, the command "show info" or "info exploit/unix/ftp/vsftpd_234_backdoor" is executed. This command provides detailed information about the exploit's functionality, scope, and operational characteristics, as shown in Figure 19.

Figure 18. Msfconsole Search Results for Vsftpd

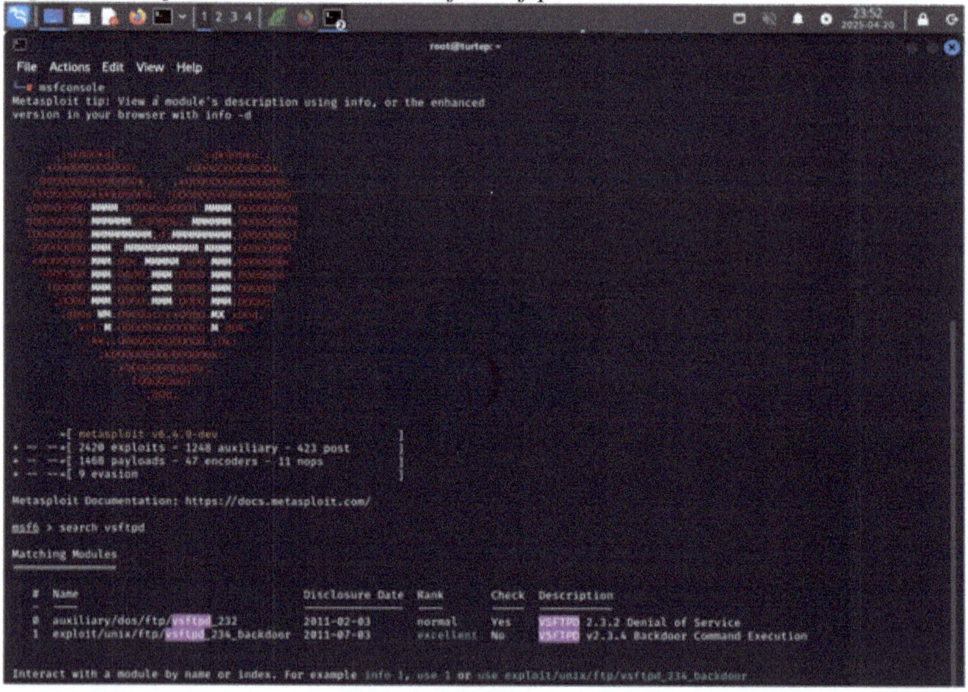

Figure 19. Information Screen of vsftpd v2.3.4 Exploit on the Msfconsole

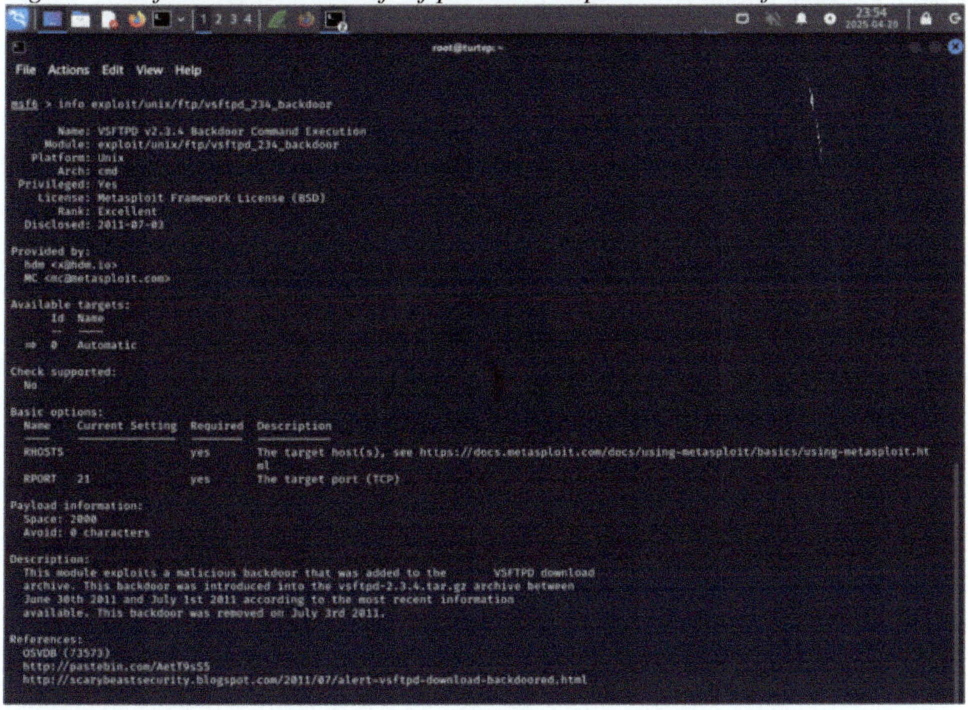

After this configuration, the stage of selecting and confirming the malicious payload used by the exploit is performed. Once a suitable payload is selected, it becomes apparent that no additional configuration parameters are required for execution. By examining the available payloads using the "show payloads" command, the correctness of the configuration settings can be verified.

After completing all configuration options, the exploitation process is initiated by executing the "exploit" command. This command creates a command shell session on the target system. Access to the system was verified by executing commands such as "ls" and "whoami". The results revealed that the session possessed root privileges.

Additionally, the commands "pwd" and "ifconfig" were executed to further verify successful system compromise. The "pwd" command confirmed that the working directory was the root directory, while "ifconfig" displayed the IP address of the compromised Metasploitable machine.

Figure 20 demonstrates the practical implementation of reconnaissance, vulnerability assessment, and exploitation techniques within the context of red team operations in cybersecurity. Careful vulnerability analysis and controlled exploitation enable red teams to better understand attacker methodologies and significantly strengthen organisational defensive capabilities.

Figure 20. Running the vsftpd v2.3.4 Exploit

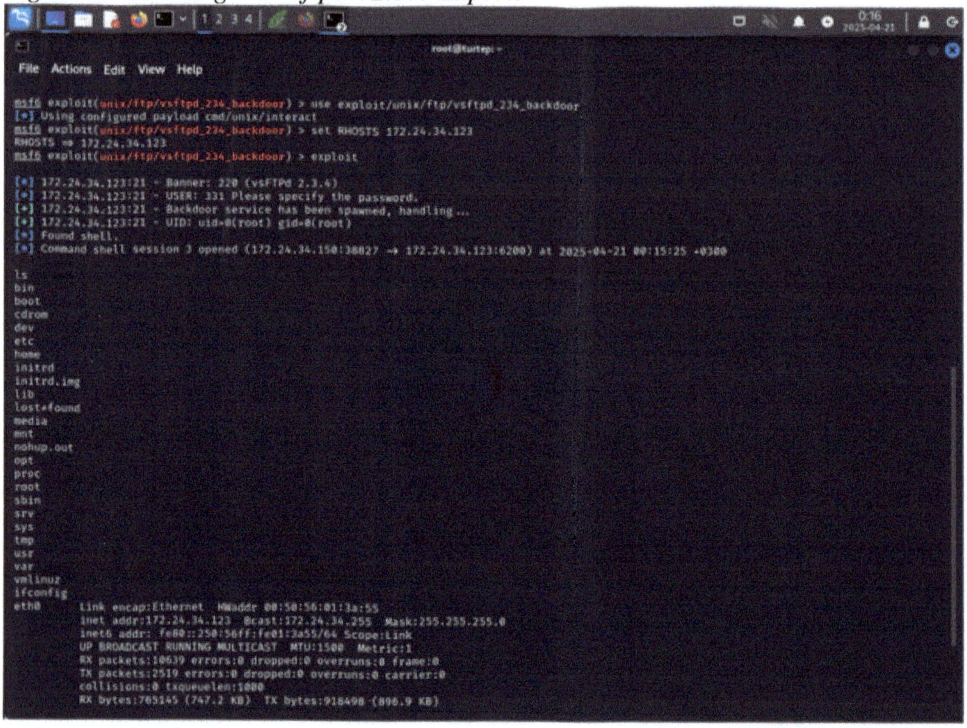

Bindshell Exploitation

For this stage, a connection attempt was made via TCP port 1524. If authentication mechanisms are absent, this port may provide direct root shell access to the target system. The Netcat utility, which allows network connections to be established over TCP and UDP protocols, was used for this purpose (Armstrong, 2001).

Netcat can both listen for incoming connections and initiate connections to remote hosts. The syntax used to establish the connection is as follows:

nc <IP address> <port>

The use of this tool is illustrated in Figure 21. Exploitation is considered successful when the shell running on the Metasploitable machine accepts a connection from a remote client. Listing files within the root directory and verifying the IP address confirmed that root-level access had been obtained.

This vulnerability exists due to the complete absence of authentication mechanisms. Although such configurations are uncommon, they may occur in systems that are improperly configured. In some cases, administrators may intentionally enable such access for remote maintenance purposes but neglect to implement proper authentication controls.

This scenario demonstrates that misconfigurations remain a significant attack vector, whether intentional or accidental. During red team engagements, all potential entry points into the target system must be carefully examined. The primary objective is to identify and exploit existing vulnerabilities in order to evaluate the security posture of the system.

Figure 21. Root Access with Netcat

Exploiting the Telnet Vulnerability

Another attack on the Metasploitable machine targets the Telnet service running on the target system. This vulnerability becomes exploitable due to information disclosure during the service interaction process. As shown in Figure 22, the Telnet service is identified as running on port 23. However, the version information displayed as "Linux telnetd" does not provide sufficiently detailed information for precise vulnerability identification.

Figure 22. Running Searchsploit Tool for Linux telnetd

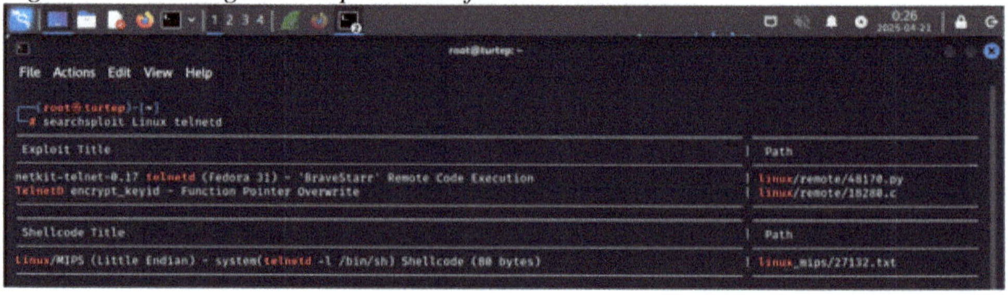

At this stage, instead of continuing with exploit database research, direct interaction with the service can be considered as an alternative reconnaissance technique. Figure 23 illustrates attempts to establish a direct Telnet connection to the target system.

Since the Telnet service requires authentication through a username and password, default credentials were attempted by connecting directly to the Telnet port of the target machine. The Telnet banner unexpectedly revealed not only standard service information but also the login credentials "msfadmin/msfadmin". These credentials correspond to the default user account of the Metasploitable system and allowed successful authentication.

After logging into the system, it was observed that the authenticated user account was "msfadmin" rather than the root account. Privilege escalation was therefore performed using the command "sudo su", followed by the password "msfadmin" revealed in the Telnet banner, which resulted in successful elevation to root privileges.

Figure 23. Exploitation of Telnet Vulnerabilities

Samba Vulnerability Exploitation

As shown in Figure 24, the Searchsploit tool was used to identify possible exploitation techniques related to different Samba versions. In order to determine the exact version of Samba running on the target machine, the Metasploit auxiliary module "auxiliary/scanner/smb/smb_version" was selected and executed.

The smb_version auxiliary scanner module was configured to scan the target IP address, and the results revealed that the Samba version running on the target system was 3.0.20. With this information, the Searchsploit tool was executed again, this time filtering results according to the identified version.

The search returned four potential exploit entries. Among these, the module "exploit/multi/samba/usermap_script_command_execution" was identified as the most promising option. After configuring the required parameters for this module, a command shell was successfully opened on the target system, confirming successful exploitation of the Samba vulnerability.

Now that the exact Samba version was known, the Searchsploit tool was used again to examine other available exploits, as shown in Figure 25. Among the identified entries, the exploit located at the path "unix/remote/16320.rb" was considered the most suitable. This exploit belongs to the Metasploit Framework and is compatible with Samba versions in the 3.x–4.x range. It is an executable exploit written in Ruby.

In contrast, files with the .txt extension cannot be executed directly and require manual processing before use. In real-world red team penetration testing scenarios within corporate environments, version information about the target system is carefully documented in a detailed security report, and additional vulnerabilities are analysed by referencing known exploits associated with the identified software versions.

Figure 24. Searchsploit Scan Result for "Samba 3.0.20"

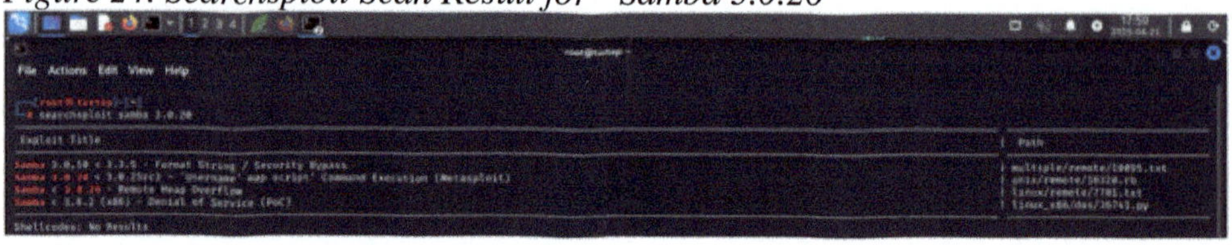

Figure 25. Configuration Options for Samba Vulnerability

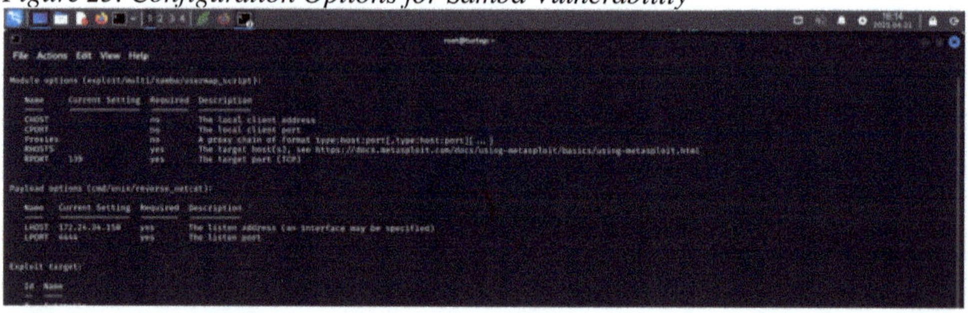

Figure 26 illustrates the configuration options required to execute the Samba exploit. The only missing parameter is "RHOST", which represents the target system's IP address. Setting the RHOST value to the IP address of the Metasploitable machine enables the exploit to run successfully.

The Samba vulnerability was successfully exploited to obtain a command shell on the target system. The "whoami" command was executed to verify the authorisation level, confirming that the compromised account possessed root privileges. This result demonstrates that the target system had been fully compromised.

Figure 26. Exploitation with RHOST Settings and Samba Vulnerability

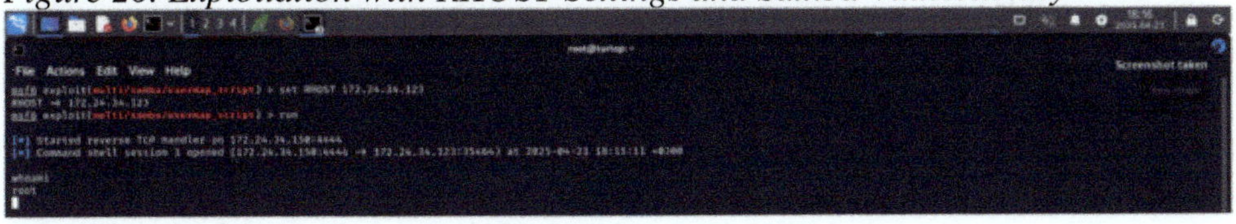

SSH Brute Force Attack

As shown in Figure 27, a brute-force attack targeting the SSH service is conducted using a helper module within the Metasploit Framework. A brute-force attack involves systematically attempting numerous combinations of usernames and passwords in order to discover valid authentication credentials.

This method typically involves sending a large number of credential combinations to the target system until the correct login information is identified. The configuration also specifies the files required for the attack, including username and password wordlists.

Brute-force attacks are particularly effective when systems rely on weak, predictable, or default credentials. Passwords such as "password123" or "admin" are frequently targeted because they are easily guessed.

In this demonstration scenario, the username and password used for SSH authentication on the target machine correspond to the default credentials "msfadmin/msfadmin". The attack can be performed using any Metasploit auxiliary module capable of testing SSH login credentials.

To launch the brute-force attack, the module configuration includes parameters such as the target IP address, username and password wordlist files, and the execution speed of the attack module. This configuration process is illustrated in Figure 27.

Figure 27. Password and Username Configuration

Figure 28 shows the contents of the prepared credential files, each containing a list of possible usernames and passwords. Before launching the attack, these text files must be prepared so that they can be used as input for the brute-force process.

Once the attack is launched, the Metasploit Framework systematically tests each username–password combination against the SSH service running on the target system. When the correct credentials are identified, the framework displays a success message indicating that unauthorised access has been achieved.

After discovering valid credentials, the active session must be captured and used to interact with the target system.

Figure 28. Brute Force Attacks

After identifying the correct credentials, the next stage involves interacting with the compromised system. The command "sessions" is used to display all active sessions established by the framework. In this scenario, one SSH session is displayed, originating from the IP address of the Metasploitable machine.

To interact with the session, the command "sessions -i 1" is executed, where "1" represents the session ID. Once the session is activated, commands can be executed directly on the target system shell.

For example, running the command "whoami" confirms that the current authenticated user is "msfadmin". To perform privilege escalation, the command "sudo su" is executed, followed by the password "msfadmin". Running "whoami" again confirms that root privileges have been successfully obtained, as illustrated in Figure 29.

Although this demonstration appears relatively simple, real-world brute-force attacks often involve significantly larger and more diverse credential lists. In this case, the correct credentials were intentionally included within the wordlists for demonstration purposes, enabling the attack process to be clearly illustrated.

Figure 29. Exploitation of the Target Machine with Created Sessions

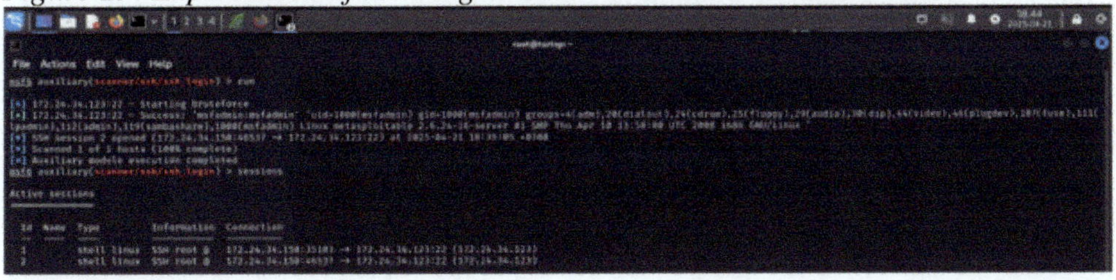

Exploiting Distcc Daemon Vulnerability

A commonly used exploit targets port 3632 within the Metasploit Framework. This exploit, known as “distcc exec” or “Daemon command execution”, is rated as “excellent” and exploits a documented vulnerability that allows arbitrary command execution on systems running the distccd service.

Since the target system was identified as running distccd on port 3632, this exploit can be applied directly. The exploit description provides information such as the vulnerability disclosure date, severity rating, and operational details.

After selecting the exploit module, its details were examined using the “show info” command. As illustrated in Figure 30, the description confirms that:

“This module exploits a documented vulnerability to execute arbitrary commands on any system running distccd.”

Figure 30. Distcc Daemon Command Execution Information

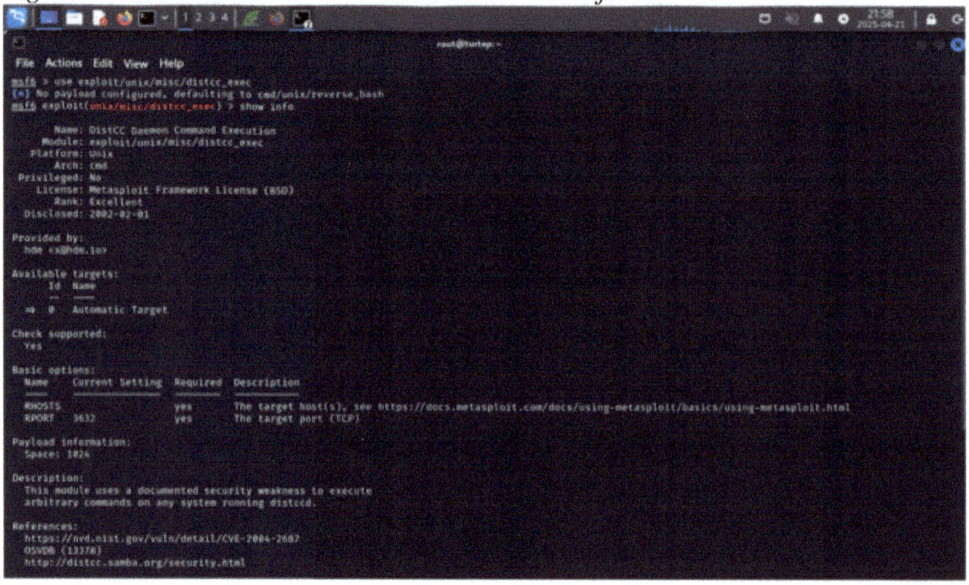

The configuration options for the exploit are displayed using the "show options" command. During configuration, the target IP address (RHOST) is set to the Metasploitable machine's IP address.

The available payloads can be listed using the "show payloads" command. For this scenario, the payload "cmd/unix/reverse" was selected, which establishes a reverse shell connection between the target system and the attacking machine.

In this configuration, LHOST represents the IP address of the attacking system (Kali Linux), while RHOST represents the IP address of the target machine. Once the payload is selected and all parameters are configured correctly, the exploit can be executed, as shown in Figure 31.

Figure 31. Command Shell Access After Successful Exploitation

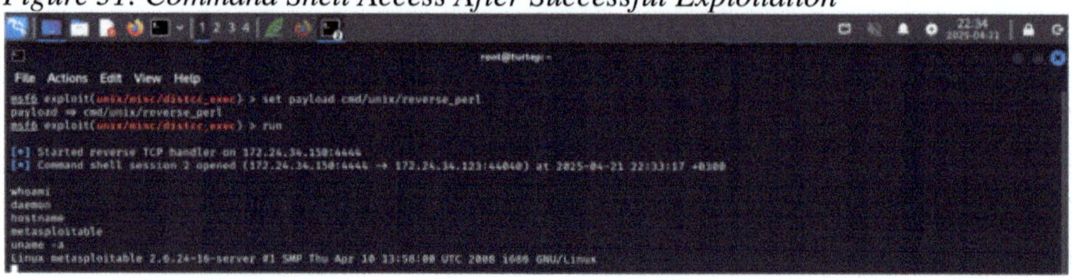

After successful exploitation, a command shell is opened on the target machine. Commands such as "whoami", "ls", and "hostname" are executed to verify successful access.

In addition to reverse shell payloads, alternative payloads such as "bind_ruby" can also be used to compromise the system. Figure 32 illustrates another successful exploitation using the "bind_ruby" payload on port 3632. In this instance, the authenticated user is identified as "daemon", which belongs to the Metasploitable system in this experimental scenario.

Figure 32. Distcc Exploitation with Bind_ruby Payload

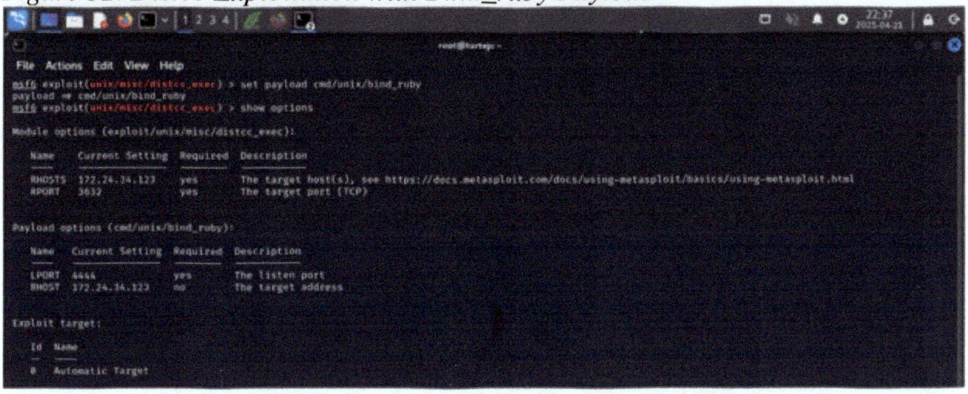

UnrealIRCd Vulnerability Exploitation

Ports 6667 and 6697 indicate that the Internet Relay Chat (IRC) service is running using the UnrealIRCd software. A search conducted within the Metasploit Framework identified a single exploit module written in Ruby.

This exploit specifically targets UnrealIRCd version 3.2.8, enabling command execution through a malicious backdoor embedded within the software distribution archive. Further investigation confirmed that this vulnerability is rated as "excellent" and was publicly disclosed in 2010.

After selecting the exploit, its configuration options are reviewed and the necessary parameters are set, including:

- RHOSTS – the target IP address
- LHOST – the local IP address of the attacking machine (Kali Linux)
- Payload – the malicious payload used to establish system access

Once the payload and parameters are correctly configured, the exploit "unix/irc/unreal_ircd_3281_backdoor" is executed, as shown in Figure 33 and Figure 34.

Figure 33. UnrealIRCd Exploit Setup

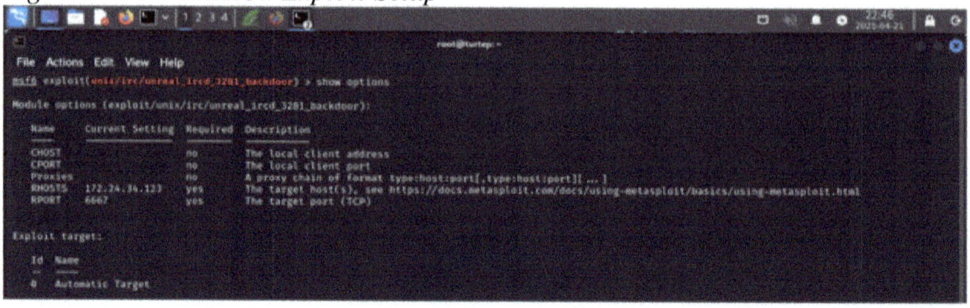

Figure 34. Exploitation of UnrealIRCd Vulnerability

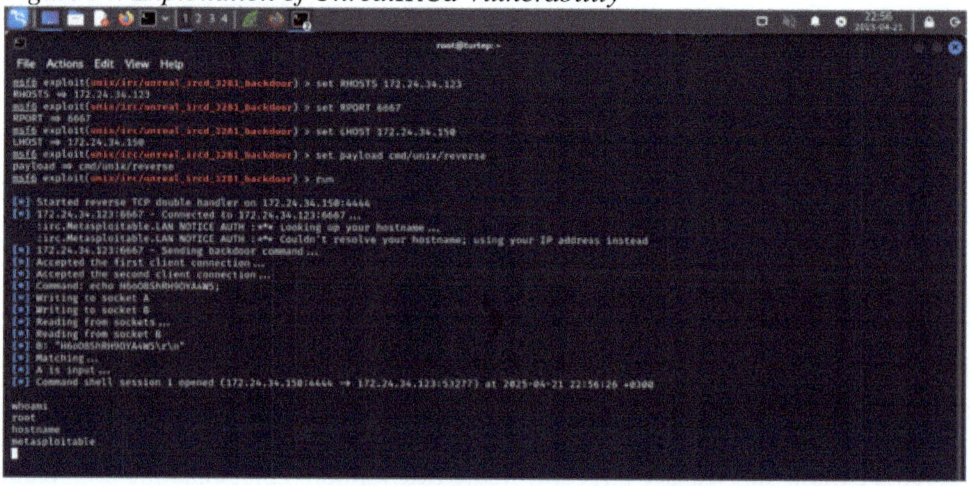

VNC Exploitation

Port 5900, which is open on the Metasploitable virtual machine, corresponds to the Virtual Network Computing (VNC) service. VNC is a remote desktop sharing system that allows users to graphically control another computer over a network (Richardson et al., 1998).

VNC operates using a client–server architecture, where the server shares the remote screen while the client displays and controls it through user input.

However, VNC services are often configured with weak or default credentials, making them attractive targets for attackers. In particular, VNC servers operating on port 5900 may be vulnerable to unauthorised access if proper authentication mechanisms are not enforced.

Initial searches conducted using searchsploit and msfconsole did not identify a direct exploit for the VNC service in Kali Linux. However, the module "exploit/multi/vnc/vnc_keyboard_exec" was identified as a potentially viable option, as it supports multiple operating systems.

As shown in Figure 35, a connection to the Metasploitable system was attempted using the command "vncviewer 172.24.34.123", which triggered the password authentication mechanism. After several attempts using common passwords such as "password" and "123456", the correct password "password" was successfully identified, allowing unauthorised access to the VNC server.

Figure 35. Virtual Network Computing (VNC) Exploitation

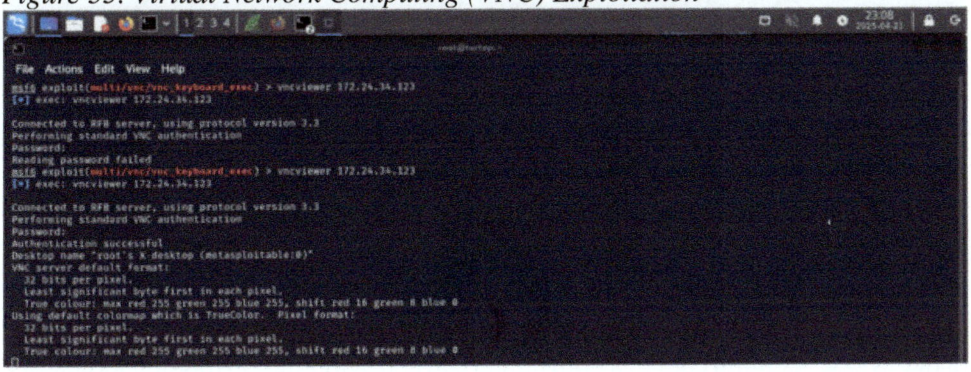

Java-Remote Method Invocation (RMI) Exploitation

Another successfully exploited port is port 1099, associated with the Java Remote Method Invocation (RMI) service. A search conducted through Msfconsole identified four modules related to this service.

Two of these modules are exploit modules, although one of them only establishes a connection and does not create a session for exploitation. Therefore, the module "exploit/multi/misc/java_rmi_server" was selected for this attack.

After selecting the module, the configuration options were examined and the necessary parameters were set. The RHOST parameter was assigned the IP address of the Metasploitable system, while LHOST was set to the IP address of the Kali Linux attacking machine.

Figure 36 illustrates the successful exploitation of port 1099, where the target machine's IP address is confirmed and access to the system's file structure is obtained.

Figure 36. Java-RMI Exploitation

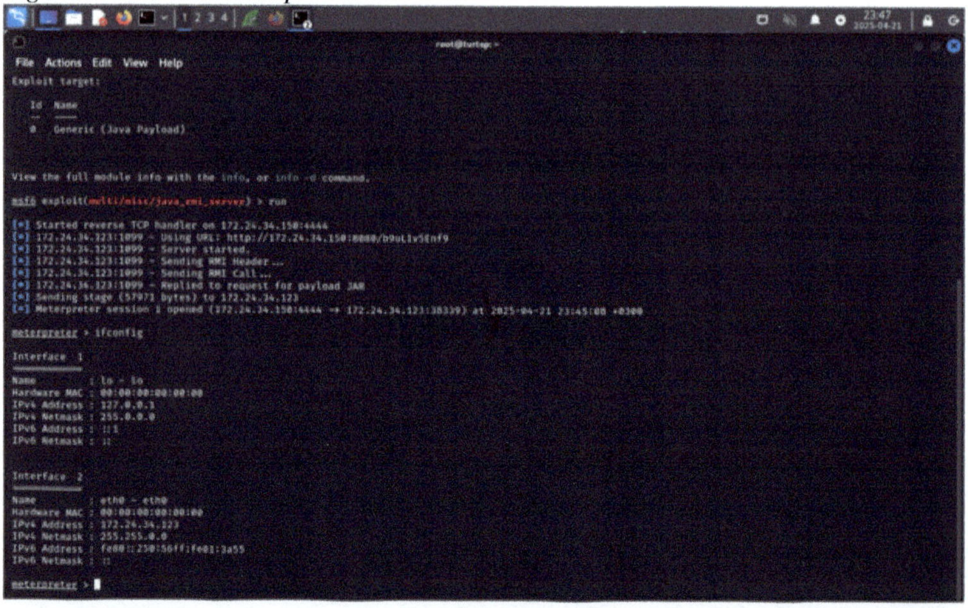

This process reveals the Unix/Linux file system structure of the compromised system, including file permissions, sizes, and modification timestamps. Each entry in the "Mode" column contains both numerical and symbolic permission indicators, representing access rights for files and directories.

The "Size" column indicates the file size in bytes, while directories typically occupy 4096 bytes. The "Type" column identifies whether an entry is a directory ("dir") or a regular file ("fil"), and the "Last Modified" column records the most recent modification date and time.

During red team operations, analysing file system structure, permissions, and modification timestamps is critical not only for system compromise but also for post-exploitation activities. The real risk arises when attackers gain the ability to manipulate the internal structure of the system, including editing, deleting, or copying sensitive files.

Understanding file permissions enables red team analysts to identify potential privilege escalation opportunities, while file sizes and modification dates may reveal frequently accessed or recently modified files that could contain valuable information for further analysis or exploitation.

CLASSIFICATION OF VULNERABILITIES BY NESSUS AND SOLUTION STRATEGIES

Nessus is a highly effective and visually intuitive vulnerability scanning tool. As shown in Figure 37, once the scan of the Metasploitable target machine is completed, the identified vulnerabilities are categorised and presented through a series of graphical visualisations together with detailed scan results.

Figure 37. Nessus scan result on Metasploitable machine

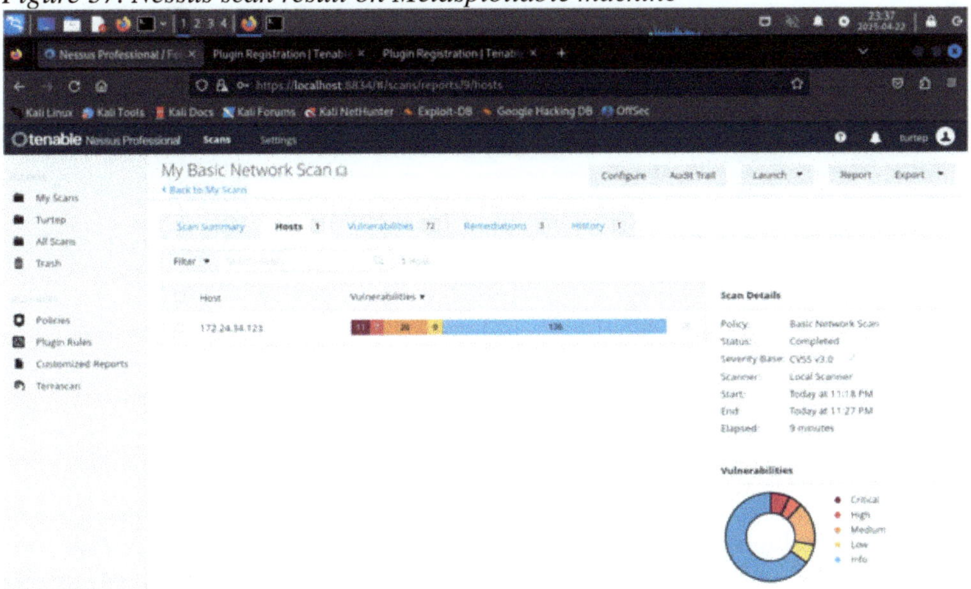

After scanning the Metasploitable machine with Nessus, a total of 11 critical, 7 high, 26 medium, and 9 low-level vulnerabilities, together with 136 information disclosure issues, were identified, as shown in Figure 38. Detailed information regarding each vulnerability can be accessed through the Nessus interface. As observed, several of the critical vulnerabilities detected were successfully exploited during the red team exercise. Many of the vulnerabilities exploited are categorised as critical, particularly because they enable root-level access to the target servers.

Figure 38. Critical vulnerabilities of the Metasploitable machine detected by Nessus

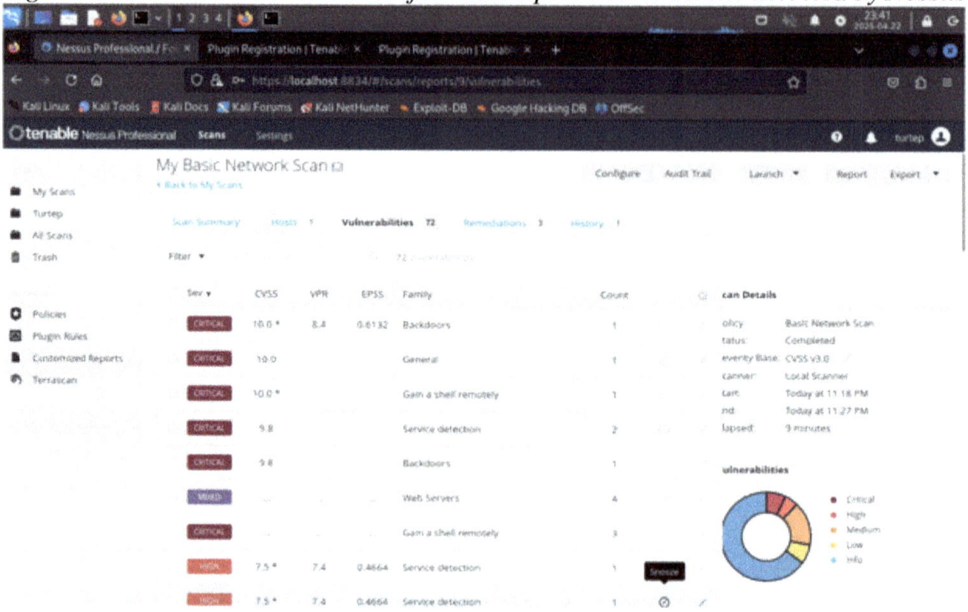

Network File System (NFS) Shared Directory Information Disclosure

One of the high-risk security vulnerabilities detected during the Nessus vulnerability scan is "NFS Exported Share Information Disclosure", which affects the Metasploitable machine, as shown in Figure 39. This vulnerability may allow unauthorised users to access sensitive information.

The remote server exposes NFS shares and permits the scanning client to access these shared directories. Due to this configuration, malicious actors may gain additional opportunities to exploit the system, potentially resulting in unauthorised file access and modification on the remote host. The recommended mitigation strategy is to configure the NFS service so that it accepts requests only from trusted clients, thereby reducing the risk of unauthorised access and preventing further exploitation of the vulnerability.

This vulnerability, identified on the Metasploitable system via UDP port 2049, clearly indicates a serious security misconfiguration and requires further investigation as well as corrective security measures. Such vulnerabilities must be addressed promptly to mitigate the risk of unauthorised access and potential data breaches.

Figure 39. NFS shared directory information disclosure

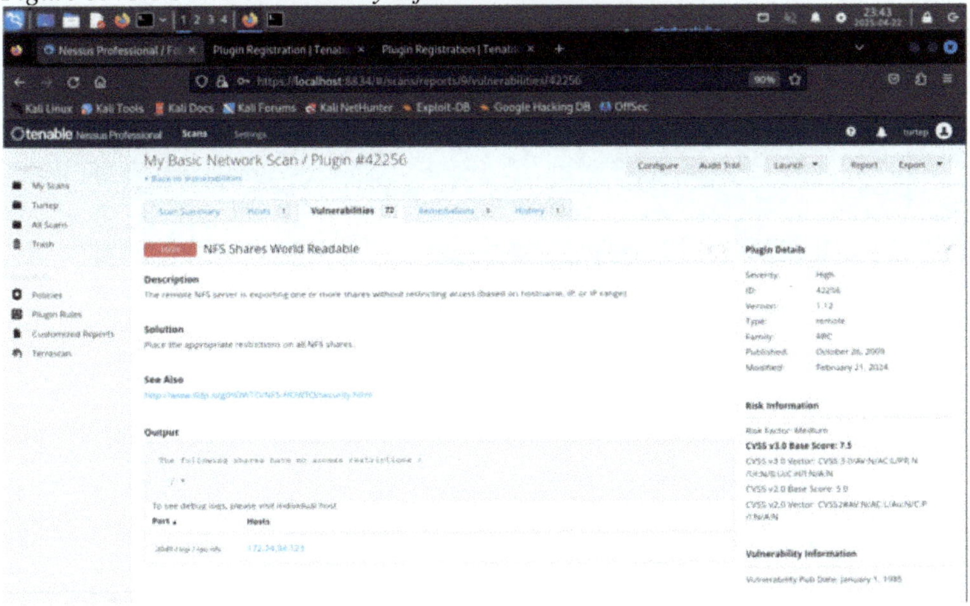

VNC Server Password Vulnerability

During the Nessus vulnerability assessment conducted on the Metasploitable machine, it was determined that the VNC server was configured with weak default credentials, as illustrated in Figure 40. The Nessus tool successfully authenticated using the password "password" over TCP port 5900, demonstrating the presence of a weak authentication mechanism.

This finding highlights the critical importance of implementing strong password policies during system deployment, whether for individual users or organisational infrastructures. Even the most advanced security mechanisms can be undermined if authentication credentials are poorly configured or weakly protected.

The successful exploitation attempts and the information obtained during the reconnaissance phase clearly demonstrate the necessity of strengthening system security practices. Red team exercises are particularly valuable in this context, as they provide critical insights into potential weaknesses within the target environment.

Each vulnerability identified reveals different aspects of the network structure and security posture of the target system. The presence of multiple services operating on different network ports indicates that various attack vectors may exist depending on the configuration and functionality of these services. If services are improperly configured or deployed without adequate security controls, they may introduce exploitable vulnerabilities. Therefore, developing and implementing proactive remediation strategies is essential for mitigating potential security risks.

Figure 40. VNC server as critical vulnerability due to a weak password

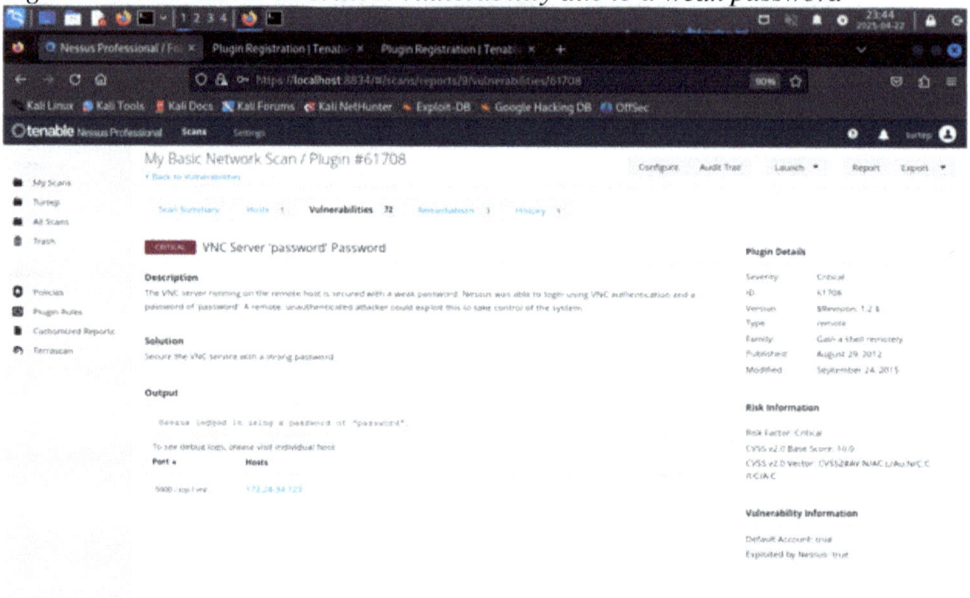

FINDINGS AND DISCUSSION

Ethical attackers are not merely individuals possessing technical expertise; they are professionals who operate within legal and ethical frameworks while prioritising societal benefit. These specialists simulate the tools, techniques, and procedures used by malicious attackers in order to strengthen organisational security defences. Ethical hacking therefore requires not only advanced technical competence but also a high level of ethical responsibility and professional awareness.

In this study, cybersecurity tools including Kali Linux, Metasploitable, Nessus, Wireshark, and Nmap were deployed within a virtual environment using VMware Workstation. Red team exercises were conducted to identify open ports, active services, and associated vulnerabilities.

Some of the vulnerabilities identified were caused by weak authentication credentials in services such as Tomcat and Vsftpd, while others resulted from exploitable weaknesses in services including Bindshell, Telnet, Samba, SSH, Distccd, UnrealIRCd, VNC, and Java-RMI. By successfully exploiting these vulnerabilities, the primary objective of the red team exercise, evaluating the resilience of the defensive infrastructure, was achieved.

The practical activities conducted in this study demonstrate the critical importance for organisations to identify vulnerabilities and implement appropriate mitigation strategies. Since not all vulnerabilities pose the same level of risk, it is essential to classify vulnerabilities according to their severity and prioritise remediation accordingly.

Within this study, Nessus and Nmap were utilised to detect and categorise vulnerabilities according to their criticality levels. A total of 11 critical, 7 high, 26 medium, and 9 low-level vulnerabilities, along with 136 information disclosure issues, were identified. Several of these vulnerabilities were subsequently exploited using tools such as Nmap and Msfconsole. The recommended remediation strategies based on the detected open ports emphasise the necessity of adopting a proactive security approach to protect network infrastructures.

Despite the valuable insights obtained, this study has several limitations. The attack scenario implemented using the Metasploitable platform does not fully replicate the complexity of real-world cyber threats. For instance, the extremely weak passwords configured for services such as Tomcat and the ease with which many vulnerabilities can be detected through Nmap scanning create a simplified experimental environment compared with real operational systems.

Furthermore, the practical execution of red team activities was limited to personal network environments due to legal and ethical considerations. Nevertheless, the study systematically documented the vulnerability exploitation process, malicious payload analysis, auxiliary tool usage, configuration procedures, and post-exploitation activities conducted within the simulated target network.

CONCLUSION

This chapter examined cyber-attack methodologies with a particular focus on red team approaches. Red teaming provides a systematic method for evaluating the security posture of organisations by simulating the techniques and strategies employed by real-world cyber attackers. These practices demonstrate how a target system may be compromised through structured analysis, strategic planning, and technical exploitation techniques.

In this study, security testing frameworks including OSSTMM, PTES, and ISSAF were considered as foundational references for cybersecurity assessment, ethical hacking procedures, penetration testing phases, scenario development, and the execution of red team operations.

During the implementation phase, controlled penetration testing scenarios were conducted using virtualisation and security testing tools such as VMware Workstation, Kali Linux, and Metasploitable. Through these simulations, security vulnerabilities were successfully exploited, vulnerability severity levels were analysed, and mitigation strategies were proposed to address potential cyber threats.

As future work, advanced cybersecurity techniques such as machine learning-based anomaly detection and the integration of block chain technologies in network security environments may be further investigated. These approaches may contribute to the development of more intelligent and adaptive cybersecurity solutions. In addition, time-dependent performance evaluations of the proposed vulnerability mitigation strategies could be conducted in order to develop more effective defensive mechanisms for organisational systems.

ACKNOWLEDGMENT

Some parts of this chapter were produced from the first author's master's project. This research received no specific grant from any funding agency in the public, commercial, or not-for-profit sectors.

REFERENCES

Abu-Shaqra, R. (2020). Technoethics and sensemaking: Risk assessment and knowledge management of Ethical Hacking in a sociotechnical society. [Doctoral dissertation, University of Ottowa]. DOI: 10.20381/ruor-24626

Ajami, R., & Dinh, A. V. (2011). Embedded Network Firewall on FPGA. *2011 Eighth International Conference on Information Technology: New Generations*, 1041-1043. DOI: 10.1109/ITNG.2011.178

Armstrong, T. (2001, February 15). *Netcat – The TCP/IP Swiss Army Knife. SANS Institute*. https://www.sans.org/white-papers/952/

Cisco. (2024). *What Is Social Engineering in Cyber Security?* https://www.cisco.com/c/en/us/products/security/what-is-social-engineering.html

Engström, V., & Lagerström, R. (2022). Two Decades of Cyberattack Simulations: A Systematic Literature Review. *Computers & Security*, *116*, 102681. Advance online publication. DOI: 10.1016/j.cose.2022.102681

ENISA. (2019). *Red Teaming - Threat-led Penetration Testing*. https://www.enisa.europa.eu/publications/threat-led-penetration-testing

Heiding, F., Katsikeas, S., & Lagerström, R. (2023). Research communities in cyber security vulnerability assessments: A comprehensive literature review. *Computer Science Review*, *48*, 100551. Advance online publication. DOI: 10.1016/j.cosrev.2023.100551

Herzog, P. (2010). OSSTMM 3: *The Open Source Security Testing Methodology Manual (v3.0)*. https://www.isecom.org/OSSTMM.3.pdf

Holik, F., Horalek, J., Marik, O., Neradova, S., & Zitta, S. (2014). Effective penetration testing with Metasploit framework and methodologies. *Proceedings of 2014 IEEE 15th International Symposium on Computational Intelligence and Informatics (CINTI)* (pp. 237-242). DOI: 10.1109/CINTI.2014.7028682

Insecure.Org. (n.d.). *Nmap: the network mapper*. https://nmap.org

KaliLinux. (2025). *The most advanced penetration testing distribution.* https://www.kali.org/

Kardos, M., & Dexter, P. (2017). *A simple handbook for non-traditional red teaming.* https://www.dst.defence.gov.au/sites/default/files/publications/documents/DST-Group-TR-3335.pdf

Kraemer, S., Carayon, P., & Duggan, R. (2004). Red Team Performance for Improved Computer Security. *Proceedings of the Human Factors and Ergonomics Society Annual Meeting, 48*(14), 1605–1609. DOI: 10.1177/154193120404801410

Lachkov, P., Tawalbeh, L., & Bhatt, S. (2022). Vulnerability assessment for applications security through penetration simulation and testing. *Journal of Web Engineering, 21*(7), 2187–2208. DOI: 10.13052/jwe1540-9589.2178

Li, Y., Li, W., & Jiang, C. (2010). A survey of virtual machine systems: Current technology and future trends. *Proceedings of 2010 Third International Symposium on Electronic Commerce and Security* (pp. 332-336). DOI: 10.1109/ISECS.2010.80

Lyon, G. (2009). *Nmap Network Scanning: The Official Nmap Project Guide to Network Discovery and Security Scanning.* https://nmap.org/book/toc.html

Mani, V. (2022). *Strengthening cybersecurity with red team engagements.* https://www.isaca.org/resources/isaca-journal/issues/2022/volume-1/strengthening-cybersecurity-with-red-team-engagements

Microsoft Security Response Center. (13 May 2017). *Customer Guidance for WannaCrypt attacks.* https://www.microsoft.com/en-us/msrc/blog/2017/05/customer-guidance-for-wannacrypt-attacks

Mohurle, S., & Patil, M. (2017). A brief study of WannaCry threat: Ransomware attack 2017. *International Journal of Advanced Research in Computer Science, 8*(5), 1938–1940.

Mosse Cyber Security Institute. (2022, April). *Using Netcat as a Reverse Shell.* https://library.mosse-institute.com/articles/2022/04/using-netcat-as-a-reverse-shell/using-netcat-as-a-reverse-shell.html

Postel, J. (1980). *User Datagram Protocol.* https://datatracker.ietf.org/doc/html/rfc768

Postel, J. (1981). *Transmission Control Protocol.* https://datatracker.ietf.org/doc/html/rfc793

PTES. (2014). *Penetration Testing Execution Standard (PTES).* http://www.pentest-standard.org/index.php/Main_Page

Rapid7. (2018). *VSFTPD v2.3.4 Backdoor Command Execution.* https://www.rapid7.com/db/modules/exploit/unix/ftp/vsftpd_234_backdoor/

Rapid7. (n.d.). *Metasploit Framework.* https://www.metasploit.com/

Richardson, T., Stafford-Fraser, Q., Wood, K. R., & Hopper, A. (1998). Virtual Network Computing. *IEEE Internet Computing*, *2*(1), 33–38. DOI: 10.1109/4236.656066

Rusdan, D., Manurung, R., & Genta, G. (2020). *Information Systems Security Assessment Framework.* ISSAF.

Scarfone, K., & Mell, P. (2007). *Guide to Intrusion Detection and Prevention Systems (IDPS).* https://nvlpubs.nist.gov/nistpubs/Legacy/SP/nistspecialpublication800-94.pdf DOI: 10.6028/NIST.SP.800-94

Sharma, M., & Ravichandra, S. (2023). Design and Implementation of a Mechanism to Identify and Defend Against ARP Spoofing. *Proceedings of 2023 14th International Conference on Computing Communication and Networking Technologies (ICCCNT)* (pp. 1-6). IEEE. DOI: 10.1109/ICCCNT56998.2023.10308362

Sharpe, R., Warnicke, E., & Lamping, U. (2024). *Wireshark user's guide (Version 4.2).* https://www.wireshark.org/docs/wsug_html_chunked/

Singh, R., Tripathi, P., & Singh, R. (2014). A Survey on TCP (Transmission Control Protocol) and UDP (User Datagram Protocol) over AODV Routing Protocol. *International Journal of Research*, *1*(7), 26–33.

TechTarget. (2023). *What is a zero-day vulnerability?* https://www.techtarget.com/searchsecurity/definition/zero-day-vulnerability

Tenable, Inc. (2025). *Nessus vulnerability scanner.* https://www.tenable.com/products/nessus

Thapa, R., Sehl, B., Gupta, S., & Goyal, A. (2022). Security of operating system using the Metasploit framework by creating a backdoor from remote setup. *Proceedings of 2022 2nd International Conference on Advance Computing and Innovative Technologies in Engineering (ICACITE)* (pp. 2618-2620). DOI: 10.1109/ICACITE53722.2022.9823460

Yanalitis, M. (2014). *Red Teaming: Approach, Rationale, and Risks.* https://www.researchgate.net/profile/Mark-Yanalitis-2/publication/259546738_Red_Teaming_Approach_Rationale_and_Risks/links/0c96052c6e6a18dd8e000000/Red-Teaming-Approach-Rationale-and-Risks.pdf

Yulianto, S., Soewito, B., Gaol, F. L., & Kurniawan, A. (2025). Enhancing cybersecurity resilience through advanced red-teaming exercises and MITRE ATT&CK framework integration: A paradigm shift in cybersecurity assessment. *Cyber Security and Applications*, *3*, 100077. DOI: 10.1016/j.csa.2024.100077

ADDITIONAL READING

Maurushat, A. (2019). *Ethical hacking*. University of Ottawa Press.

Messier, R. (2024). *Learning Kali Linux: security testing, penetration testing & ethical hacking* (2nd ed.). O'Reilly Media, Inc.

Solomon, M., & Oriyano, S.-P. (2022). *Ethical hacking: techniques, tools, and countermeasures* (4th ed.). Jones & Bartlett Learning, LLC.

Trim, P. R. J., & Lee, Y.-I. (2025). *Cyber security management and strategic intelligence*. Routledge. DOI: 10.4324/9781003570905

KEY TERMS AND DEFINITIONS

Cyber Attack: An unauthorised action performed against computer infrastructure to compromise the confidentiality, integrity, or availability of the computer infrastructure's content.

Ethical Hacking: An authorised attempt to gain unauthorised access to a computer system, application, or data using the strategies and actions of malicious attackers. This way, it helps to identify security vulnerabilities that can then be resolved before a malicious attacker has the opportunity to exploit them.

Penetration Testing: An authorised simulated cyber attack on a computer system, performed to evaluate the security of the system.

Vulnerabilities: Flaws or weaknesses in the design, implementation, or management of a system that can be exploited by a malicious actor to compromise its security.

Compilation of References

Abdollahi, A., Arzandeh, S. B., & Sheibani, M. (2024). Privacy and safety of narrowband internet of things devices. *Telkomnika*, *22*(4), 969–975. DOI: 10.12928/telkomnika.v22i4.26279

Abduljalil, J. M., & Abduljalil, B. M. (2020). *Epidemiology, genome, and clinical features of the pandemic SARS-CoV-2: a recent view*. New Microb. New Infect., DOI: 10.1016/j.nmni.2020.100672

Abu-Shaqra, R. (2020). Technoethics and sensemaking: Risk assessment and knowledge management of Ethical Hacking in a sociotechnical society. [Doctoral dissertation, University of Ottowa]. DOI: 10.20381/ruor-24626

Aceto, G., Persico, V., & Pescapé, A. (2020). Industry 4.0 and health: Internet of things, big data, and cloud computing for Healthcare 4.0. *Journal of Industrial Information Integration*, *18*, 100129. DOI: 10.1016/j.jii.2020.100129

Adejumo, A., & Ogburie, C. (2025). The role of cybersecurity in safeguarding finance in a digital era. *World Journal of Advanced Research and Reviews, 25.*

Aftab, S. O., Ghouri, M. Z., Masood, M. U., Haider, Z., Khan, Z., Ahmad, A., & Munawar, N. (2020). Analysis of SARS-CoV-2 RNA-dependent RNA polymerase as a potential therapeutic drug target using a computational approach. *Journal of Translational Medicine*, *18*(1), 1–15. DOI: 10.1186/s12967-020-02439-0 PMID: 32635935

Agarwal, A., & Nene, M. J. (2025). Advancing Trustworthy AI: A Comparative Evaluation of AI Robustness Toolboxes. *SN Computer Science*, *6*(3), 1–16. DOI: 10.1007/s42979-025-03785-w

Ahmed, M., & Qamar, F. (2022). Automated penetration testing: Techniques and challenges. *International Journal of Cyber-Security and Digital Forensics*, *11*(1), 45–58.

Ahn, G. H., Kim, K., Park, W., & Shin, D. (2022). Malicious File Detection Method using Machine Learning and Interworking with MITRE ATT&CK Framework. *Applied Sciences (Basel, Switzerland), 12*(21), 10761. Advance online publication. DOI: 10.3390/app122110761

Ajami, R., & Dinh, A. V. (2011). Embedded Network Firewall on FPGA. *2011 Eighth International Conference on Information Technology: New Generations*, 1041-1043. DOI: 10.1109/ITNG.2011.178

Ali, A., Khan, M. A., Farid, K., Akbar, S. S., Taher, A. I., & Ghazal, M.. (2023). The effect of artificial intelligence on cybersecurity. *2023 International Conference on Business Analytics for Technology and Security (ICBATS)*, Dubai, United Arab Emirates, pp. 1–7. DOI: 10.1109/ICBATS57792.2023.10111151

Allen, B. (2022). *Practical cybersecurity architecture: A guide to creating and implementing robust designs for cybersecurity practitioners*. Packt Publishing.

Aloqaily, M., Kanhere, S., Bellavista, P., & Nogueira, M. (2022). Special issue on cybersecurity Management in the era of AI. *Journal of Network and Systems Management, 30*(3), 39–37. DOI: 10.1007/s10922-022-09659-3

Alotaibi, S., Mehmood, R., & Katib, I. (2020). The role of big data and twitter data analytics in healthcare supply chain management. *Smart Infrastructure and Applications: Foundations for Smarter Cities and Societies,* 267-279.

Alrahbi, D. A., Khan, M., Gupta, S., Modgil, S., & Jabbour, C. J. C. (2021). Health-care information technologies for dispersed knowledge management. *Journal of Knowledge Management*. Advance online publication. DOI: 10.1108/JKM-10-2020-0786

Al-Sinani, H. S., & Mitchell, C. J. (2024). *AI-augmented ethical hacking: A practical examination of manual exploitation and privilege escalation in Linux environments*. ACM Transactions on Privacy and Security, 27(1), Article 7.

Al-Sinani, H. S., & Mitchell, C. J. (2024). AI-enhanced ethical hacking: A Linux-focused experiment [Technical report]. arXiv. https://doi.org//arXiv.2410.05105DOI: 10.48550

Al-Sinani, H. S., & Mitchell, C. J. (2024). AI-enhanced ethical hacking: A Linux-focused experiment. *IEEE Transactions on Dependable and Secure Computing*.

Al-Sinani, H. S., Mitchell, C. J., Sahli, N., & Al-Siyabi, M. (2025). Unleashing AI in ethical hacking. In Martinelli, F., & Rios, R. (Eds.), Lecture Notes in Computer Science: Vol. 15235. *Security and trust management*. Springer., DOI: 10.1007/978-3-031-76371-7_10

Anandh, S. (2025). Ethical Hacking And Penetration Testing. *ERES International Journal of Computer Networks.*, *13*(4), 1–6. DOI: 10.62346/ijcn_q4_v13_no4_25_02

Andress, J. (2021). *The basics of information security: Understanding the fundamentals of InfoSec in theory and practice* (3rd ed.). Syngress.

Anthony, A. (2023). Cyber resilience must focus on marginalized individuals, not just institutions, carnegie endowment for international peace. Available at: https://carnegieendowment.org/research/2023/03/cyber-resilience-must-focus-on-marginalized-individuals-not-just-institutions?lang=en (Accessed July 2, 2024).

Arinze, C. A., Ajala, O. A., Okoye, C. C., Ofodile, O. C., & Daraojimba, A. I. (2024). *Evaluating the integration of advanced IT solutions for emission reduction in the oil and gas sector.* Engineering Science and Technology Journal., DOI: 10.51594/estj/v5i3.862

Armstrong, T. (2001, February 15). *Netcat – The TCP/IP Swiss Army Knife. SANS Institute.* https://www.sans.org/white-papers/952/

Asif, F., Sohail, F., Butt, Z. H., Nasir, F., & Asgar, N. (2024). Ethical hacking and its role in cybersecurity. *Journal of Network and Computer Applications.*

Attaullah, H. M., Memon, S., Erkan, O. F., & Khawar, R. (2024, January). IoT Based Systems and Services: Recent Security Concerns and Feasible Solutions. In 2024 IEEE 1st Karachi Section Humanitarian Technology Conference (KHI-HTC) (pp. 1-6). IEEE.

Au-Yong-Oliveira, M., Pesqueira, A., Sousa, M. J., Dal Mas, F., & Soliman, M. (2021). The potential of big data research in health care for medical doctors' learning. *Journal of Medical Systems*, *45*(1), 1–14. DOI: 10.1007/s10916-020-01691-7 PMID: 33409620

Awonuga, K. F., Nwankwo, E. E., Oladapo, J. O., Okoye, C. C., Odunaiya, O. G., & Uzondu, C. S. (2024). *Driving sustainable growth in SME manufacturing: The role of digital transformation, project, and capture management. International Journal of Science and Research Archives.* IJSRA., DOI: 10.30574/ijsra.2024.11.1.0270

Ayas, M. S., Ayas, S., & Djouadi, S. M. (2022). Projected Gradient Descent Adversarial Attack and Its Defense on a Fault Diagnosis System. *2022 45th International Conference on Telecommunications and Signal Processing, TSP 2022.* DOI: 10.1109/TSP55681.2022.9851334

Azadegan, A., Mellat Parast, M., Lucianetti, L., Nishant, R., & Blackhurst, J. (2020). Supply chain disruptions and business continuity: An empirical assessment. *Decision Sciences*, *51*(1), 38–73. DOI: 10.1111/deci.12395

Bacci, G., Picchi, O. M., Luise, M., Casali, C., & Andrenacci, M. (2024, September). Vulnerability of 3GPP's NB-IoT Standard in the Presence of Jamming: The Satellite Scenario. In 2024 IEEE 25th International Workshop on Signal Processing Advances in Wireless Communications (SPAWC) (pp. 486-490). IEEE.

Bajantri, G., & Shariff, N. (2024). Machine learning algorithms for robust software vulnerability detection. (2024) *International Conference on Innovation and Novelty in Engineering and Technology (INNOVA)*, 1–7. DOI: 10.1109/INNOVA63080.2024.10846984

Balch, J. A., Ruppert, M. M., Loftus, T. J., Guan, Z., Ren, Y., Upchurch, G. R., Ozrazgat-Baslanti, T., Rashidi, P., & Bihorac, A. (2023). Machine learning–enabled clinical information systems using fast healthcare interoperability resources data standards: Scoping review. *JMIR Medical Informatics*, *11*, e48297. DOI: 10.2196/48297 PMID: 37646309

Balding, B. (2021). *Practical cloud security: A guide for secure design and deployment*. O'Reilly Media.

Banerjee, A., Chakraborty, C., Kumar, A., & Biswas, D. (2020). Emerging trends in IoT and big data analytics for biomedical and health care technologies. *Handbook of data science approaches for biomedical engineering,* 121-152.

Baniecki, H., & Biecek, P. (2024). Adversarial attacks and defenses in explainable artificial intelligence: A survey. *Information Fusion, 107*, 102303. Advance online publication. DOI: 10.1016/j.inffus.2024.102303

Basak, S., Chatterjee, P., Biswas, D., Bhadra, P., & Das, R. (2024). Introduction to AI and ML Technologies and Their Potential Applications in Cybersecurity. In *Strategies for E-Commerce Data Security: Cloud, Blockchain, AI, and Machine Learning* (pp. 277-309). IGI Global. DOI: 10.4018/979-8-3693-6557-1.ch012

Basile, L. J., Carbonara, N., Pellegrino, R., & Panniello, U. (2022). Business intelligence in the healthcare industry: The utilization of a data-driven approach to support clinical decision making. *Technovation*. Advance online publication. DOI: 10.1016/j.technovation.2022.102482

Bello, A. B., Ogundipe, A. O., George, A. A., & Anifowose, O. (2025). The role of AI and machine learning in cybersecurity: Advancements in threat detection, anomaly detection and automated response. *International Journal of Science and Research Archive, 14*(2), 1587–1597. DOI: 10.30574/ijsra.2025.14.2.0542

Benson, T., & Grieve, G. (2021). *Principles of health interoperability*. Springer International. DOI: 10.1007/978-3-030-56883-2

Bergsten, S., & Rivas, P. (2019). Societal benefits and risks of artificial intelligence: a succinct survey. Available at: https://www.semanticscholar.org/paper/Societal-Benefits-and-Risks-of-Artificial-%3A-A-Bergsten-Rivas/fc38e40fd709429633b31436814334cc7edb0092 (Accessed July 4, 2024).

Bhatt, V., & Chakraborty, S. (2023). Improving service engagement in healthcare through internet of things based healthcare systems. *Journal of Science and Technology Policy Management, 14*(1), 53–73. DOI: 10.1108/JSTPM-03-2021-0040

Biancone, P., Secinaro, S., Marseglia, R., & Calandra, D. (2021). E-health for the future. Managerial perspectives using a multiple case study approach. *Technovation*. Advance online publication. DOI: 10.1016/j.technovation.2021.102406

Blauth, T. F., Gstrein, O. J., & Zwitter, A. (2022). Artificial Intelligence Crime: An Overview of Malicious Use and Abuse of AI. *IEEE Access : Practical Innovations, Open Solutions, 10*, 77110–77122. Advance online publication. DOI: 10.1109/ACCESS.2022.3191790

Blythe, M., Andersen, K., Clarke, P., Clarke, R., & Wright, P. C. (2016). 'Anti-solutionist strategies: seriously silly design fiction', In *Proceedings of the 2016 CHI conference on human factors in computing systems*. New York, NY, USA: Association for Computing Machinery (CHI '16), pp. 4968–4978. DOI: 10.1145/2858036.2858482

Böttinger, K., Godefroid, P., & Singh, R. (2018). Deep reinforcement fuzzing. 2018 IEEE Security and Privacy Workshops (SPW), 116–122. DOI: 10.1109/SPW.2018.00026

Bran, E., Rughini , C., Nadoleanu, G., & Flaherty, M. G. (2023). 'The emerging social status of generative AI: vocabularies of AI competence in public discourse', In 2023 24th International Conference on Control Systems and Computer Science (CSCS), Bucharest, Romania. DOI: 10.1109/CSCS59211.2023.00068

Calderon, R. (2019). The benefits of artificial intelligence in cybersecurity, economic crime forensics capstones. Available at: https://digitalcommons.lasalle.edu/ecf_capstones/36

Caldwell, T. (2011). Ethical hackers: Putting on the white hat. *Network Security, 2011*(7). DOI: 10.1016/S1353-4858(11)70075-7

Cambosuela, L., Kaur, M., & Astya, R. (2024, March). The vulnerabilities and risks of implementing internet of things (IoT) in cyber security. In 2024 11th International Conference on Reliability, Infocom Technologies and Optimization (Trends and Future Directions)(ICRITO) (pp. 1-5). IEEE.

Campoverde-Fordon, M., & Andersen, B. (2024). Analysis of LoRaWAN and NB-IoT for Critical and Massive Communication Check for updates. In The Seventh International Conference on Safety and Security with IoT: SaSeIoT 2023 (p. 35). Springer Nature.

Çaylı, O. (2024). *AI-enhanced cybersecurity: Vulnerability-based prevention, defense, and mitigation using generative AI*. Orclever Proceedings of Research and Development., DOI: 10.56038/oprd.v5i1.616

Cerchione, R., Centobelli, P., Riccio, E., Abbate, S., & Oropallo, E. (2023). Blockchain's coming to hospital to digitalise healthcare services: Designing a distributed electronic health record ecosystem. *Technovation*, *120*, 102480. DOI: 10.1016/j.technovation.2022.102480

Chacko, S., & Job, M. D. (2018, August). Security mechanisms and Vulnerabilities in LPWAN. [). IOP Publishing.]. *IOP Conference Series. Materials Science and Engineering*, *396*, 012027. DOI: 10.1088/1757-899X/396/1/012027

Chakraborty, D., & Paul, J. (2022). Healthcare apps' purchase intention: A consumption values perspective. *Technovation*. Advance online publication. DOI: 10.1016/j.technovation.2022.102481

Chao, K., Sarker, M. N. I., Ali, I., Firdaus, R. R., Azman, A., & Shaed, M. M. (2023). Big datadriven public health policy making: Potential for the healthcare industry. *Heliyon*, *9*(9), e19681. DOI: 10.1016/j.heliyon.2023.e19681 PMID: 37809720

Chatzopoulou, S., Eriksson, N. L., & Eriksson, D. (2020). Improving risk assessment in the European food safety authority: Lessons from the European Medicines Agency. *Frontiers in Plant Science*, *11*, 488663. DOI: 10.3389/fpls.2020.00349 PMID: 32318080

Chaudhari, B. S., Zennaro, M., & Borkar, S. (2020). LPWAN technologies: Emerging application characteristics, requirements, and design considerations. *Future Internet*, *12*(3), 46. DOI: 10.3390/fi12030046

Chauhan, R., Singh, R., Bartwal, R., Rawat, R., & Dhanalakshmi, R. (2024). An investigation of ethical hacking: White-hat hackers. *Challenges in Information, Communication and Computing Technology*, 769–774. DOI: 10.1201/9781003559085-132

Chen, J., Zhang, X., Zhang, R., Wang, C., & Liu, L. (2021). De-Pois: An Attack-Agnostic Defense against Data Poisoning Attacks. *IEEE Transactions on Information Forensics and Security*, *16*, 3412–3425. Advance online publication. DOI: 10.1109/TIFS.2021.3080522

Chen, Y., Sambo, Y. A., Onireti, O., & Imran, M. A. (2022). A survey on LPWAN-5G integration: Main challenges and potential solutions. *IEEE Access : Practical Innovations, Open Solutions, 10*, 32132–32149. DOI: 10.1109/ACCESS.2022.3160193

Chen, Y., Zhu, X., Gong, X., Yi, X., & Li, S. (2023). Data Poisoning Attacks in Internet-of-Vehicle Networks: Taxonomy, State-of-The-Art, and Future Directions. *IEEE Transactions on Industrial Informatics, 19*(1), 20–28. Advance online publication. DOI: 10.1109/TII.2022.3198481

Chiruvella, V., & Guddati, A. K. (2021). Ethical issues in patient data ownership. *Interactive Journal of Medical Research, 10*(2), e22269. DOI: 10.2196/22269 PMID: 34018968

Cisco. (2024). *What Is Social Engineering in Cyber Security?* https://www.cisco.com/c/en/us/products/security/what-is-social-engineering.html

Cobianchi, L., Dal Mas, F., & Angelos, P. (2021). One size does not fit all–translating knowledge to bridge the gaps to diversity and inclusion of surgical teams. *Annals of Surgery, 273*(2), e34–e36. DOI: 10.1097/SLA.0000000000004604 PMID: 33201134

Cobianchi, L., Dal Mas, F., Peloso, A., Pugliese, L., Massaro, M., Bagnoli, C., & Angelos, P. (2020). Planning the full recovery phase: An antifragile perspective on surgery after COVID-19. *Annals of Surgery, 272*(6), e296–e299. DOI: 10.1097/SLA.0000000000004489 PMID: 32941268

Cobianchi, L., Pugliese, L., Peloso, A., Dal Mas, F., & Angelos, P. (2020). To a new normal: Surgery and COVID-19 during the transition phase. *Annals of Surgery, 272*(2), e49–e51. DOI: 10.1097/SLA.0000000000004083 PMID: 32675493

Coccia, M. (2020). Global Encyclopedia of Public Administration, Public Policy, and Governance. *Springer Nature Switzerland AG.* Disruptive technologies for industrial and corporate change; pp. 1–7.

Coleman, C. (2021). *The art of network penetration testing*. No Starch Press.

Colombo, F., Oderkirk, J., & Slawomirski, L. (2020). Health information systems, electronic medical records, and big data in global healthcare: Progress and challenges in oecd countries. *Handbook of Global Health,* 1-31

Conklin, A., White, G. B., Cothren, C., Williams, R. L., & Davis, D. (2018). *Principles of computer security: CompTIA Security+ and beyond* (5th ed.). McGraw-Hill Education.

Cozzoli, N., Salvatore, F. P., Faccilongo, N., & Milone, M. (2022). How can big data analytics be used for healthcare organization management? Literary framework and future research from a systematic review. *BMC Health Services Research, 22*(1), 809. DOI: 10.1186/s12913-022-08167-z PMID: 35733192

Dai, T., & Tayur, S. (2020). Healthcare operations management: A snapshot of emerging research. *Manufacturing & Service Operations Management, 22*(5), 869–887. DOI: 10.1287/msom.2019.0778

Debicha, I., Cochez, B., Kenaza, T., Debatty, T., Dricot, J. M., & Mees, W. (2023). Adv-Bot: Realistic adversarial botnet attacks against network intrusion detection systems. *Computers & Security, 129*, 103176. Advance online publication. DOI: 10.1016/j.cose.2023.103176

Desetty, A. G. (2024). *Unveiling Hidden Threats with ML-Powered User and Entity Behavior Analytics (UEBA). Turkish Journal of Computer and Mathematics Education.* TURCOMAT., DOI: 10.61841/turcomat.v15i1.14394

Deviant Ollam. (2021). *Practice makes perfect: Lockpicking, red teaming, and hacker culture*. No Starch Press.

Dhanjani, N. (2015). *Abusing the Internet of Things: Blackouts, Freakouts, and Stakeouts*. O'Reilly Media.

Ding, A. Y., De Jesus, G. L., & Janssen, M. (2019). Ethical hacking for IoT security: A first look into bug bounty programs and responsible disclosure. *Government Information Quarterly, 36*(2), 273–282.

Drago, C., Gatto, A., & Ruggeri, M. (2021). Telemedicine as technoinnovation to tackle COVID-19: A bibliometric analysis. *Technovation*. Advance online publication. DOI: 10.1016/j.technovation.2021.102417

Duggineni, S. S. (2023). *Data integrity as a code*. DIAC.

Durgaraju, S., Vel, D. V. T., & Madathala, H. (2025). The evolution of cyber threats and defenses: A review of innovations and challenges. 2025 6th International Conference on Mobile Computing and Sustainable Informatics (ICMCSI), 117–123. DOI: 10.1109/ICMCSI64620.2025.10883230

EC-Council. (2023). *Certified Ethical Hacker (CEH) v12 official courseware*. EC-Council Press.

Egbedion, G. (2024). Impact Of Vulnerability Management And Penetration Testing On Security-Informed It Project Planning And Implementation. *Journal of Engineering Science and Technology., 11*, 16821–16828.

El Houda, Z. A. (2024). Cyber Threat Actors Review: Examining the Tactics and Motivations of Adversaries in the Cyber Landscape. In *Cyber Security for Next-Generation Computing Technologies*. DOI: 10.1201/9781003404361-5

Enck, W., Gilbert, P., Chun, B. G., Cox, L. P., Jung, J., McDaniel, P., & Sheth, A. N. (2014). TaintDroid: An information-flow tracking system for realtime privacy monitoring on smartphones. [TOCS]. *ACM Transactions on Computer Systems*, *32*(2), 1–29. DOI: 10.1145/2619091

Engström, V., & Lagerström, R. (2022). Two Decades of Cyberattack Simulations: A Systematic Literature Review. *Computers & Security*, *116*, 102681. Advance online publication. DOI: 10.1016/j.cose.2022.102681

ENISA. (2019). *Red Teaming - Threat-led Penetration Testing*. https://www.enisa.europa.eu/publications/threat-led-penetration-testing

Eshita, M., Ashutosh, G., & Nidhi, G. (2016). Artificial Intelligence Impact on Cyber Security. *Journal of Management and IT*, *7*, 100–107.

European Union. (2016). *General Data Protection Regulation (GDPR)*. https://eur-lex.europa.eu/eli/reg/2016/679/oj

Fahy, N., Mauer, N., & Panteli, D. (2021). *European support for improving health and care systems.*

Fan, L., Khairuddin, A. S. M., Liu, H., & Hasikin, K. B. (2025). Perceptual Carlini-Wagner Attack: A Robust and Imperceptible Adversarial Attack Using LPIPS. *IEEE Access : Practical Innovations, Open Solutions*, *13*, 1–1. DOI: 10.1109/ACCESS.2025.3588113

Fast, E., & Horvitz, E. (2017). Long-term trends in the public perception of artificial intelligence. Proc. AAAI Conf. Artif. Intell. 31, 963–969. DOI: 10.1609/aaai.v31i1.10635

Filipovich, I., & Kovalev, V. (2023). Dependence of the results of adversarial attacks on medical image modality, attack type, and defense methods. *Diagnostic Biomedical Signal and Image Processing Applications with Deep Learning Methods*, 179–195. DOI: 10.1016/B978-0-323-96129-5.00004-4

Flannery, B. T., Sandler, H. M., Lal, P., Feldman, M. D., Santa-Rosario, J. C., Pathak, T., Mirtti, T., Farre, X., Correa, R., Chafe, S., Shah, A., Efstathiou, J. A., Hoffman, K., Hallman, M. A., Straza, M., Jordan, R., Pugh, S. L., Feng, F., & Madabhushi, A. (2025). Stress testing deep learning models for prostate cancer detection on biopsies and surgical specimens. *The Journal of Pathology*, *265*(2), 146–157. DOI: 10.1002/path.6373 PMID: 39660731

Flother, F., Moose, C., & Tavernelli, I. (2020). IBM Institute for Business Value-Institute for Business Value. *Expert Insights Exploring Quantum Computing Use Cases for Life Sciences: Decoding Secrets of Genomes, Drugs, and Proteins.*https://www.ibm.com/downloads/cas/EVBKAZGJ

Fortes, P. R. B., Baquero, P. M., & Amariles, D. R. (2022). Artificial intelligence risks and algorithmic regulation. *European Journal of Risk Regulation, 13*(3), 357–372. DOI: 10.1017/err.2022.14

Gamal, A., Barakat, S., & Rezk, A. (2021). Standardised electronic health record data modeling and persistence: A comparative review. *Journal of Biomedical Informatics, 114*, 103670. DOI: 10.1016/j.jbi.2020.103670 PMID: 33359548

Ganesan, S., Shanmugaraj, G., & Indumathi, A. (2023). A Survey of Data Mining and Machine Learning-Based Intrusion Detection System for Cyber Security. *Risk Detection and Cyber Security for the Success of Contemporary Computing*, 52-74.

Ghimire, S., & Thapaliya, S. (2024). Al-driven cybersecurity: Mitigating prompt injection attacks through adversarial machine learning. *NPRC Journal of Multidisciplinary Research, 1*(8), 63–69. DOI: 10.3126/nprcjmr.v1i8.73029

Gong, C., & Ribiere, V. (2020). Developing a unified definition of digital transformation. *Technovation*. Advance online publication. DOI: 10.1016/j.technovation.2020.102217

Gong, X., Chen, Y., Wang, Q., & Kong, W. (2023). Backdoor Attacks and Defenses in Federated Learning: State-of-the-Art, Taxonomy, and Future Directions. *IEEE Wireless Communications, 30*(2), 114–121. Advance online publication. DOI: 10.1109/MWC.017.2100714

Gopalsamy, M., & Dastageer, B. (2025). The Role of Ethical Hacking and AI in Proactive Cyber Defense. *Current Approaches and Future Perspectives., 10*, 482–489. DOI: 10.5281/zenodo.14916984

Gracious, L. A. (2025). The Convergence of Artificial Intelligence and Cybersecurity: Technologies, Challenges, and Future Directions. In *Deep Learning Innovations for Securing Critical Infrastructures* (pp. 463–476). IGI Global Scientific Publishing. DOI: 10.4018/979-8-3373-0563-9.ch028

Grigorescu, O., Nica, A., Dascalu, M., & Rughinis, R. (2022). CVE2ATT&CK: BERT-Based Mapping of CVEs to MITRE ATT&CK Techniques. *Algorithms, 15*(9), 314. DOI: 10.3390/a15090314

Grimes, R. A. (2021). *Hacking the hacker: Learn from the experts who take down hackers*. Wiley.

Guo, N., Li, X., Yin, H., & Gao, Y. (2019). VulHunter: An automated vulnerability detection system based on deep learning and bytecode. In *Proceedings of the International Conference on Cloud Computing and Security* (pp. 199–218). DOI: 10.1007/978-3-030-41579-2_12

Gupta, B., Agrawal, D. P., & Yamaguchi, S. (2022). *Handbook of computer networks and cybersecurity*. Springer.

Hamed, O., Amer, M., & Bejaoui, T. (2024). Survey on advancements in machine learning for natural language processing. *2024 International Symposium on Networks, Computers and Communications (ISNCC)*, 1–6. DOI: 10.1109/ISNCC62547.2024.10759035

Hansen, J., Wilson, P., Verhoeven, E., Kroneman, M., Kirwan, M., Verheij, R., & van Veen, E.-B. (2021). *Assessment of the EU Member States' rules on health data in the light of GDPR*

Hansson, S. O., Belin, M. Å., & Lundgren, B. (2021). Self-Driving Vehicles—An Ethical Overview. *Philosophy & Technology*, *34*(4), 1383–1408. DOI: 10.1007/s13347-021-00464-5

Happe, A., & Cito, J. (2023). Understanding Hackers' Work: An Empirical Study of Offensive Security Practitioners. *ESEC/FSE 2023 - Proceedings of the 31st ACM Joint Meeting European Software Engineering Conference and Symposium on the Foundations of Software Engineering*. DOI: 10.1145/3611643.3613900

Hartzog, W., & Richards, N. (2020). *Privacy's constitutional moment and the limits of data protection.*

Haryono, S. A., Thung, F., Lo, D., Lawall, J., & Jiang, L. (2021). Characterization and automatic updates of deprecated machine-learning API usages. *2021 IEEE International Conference on Software Maintenance and Evolution (ICSME)*, 137–147. DOI: 10.1109/ICSME52107.2021.00019

Hashemzadeh, A., Avan, A., Ferns, G. A., & Khazaei, M. (2020). Vaccines based on virus-like nano-particles for use against Middle East Respiratory Syndrome (MERS) coronavirus. *Vaccine*, *38*(36), 5742–5746. DOI: 10.1016/j.vaccine.2020.07.003 PMID: 32684497

Hassan, M., Awan, F. M., Naz, A., deAndrés-Galiana, E. J., Alvarez, O., Cernea, A., Fernández-Brillet, L., Fernández-Martínez, J. L., & Kloczkowski, A. (2022). Innovations in genomics and big data analytics for personalized medicine and health care: A review. *International Journal of Molecular Sciences*, *23*(9), 4645. DOI: 10.3390/ijms23094645 PMID: 35563034

Heiding, F., Katsikeas, S., & Lagerström, R. (2023). Research communities in cyber security vulnerability assessments: A comprehensive literature review. *Computer Science Review*, *48*, 100551. Advance online publication. DOI: 10.1016/j.cosrev.2023.100551

He, L., Wang, Z., Yang, S., Liu, T., & Huang, Y. (2024). Generalizing Projected Gradient Descent for Deep-Learning-Aided Massive MIMO Detection. *IEEE Transactions on Wireless Communications*, *23*(3), 1827–1839. Advance online publication. DOI: 10.1109/TWC.2023.3292124

Helkala, K., Cook, J., Lucas, G., Pasquale, F., Reichberg, G., & Syse, H. (2023). AI in cyber operations: Ethical and legal considerations for end-users. In Sipola, T., Kokkonen, T., & Karjalainen, M. (Eds.), *Artificial intelligence and cybersecurity*. Springer., DOI: 10.1007/978-3-031-15030-2_9

Herzog, P. (2010). OSSTMM 3: *The Open Source Security Testing Methodology Manual (v3.0)*. https://www.isecom.org/OSSTMM.3.pdf

Holik, F., Horalek, J., Marik, O., Neradova, S., & Zitta, S. (2014). Effective penetration testing with Metasploit framework and methodologies. *Proceedings of 2014 IEEE 15th International Symposium on Computational Intelligence and Informatics (CINTI)* (pp. 237-242). DOI: 10.1109/CINTI.2014.7028682

Hossain, M. I., & Markendahl, J. I. (2021). Comparison of LPWAN technologies: Cost structure and scalability. *Wireless Personal Communications*, *121*(1), 887–903. DOI: 10.1007/s11277-021-08664-0

Hu, Q. (2021). A survey of adversarial example toolboxes. *Proceedings - 2021 2nd International Conference on Computing and Data Science, CDS 2021*, 603–608. DOI: 10.1109/CDS52072.2021.00109

Hu, Z., Beuran, R., & Tan, Y. (2020). Automated penetration testing using deep reinforcement learning. 2020 IEEE European Symposium on Security and Privacy Workshops (EuroS&PW), 2–10. DOI: 10.1109/EuroSPW51379.2020.00010

Hu, H., Salcic, Z., Sun, L., Dobbie, G., Yu, P. S., & Zhang, X. (2023). Membership Inference Attacks on Machine Learning: A Survey. *ACM Computing Surveys*, *54*(11s), 1–37. Advance online publication. DOI: 10.1145/3523273

Hutter, R., & Hutter, M. (2021). Chances and risks of artificial intelligence—A concept of developing and exploiting machine intelligence for future societies. *Applied System Innovation*, *4*(2), 1–19. DOI: 10.3390/asi4020037

Hu, W., Shao, C., & Zhang, W. (2025). Predicting U.S. bank failures and stress testing with machine learning algorithms. *Finance Research Letters*, *75*, 106802. DOI: 10.1016/j.frl.2025.106802

Ienca, M., & Vayena, E. (2020). On the responsible use of digital data to tackle the COVID-19 pandemic. *Nature Medicine*, *26*(4), 463–464. DOI: 10.1038/s41591-020-0832-5 PMID: 32284619

Iftikhar, U., Rashid, H., & Attaullah, H. M. (2025). Future Emerging Challenges and Innovations in Next Gen-Cybersecurity and Information Systems Security. In Rehman, F., Khan, I. U., Arshi, O., & Gupta, S. K. (Eds.), *Emerging Trends in Information System Security Using AI & Data Science for Next-Generation Cyber Analytics. Information Systems Engineering and Management* (Vol. 32). Springer., DOI: 10.1007/978-3-031-81481-5_12

Ilić, N., Dašić, D., Vucetic, M., Makarov, A., & Petrović, R. (2023). Distributed web hacking by adaptive consensus-based reinforcement learning. *Artificial Intelligence*, *326*, 104032. DOI: 10.1016/j.artint.2023.104032

Insecure.Org. (n.d.). *Nmap: the network mapper*. https://nmap.org

Iqbal, M., Abdullah, A. Y. M., & Shabnam, F. (2020, June). An application based comparative study of LPWAN technologies for IoT environment. In 2020 IEEE Region 10 Symposium (TENSYMP) (pp. 1857-1860). IEEE. DOI: 10.1109/TENSYMP50017.2020.9230597

Iridium Communications. (2024). Iridium makes strides in NB-IoT NTN with 3GPP Release 19 inclusion.

ITU-R. (2015). Framework and overall objectives of the future development of IMT for 2020 and beyond. Recommendation ITU-R M.2083-0.

Jacks, B. S., Ajala, O. A., Lottu, O. A., & Okafor, E. S.Boma Sonimiteim JacksOlakunle Abayomi AjalaOluwaseun Augustine LottuEnyinaya Stefano Okafor. (2024). Theoretical frameworks for ICT for development: Impact assessment of telecommunication infrastructure projects in Africa and the US. *World Journal of Advanced Research and Reviews*, *21*(3), 394–400. DOI: 10.30574/wjarr.2024.21.3.0721

Jambol, D. D., Sofoluwe, O. O., Ukato, A., & Ochulor, O. J. (2024). Enhancing oil and gas production through advanced instrumentation and control systems. *GSC Advanced Research and Reviews,* 19(3), 043-056

Jamil, D., & Khan, M. N. A. (2011). Is ethical hacking ethical. *International Journal of Engineering Science and Technology*, *3*(5), 3–758. DOI: 10.48175/IJARSCT-12421</jrn>

Joel, O. T., & Oguanobi, V. U. (2024a). Entrepreneurial leadership in startups and SMEs: Critical lessons from building and sustaining growth. *International Journal of Management & Entrepreneurship Research, 6*(5), 1441–1456. DOI: 10.51594/ijmer.v6i5.1093

Joel, O. T., & Oguanobi, V. U. (2024c). Leadership and management in high-growth environments: Effective strategies for the clean energy sector. *International Journal of Management & Entrepreneurship Research, 6*(5), 1423–1440. DOI: 10.51594/ijmer.v6i5.1092

Joel, O. T., & Oguanobi, V. U. (2024d). Navigating business transformation and strategic decision-making in multinational energy corporations with geodata. *International Journal of Applied Research in Social Sciences, 6*(5), 801–818. DOI: 10.51594/ijarss.v6i5.1103

Johnson, D., & Harris, T. (2021). *Implementing DevSecOps in the enterprise: A practical guide*. Springer.

Jyothsna, V., Sandhya, E., Kamalapuram, K. B., & Bhasha, P. (2025). AI-Driven Threat Detection in Cloud Environments. In Convergence of Cybersecurity and Cloud Computing (pp. 261-284). IGI Global Scientific Publishing.

Kabay, M. E. (2020). Ethical issues in cybersecurity. In Kabay, M. E. (Ed.), *Cybersecurity for dummies* (pp. 345–365). Wiley.

KaliLinux. (2025). *The most advanced penetration testing distribution*. https://www.kali.org/

Kardos, M., & Dexter, P. (2017). *A simple handbook for non-traditional red teaming*. https://www.dst.defence.gov.au/sites/default/files/publications/documents/DST-Group-TR-3335.pdf

Kathe, P. H., & Lotankar, A. P. (2020). "Penetration Testing: A Practical Guide." A practical resource outlining methodologies and best practices in penetration testing. DOI: https://www.doi.org/10.56726/IRJMETS62634

Khanam, S., Ahmedy, I. B., Idris, M. Y. I., Jaward, M. H., & Sabri, A. Q. B. M. (2020). A survey of security challenges, attacks taxonomy and advanced countermeasures in the internet of things. *IEEE Access : Practical Innovations, Open Solutions, 8*, 219709–219743. DOI: 10.1109/ACCESS.2020.3037359

Kim, D., & Solomon, M. G. (2022). *Fundamentals of information systems security* (4th ed.). Jones & Bartlett Learning.

Kirubai, J. C. D., & Priscila, S. S. (2024). Artificial Neural Network-Based Efficient Cyber Hacking Detection System Using Deep Learning Approaches. In Explainable AI Applications for Human Behavior Analysis (pp. 205-223). IGI Global.

Knowles, W., Prince, D., Hutchison, D., Disso, J. F. P., & Jones, K. (2015). A survey of cyber security management in industrial control systems. *International Journal of Critical Infrastructure Protection*, *9*, 52–80. DOI: 10.1016/j.ijcip.2015.02.002

Kolade, T. M., Obioha-Val, O. A., Balogun, A. Y., Gbadebo, M. O., & Olaniyi, O. O. (2025). AI-driven open-source intelligence in cyber defense: A double-edged sword for national security. *Asian Journal of Research in Computer Science*, *18*(1), 133–153. DOI: 10.9734/ajrcos/2025/v18i1554

Kong, Z., Xue, J., Wang, Y., Huang, L., Niu, Z., & Li, F. (2021). A Survey on Adversarial Attack in the Age of Artificial Intelligence. *Wireless Communications and Mobile Computing*, *2021*(1), 4907754. Advance online publication. DOI: 10.1155/2021/4907754

Kott, A., Wang, C., & Erbacher, R. (2022). *Cyber defense and situational awareness*. Springer.

Koushal, H., Kaur, R., & Kaur, C. (2025). *The relative review of machine learning in natural language processing (NLP)*. International Journal of Scientific Research in Computer Science, Engineering and Information Technology., DOI: 10.32628/CSEIT251112399

Kraemer, S., Carayon, P., & Duggan, R. (2004). Red Team Performance for Improved Computer Security. *Proceedings of the Human Factors and Ergonomics Society Annual Meeting*, *48*(14), 1605–1609. DOI: 10.1177/154193120404801410

Krishna, R. R., Priyadarshini, A., Jha, A. V., Appasani, B., Srinivasulu, A., & Bizon, N. (2021). State-of-the-art review on IoT threats and attacks: Taxonomy, challenges and solutions. *Sustainability (Basel)*, *13*(16), 9463. DOI: 10.3390/su13169463

Krupka, L., Vojtech, L., & Neruda, M. (2016, December). The issue of LPWAN technology coexistence in IoT environment. In 2016 17th International Conference on Mechatronics-Mechatronika (ME) (pp. 1-8). IEEE.

Kumar, S., Menezes, A., Giri, S., & Kotikela, S. D. (2024). What the phish! Effects of AI on phishing attacks and defense. International Conference on AI Research. DOI: 10.34190/icair.4.1.3224

Kumar, J. R. R., Bhalke, D. G., Nikam, S., & Chobe, S. (2023). Evaluation of the extent and demanding roles of ethical hacking in cybersecurity. *International Journal of Cybersecurity Intelligence and Cybercrime*, *6*(1), 21–33.

Kumawat, P. P. P. J. V. "Ethical Hacking: White Hat Hackers," in *SCRS Proceedings of International Conference of Undergraduate Students (SCRS)*, 2021. DOI:DOI: 10.48175/IJARSCT-12422

LA, A. G. (2026). Machine Learning for Threat Detection: A Comprehensive Survey on Anomaly Detection Techniques. *Improving Threat Detection, Network Security, and Incident Response With AI*, 235-268.

Lachkov, P., Tawalbeh, L., & Bhatt, S. (2022). Vulnerability assessment for applications security through penetration simulation and testing. *Journal of Web Engineering, 21*(7), 2187–2208. DOI: 10.13052/jwe1540-9589.2178

Lancieri, F. (2022). *Narrowing data protection's enforcement gap.*

Leslie, D., Rincón, C., Briggs, M., Perini, A., Jayadeva, S., Borda, A., Bennett, S. J., Burr, C., Aitken, M., Katell, M., Fischer, C., & Wong, J. (2024). AI fairness in practice. DOI: 10.2139/ssrn.4731838

Li, J. (2018). Cyber security meets artificial intelligence: A survey. *Frontiers of Information Technology & Electronic Engineering, 19*(12), 1462–1474. DOI: 10.1631/FITEE.1800573

Li, S., Surineni, K., & Prabhakaran, N. (2025). Kamalakar Surineni, Nishant Prabhakaran, Cyber-Attacks on Hospital Systems: A Narrative Review. *The American Journal of Geriatric Psychiatry. Open Science, Education, and Practice*, *7*, 30–39. DOI: 10.1016/j.osep.2025.03.002

Li, Y., Li, W., & Jiang, C. (2010). A survey of virtual machine systems: Current technology and future trends. *Proceedings of 2010 Third International Symposium on Electronic Commerce and Security* (pp. 332-336). DOI: 10.1109/ISECS.2010.80

Lomonaco, V., De Caro, V., Gallicchio, C., Carta, A., Sardianos, C., Varlamis, I., Tserpes, K., Coppola, M., Marmpena, M., Politi, S., Schoitsch, E., & Bacciu, D. (2023). AI-Toolkit: A microservices architecture for low-code decentralized machine intelligence. *2023 IEEE International Conference on Acoustics, Speech, and Signal Processing Workshops (ICASSPW)*, 1–5. DOI: 10.1109/ICASSPW59220.2023.10193222

Looi, J. C. L., Bonner, D., & Maguire, P. (2021). Maslow's hammer: Considering the perils of solutionism in mental healthcare and psychiatric practice. *Australasian Psychiatry, 29*(6), 687–689. DOI: 10.1177/10398562211005438 PMID: 34014790

Lu, T., Zhang, L., & Fu, Y. (2018). A novel immune-inspired shellcode detection algorithm based on hyperellipsoid detectors. *Security and Communication Networks, 2018*, 1–10. DOI: 10.1155/2018/2063089

Lutkevich, B. (2019). What is HIPAA (Health Insurance Portability and Accountability Act)? In *WhatIs.com*.

Luttgens, J., Pepe, M., & Mandia, K. (2016). *Incident response & computer forensics* (3rd ed.). McGraw-Hill Education.

Lyon, G. (2009). *Nmap Network Scanning: The Official Nmap Project Guide to Network Discovery and Security Scanning*. https://nmap.org/book/toc.html

Mahadev Madgule, N. (2023). Mechanical properties and microstructure of activated TIG welded similar joints of Inconel alloys by desirability approaches. *Materials Today: Proceedings*, *77*, 528–533. DOI: 10.1016/j.matpr.2022.12.250

Mandal, P. (2024). NB-IoT: Analytical Perspective of IP Data Delivery Variants. *Internet Technology Letters*, *7*(6), 594. DOI: 10.1002/itl2.594

Mani, V. (2022). *Strengthening cybersecurity with red team engagements.* https://www.isaca.org/resources/isaca-journal/issues/2022/volume-1/strengthening-cybersecurity-with-red-team-engagements

Marri, R., Varanasi, S., & Kalidindi Chaitanya, S. V. (2024). Integrating Security Information and Event Management (SIEM) with Data Lakes and AI: Enhancing Threat Detection and Response. Journal of Artificial Intelligence General Science. DOI: 10.60087/jaigs.v6i1.239

Martínez-Román, J. A., Gamero, J., Tamayo, J. A., & Delgado-González, L. (2020). Empirical analysis of organizational archetypes based on generation and adoption of knowledge and technologies. *Technovation*, *96-97*, 102145. Advance online publication. DOI: 10.1016/j.technovation.2020.102145

Martínez-Vergara S.J., Valls-Pasola J. (2020). Clarifying the disruptive innovation puzzle: a critical review. *Eur. J. Innovat. Manag.* .DOI: 10.1108/EJIM-07-2019-0198

Massaro, M. (2021). Digital transformation in the healthcare sector through blockchain technology. Insights from academic research and business developments. *Technovation*. Advance online publication. DOI: 10.1016/j.technovation.2021.102386

McKeown, A., Mourby, M., Harrison, P., Walker, S., Sheehan, M., & Singh, I. (2021). Ethical issues in consent for the reuse of data in health data platforms. *Science and Engineering Ethics*, *27*(1), 1–21. DOI: 10.1007/s11948-021-00282-0 PMID: 33538942

Mekki, K., Bajic, E., Chaxel, F., & Meyer, F. (2018, March). Overview of cellular LPWAN technologies for IoT deployment: Sigfox, LoRaWAN, and NB-IoT. In 2018 ieee international conference on pervasive computing and communications workshops (percom workshops) (pp. 197-202). IEEE.

Mekki, K., Bajic, E., Chaxel, F., & Meyer, F. (2019). A comparative study of LPWAN technologies for large-scale IoT deployment. *ICT Express*, *5*(1), 1–7. DOI: 10.1016/j.icte.2017.12.005

Melchiorre, M. G., Papa, R., Quattrini, S., Lamura, G., Barbabella, F., & Consortium, I. E. (2020). Integrated care programs for people with multimorbidity in European countries: eHealth adoption in health systems. *BioMed Research International*, *2020*(1), 2020. DOI: 10.1155/2020/9025326 PMID: 32337283

Mellado, D., Fernández-Medina, E., & Piattini, M. (2021). A systematic review of secure software development lifecycle models. *Computer Standards & Interfaces*, *82*, 103561. DOI: 10.1016/j.csi.2021.103561

Meriton, R., Bhandal, R., Graham, G., & Brown, A. (2021). An examination of the generative mechanisms of value in big data-enabled supply chain management research. *International Journal of Production Research*, *59*(23), 7283–7310. DOI: 10.1080/00207543.2020.1832273

Microsoft Security Response Center. (13 May 2017). *Customer Guidance for WannaCrypt attacks.* https://www.microsoft.com/en-us/msrc/blog/2017/05/customer-guidance-for-wannacrypt-attacks

Microsoft. (2020). *STRIDE threat model.* Microsoft Docs. https://learn.microsoft.com/en-us/security/compass/stride-threat-modeling

Mishra, R., Varshney, G., & Singh, S. (2025). Jailbreaking Generative AI: Empowering Novices to Conduct Phishing Attacks. ArXiv, abs/2503.01395. /arXiv.2503.01395DOI: 10.1109/DSN-S65789.2025.00022

Mmaduekwe, E. M., Stanley, U. M., Kessie, J. D., & Salawudeen, M. D. (2023). *Adversarial machine learning in cybersecurity: Mitigating evolving threats in AI-powered defense systems.* World Journal of Advanced Engineering Technology and Sciences., DOI: 10.30574/wjaets.2023.10.2.0294

Modesti, P., Golightly, L., Holmes, L., Opara, C., & Moscini, M. (2024). *Bridging the gap: A survey and classification of research-informed ethical hacking tools.* Computers & Security, Elsevier.

Mohammadian, H., Lashkari, A. H., & Ghorbani, A. A. (2024). Poisoning and evasion: Deep learning-based NIDS under adversarial attacks. *21st Annual International Conference on Privacy, Security and Trust (PST)*, 1–9. DOI: 10.1109/PST62714.2024.10788064

Mohammed, C. P., & Chopra, S. R. NB-IoT vs Lora: A Practical Analysis in Terms of Power Consumption. In *Intelligent Circuits and Systems for SDG 3–Good Health and well-being* (pp. 546–552). CRC Press. DOI: 10.1201/9781003521716-60

Mohurle, S., & Patil, M. (2017). A brief study of WannaCry threat: Ransomware attack 2017. *International Journal of Advanced Research in Computer Science*, *8*(5), 1938–1940.

Moore, T. (2021). *Cybersecurity law and regulation*. Routledge.

Moriniello, F., Martí-Testón, A., Muñoz, A., Silva Jasaui, D., Gracia, L., & Solanes, J. E. (2024). Exploring the relationship between the coverage of AI in WIRED magazine and public opinion using sentiment analysis. *Applied Sciences (Basel, Switzerland)*, *14*(5), 1994. DOI: 10.3390/app14051994

Mosse Cyber Security Institute. (2022, April). *Using Netcat as a Reverse Shell.* https://library.mosse-institute.com/articles/2022/04/using-netcat-as-a-reverse-shell/using-netcat-as-a-reverse-shell.html

Mullins, A., O'Donnell, R., Mousa, M., Rankin, D., Ben-Meir, M., Boyd-Skinner, C., & Skouteris, H. (2020). Health outcomes and healthcare efficiencies associated with the use of electronic health records in hospital emergency departments: A systematic review. *Journal of Medical Systems*, *44*(12), 200. DOI: 10.1007/s10916-020-01660-0 PMID: 33078276

Muthalagu, R., Malik, J., & Pawar, P. M. (2025). Detection and prevention of evasion attacks on machine learning models. *Expert Systems with Applications*, *266*, 126044. DOI: 10.1016/j.eswa.2024.126044

Nabi, F., Zhou, X., Iftikhar, U., & Attaullah, H. M. (2024). A Case Study of Cyber Subversion Attack based Design Flaw in Service Oriented Component Application Logic. *Journal of Cyber Security Technology*, *8*(3), 204–228. DOI: 10.1080/23742917.2023.2261169

Naik, N. (2018, October). LPWAN technologies for IoT systems: choice between ultra narrow band and spread spectrum. In 2018 IEEE international systems engineering symposium (ISSE) (pp. 1-8). IEEE.

Nandi, S., Bhaduri, S., Das, D., Ghosh, P., Mandal, M., & Mitra, P. (2024). Deciphering the lexicon of protein targets: A review on multifaceted drug discovery in the era of artificial intelligence. *Molecular Pharmaceutics*, *21*(4), 1563–1590. DOI: 10.1021/acs.molpharmaceut.3c01161 PMID: 38466810

Naqvi, S. M. A., Shabaz, M., Khan, M. A., & Hassan, S. I. (2023). Adversarial Attacks on Visual Objects Using the Fast Gradient Sign Method. *Journal of Grid Computing*, *21*(4), 52. Advance online publication. DOI: 10.1007/s10723-023-09684-9

Ng, K. H., & Bezak, E. (2020). Prejudice in science – lessons from the coronavirus story. *Physica Medica*, *75*, 83–84. DOI: 10.1016/j.ejmp.2020.06.011 PMID: 32559649

Nguyen, D. (2023). How news media frame data risks in their coverage of big data and AI. Internet Policy Review. Available at: https://policyreview.info/articles/analysis/how-news-media-frame-data-risks-big-data-and-ai (Accessed July 4, 2024).

Nguyen, D., & Hekman, E. (2024). The news framing of artificial intelligence: A critical exploration of how media discourses make sense of automation. *AI & Society*, *39*(2), 437–451. DOI: 10.1007/s00146-022-01511-1

NIST. (2020). Technical Guide to Information Security Testing and Assessment (SP 800-115). National Institute of Standards and Technology. DOI: 10.6028/NIST.SP.800-115

Niu, J., Liu, P., Zhu, X., Shen, K., Wang, Y., Chi, H., Shen, Y., Jiang, X., Ma, J., & Zhang, Y. (2024). A survey on membership inference attacks and defenses in machine learning. *Journal of Information and Intelligence*, *2*(5), 404–454. Advance online publication. DOI: 10.1016/j.jiixd.2024.02.001

Niu, J., Ma, X., Chen, Y., Zhang, G., He, Z., Hou, Z., Zhu, X., Wu, G., Chen, K., & Zhang, Y. (2022). A survey on membership inference attacks and defenses in Machine Learning. *Journal of Cybersecurity*, *7*(6). Advance online publication. DOI: 10.19363/J.cnki.cn10-1380/tn.2022.11.01

Northcutt, S. (2020). *Penetration testing fundamentals*. SANS Institute. https://www.sans.org/white-papers/pen-testing/

Ochulor, O. J., Sofoluwe, O. O., Ukato, A., & Jambol, D. D. (2024). Technological innovations and optimised work methods in subsea maintenance and production. *Engineering Science & Technology Journal*, *5*(5), 1627–1642. DOI: 10.51594/estj.v5i5.1112

Odeyemi, O., Mhlongo, N. Z., Nwankwo, E. E., Uzondu, C. S., & Okoye, C. C. (2024). *Big data applications in portfolio management: A review of techniques and strategies. International Journal of Science and Research Archives*. IJSRA., DOI: 10.30574/ijsra.2024.11.1.0268

Ofodile, O. C., Oyewole, A. T., Ugochukwu, C. E., Addy, W. A., Adeoye, O. B., & Okoye, C. C. (2024). *Predictive analytics in climate finance: Assessing risks and opportunities for investors*. GSC Advanced Research and Reviews., DOI: 10.30574/gscarr.2024.18.2.0076

Ogbodo, E. U., Abu-Mahfouz, A. M., & Kurien, A. M. (2022). A survey on 5G and LPWAN-IoT for improved smart cities and remote area applications: From the aspect of architecture and security. *Sensors (Basel)*, *22*(16), 6313. DOI: 10.3390/s22166313 PMID: 36016078

Oguanobi, V. U., & Joel, O. T. (2024). Scalable business models for startups in renewable energy: Strategies for using GIS technology to enhance SME scaling. *Engineering Science & Technology Journal*, *5*(5), 1571–1587. DOI: 10.51594/estj.v5i5.1109

Oladipo, J. O., Okoye, C. C., Elufioye, O. A., Falaiye, T., & Nwankwo, E. E. (2024). *Human factors in cybersecurity: Navigating the fintech landscape. International Journal of Science and Research Archives*. IJSRA., DOI: 10.30574/ijsra.2024.11.1.0258

Olatoye F. O., Elufioye O. A., Okoye C. C., Nwankwo E. E., & Oladapo O. O. (2024). Leadership styles and their impact on healthcare management effectiveness: A review. *International Journal of Science and Research Archives (IJSRA)*. DOI: DOI: 10.30574/ijsra.2024.11.1.0271

Oriekhoe O. I., Addy W. A., Okoye C. C., Oyewole A. T., Ofodile O. C. & Ugochukwu C. E. (2024). The role of accounting in mitigating food supply chain risks and food price volatility. *International Journal of Science and Research Archives (IJSRA)*. DOI: DOI: 10.30574/ijsra.2024.11.1.0340

Ouchchy, L., Coin, A., & Dubljević, V. (2020). AI in the headlines: The portrayal of the ethical issues of artificial intelligence in the media. *AI & Society*, *35*(4), 927–936. DOI: 10.1007/s00146-020-00965-5

OWASP Foundation. (2023). *OWASP testing guide v4*. https://owasp.org/www-project-web-security-testing-guide/

Padmanaban, H. (2024). Navigating the Complexity of Regulations: Harnessing AI/ML for Precise Reporting. *Journal of Artificial Intelligence General science (JAIGS)*, 3(1), 49-61.

Page, J., Bain, M., & Mukhlish, F. (2018). *'The risks of low level narrow artificial intelligence', in 2018 IEEE international conference on intelligence and safety for robotics (ISR). 2018 IEEE international conference on intelligence and safety for robotics.* ISR.

Pan, Z., Yu, W., Yi, X., Khan, A., Yuan, F., & Zheng, Y. (2019). Recent Progress on Generative Adversarial Networks (GANs): A Survey. *IEEE Access : Practical Innovations, Open Solutions*, *7*, 36322–36333. Advance online publication. DOI: 10.1109/ACCESS.2019.2905015

Paradhi, D., Ansari, M. N., & More, S. (2024). Anomaly detection in network traffic using unsupervised machine learning. International Journal of Advanced Research in Science. *Tongxin Jishu*, 418–425. Advance online publication. DOI: 10.48175/IJARSCT-19264

Patel, A., Vyas, A., & Bhatia, K. (2023). *Offensive automation in cybersecurity: Building tools and scripting techniques.* Packt Publishing.

Patil, S., Jangra, A., Bhale, M., Raina, A., & Kulkarni, P. "Ethical hacking: The need for cyber security.," in *IEEE International Conference on Power, Control, Signals and Instrumentation Engineering (ICPCSI)*, Chennai, 2017. DOI: 10.1109/ICPCSI.2017.8391982

Patterson, C., Nurse, J., & Franqueira, V. (2023). Learning from cyber security incidents: A systematic review and future research agenda. *Computers & Security*, *132*, 103309. DOI: 10.1016/j.cose.2023.103309

PCI Security Standards Council. (2022). *Information supplement: Penetration testing guidance.* https://www.pcisecuritystandards.org/

Pérez-Castillo, R., Serrano, M. A., & Piattini, M. (2021). Software modernization to embrace quantum technology. *Advances in Engineering Software*, *151*, 102933. Advance online publication. DOI: 10.1016/j.advengsoft.2020.102933

Perez-Pozuelo, I., Spathis, D., Clifton, E. A., & Mascolo, C. (2021). Wearables, smartphones, and artificial intelligence for digital phenotyping and health. In *Digital health* (pp. 33–54). Elsevier. DOI: 10.1016/B978-0-12-820077-3.00003-1

Perez-Pozuelo, I., Spathis, D., Gifford-Moore, J., Morley, J., & Cowls, J. (2021). Digital phenotyping and sensitive health data: Implications for data governance. *Journal of the American Medical Informatics Association : JAMIA*, *28*(9), 2002–2008. DOI: 10.1093/jamia/ocab012 PMID: 33647989

Postel, J. (1980). *User Datagram Protocol.* https://datatracker.ietf.org/doc/html/rfc768

Postel, J. (1981). *Transmission Control Protocol.* https://datatracker.ietf.org/doc/html/rfc793

Prabhu, D., & Sudha, L. MR, P. K., Adaikkammai, A., Aparna, P., & Sathya, V. (2025). Machine Learning in Cybersecurity: Challenges, Applications, and Future Directions. *Exploiting Machine Learning for Robust Security*, 25-48.

Prasad, N., Diro, A., Warren, M., & Fernando, M. (2025). A survey of cyber threat attribution: Challenges, techniques, and future directions. *Computers & Security, 157*, 104606. DOI: 10.1016/j.cose.2025.104606

Prümmer, J., van Steen, T., & van den Berg, B. (2024). A systematic review of current cybersecurity training methods. *Computers & Security, 136*, 103585. Advance online publication. DOI: 10.1016/j.cose.2023.103585

PTES. (2014). *Penetration Testing Execution Standard (PTES).* http://www.pentest-standard.org/index.php/Main_Page

Pu, G., Wang, L., Shen, J., & Dong, F. (2021). A hybrid unsupervised clustering-based anomaly detection method. *Tsinghua Science and Technology, 26*(2), 146–153. Advance online publication. DOI: 10.26599/TST.2019.9010051

Qiu, S., Liu, Q., Zhou, S., & Wu, C. (2019). Review of artificial intelligence adversarial attack and defense technologies. In *Applied Sciences (Switzerland)* (Vol. 9, Issue 5). DOI: 10.3390/app9050909

Rajalingam, R., & Kavitha, K. (2024). Original Research Article An efficient network optimized machine learning architecture framework for detection of malwares in IOT (NB-IOT) systems. *Journal of Autonomous Intelligence, 7*(5).

Rajamäki, J., McMenamin, S., & Tiitta, K. (2024). The importance of open-source intelligence in assessing risks of cyberattacks. Information & Security. *International Journal (Toronto, Ont.), 55*(1), 15–31. DOI: 10.11610/isij.5511

Ramakrishnan, T., Mohan Gift, M. D., Chitradevi, S., Jegan, R., & Subha Hency Jose, P. Nagaraja, Rajneesh Sharma H.N., Selvakumar P., Sintayehu Mekuria Hailegiorgis, (2022). "Study of Numerous Resins Used in Polymer Matrix Composite Materials", Advances in Materials Science and Engineering, vol. 2022, Article ID 1088926, 8 pages, 2022. DOI: 10.1155/2022/1088926

Ramalingam, R., Arthi, K., Bhavani, M. M., & Sunitha, T. (2025). AI-Enhanced Security Information and Event Management (SIEM) System. In *Deep Learning Innovations for Securing Critical Infrastructures* (pp. 75-94). IGI Global Scientific Publishing.

Rapid7. (2018). *VSFTPD v2.3.4 Backdoor Command Execution*. https://www.rapid7.com/db/modules/exploit/unix/ftp/vsftpd_234_backdoor/

Rapid7. (n.d.). *Metasploit Framework*. https://www.metasploit.com/

Rayhan, A. (2024). The Role of Ethical Hacking in Modern Cybersecurity Practices. DOI: 10.13140/RG.2.2.16619.55841

Rehman, A., Naz, S., & Razzak, I. (2022). Leveraging big data analytics in healthcare enhancement: Trends, challenges and opportunities. *Multimedia Systems*, *28*(4), 1339–1371. DOI: 10.1007/s00530-020-00736-8

Ribeiro, D., Fonte, V., Ramos, L. F., & Silva, J. M. (2025). Assessing the information security posture of online public services worldwide: Technical insights, trends, and policy implications. *Government Information Quarterly*, *42*(2), 102031. Advance online publication. DOI: 10.1016/j.giq.2025.102031

Richardson, T., Stafford-Fraser, Q., Wood, K. R., & Hopper, A. (1998). Virtual Network Computing. *IEEE Internet Computing*, *2*(1), 33–38. DOI: 10.1109/4236.656066

Rigaki, M., & Garcia, S. (2024). A Survey of Privacy Attacks in Machine Learning. *ACM Computing Surveys*, *56*(4), 1–34. Advance online publication. DOI: 10.1145/3624010

Rodríguez Llerena, A. E. (2020). Fundamental Tools for Ethical Hacking. http: // scielo. sld.cu/pdf/rcim/v12n1/1684 - 1859 - rcim - 12 - 01 - 116.pdf

Roger, A. (2021). *Grimes, "Brute-Force Attacks," in Hacking Multifactor Authentication*. Wiley., DOI: 10.1002/9781119672357.ch14

Rohde & Schwarz. (2023). NB-IoT and 3GPP evolution white paper. https://www.rohde-schwarz.com (navigate via search: "NB-IoT Release 18")

Rubio-Aparicio, J., Cerdan-Cartagena, F., Suardiaz-Muro, J., & Ybarra-Moreno, J. (2019). Design and implementation of a mixed IoT LPWAN network architecture. *Sensors (Basel)*, *19*(3), 675. DOI: 10.3390/s19030675 PMID: 30736405

Ruckenstein, M., & Pantzar, M. (2018). Beyond the quantified self: Thematic exploration of a dataistic paradigm. *New Media & Society*, *19*(3), 401–418. DOI: 10.1177/1461444815609081

Rughini , C., & Flaherty, M. G. (2022). The social bifurcation of reality: Symmetrical construction of knowledge in lay science-distrusting and science-trusting discourses. *Frontiers in Sociology*, *7*, 782851. DOI: 10.3389/fsoc.2022.782851 PMID: 35224088

Rusdan, D., Manurung, R., & Genta, G. (2020). *Information Systems Security Assessment Framework*. ISSAF.

Saxena, D., & Cao, J. (2021). Generative Adversarial Networks (GANs). In *ACM Computing Surveys* (Vol. 54, Issue 3). DOI: 10.1145/3446374

Scarfone, K., & Mell, P. (2007). *Guide to Intrusion Detection and Prevention Systems (IDPS)*. https://nvlpubs.nist.gov/nistpubs/Legacy/SP/nistspecialpublication800-94 .pdf DOI: 10.6028/NIST.SP.800-94

Seara, J. P., & Serrão, C. (2024). Automation of System Security Vulnerabilities Detection Using Open-Source Software. *Electronics (Basel)*, *13*(5), 873. DOI: 10.3390/electronics13050873

Sestino, A., Prete, M. I., Piper, L., & Guido, G. (2020). Internet of Things and Big Data as enablers for business digitalization strategies. *Technovation*, *98*, 102173. Advance online publication. DOI: 10.1016/j.technovation.2020.102173

Shanthi, R. R., Sasi, N. K., & Gouthaman, P. (2023). *A new era of cybersecurity: the influence of artificial intelligence. 2023 international conference on networking and communications*. ICNWC.

Sharma, P., & Gupta, H. (2024). Emerging Cyber Security Threats and Security Applications in Digital Era. In *2024 11th International Conference on Reliability, Infocom Technologies and Optimization (Trends and Future Directions)(ICRITO)* (pp. 1-6). IEEE. DOI: 10.1109/ICRITO61523.2024.10522181

Sharma, M., & Ravichandra, S. (2023). Design and Implementation of a Mechanism to Identify and Defend Against ARP Spoofing. *Proceedings of 2023 14th International Conference on Computing Communication and Networking Technologies (ICCCNT)* (pp. 1-6). IEEE. DOI: 10.1109/ICCCNT56998.2023.10308362

Sharpe, R., Warnicke, E., & Lamping, U. (2024). *Wireshark user's guide (Version 4.2)*. https://www.wireshark.org/docs/wsug_html_chunked/

Shaygan, A., & Daim, T. (2021). Technology management maturity assessment model in healthcare research centers. *Technovation*. Advance online publication. DOI: 10.1016/j.technovation.2021.102444

Shinde, S. S., & Shivalkar, S. J. (2025). AI to predict zero day vulnerabilities. [IJSREM]. *International Journal of Scientific Research in Engineering and Management*, *9*(1), 1–9. DOI: 10.55041/IJSREM40510

Shostack, A. (2014). *Threat modeling: Designing for security*. Wiley.

Shrivastava, U., Song, J., Han, B. T., & Dietzman, D. (2021). Do data security measures, privacy regulations, and communication standards impact the interoperability of patient health information? A cross-country investigation. *International Journal of Medical Informatics, 148*, 104401. DOI: 10.1016/j.ijmedinf.2021.104401 PMID: 33571743

Shubham, , & Sodhi, , R. SKaur, , P. (2024). Measures and security to avoid ethical hacking. *International Journal of Information Security and Privacy, 18*(1), 11–20.

Shubham, , & Sodhi, , R. SKaur, , P. (2024). Measures and security to avoid ethical hacking. *Journal of Information Security Research, 13*(1), 44–51.

Siddiq, M. (2022). Use of machine learning to predict patient developing a disease or condition for early diagnose. *International Journal of Multidisciplinary Sciences and Arts, 1*(1). Advance online publication. DOI: 10.47709/ijmdsa.v1i1.2271

Singh, R., Tripathi, P., & Singh, R. (2014). A Survey on TCP (Transmission Control Protocol) and UDP (User Datagram Protocol) over AODV Routing Protocol. *International Journal of Research, 1*(7), 26–33.

Sinha, A. R., Singla, K., & Victor, T. M. M. (2023). Artificial intelligence and machine learning for cybersecurity applications and challenges. *Risk Detection and Cyber Security for the Success of Contemporary Computing*, 109-146.

Skoudis, E., & Liston, T. (2021). *Counter hack reloaded: A step-by-step guide to computer attacks and effective defenses* (2nd ed.). Pearson Education.

Snyder, C. (2021). *Cybersecurity incident response: How to contain, eradicate, and recover from incidents*. Apress.

Song, Y., Lin, J., Tang, M., & Dong, S. (2017). An Internet of energy things based on wireless LPWAN. *Engineering (Beijing), 3*(4), 460–466. DOI: 10.1016/J.ENG.2017.04.011

Spanò, R., Massaro, M., & Iacuzzi, S. (2021). Blockchain for value creation in the healthcare sector. *Technovation*. Advance online publication. DOI: 10.1016/j.technovation.2021.102440

Sreenivasulu, A., & Manimozhi, T. Satheesh kumar P. and Singh P.,(2022). "The Model of Smart Sensing Device For Sensitive Nanoclusters Modification in Sensing Properties," 2022 2nd International Conference on Advance Computing and Innovative Technologies in Engineering (ICACITE), Greater Noida, India, 2022, pp. 1043-1047, DOI: 10.1109/ICACITE53722.2022.9823846

Stanco, G., Navarro, A., Frattini, F., Ventre, G., & Botta, A. (2024). A comprehensive survey on the security of low power wide area networks for the Internet of Things. *ICT Express, 10*(3), 519–552. DOI: 10.1016/j.icte.2024.03.003

Stanger, J. (2023). *CompTIA PenTest+ Certification All-in-One Exam Guide (Exam PT0-002)*. McGraw-Hill Education.

Stephanie, L., & Sharma, R. S. (2020). Digital health eco-systems: An epochal review of practice-oriented research. *International Journal of Information Management, 53*, 102032. Advance online publication. DOI: 10.1016/j.ijinfomgt.2019.10.017

Stewart, J. M., Chapple, M., & Gibson, D. (2021). *CISSP (ISC)2 Certified Information Systems Security Professional Official Study Guide* (9th ed.). Wiley.

Stilgoe, J. (2021). How can we know a self-driving car is safe? *Ethics and Information Technology, 23*(4), 635–647. DOI: 10.1007/s10676-021-09602-1

Stouffer, K., Falco, J., & Scarfone, K. (2015). *Guide to industrial control systems (ICS) security* (NIST Special Publication 800-82 Rev. 2). National Institute of Standards and Technology. DOI: 10.6028/NIST.SP.800-82r2

Strauß, S. (2018). From big data to deep learning: A leap towards strong AI or "Intelligentia Obscura"? *Big Data and Cognitive Computing, 2*(3), 16. DOI: 10.3390/bdcc2030016

Sugumaran, K. M. D., Pandiyarajan V., Y. B S, and M. S, (2024). "Analysis of Electromyography Signals for Control of Mechanical Prosthesis using Machine Learning Techniques," 2024 2nd International Conference on Intelligent Data Communication Technologies and Internet of Things (IDCIoT), Bengaluru, India, 2024, pp. 1059-1067, DOI: 10.1109/IDCIoT59759.2024.10467707

Suman, A., Suman, P., Padhy, S., & Qureshi, S. G. (2025). 16 Cyber Risk Management in IoT Security. Cyberology: An Optimized Approach to the Cyber-World, 264.

Sunku Mohan, V., Sankaran, S., Buyya, R., & Achuthan, K. (2025). Leveraging Fog Computing for Security-Aware Resource Allocation in Narrowband Internet of Things. *Software, Practice & Experience, 55*(4), 683–713. DOI: 10.1002/spe.3392

Suresh, H. (2023). *Pooja M R*. Ethical Framework for Cyber Security, Journal of Network Security and Data Mining., DOI: 10.5281/ZENODO.7550038

Syafitri, W., Shukur, Z., Mokhtar, U. A., Sulaiman, R., & Ibrahim, M. A. (2022). Social Engineering Attacks Prevention: A Systematic Literature Review. *IEEE Access : Practical Innovations, Open Solutions, 10*, 39325–39343. DOI: 10.1109/ACCESS.2022.3162594

Tamiminia, H., Salehi, B., Mahdianpari, M., Quackenbush, L., Adeli, S., & Brisco, B. (2020). Google Earth Engine for geo-big data applications: A meta-analysis and systematic review. *ISPRS Journal of Photogrammetry and Remote Sensing, 164*, 152–170. DOI: 10.1016/j.isprsjprs.2020.04.001

Tan, F. T. C., Ondrus, J., Tan, B., & Oh, J. (2020). Digital transformation of business ecosystems: Evidence from the Korean pop industry. *Information Systems Journal, 30*(5), 866–898. DOI: 10.1111/isj.12285

Tariq, M. U. (2024). Enhancing cybersecurity protocols in modern healthcare systems: Strategies and best practices. In *Transformative Approaches to Patient Literacy and Healthcare Innovation* (pp. 223–241). IGI Global. DOI: 10.4018/979-8-3693-3661-8.ch011

Tayefi, M., Ngo, P., Chomutare, T., Dalianis, H., Salvi, E., Budrionis, A., & Godtliebsen, F. (2021). Challenges and opportunities beyond structured data in analysis of electronic health records. *Wiley Interdisciplinary Reviews: Computational Statistics, 13*(6), e1549. DOI: 10.1002/wics.1549

TechTarget. (2023). *What is a zero-day vulnerability?* https://www.techtarget.com/searchsecurity/definition/zero-day-vulnerability

Teichmann, F. M., & Boticiu, S. R. (2023). An overview of the benefits, challenges, and legal aspects of penetration testing and red teaming. *International Cybersecurity Law Review, 4*(4), 387–397. Advance online publication. DOI: 10.1365/s43439-023-00100-2

Tenable, Inc. (2025). *Nessus vulnerability scanner.* https://www.tenable.com/products/nessus

Thapa, R., Sehl, B., Gupta, S., & Goyal, A. (2022). Security of operating system using the Metasploit framework by creating a backdoor from remote setup. *Proceedings of 2022 2nd International Conference on Advance Computing and Innovative Technologies in Engineering (ICACITE)* (pp. 2618-2620). DOI: 10.1109/ICACITE53722.2022.9823460

Tian, Z., Cui, L., Liang, J., & Yu, S. (2023). A Comprehensive Survey on Poisoning Attacks and Countermeasures in Machine Learning. *ACM Computing Surveys, 55*(8), 1–35. Advance online publication. DOI: 10.1145/3551636

Towett, G., Snead, R. S., Grigoryan, K., & Marczika, J. (2023). Geographical and practical challenges in the implementation of digital health passports for cross-border COVID-19 pandemic management: A narrative review and framework for solutions. *Globalization and Health*, *19*(1), 98. DOI: 10.1186/s12992-023-00998-7 PMID: 38066568

Truong, N. B., Sun, K., Lee, G. M., & Guo, Y. (2020). GDPR-Compliant Personal Data Management: A Blockchain-Based Solution. *IEEE Transactions on Information Forensics and Security*, *15*, 1746–1761. Advance online publication. DOI: 10.1109/TIFS.2019.2948287

U.S. Department of Health and Human Services. (2023). *HIPAA Security Rule*. https://www.hhs.gov/hipaa/for-professionals/security/index.html

Uddin, M. S. (2024). Addressing IoT Security Challenges through AI Solutions. *International Journal of Computer Applications*, *186*(45), 50–55. DOI: 10.5120/ijca2024924107

Ukato, A., Sofoluwe, O. O., Jambol, D. D., & Ochulor, O. J. (2024). Optimising maintenance logistics on offshore platforms with AI: Current strategies and future innovations.

Untawale, T. (2021). Importance of cyber security in digital era. *International Journal for Research in Applied Science and Engineering Technology*, *9*(8), 963–966. DOI: 10.22214/ijraset.2021.37519

Uzougbo, N. S., Ikegwu, C. G., & Adewusi, A. O. (2024). International enforcement of cryptocurrency laws: Jurisdictional challenges and collaborative solutions. *Magna Scientia Advanced Research and Reviews,* 11(1), 068-083

Vacca, J. R. (2020). *Computer and information security handbook* (4th ed.). Academic Press.

van Dijck, J. (2014). Datafication, dataism and dataveillance: Big data between scientific paradigm and ideology. *Surveillance & Society*, *12*(2), 197–208. DOI: 10.24908/ss.v12i2.4776

Varshney, M., Kumar, A., Ganguli, R., Umer, S., Sonkar, S. S., & Molla, N. (2023). Ethical hacking: Enhancing cybersecurity through offensive security practices. *Journal of Cybersecurity and Privacy*, *3*(2), 115–129.

Vásquez-Venegas, C., Wu, C., Sundar, S., Prôa, R., Beloy, F. J., Medina, J. R., McNichol, M., Parvataneni, K., Kurtzman, N., Mirshawka, F., Aguirre-Jerez, M., Ebner, D. K., & Celi, L. A. (2024). Detecting and Mitigating the Clever Hans Effect in Medical Imaging: A Scoping Review. *Journal of Imaging Informatics in Medicine*, *2024*(4), 1–17. DOI: 10.1007/s10278-024-01335-z PMID: 39643820

Verma, R. K. (2025). Enhancing Carbon Sequestration Monitoring Through Machine Learning: Challenges and Opportunities. *Advanced Systems for Monitoring Carbon Sequestration*, 301-320.

Verma, R. K., & Kishor, K. (2024). Innovative Solutions: Exploring Federated Learning-Based Resource Virtualization with AR Integration in Healthcare Environments. In *Federated Learning for Smart Communication using IoT Application* (pp. 155-177). Chapman and Hall/CRC.

Verma, R. K., Verma, R. K., Chaudhary, A., Bhati, H., & Bisht, G. (2025). "Advanced AI & ML Applications in Satellite Image Processing & Industry," *2025 3rd International Conference on Disruptive Technologies (ICDT)*, Greater Noida, India, pp. 66-69, DOI: 10.1109/ICDT63985.2025.10986339

Verma, R. K., & Kishor, K. (2024). Image processing applications in agriculture with the help of AI. In *Infrastructure Possibilities and Human-Centered Approaches With Industry 5.0* (pp. 162–181). IGI Global Scientific Publishing. DOI: 10.4018/979-8-3693-0782-3.ch010

Verma, R. K., Kishor, K., & Galletta, A. (2024). Federated Learning Shaping the Future of Smart City Infrastructure. In *Federated Learning for Smart Communication using IoT Application* (pp. 196–216). Chapman and Hall/CRC. DOI: 10.1201/9781003489368-10

Verma, R. K., Kishor, K., & Jha, S. K. (2024). Big Data Analytics in Bioinformatics and Healthcare. In *Applications of Parallel Data Processing for Biomedical Imaging* (pp. 25–43). IGI Global. DOI: 10.4018/979-8-3693-2426-4.ch002

Vijayakumar, G., Rajkumar, M., Rajiv Chandar, N., Selvakumar, P., & Duraisamy, R. (2024). Muniyandi Rajkumar, Rajiv Chandar N, Selvakumar P and Ramesh Duraisamy, (2024). Environmentally friendly TDS removal from waste water by electrochemical ion exchange batch-type recirculation (EIR) technique. *Environmental Science. Water Research & Technology*, *10*(4), 826–835. DOI: 10.1039/D3EW00793F

Villalón-Huerta, A., Ripoll-Ripoll, I., & Marco-Gisbert, H. (2022). A Taxonomy for Threat Actors' Delivery Techniques. *Applied Sciences (Basel, Switzerland)*, *12*(8), 3929. Advance online publication. DOI: 10.3390/app12083929

Villegas-Ch, W., Jaramillo-Alcázar, A., & Luján-Mora, S. (2024). Evaluating the Robustness of Deep Learning Models against Adversarial Attacks: An Analysis with FGSM, PGD and CW. *Big Data and Cognitive Computing 2024, Vol. 8, Page 8, 8*(1), 8. DOI: 10.3390/bdcc8010008

Wang, J., Huang, M., Nie, Y., & Li, J. (2021). Static analysis of source code vulnerability using machine learning techniques: A survey. 2021 4th International Conference on Artificial Intelligence and Big Data (ICAIBD), 76–86. DOI: 10.1109/ICAIBD51990.2021.9459075

Wang, H., Yu, B., Chen, X., & Yan, H. (2022). Global pattern and determinants of COVID-19 vaccine coverage and progression: a global ecological study. Soc. Sci. Electr. Publish. Pres. Soc. Sci. Res. Netw. DOI: 10.2139/ssrn.4046662

Wang, S., Ko, R. K. L., Bai, G., Dong, N., Choi, T., & Zhang, Y. (2024). Evasion Attack and Defense on Machine Learning Models in Cyber-Physical Systems: A Survey. *IEEE Communications Surveys and Tutorials, 26*(2), 930–966. Advance online publication. DOI: 10.1109/COMST.2023.3344808

Wang, Z., Li, S., Zhang, L., Hu, C., & Yan, L. (2024). A Red Team automated testing modeling and online planning method for post-penetration. *Computers & Security, 144*, 103945. DOI: 10.1016/j.cose.2024.103945

Wang, Z., Ma, J., Wang, X., Hu, J., Qin, Z., & Ren, K. (2023). Threats to Training: A Survey of Poisoning Attacks and Defenses on Machine Learning Systems. *ACM Computing Surveys, 55*(7), 1–36. Advance online publication. DOI: 10.1145/3538707

Weerasinghe, K., Scahill, S. L., Pauleen, D. J., & Taskin, N. (2022). Big data analytics for clinical decision-making: Understanding health sector perceptions of policy and practice. *Technological Forecasting and Social Change, 174*, 121222. DOI: 10.1016/j.techfore.2021.121222

Weidman, G. (2020). *Advanced penetration testing: Hacking the world's most secure networks*. No Starch Press.

Williams, P., Rojas, P., & Bayoumi, M. (2019, August). Security taxonomy in iot–a survey. In 2019 IEEE 62nd International Midwest Symposium on Circuits and Systems (MWSCAS) (pp. 560-565). IEEE. DOI: 10.1109/MWSCAS.2019.8884913

Williamson, S. M., & Prybutok, V. (2024). Balancing privacy and progress: A review of privacy challenges, systemic oversight, and patient perceptions in AI-Driven healthcare. *Applied Sciences (Basel, Switzerland), 14*(2), 675. DOI: 10.3390/app14020675

Wimelius, H., Mathiassen, L., Holmström, J., & Keil, M. (2021). A paradoxical perspective on technology renewal in digital transformation. *Information Systems Journal, 31*(1), 198–225. DOI: 10.1111/isj.12307

Winkler, I., & Gomes, A. (2022). *Advanced persistent security: A cyberwarfare approach to implementing adaptive enterprise protection, detection, and reaction strategies*. Syngress.

Xue, M., Yuan, C., Wu, H., Zhang, Y., & Liu, W. (2020). Machine Learning Security: Threats, Countermeasures, and Evaluations. *IEEE Access : Practical Innovations, Open Solutions, 8*, 74720–74742. Advance online publication. DOI: 10.1109/ACCESS.2020.2987435

Yaacoub, J. P. A., Noura, H. N., Salman, O., & Chehab, A. (2023). Ethical hacking for IoT: Security issues, challenges, solutions and recommendations. *Internet of Things and Cyber-Physical Systems, 3*, 280–308. DOI: 10.1016/j.iotcps.2023.04.002

Yamini, B. MAY, P. M. A., Shobana, R., TP, A., & Nalini, M. (2024, December). Cybersecurity: Strategies, Sector-Specific Challenges, and Future Prospects. In *2024 4th International Conference on Ubiquitous Computing and Intelligent Information Systems (ICUIS)* (pp. 1338-1345). IEEE.

Yanalitis, M. (2014). *Red Teaming: Approach, Rationale, and Risks*. https://www.researchgate.net/profile/Mark-Yanalitis-2/publication/259546738_Red_Teaming_Approach_Rationale_and_Risks/links/0c96052c6e6a18dd8e000000/Red-Teaming-Approach-Rationale-and-Risks.pdf

Yang, F., & Gu, S. (2021). Industry 4.0, a revolution that requires technology and national strategies. *Complex & Intelligent Systems, 7*(3), 1311–1325. DOI: 10.1007/s40747-020-00267-9

Yash, T., Dinki, , & Kumar, , SSharma, , K. (2022). *Ethical hacking: A technique to enhance information security*. In *Proceedings of the IEEE International Conference on Computing, Communication, and Intelligent Systems* (pp. 245–250). DOI: 10.1109/COM-IT-CON54601.2022.9850601

Young, A. (2023). *The pentester blueprint: Starting a career as an ethical hacker*. Wiley.

Yuan, X., Yang, C., He, Q., Chen, J., Yu, D., Li, J., Zhai, S., Qin, Z., Du, K., Chu, Z., & Qin, P. (2020). Current and perspective diagnostic techniques for COVID-19. *ACS Infectious Diseases, 6*(8), 1998–2016. DOI: 10.1021/acsinfecdis.0c00365 PMID: 32677821

Yulianto, S., Soewito, B., Gaol, F. L., & Kurniawan, A. (2025). Enhancing cybersecurity resilience through advanced red-teaming exercises and MITRE ATT&CK framework integration: A paradigm shift in cybersecurity assessment. *Cyber Security and Applications*, *3*, 100077. DOI: 10.1016/j.csa.2024.100077

Zardari, S., Nisar, N., Fatima, Z., & Dhirani, L. L. (2023, January). Iot–assets taxonomy, threats assessment and potential solutions. In *2023 Global Conference on Wireless and Optical Technologies (GCWOT)* (pp. 1-8). IEEE. DOI: 10.1109/GCWOT57803.2023.10064657

Zaydi, M., & Maleh, Y. (2025). EMPOWERING RED TEAMS WITH GENERATIVE AI: TRANSFORMING PENETRATION TESTING THROUGH ADAPTIVE INTELLIGENCE. *EDPACS*, *70*(2), 41–66. DOI: 10.1080/07366981.2024.2439628

Zeadally, S., Siddiqui, F., Baig, Z., & Ibrahim, A. (2020). Smart healthcare: Challenges and potential solutions using internet of things (IoT) and big data analytics. *PSU Research Review*, *4*(2), 149–168. DOI: 10.1108/PRR-08-2019-0027

Zhai, Y., Yan, J., Zhang, H., & Lu, W. (2020). Tracing the evolution of AI: Conceptualization of artificial intelligence in mass media discourse. *Information Discovery and Delivery*, *48*(3), 137–149. DOI: 10.1108/IDD-01-2020-0007

Zhang, D., Jain, K., & Singh, P. (2024). Guarding Against ChatGPT Threats: Identifying and Addressing Vulnerabilities. 2024 IEEE 7th International Conference on Multimedia Information Processing and Retrieval (MIPR), 612–615 DOI: 10.1109/MIPR62202.2024.00104

Zhang, A., Xing, L., Zou, J., & Wu, J. C. (2022). Shifting machine learning for healthcare from development to deployment and from models to data. *Nature Biomedical Engineering*, *6*(12), 1330–1345. DOI: 10.1038/s41551-022-00898-y PMID: 35788685

Zhang, J., Dongdong, C., Huang, Q., Liao, J., Zhang, W., Feng, H., Hua, G., & Yu, N. (2022). Poison Ink: Robust and Invisible Backdoor Attack. *IEEE Transactions on Image Processing*, *31*, 5691–5705. Advance online publication. DOI: 10.1109/TIP.2022.3201472 PMID: 36040942

Zhang, J., Qian, W., Nie, R., Cao, J., & Xu, D. (2023). Generate adversarial examples by adaptive moment iterative fast gradient sign method. *Applied Intelligence*, *53*(1), 1101–1114. Advance online publication. DOI: 10.1007/s10489-022-03437-z

Zhang, K., Yuan, X., & Lu, W. (2021). *Embedded system security: Threats, vulnerabilities, and countermeasures*. Elsevier.

Zhang, Z., Liu, Q., Huang, Z., Wang, H., Lee, C. K., & Chen, E. (2023). Model Inversion Attacks Against Graph Neural Networks. *IEEE Transactions on Knowledge and Data Engineering*, *35*(9), 8729–8741. Advance online publication. DOI: 10.1109/TKDE.2022.3207915

Zhou, S., Zhu, T., Ye, D., Yu, X., & Zhou, W. (2024). Boosting Model Inversion Attacks With Adversarial Examples. *IEEE Transactions on Dependable and Secure Computing*, *21*(3), 1451–1468. Advance online publication. DOI: 10.1109/TDSC.2023.3285015

Zhou, Y., Ma, X., Zhang, W., & Tang, Y. (2021). Machine learning for cybersecurity: Threat detection and mitigation. *ACM Computing Surveys*, *54*(10), 1–36. DOI: 10.1145/3395046

Zinner, M., Dahlhausen, F., Boehme, P., Ehlers, J., Bieske, L., & Fehring, L. (2021). Quantum computing's potential for drug discovery: Early stage industry dynamics. *Drug Discovery Today*, *26*(7), 1680–1688. DOI: 10.1016/j.drudis.2021.06.003 PMID: 34119668

About the Contributors

Shafiullah Khan got PhD from Middlesex University UK in March 2011. Currently he is working as Professor cybersecurity, Abdullah Al Salem University, Kuwait. He is also affiliated with Institute of Computing, Kohat University of Science and Technology Pakistan.

Ali Almutairi is working as Prof. Electrical Engineering, Abdullah Al Salem University

Jaime Lloret is working as Prof. Politecnia De Valencia, Spain. He is chair of many IEEE committees and councils

***

Iroda Abdullaeva is a faculty member at the Department of Philosophy at Urgench State University, Urgench, Uzbekistan. She has a background in philosophical sciences and is engaged in teaching and research in areas related to ethics, social philosophy, and cultural studies. Abdullaeva contributes to academic initiatives and conferences, and her research interests include moral philosophy, philosophical traditions in Central Asia, and their relevance to modern society.

Munir Ahmad is a seasoned professional in the realm of Spatial Data Infrastructure (SDI), Geo-Information Productions, Information Systems, and Information Governance, boasting over 25 years of dedicated experience in the field. With a PhD in Computer Science, Dr. Ahmad's expertise spans Spatial Data Production, Management, Processing, Analysis, Visualization, and Quality Control. Throughout his career, Dr. Ahmad has been deeply involved in the development and deployment of SDI systems specially in the context of Pakistan, leveraging his proficiency in Spatial Database Design, Web, Mobile & Desktop GIS, and Geo Web Services Architecture. His contributions to Volunteered Geographic Information

(VGI) and Open Source Geoportal & Metadata Portal have significantly enriched the geospatial community. As a trainer and researcher, Dr. Ahmad has authored over 50 publications, advancing the industry's knowledge base and fostering innovation in Geo-Tech, Data Governance, and Information Infrastructure, and Emerging Technologies. His commitment to Research and Development (R&D) is evident in his role as a dedicated educator and mentor in the field.

Hafiz Muhammad Attaullah is a cybersecurity researcher and educator with extensive experience in offensive security, AI-driven SecOps, and academic instruction. He is currently pursuing a Ph.D. in Computer Science with a specialization in Cybersecurity at Multimedia University, Malaysia. His research focuses on NB IoT security, anomaly-based intrusion detection systems for UAV networks. He serves as the Head of Offensive Security and Senior Cybersecurity Consultant at NanoTechx, where he has led the development of several award-winning security solutions. He is also a Senior Lecturer and Final Year Project (FYP) Head at Mohammad Ali Jinnah University (MAJU), Karachi. His prior roles include Red Team Lead at Greens Fin (Meezan Bank) and Research Scientist at AI EYS, where he contributed to AI-integrated security solutions.

Lumbini Bhaumik has been working as an Assistant Professor in Asansol Engineering College, Asansol, West Bengal, India. She has 17+ years of experience in teaching. She's passionate about research in AI and Machine Learning, and constantly upgrades her skills.

Aswini C has completed B.Tech from Ganadipathy Tulsis Jain Engineering College; M.E from College of Engineering & Ph D in Information and Communication Engineering from Anna University, Chennai. She has 12 years of teaching experience. Currently working as Assistant Professor in the Department of IT, Government College of Technology, Coimbatore,, Tamilnadu, India. Her research area includes Software Defined Networking & Machine Learning.

Saranya G is working as an Assistant Professor in the Department of Computer Science and Engineering at S.A. Engineering College. She is dedicated to teaching and mentoring students in core areas of computer science. Her academic interests include emerging technologies and innovative teaching methodologies. She actively contributes to research and academic development through publications and participation in conferences. With a passion for knowledge sharing, she strives to inspire students towards excellence in engineering education.

Oindrilla Ghosh is a Research Scholar hailing from the School of Law at Christ (Deemed to be University) Bangalore, India, focuses her research on health of tribal communities. Her work includes total 38 publications on Neuroscience on Organizational Behavior at IGI Global Scientific Publishing and also Environmental Disasters that are indexed in SCOPUS and Web of Sciences conference proceedings. She completed her early education at Loreto Day School, Bowbazar and went on to achieve distinction in her undergraduate (B.A/LL.B) and postgraduate (LL.M) studies at Calcutta University. Having served as an Assistant Professor of Law at Kingston Law College,Barasat, Kolkata, Ghosh has actively participated in numerous National Conferences, International Conferences, UN Global Summits, webinars, and seminars organized by prestigious academic institutions. Her expertise lies in health perspectives, environmental studies, human behavior, and related areas. Additionally, she has conducted various workshops, lectures in educational institutions, and is engaged with NGO's to help the needy.

Mayur Jariwala is an experienced IT professional with over 15 years of expertise in managing complex technology-driven projects. His background spans product design, system integration, and IT infrastructure management, with a strong focus on delivering solutions that meet both business and technical requirements. Mayur has a deep understanding of both traditional Waterfall and Agile methodologies, making him adept at leading cross-functional teams through all phases of the project lifecycle. Currently pursuing a PhD in Information Technology at the University of the Cumberlands, Mayur's academic and professional journey is rooted in the intersection of technology and project management. He holds master's degrees in Information Technology and Project Management, as well as Business Administration, and is certified as a Project Management Professional (PMP)®, Lean Six Sigma Green Belt, and SAFe® 5 Scrum Master. Mayur's contributions to the field extend beyond project management. He is an active researcher and author, with a focus on the integration of AI and cybersecurity in IT frameworks. His publications include "The Cyber Security Roadmap: A Comprehensive Guide to Cyber Threats, Cyber Laws, and Cyber Security Training for a Safer Digital World," as well as numerous research articles on cutting-edge topics like blockchain's potential in space missions and AI's role in enhancing IT project management. Mayur also serves as a reviewer for several IT journals and contributes to the Project Management Institute's AI content, reflecting his commitment to advancing the fields of information technology, AI, and cybersecurity.

Sowmya K is an Assistant Professor in the Department of MCA at Nitte Meenakshi Institute of Technology (NMIT), Bengaluru. I have over 13 years of teaching experience in the field of Computer Applications and Information Technology. My academic and research interests span areas such as software development, data analytics, and emerging technologies. I have published more than 10 research papers in Scopus-indexed journals and conferences, reflecting my active engagement in scholarly work. With a strong commitment to student-centered teaching and innovation in learning, I continue to contribute significantly to both academic and research communities.

Binod Kumar is a graduate student known for his academic excellence, with his total 27 scholarly works indexed in Scopus database on Neuroscience in Organizational Behavior, Neuromarketing and AI Applications on Wildlife Conservation. Hailing from Ranchi, Jharkhand in India, Binod is currently pursuing a Master of Laws (LL.M) at the prestigious Radha Govind University. His passion for technology and innovation along with climate changes is evident through his high academic performance and numerous projects. Binod has a keen interest in artificial intelligence, machine learning, neuropsychology, climate changes and disaster management, fields in which he has undertaken several research projects. He is particularly fascinated by the potential of AI to solve real-world problems and is dedicated to learning and applying new techniques in these areas. He volunteers at local NGOs, teaching underprivileged children basic computer skills. With a strong foundation in law and a commitment to making a positive impact, Binod Kumar is poised to become a future leader in the legal industry.

Zokir Mamadiyarov is a Professor of Economics at Mamun University, Khiva, Uzbekistan, and also serves as Professor at the Department of Finance and Tourism at Termez University of Economics and Service, Termez, Uzbekistan. He earned his academic qualifications in economics and finance and has over two decades of teaching and research experience in higher education. Prof. Mamadiyarov is a member of several national and regional academic initiatives and actively participates in conferences and journal publications. His primary research interests cover economic policy, financial systems, tourism management, and sustainable regional development.

Gularam Masharipova is a lecturer at the Department of Social Science at Alfraganus University, Tashkent, Uzbekistan. She is engaged in academic and educational activities in the field of social sciences, with a focus on contemporary social issues and their impact on education and society. Masharipova actively participates in teaching and academic discussions, and her research interests include social development, education, and the role of values in shaping civic consciousness.

Ponnuviji N. P. is a faculty member in the Department of Computer Science and Engineering at R M K College of Engineering and Technology, Puduvoyal, Tamil Nadu, India. She is engaged in teaching core computer science subjects and supporting students' academic development. Her interests focus on strengthening technical knowledge and practical problem-solving skills among learners.

S. Gladson Oliver is an Assistant Professor in the Department of Information Technology at Government College of Technology, Coimbatore. His research interests include cybersecurity, penetration testing, and secure software development. He has published several research articles in reputed journals and has experience in teaching and academic research in the field of information security.

P. Selvakumar is currently an Associate Professor in the Department of Science and Humanities at Nehru Institute of Technology, Coimbatore, Tamil Nadu, India. Prior to joining Nehru Institute of Technology, he held positions as an Assistant Professor in the Department of Science and Humanities various engineering colleges in Coimbatore, Tamil Nadu, India, spanning from 2011 to 2023. Dr.P. Selvakumar's academic and research interests lie primarily in the field of phytochemistry. He has made significant contributions to his field, with an impressive record that includes 30 journal publications, 12 patents, and 20 conference papers. Additionally, he has organized 5 seminars and conferences, further demonstrating his commitment to academic and scientific exchange. Throughout his career, Dr. P.Selvakumar has been recognized for his dedication and excellence in teaching, having been honored with several awards, including the Best Teacher Awards. He holds a prominent position in the academic community, contributing actively to research.

Al-Sakib Khan Pathan is a Professor at CSE department, United International University (UIU), Bangladesh. He received PhD in Computer Engineering in 2009 from Kyung Hee University, South Korea and B.Sc. in Computer Science and Information Technology from Islamic University of Technology (IUT), Bangladesh in 2003. In his academic career so far, he worked as a faculty member in Independent University, Bangladesh (2020-2021), Southeast University, Bangladesh (2015-2020), International Islamic University Malaysia (IIUM), Malaysia during 2010-2015; at BRACU, Bangladesh during 2009-2010, and at NSU, Bangladesh during 2004-2005. He has served as a General Chair, Organizing Committee member, and Technical Program Committee member in numerous international conferences/workshops like INFOCOM, CCGRID, GLOBECOM, ICC, etc. He was awarded the IEEE Outstanding Leadership Award for his role in IEEE GreenCom 13 conference. Among various editorial roles, he is currently serving as the Editor-in-Chief of International Journal of Computers and Applications and Journal of Cyber Security Technology, Taylor & Francis, UK; Associate Editor of Connection Science, T&F; Editor of Ad Hoc and Sensor Wireless

Malavika R. is currently an Assistant Professor at Department of Information Technology, Government College of Technology in Coimbatore-641013, Tamilnadu, India. She Obtained her M.Tech Information Technology Degree from Anna University, Coimbatore and her Doctoral degree from Anna University, Chennai. Her area of interest include Software Defined Networking, Network optimization, Computer Networks. She has journal articles in her credit and also she worked as reviewer in many reputed journals.

Siva Subramanian R is an Associate Professor in the Department of Computer Science and Engineering at SRM Institute of Science and Technology, Tiruchirappalli. He specializes in computer science research with a focus on emerging technologies and innovative teaching practices. His academic contributions include guiding students in advanced computing concepts and publishing research papers in reputed journals. He is actively engaged in departmental and institutional development activities, fostering a collaborative learning environment. With a commitment to excellence, he continues to contribute to both academia and research in the field of computer science.

Giriprasad S. is an academic professional serving as an Assistant Professor in the Department of Electronics and Communication Engineering at SRM Institute of Science and Technology. He is actively engaged in teaching, research, and mentoring students in the field of electronics and communication engineering. His professional contributions reflect a strong commitment to academic excellence, technical education, and the overall development of students in electronics and communication engineering.

Swapna Siddamsetti is an accomplished academician currently serving as the Head of the Department of Computer Science and Engineering at Neil Gogte Institute of Technology, Hyderabad, Telangana (Postal Code: 500092). With 17 years of rich teaching experience, she has made significant contributions to engineering education and academic leadership. Her scholarly work includes the publication of 40 research papers in various reputed national and international journals, reflecting her strong research orientation and expertise. In addition to her publications, she has demonstrated a keen interest in innovation and intellectual property by filing 25 patents, underscoring her commitment to research, development, and technological advancement.

Dharmendra Singh is a distinguished academician, researcher, and administrator with over 21 years of exemplary contributions to education, research, and institutional leadership. Currently serving as Professor and Associate Director at the School of Management Science, Lucknow, Dr. Singh is a beacon of academic excellence, driving innovation and fostering intellectual growth in the fields of Mathematics, Artificial Intelligence, and interdisciplinary applications. Dr. Singh's academic journey is marked by a robust foundation in Mathematics. He earned his Ph.D. in Mathematics from the prestigious University of Lucknow, Uttar Pradesh, where he developed a deep expertise in analytical and computational methodologies. His academic credentials are further strengthened by an M.Sc. and B.Sc. in Mathematics from DDU Gorakhpur University, Uttar Pradesh, equipping him with a solid grounding in theoretical and applied sciences. As Professor and Associate Director at the School of Management Science, Lucknow, Dr. Singh plays a pivotal role in shaping academic curricula, fostering research innovation, and mentoring future scholars. His leadership extends to strategic administration, where he ensures the alignment of institutional goals with academic excellence. Dr. Singh has successfully supervised two M.Phil. students, guiding them toward academic and professional success with a focus on rigorous scholarship and critical thinking. Dr. Singh is a prolific researcher whose work has significantly advanced the fields of Mathematics, Artificial Intelligence, and their applications. He has authored over 43 research papers published in high-impact SCOPUS, journals and conferences, contributing to global academic discourse.

Suguna T received her B.Tech Degree from Madras University in 2004, M.Tech and Ph.D degree from Anna University in 2011 and 2022 respectively. She has 19 years of teaching experience. Currently working as Assistant Professor in the Department of Information Technology, Government College of Technology, Coimbatore, Tamilnadu, India. Her research area includes Image Processing, Machine Learning, Information Security and Artificial Intelligence

Gurkan Tuna is a Professor at the Department of Computer Technologies of Trakya University (2006–. . ..). He has authored several papers in international conference proceedings and refereed journals, and has been actively serving as a reviewer for international journals and conferences. His current research interests include cyber security and machine learning.

Venkata Ramana Kaneti is an Assistant Professor in the Department of Computer Science and Engineering at VNR Vignana Jyothi Institute of Engineering and Technology, Hyderabad, India. His research interests include artificial intelligence, machine learning, and data-driven systems. He has contributed to publications and academic activities in advancing emerging technologies in computer science.

Raj Kishor Verma is a seasoned academician and researcher with over 12 years of teaching experience in the field of Computer Science and Engineering

(CSE). He is currently pursuing a Ph.D. in CSE from Galgotias University, focusing on developing innovative solutions to address contemporary challenges in technology. Raj Kishor Verma holds an M.Tech. in Mobile Computing from the Central University of Jharkhand, where he gained expertise in Automatic Text Summarization by the using Python, mobile systems, and pervasive computing. He completed his B.Tech. in Computer Science and Engineering from RVS College of Engineering & Technology, Jamshedpur, building a strong academic foundation. Throughout his career, Raj Kishor Verma has demonstrated excellence in teaching and research. He has published four research papers in Scopus-indexed journals, contributing significantly to fields such as mobile computing, artificial intelligence, wireless networks, and emerging technologies. He is actively working on additional research projects to advance knowledge in his domain. Currently, he serves as an Assistant Professor at ABES Institute of Technology (ABESIT),

Hakkı Yılgın has received his MSc in cyber security from Ahmet Yesevi University, Ankara, Türkiye. He has been working for a well-known cloud provider in Türkiye. His current research interests include cloud computing and cyber security.

Index

www.ingramcontent.com/pod-product-compliance
Ingram Content Group UK Ltd.
Pitfield, Milton Keynes, MK11 3LW, UK
UKHW050844101026
15624UKWH00018B/499